COMIC DRAMA IN THE LOW COUNTRIES, c.1450–1560

A CRITICAL ANTHOLOGY

*The publishers gratefully acknowledge the support
of the Dutch Foundation for Literature.*

Comic Drama
in the Low Countries, c.1450–1560

A Critical Anthology

Edited and Translated by

Ben Parsons and Bas Jongenelen

D. S. BREWER

First published 2012

D. S. Brewer, Cambridge

ISBN 978-1-84384-291-0

D. S. Brewer is an imprint of Boydell & Brewer Ltd
PO Box 9, Woodbridge, Suffolk IP12 3DF, UK
and of Boydell & Brewer Inc.
668 Mount Hope Ave, Rochester, NY 14620, USA
website: www.boydellandbrewer.com

A CIP catalogue record for this book is available
from the British Library.

The publisher has no responsibility for the continued existence or accuracy of URLs for external or third-
party internet websites referred to in this book, and does not guarantee that any content on such websites is,
or will remain, accurate or appropriate.

Papers used by Boydell & Brewer Ltd are natural, recyclable products
made from wood grown in sustainable forests

Typeset in Garamond by Word and Page, Chester, UK

Printed and bound by
CPI Group (UK) Ltd, Croydon, CR0 4YY

CONTENTS

ILLUSTRATIONS

TRANSLATORS' NOTE

The following collection is not intended to provide an exhaustive overview of comic drama in the early-modern Netherlands. In fact, given the sheer quantity of surviving texts, such a project would scarcely be achievable within a single volume. According to W. M. Hummelen, who produced the authoritative catalogue of extant Dutch drama back in the 1960s, there are at least seventy-nine plays from the fifteenth and sixteenth centuries that can be categorised as 'farces' (*kluchten*).[1] The true number may in fact be even higher. Femke Kramer has noted that Hummelen's tally is a fairly conservative estimate, as the boundaries between genres were not as clear-cut as he seems to assume: comic themes and episodes appear in a number of further texts, as does the label *klucht* itself, meaning that at least a hundred further plays might also be admitted into the grouping.[2] Moreover, since neither writer considers the numerous monologues that have survived from the period, even though these were undoubtedly composed for dramatic performance, the canon of early-modern comedy can be expanded further still.

Given this embarrassment of comic riches, the present selection has not attempted to survey the literature of the period as a whole, or to make large generalisations about it; on the contrary, it has tried to give a sense of its diversity. To this end, we have chosen plays primarily for their variety: we have, for instance, included some from the most highly regarded playwrights of the era, such as the Bruges poet Cornelis Everaert, along with pieces that have been overlooked, neglected, or even treated with active disdain. Likewise, not all of the pieces have been selected for their typicality. Some, such as the *Mock-Sermon on Saint Nobody*, do exemplify specific genres or particular styles of performance, whereas others are more singular or eccentric, such as the puzzling *This is the Madness*. Other texts, like *The Barefoot Brothers* and *The Oath of Master Pawnbroker*, have been selected primarily for the contexts in which they were staged, with the latter taking place at a well-documented and elaborate festival, and the former initiating an official crackdown on dramatic performance. But more importantly, we have interpreted drama in a fairly broad sense here. Half of the texts we have chosen are comic monologues, designed for performance by one speaker, most likely a semi-professional fool or *zot*. While these are not stage-plays in any traditional sense, they were undoubtedly an important aspect of dramatic practice in the period, and are often no less interesting than the more conventionally theatrical *kluchten*. We hope that the inclusion of several of these pieces will underscore their value as witnesses to early-modern dramatic tradition.

---

[1] W. M. H. Hummelen, *Repertorium van het rederijkersdrama 1500–ca. 1620* (Assen, 1968), 25.

[2] Femke Kramer, *Mooi vies, knap lelijk: Grotesk realisme in rederijkerskluchten* (Hilversum, 2009), 82–3.

Our translation policy likewise needs some explanation. The Dutch poets of the Renaissance period saw themselves above all else as devotees of formal oratory, a fact commemorated in the name they invariably applied to themselves: *rederijkers*, or 'rhetoricians'. Accordingly they were, to the exasperation of at least one modern commentator, much concerned with cultivating highly elaborate forms in their verse, favouring complex poetic schemes with densely interwoven rhymes and patterns of repetition.[3] This habit crossed over into their drama: a number of the plays featured here incorporate *rondelen* into their dialogue, a Dutch offshoot of the French *rondeau*, which consists of eight lines, two rhymes and a repeated burden. Other, no less polished forms also make their way into their dramas: a further example is the *refrein*, an even more elaborate framework of around fourteen lines which occurs in plays throughout the period, including one of the best known, *Mariken van Nieumeghen* (*c.*1515). These forms, despite their technical sophistication and the deftness with which the *rederijkers* often handled them, hardly lend themselves to lucid translation. For the sake of clarity, therefore, we have not attempted to replicate the ornate forms of *rederijker* verse in our own translation. Instead we have opted for an unrhymed rendering of the texts, in clear modern English. As a matter of fact, our main concern in translating these pieces has been to make them as accessible and fluent as possible; clarity has been our guiding principle throughout. Although we have tried to follow the original Dutch as closely as possible in lexis, sentence structure and meaning, we have not allowed this to interfere with the smoothness of the translation. Wherever the Dutch contains syntax or phrases that cannot be easily transposed into modern English without sacrificing coherence, we have not hesitated to reorder the language or turn to a more idiomatic mode of translation. For instance, we have often felt it necessary to move verbs to the beginnings of their sentences, in accordance with standard modern English syntax, especially where line-division would occlude the sense of a more literal translation. We have also tried to annotate each text as fully as possible. The culture the *rederijkers* inhabited was rich in its own folklore and ideas, as any glance at the work of Breugel or Bosch will demonstrate. Not all of these meanings and allusions are immediately intelligible to the modern-day reader; we therefore hope that our notes will give some degree of access to this complex culture.

However, our intention is not to replace the original texts with our own versions and interpretations, but to help readers to appreciate them in their own right. To assist in this end, we have included the original Dutch pieces in facing text. For these, we are indebted to a number of scholars in the Low Countries, who have allowed us to reproduce their editions of the plays. We would like to express our sincere gratitude to the following for granting the relevant permissions: Herman Pleij, for allowing us to use his editions of *The Guild of the Blue Barge*, *A Mock-Sermon on Saint Nobody*, *A Wise and Wonderful Prognostication* and *The Oath of Master Pawnbroker*; Mw. M. Zandee-Salomé, for allowing us to reproduce Cornelis Kruyskamp's editions of *This is the Madness* and *Jack Sweet-tooth*. We thank Cees Klapwijk, of the website Digitale Bibliotheek voor de Nederlandse Letteren (www.dbnl.org), for his assistance in locating copyright holders. The translators and publishers are grateful

---

[3]   See Reinder P. Meijer, *Literature of the Low Countries. A Short History of Dutch Literature in the Netherlands and Belgium* (The Hague, 1978), 52–3.

for permission to reproduce materials in copyright. Every effort has been made to trace the copyright holders; apologies are offered for any omission, and the publishers will be pleased to add any necessary acknowledgement in subsequent editions.

We would also like to thank Geert van Iersel and the anonymous readers at Boydell and Brewer for their comments on the translated texts; their advice and suggestions have been invaluable throughout, and this would be a much lesser collection without their counsel. Lastly, we are grateful to Caroline Palmer and all at Boydell and Brewer for their support for this project, and above all for their patience.

All biblical quotations are taken from the Douay-Rheims translation.

The Older the Hollander the More Foolish: Comedy, Foolery and the Chambers of Rhetoric in the Medieval Low Countries

THE PERIOD 1450–1570 is one of the most crucial in the history and development of the Netherlands. It saw the union of its various medieval territories under the dukes of Burgundy, numerous religious and dynastic controversies, and finally the revolt of northern provinces against Philip II of Spain in the 1560s. However, rather than focusing on the intermittent warfare, popular unrest and religious upheaval of the period, this anthology will focus on one of the most surprising outcomes of this turmoil: the rich tradition of comic literature it produced. In fact, the importance of comedy in the early-modern Low Countries is difficult to overstate. As one modern scholar has observed, comedy was a major component of Dutch-language culture throughout the era: 'It seems as though every social phenomenon of any importance in the late Middle Ages was claimed for parody ... the popular printers produced many parodies and play-texts, which attained a large readership ... playful works had a strong social impact.'[1] The prominence of comedy in the Netherlands was also noted by contemporary witnesses. The Low Countries seem to have gained a reputation for foolery among their European neighbours. Hence in his description of Flanders, published in 1613, the French soldier Pierre d'Avity makes several references to the celebratory culture of the Low Countries, noting that Flemings 'aboue all things loue banquets, and to make good cheere', even though this might lead to 'loue of wine ... somtimes more than is fit'.[2] The same tendency seems to have struck visitors from England, judging from the proverbs that enter English around this time: the phrases 'Dutch courage', 'double Dutch', 'Dutch feast' and 'Dutch gleek' all share a common emphasis on carousing and playful nonsense.[3] The prevalence of such practices even seems to have been a source of cultural pride within the Netherlands.

---

[1] 'Zoals elk maatschappelijk verschijnsel van enige betekenis in de late middeleeuwen is ook dit aangegrepen voor parodie ... de populaire drukpers heeft veel van zulke spot- en speelteksten ... voor een zo breed mogelijk publiek ... er gaat een sterk sociaal effect uit van deze vrolijke boekjes': Hinke van Kampen, Herman Pleij, Bob Stumpel, Annebel Venmans and Paul Vriesema, *Het zal koud zijn in 't water als 't vriest: zestiende-eeuwse parodieën op gedrukte jaarvoorspellingen tekstuitg. met inleiding en commentaar* (The Hague, 1980), 5.

[2] Pierre d'Avity, *The Estates, Empires, & Principallities of the World*, trans. Edward Grimeston (London, 1615), 308–9.

[3] Jonathon Green, *Slang down the Ages: The Historical Development of Slang*, rev. edn (London, 2003), 282–3.

In *The Praise of Folly* (1509), Erasmus makes Stultitia praise 'my Hollanders' because they are 'so devoted to my worship that they have commonly earned the nickname of fools, which they are not ashamed of, but even use among themselves'.[4] Alaard van Amsterdam and Hadrianus Junius also record the Dutch referring to themselves as clownish, and the custom is further reflected in a popular adage: 'the older the Brabanter the more foolish; the older the Hollander the dimmer'.[5]

To understand why comedy attained such a prominent role in the period, it is important to appreciate the social background of dramatic texts in the early-modern Low Countries. This was dominated by the organisations known as *rederijkers-kamers*, or 'chambers of rhetoric'. These lay fraternities, whose members styled themselves *rederijkers* or 'rhetoricians', had an inestimable impact on the public life of the Netherlands at the end of the Middle Ages, and on the plays that were generated out of this. As Bruce Wardropper justly states, 'by 1450 virtually the entire literary output had become the monopoly of the chambers of rhetoricians'.[6] In fact of the ten pieces included here, only *This is the Madness* lacks a demonstrable connection to the chambers, owing to its unusually early date.

The chambers themselves were a peculiarly Netherlandish institution. While they bear some comparison to similar groups in other parts of medieval Europe, such as the French *puys* or the Italian *accademie*, they also developed along their own specific lines.[7] They took their name from the halls in which they convened their meetings and held feasts for their members. This was often a jealously guarded space, which only a privileged few might enter: each chamber possessed its own ceremonial *cnape* (doorman) whose chief duty was to restrict access to the hall by non-members.[8] The rhetoricians would also compose poems for exclusive consumption within these spaces, seeing themselves as a 'limited public with refined literary tastes'.[9] This sense of elitism is no doubt derived from the social standing of the rhetoricians. The members of the chambers tended to belong to the same economic group: the so-called *middenklasse*, the artisanal and mercantile class that became increasingly powerful towards the end of the Middle Ages. While the nobility were involved in a few chambers, they tended to participate only as patrons. Aristocratic members usually served as the *prinsen* (princes) or *keisers* (emperors) of chambers,

---

[4] 'Cur enim non meos appellem, usque adeo studiosos mei cultores, ut inde uulgo cognomen emeruerint? cuius illos adeo non pudet, ut hinc uel praecipue sese iactitent': Erasmus, *Stultitiae Laus*, ed. John F. Collins (Bryn Mawr, PA, 1991), 11.

[5] Ari Wesseling, 'Dutch Proverbs and Ancient Sources in Erasmus's *Praise of Folly*', *Renaissance Quarterly* 47 (1994), 351–78 (354); 'Hoe ouder, hoe zotter Brabander; Hoe ouder, hoe botter Hollander', P. J. Harrebomée, *Spreekwoordenboek der Nederlandsche taal*, 3 vols. (Hoevelaken, 1990), 3: 400.

[6] Bruce Wardropper, 'Belgium', in *The Reader's Encyclopedia of World Drama*, ed. John Gassner and Edward Quinn (New York, 1970), 59–65 (60).

[7] See for instance the discussion in Arjan van Dixhoorn, 'Epilogue', in *The Reach of the Republic of Letters: Literary and Learned Societies in Late Medieval and Early Modern Europe*, ed. Arjan van Dixhoorn and Susie Speakman Sutch, 2 vols. (Leiden, 2008), 2: 423–62.

[8] On the duties of the *cnape*, see Prudens van Duyse, *De rederijkkamers in Nederland, hun invloed op letterkundig, politiek en zedelijk gebied*, 2 vols. (Ghent, 1900–2), 1: 42.

[9] 'Een beperkter publiek met meer uitgesproken literaire pretenties': A. van Elslander, *Het refrein in de Nederlanden tot 1600* (Ghent, 1953), 187.

their ceremonial figureheads or sponsors.[10] The bulk of the ordinary *rederijkers* were drawn from the urban professional social stratum. As Gary Waite notes, the chambers are best seen as a mouthpiece for this class, providing 'ordinary citizens with a cultural outlet that had hitherto been the sole preserve of the first two social estates'.[11] Individual chambers might in fact contain a broad cross-section of these citizens, incorporating a wide selection of different craftsmen and traders. Although some *kamers* were associated with particular professions, such as *De Corenbloem* (The Corn Flower) at Brussels or *Mariën Theeren* (To Honour Mary) at Ghent, which were dominated by tapestry-weavers and leather-workers respectively, none were officially restricted to one profession alone, on the pattern of trade-guilds.[12]

The precise origin of these companies is obscure. The chambers seem to have some connection with various urban confraternities that began to appear in the fourteenth century. An especially close prototype is found in the *schuttergilden* (shooting-guilds), groups of amateur archers that originally made up the militia in several cities, but later became largely ceremonial in their activities.[13] Along slightly different lines, at least one chamber, that of *Den Boeke* (The Book) in Brussels, was created to provide music for the ducal court: its members are first described as *pijpers* (musicians) in the city accounts.[14] What is clear, however, is that the chambers emerged as a distinct type of organisation towards the middle of the fifteenth century. The first concrete reference to a *Camer van Rhetorica* occurs in 1441 in the Flemish city of Oudenaarde, and there is evidence that other groups around this date were also carrying out functions associated with the chambers, such as the *Spelers van Herten Wilt* (Players of the Passionate Heart) at Ypres, *Den Wijngaerde* (The Vineyard) at Diksmuide, and an unnamed company at Lo.[15] At any rate, whatever their provenance, the chambers flourished throughout the fifteenth and sixteenth centuries, as some four hundred companies were founded between 1400 and 1650.[16] Most major towns boasted at

---

[10] On the hierarchy of the chambers, see Herman Pleij, *Het gevleugelde woord – Geschiedenis van de Nederlandse literatuur 1400–1650* (Amsterdam, 2007), 299; Susie Speakman Sutch, 'Dichters van de stad – De Brusselse rederijkers en hun verhouding tot de Franstalige hofliteratuur en het geleerde humanisme (1475–1522)', *De macht van het schone woord: literatuur in Brussel van de 14de tot de 18de eeuw*, ed. Jozef Janssens and Remco Sleiderink (Leuven, 2003), 141–59.

[11] Gary K. Waite, *David Joris and Dutch Anabaptism, 1524–1543* (Waterloo, Ontario, 1990), 13.

[12] Marc Beyaert, *Opkomst en bloei van de Gentse rederijkerskamer Marien Theeren* (Ghent, 1978), 41.

[13] Andrew Brown and Graeme Small, *Court and Civic Society in the Burgundian Low Countries c.1420–1530* (Manchester, 2007), 210.

[14] Dirk Coigneau, '"Den Boeck" van Brussel: een geval apart?', *Jaarboek de Fonteine* 49–50 (1999–2000), 31–44 (37).

[15] Gerard Knuvelder, *Handboek tot de geschiedenis der Nederlandse letterkunde* (Malmberg, 1978), 360; Anne-Laure van Bruaene, *Om beters wille: rederijkerskamers en de stedelijke cultuur in de Zuidelijke Nederlanden (1400–1650)* (Amsterdam, 2008), 260; E. vander Straeten, *Le Théâtre villageois et Flandre*, 2 vols. (Brussels, 1874–80), 2: 135–45.

[16] The most recent lists of the chambers are those compiled for the Digitale Bibliotheek voor de Nederlandse Letteren website, Anne-Laure van Bruaene, 'Repertorium van rederijkerskamers in de Zuidelijke Nederlanden en Luik 1400–1650', in *Digitale bibliotheek voor de Nederlandse letteren* (2005), online at www.dbnl.org/tekst/brua002repe01_01/, and Arjan van Dixhoorn, 'Repertorium van rederijkerskamers in de Noordelijke Nederlanden 1400–1650', in *Digitale bibliotheek voor de Nederlandse letteren* (2005), online at www.dbnl.

least two such organisations, and large cities contained many more: Antwerp and Amsterdam, for instance, had six and eight respectively.[17] They were also distributed widely across the Netherlands. While the majority were concentrated in the south, especially Flanders, Holland and Brabant, there is evidence of a vibrant rhetorical culture as far north as Groningen and Friesland.[18] Likewise, although predominantly an urban phenomenon, groups did emerge in more rural areas, such as *De Terwebloem* (The Wheatflower), first recorded in 1564, and associated with the village of Poeldijk in the agricultural region of Westland.[19]

For much of the sixteenth century the chambers enjoyed a considerable heyday, playing a central role in the cultural life of their communities. Being comprised of prosperous traders, with a degree of political and economic power, they could usually rely on the support of the *raden* (ruling councils) of the cities they occupied. A measure of their importance is the transmission of their texts outside the Low Countries. A number of *rederijker* plays were exported by enterprising printers in Flanders: two of the most famous are *Elkerlijc* and *Mariken van Nieumeghen*, which were both translated into English and other languages in the first decades of the sixteenth century.[20] The prestige and influence of the chambers began to decline at the turn of the seventeenth century. Several lost their official privileges in the 1580s and 1590s, as they faced opposition from Calvinist and Mennonite ministers in the newly formed United Provinces, and from the Catholic authorities in Spanish-controlled territories.[21] Nevertheless, new chambers were still being formed even at this point, and a number were even revived. For instance, *De Barbaristen* (Followers of Saint Barbara) was founded in *c.*1620 at Asse in Brabant, probably at the instigation of Hendrik van Caelen, future bishop of Roermond.[22]

org/tekst/dixh002repe01_01/. An earlier, less complete catalogue is given in Jan te Winkel, *De ontwikkelingsgang der Nederlandsche letterkunde*, 7 vols. (Haarlem, 1922–7), 1: 355–6.

[17]   See A. Keersmaekers, 'Geschiedenis van de Antwerpsche rederijkerskamers in de jaren 1585–1635', *Bijdragen tot de geschiedenis* 4 (1952), 123–56, 187–227; Te Winkel, *De ontwikkelingsgang der Nederlandsche letterkunde*, 3: 247–59.

[18]   Arjan van Dixhoorn, *Lustige geesten: rederijkers in de noordelijke nederlanden (1480–1650)* (Amsterdam, 2009), especially 57–160.

[19]   F. C. van Boheemen and T. C. J. van der Heijden, *Retoricaal memoriaal: bronnen voor de geschiedenis van de Hollandse rederijkerskamers van de middeleeuwen tot het begin van de achttiende eeuw* (Delft, 1999), 732–3.

[20]   See Ben Parsons, 'Dutch Influences on English Literary Culture in the Early Renaissance, 1470–1650', *Literature Compass* 4 (2007), 1577–96; Therese Decker and Martin W. Walsh, *Mariken van Nieumeghen: A Bilingual Edition* (Columbia, 1994); Clifford Davidson, Martin W. Walsh and Ton J. Broos, eds., *Everyman and its Dutch Original, Elckerlijc* (Kalamazoo, 2007). Further evidence for the transmission of *rederijker* drama is explored in Leonard Forster, 'Literary Relations between the Low Countries, England and Germany', *Dutch Crossing* 24 (1984), 16–31; Alexandra F. Johnston, 'Traders and Playmakers: English Guildsmen and the Low Countries', in *England and the Low Countries in the Late Middle Ages*, ed. Caroline M. Barron and Nigel Saul (New York, 1995), 99–114; Alexandra F. Johnston, 'The Continental Connection: A Reconsideration', in *The Stage as Mirror: Civic Theatre in Late Medieval Europe*, ed. A. E. Knight (Cambridge, 1997), 7–24.

[21]   Willem Frijhoff and Marijke Spies, *Dutch Culture in a European Perspective*, 2 vols. (Assen, 2004), 2: 553–4.

[22]   M. Sacré, 'Het voormalig Dorpstooneel in Brabant volgens onuitgegeven bewijsstukken',

Given the number and geographic range of these fraternities, it is difficult to reduce their exact functions to a handful of generalisations. The portrait is complicated still further by the emergence of unofficial chambers, such as *Het Leliken van Calvarien* (The Lily of Calvary) at Antwerp, which was suppressed in 1562, or the group of nine *rederijkers* arrested at Amsterdam in 1533, on charges of founding a chamber 'sonder wete van den gerechte' ('without the knowledge of the proper authorities').[23] Nevertheless, there are some features and functions that are common to the majority of *kamers*, and most were founded with a particular design in mind. In the first place, the chambers' chief role was to oversee the ceremonial and celebratory life of their cities, producing plays and poetry for religious and civic occasions. This obligation is neatly summarised by the founding statutes of *Mariën Theeren*, drawn up in 1478. The articles state that the 'deacon and officers' of the chamber 'are bound . . . to play dramas, perform tableaux or do other things . . . on any feast-day that pertains to this city, and that we or our legal rulings desire'.[24] As the unspecific language used here might suggest, this duty could take a range of possible forms. On the one hand, chambers were called on to provide entertainments and spectacles on the various festival occasions that were part of the medieval ritual year. These might include such occasions as *Paasfeest* (Easter), *Kerstmis* (Christmas), or the feast-days of saints with local significance. Some chambers were even formed expressly to stage plays on specific dates: in 1514 *De Kruisbroeders* (The Cross-brothers) were founded at Kortrijk, specifically to perform the traditional passion play on Corpus Christi.[25]

Several of the texts in the present collection clearly emanate from such a seasonal context. Many of the monologues presented here are self-evidently related to *Vastenavond*, the Netherlands' equivalent of Carnival or Shrovetide. As elsewhere in Europe, this was an occasion for playful, bawdy inversion of given standards, or 'temporary liberation . . . from the established order' as Bakhtin puts it.[26] The performance of comic monologues was one way in which this liberation was achieved, as parodic speeches were often issued by fool-kings and fool-preachers as part of the provisional authority they were given over celebrants.[27] In this anthology, *The Oath of Master Pawnbroker* and *A Mock-Sermon on Saint Nobody* provide particularly vivid instances of this custom.

De Brabander 1 (1919), 3–8; Guido Marnef, *Het calvinistisch bewind te Mechelen 1580–1585*, Standen en Landen 87 (Kortrijk, 1987), 295–7.

[23] A. van Elslander, V. Speeckaert and J. Vuyst, 'Lijst van Zuid-Nederlandsche rederijkerskamers uit de XVe en XVIe eeuw', *Jaarboek de Fonteine* 2 (1944), 29–60 (24–5); J. A. Worp, *Geschiedenis van den Amsterdamschen schouwburg 1496–1772* (Amsterdam, 1920), 7.

[24] 'De dekin met zijnen proviserers ghehouden zijn . . . het ware van spele te spelene, figuren te tooghene, of andersins . . . waert zo dat dezer stede eenighe feeste toequame, ende dat wy of onse naercommeren in wette begheerden': P. Blommaert, 'Beknopte geschiedenis der Kamers van Rhetorica te Gent', *Belgisch museum voor de Nederduitsche tael- en letterkunde en de geschiedenis des vaderlands* (1837), 417–44 (437).

[25] G. D. J. Schotel, *Geschiedenis der rederijkers in Nederland*, 2 vols. (Amsterdam, 1862–71), 1: 109.

[26] Mikhail Bakhtin, *Rabelais and his World*, trans. Hélène Iswolsky (Bloomington, 1984), 10.

[27] See Herman Pleij, *De eeuw van de zotheid: over de nar als maatschcappelijk houvast in de vroegmoderne tijd* (Amsterdam, 2007).

Alongside these yearly events, chambers might also be called on to stage occasional celebrations. These could be large-scale, such as the public festivities held in 1559 at Maastricht, Brussels and elsewhere to mark the Peace of Cateau-Cambrésis, or in 1526 at Bruges to honour the Treaty of Madrid.[28] Along similar lines, in 1511 the rhetorician Jan Smeken of the Brussels chamber *De Lelie* (The Lily) produced a poem-pamphlet to commemorate the city's 'snowman festival', which saw various ice sculptures installed around the city, including figures of Samson, Roland, Hercules, 'a trio of distinguished gentlemen playing at dice ... a war-elephant, fools, a sort of Manneken Pis, naked frolicking lovers, a lustful whore, a man-in-the-moon'.[29] The chambers also staged processions, typically to mark the visit of a foreign or local dignitary. Hence *De Blauwe Acoleyen* (The Blue Columbine) took responsibility for Phillip the Handsome's *blijde inkomst* (official entry) into Rotterdam in 1497, and performed a similar function when Henrietta Maria, wife of Charles I of England, visited Holland in 1642.[30] On the other hand, the *rederijkers* would also host relatively low-key and private events. A number of surviving plays were composed for wedding-feasts or ordination ceremonies.[31] The fraternities might also perform entertainments to accompany other civic rituals and games: for instance, in 1483 the shooting-guild of Sluis attended a contest in Hulst, and apparently brought with them the 'Gild van der Retorycke en esbatementers van der zelver stede' ('guild of Rhetoric and farce-players from the same city').[32] As this statement implies, comedy was often the preferred mode in these entertainments.

The chambers themselves seem to have regarded their overall duties in two principal ways. In the first place, they had an important devotional purpose. Several seem to have developed out of the earlier lay brotherhoods organised under direct supervision of the clergy, and the groups as a whole retained a keen religious sensibility. They invariably had their own chapels for members, such as Sint-Hilariuskapel in Maastricht, used by *Onsser Liever Vrouwen en de Heilige Drie Koningen* (Our Lady and the Three Holy Kings).[33] They also seem to have regarded membership of a chamber as a service to God, akin to membership of a religious order. This spiritual focus

---

[28] J. Notermans, 'Ambachtslieden en rederijkers spelen in Tricht toneel', *Handelingen van de Kon zuidned maatschappij voor taal- en letterkunde en geschiedenis* 12 (1958), 211–22; Van Bruaene, *Om beters wille*, 115–17; J. W. Muller and L. Scharpé, *Spelen van Cornelis Everaert*, 3 vols. (Leiden, 1898–1920), 3: 573.

[29] 'Een drietal voorname heren die aan het dobbelen zijn ... een vechtolifant, zotten, een soort Manneken Pis, naakt vrijende gelieven, een wulpse hoer, het mannetje van in maan': Herman Pleij, *De sneeuwpoppen van 1511. Literatuur en stadscultuur tussen middeleeuwen en moderne tijd* (Amsterdam, 1988), 9–10.

[30] Herman Brinkman, *Dichten uit liefde: literatuur in Leiden aan het einde van de middeleeuwen* (Hilversum, 1997), 82; On Henrietta Maria's journey to Holland, see Keith L. Sprunger, *Dutch Puritanism: A History of English and Scottish Churches of the Netherlands* (Leiden, 1982), 381.

[31] Willem van Eeghem, *Drie schandaleuse spelen (Brussel 1559)* (Antwerp, 1937), 41–56; W. M. H. Hummelen, *Repertorium van het rederijkersdrama 1500–ca. 1620* (Assen, 1968), 25.

[32] P. J. Meertens, *Letterkundig leven in Zeeland in de zestiende en de eerste helft der zeventiende eeuw* (Amsterdam, 1943), 128–9.

[33] J. van Rensch, 'Broederschappen in Maastricht 1400–1850', in *Hemelse trektochten. Broederschappen in Maastricht 1400–1850*, ed. T. J. van Rensch, A. M. Koldeweij, R. M. de la Haye, M. L. de Kreek (Maastricht, 1990), 7–88 (79–80).

is especially clear from the iconography associated with the chambers. Each chamber represented itself in three particular ways: with its name, its moralistic *zinspreuk* (motto), and its *blazoen*, the insignia of the chamber, usually mounted in a distinctive diamond-shaped panel. All of these emblems were used to declare the religious commitment of the chamber. The name, for instance, invariably had devotional significance. Several chambers took the names of popular saints: Anne at Hasselt, Agatha at 's-Hertogenbosch, Catherine at Aalst and John the Baptist at Tielt. Even when less overtly religious titles were used, clear allegorical implications remained. Most chambers were named after flowers of various kinds, and the majority of these had scriptural resonances. Hence chambers at Leuven, Tongeren, Nordwijk, Diest and elsewhere took the name *De Lelie* (The Lily), in allusion to the Sermon on the Mount, while groups at Schiedam, Ypres and Hasselt were designated *De Roose* (The Rose), a common symbol of martyrdom.[34] The *blazoen* further reinforced this focus. As Albert Heppner has noted, while these symbols are quasi-heraldic in character and function, as 'the guild brethren were as proud of their *blazoen* as knights of their coats-of-arms', they were primarily informed by religious concerns, since the *blazoen* itself was 'not heraldic but represented naturalistically the patron saint of the guild'.[35] The chambers clearly conceived their projects in devotional terms, as the symbols they used to represent themselves expressed pious dedication above all.

Alongside the devotional function they held for their members, the chambers saw themselves as performing an instructive role for the towns and cities they inhabited. As Waite aptly observes, they considered their practices 'as services to their urban community' and themselves as 'teachers and agents of communication . . . between God and the people'.[36] The chambers were, in other words, not merely concerned with their own salvation, but with the spiritual welfare of their communities at large. This educative intent is again clear from their iconography. As Nelleke Moser has shown, Pentecost had a special resonance for the groups, serving as a recurrent point of reference in their emblems, in order to stress their own comparable dissemination of knowledge.[37] Numerous fraternities, including those at Oudenburg, Bruges, Diksmuide and Ypres, were named in honour of the *Heilige Geest*, while the badge of *De Blauwe Acoleyen* at Rotterdam showed the Apostles receiving the gift of tongues, with the motto 'Met minnen versaemt' ('Gathered with love'). Their poetry also repeatedly stressed the connection between the Holy Spirit and rhetoric. Hence Anthonis de Roovere, writing in *c.*1480, explicitly claims that oratory was 'granted to the students of rhetoric with fire by the Holy Spirit'.[38]

[34] E. van Autenboer, 'De Lelikens wten Dale. Rederijkerskamer van Zoutleeuw', *Eigen Schoon en de Brabander* 68 (1985), 249–70

[35] Albert Heppner, 'The Popular Theatre of the Rederijkers in the Work of Jan Steen and his Contemporaries', *Journal of the Warburg and Courtauld Institutes* 3 (1939–40), 22–48 (25).

[36] Gary K. Waite, *Reformers on Stage: Popular Drama and Religious Propaganda in the Low Countries of Charles V, 1515–1556* (Toronto, 2000), 29.

[37] Nelleke Moser, *De strijd voor rhetorica* (Amsterdam, 2001), 78–85.

[38] 'Vander Rethorijcke scholieren in vieren/ Heeftse den heylighen gheest ghesticht': Anthonis de Roovere, 'Refereyn van rethorica', in *De gedichten van Anthonis de Roovere*, ed. J. J. Mak (Zwolle, 1955), 131–3. See Marijke Spies, 'Developments in Sixteenth-Century Dutch Poetics. From "Rhetoric" to "Renaissance"', in *Renaissance-Rhetorik*, ed. Heinrich F. Plett (Berlin, 1993), 72–91 (73–4).

This focus on instruction might also take a literal form. As Spaans writes, as well as being 'venues for male conviviality' many chambers also served as 'popular academies', providing 'adult men with a formalized education in vernacular linguistic skills, both written and oral, that were necessary for all those aspiring to public office'.[39] In fact, for this reason several groups, such as *Pax Vobis* (Peace to You) and *De Kersouwe* (The Daisy) at Oudenaarde, are called 'scolen van der retorijken' ('schools of rhetoric') in the earliest records.[40] As well as providing religious instruction, therefore, the chambers were also keen to propagate practical, secular knowledge, imparting good citizenship alongside Christian morality.

It is against this educational, spiritual background that the comedies of the *rederijkers* should be read. Plays were of course the chief means by which the chambers set out to serve God by instructing their communities. The performances of the *rederijkers* usually took place before the largest and widest audience possible. Pictorial sources, such as Pieter Balten's depiction of a farce-performance (Fig. 1), show plays being staged on large scaffolds, erected in emphatically public spaces such as market squares.[41] The bulk of their productions were quite explicit in their instructive aim, as the majority of plays fall under the category of *spelen van zinne* or *zinnespelen*, 'the quintessential rhetorician genre'.[42] These terms literally mean 'plays of judgement' or 'plays of the senses'. *Spelen van zinne* are in substance allegorical morality plays, of the kind that occur in several medieval European literatures. Their characters are generally personified concepts, actions or doctrines, with names such as 'Heijlige Kerck' (Holy Church), 'Simpel Gelovige' (Simple Believer), 'Verblinde Wille' (Blind Will), 'Selfs Goetduncken' (Self-discretion), 'tMinnende Hert' (The Loving Heart), and so on.[43] The didactic thrust of these pieces is of course quite overt. As Van Bruaene has noted, they were often little more than moral treatises cast in figurative terms, as each had 'a central argument which had to be proven ... by reference to the reality God created' and 'by reference to such authorities as Scripture and the Church Fathers'.[44]

---

[39]   Joke Spaans, 'Public Opinion or Ritual Celebration of Concord? Politics, Religion and Society in Competition between the Chambers of Rhetoric at Vlaardingen in 1616', in *Public Opinion and Changing Identities in the Early Modern Netherlands: Essays in Honour of Alastair Duke*, ed. Judith Pollmann and Andrew Spicer (Leiden, 2007), 189–210 (190).

[40]   D. J. van der Meersch, *Kronyk der rederykkamers van Andenaerde, van de vroegste tyder af tot omtrerit den jare 1830* (Ghent, 1844), 69.

[41]   For some general suppositions on staging, see W. M. H. Hummelen, 'Types and Methods of the Dutch Rhetoricians' Theatre', in *The Third Globe. Symposium for the Reconstruction of the Globe Playhouse*, ed. C. Walter Hodges, S. Schoenbaum and Leonard Leone (Detroit, 1979), 164–89.

[42]   Arjan van Dixhoorn, 'Writing Poetry as Intellectual Training. Chambers of Rhetoric and the Development of Vernacular Intellectual Life in the Low Countries', in *Education and Learning in the Netherlands, 1400–1600: Essays in Honour of Hilde de Ridder-Symoens*, ed. Koen Goudriaan, Jaap van Moolenbroek and Ad Tervoort (Leiden, 2004), 201–22 (208).

[43]   *Heijlige Kerck*, in W. N. M. Hüsken, B. A. M. Ramakers and F. A. M. Schaars, *Trou moet blijcken. Bronnenuitgave van de boeken der Haarlemse rederijkerskamer 'de Pellicanisten'*, 8 vols. (Assen, 1992–8), 3: 496–593.

[44]   Anne-Laure van Bruaene, '"In principio erat verbum": Drama, Devotion, Reformation and Urban Association in the Low Countries', in *Early Modern Confraternities in Europe and the Americas*, ed. Christopher F. Black and Pamela Gravestock (Aldershot, 2006), 64–80 (68).

FIGURE 1. A farce staged in a public square. Detail from Pieter Balten (attrib.), *Een opvoering van de klucht Een cluyte van Plaeyerwater op een Vlaamse kermis* ('A performance of the farce *Playerwater* at a Flemish festival'), *c*.1540. Rijksmuseum, Amsterdam.

While the comedies are not as explicit in carrying out instruction, they were nonetheless organised around the same principles. In the first place, a number of comedies deal expressly with education and training the young, such as the *Esbatement van musijcke ende rhetorijcke* ('Farce of Music and Rhetoric'), dating from *c*.1553, and *Jack Sweet-tooth*, a piece included in this collection.[45] But more importantly, the boundary between the moral *spelen van zinne* and comic forms was in practice quite porous. Around the turn of the sixteenth century, the *rederijkers* began to develop a new form of farce called the *esbattement*. Prior to this point, they had described the form as *klucht* or *sotternie*: these terms occur in the earliest surviving farces in Dutch, first appearing in such fourteenth-century texts as *Die hexe* ('The Witch') and *Drie daghe here* ('The Three-Day Lord').[46] The

[45] Hummelen, *Repertorium van het rederijkersdrama*, 32.
[46] See Hans van Dijk, 'The Drama Texts in the Van Hulthem Manuscript', in *Medieval Dutch Literature in its European Context*, ed. E. Kooper, Cambridge Studies in Medieval Literature 21 (Cambridge, 1994), 283–96. Several of the Van Hulthem pieces are translated in Johanna C. Prins,

esbattementen did not depart radically from the conventions of the earlier plays, as they were clearly conceived as an extension of the *klucht* rather than an entirely new genre. Indeed, the distinction between the two was never absolute, and it seems to have disappeared altogether by the last half of the sixteenth century.[47] But one respect in which the *esbattement* differed from the *klucht*, aside from its greater length and slightly more complex structure, was the addition of elements from the *speel van zinne*. For instance, a farce written by Cornelis Meeszoon van Hout in 1552 has a cast of characters that would not be inappropriate to an allegorical morality, such as 'Ghewoont' (Custom), 'Manier' (Fashion), 'sMenschen sin' (Man's Desire), and 'Verganckelijcke Scoonheit' (Perishable Beauty).[48] A later example is Hendrick Fay-d'herbe's *Esbatement van vier personagien* ('Farce for Four Characters'), written in 1620, which includes roles for 'Droncken Claes' (Drunken Claus) and 'Heyn de Duyvel' (Hein the Devil).[49] As Femke Kramer observes, this willingness to include personification and other allegorical elements in comedy is a uniquely Dutch innovation, as it is not present in French or German farce-traditions.[50] It also demonstrates the proximity of the moral and the comic for the *rederijkers*, as the two were not regarded as antitheses, but neighbouring concepts. *Spelen van zinne* and *kluchten* could freely exchange features, since the two were directed towards the same basic end.

Other features in the farces show further connections between the didactic and comic. The inclusion of complex rhyme-schemes, for instance, also shows a clear moral intent at work. In several of the farces there is a general fondness for the *rondeel*, a verse-form comprised of eight lines with two repeated rhymes, derived from the French *rondeau* and related to the English roundelay. Dialogue in the farces often incorporates *rondelen*, especially during the prologues of the texts. Several of the texts included here use the form, including Everaert's *The Fisherman* and the anonymous *Barefoot Brothers*, where it appears in a *lieken* sung by the characters in a chorus. However, this is not the only elaborate form to be deployed for comedic purposes by the chambers. Also important is the *refrein*, a sort of rhyming declamation with intricate patterns of repetition, which developed a fruitful subgenre known as the *refrein int zotte* (refrein of foolery).[51] The inclusion of these forms

---

Medieval Dutch Drama: Four Secular Plays and Four Farces from the Van Hulthem Manuscript, Early European Drama in Translation 4 (Asheville, NC, 2000); Therese Decker and Martin Walsh, 'Three Sotternien: Farcical Afterpieces from the Hulthem Manuscript', *Dutch Crossing* 48 (1992), 73–91

[47] J. J. Mak, *Vier excellente cluchten*, Klassieke Galerij 46 (Antwerp, 1950), v.

[48] Cornelis Meesz. van Hout, *sMenschen sin en verganckelijcke schoonheit*, ed. Cornelis Schmidt (Zwolle, 1967), 107–75. An English translation of this text is available in Elsa Strietman and Robert Potter, *Een esbattement van sMenschen sin en verganckelijcke schoonheit / Man's Desire and Fleeting Beauty*, Leeds Medieval Studies, Middle Dutch Texts and Translations Series 1 (Leeds, 1994).

[49] P. G. Witsen Geysbeek, *Biographisch anthologisch en critisch woordenboek der Nederduitsche dichters*, 6 vols. (Amsterdam, 1821–7), 2: 292–3.

[50] Femke Kramer, *Mooi vies, knap lelijk: grotesk realisme in rederijkerskluchten* (Hilversum, 2009), 51–2.

[51] See Dirk Coigneau, *Refreinen in het zotte bij de rederijkers*, 3 vols. (Ghent, 1980–3); Ben Parsons and Bas Jongenelen, 'The Refrein and the Chambers of Rhetoric in the Early Modern

in comedy is highly significant. As Reinder Meijer states, the *rederijkers* placed a great deal of importance on these 'technical games', as 'experimentation with form became one of their main concerns':

> Not only in the refrein, but in their lyrical poetry in general, the *Rederijkers* exhausted themselves in showing what could be done with form. They wrote poems in which a date was concealed, acrostics of several kinds which gave names or mottoes when one deciphered them, poems that could be read backwards, and combinations of all this . . . . Add to this their experiments with rhyme: rich rhymes, double rhymes, or long stanzas with only two rhymes, expansion of rhyming possibilities by using intricate circumlocutions instead of a simple word, and one has some idea of what these poets did to form.[52]

While such innovations might seem self-consciously playful, they were underpinned by a serious conviction. The chambers attached a strong ethical function to their elaborate, ornamented style. Metrical complexity was in fact thought to prompt ordered thinking, and as a result promote moderate behaviour. As Van Elslander summarises, there was a general sense that forms such as the *refrein* inspired 'reasoned thought' and good conduct, whereas simpler genres, such as songs, could only 'arouse, please, or stir' the emotions.[53] This can be seen in *De const van rhetoriken* ('The Art of Rhetoric'), a poetic manual written by Matthijs de Castelein in *c*.1548, which was largely responsible for popularising the ornate style amongst the *kamers*. De Castelein attributes great educative power to form: his section on the *rondeel*, for instance, begins 'Now comes the rondeel to lead us to thoughtfulness; its form supporting sense, it makes the fool wiser'.[54] The fact that comic texts contain these structures is again indicative of their basically serious intent. Comedy was deemed suitable not only for moral content, but also for the promotion of reason and moderation, via the elevated rhetorical forms it was made to contain.

A further point to mention is that the *klutchen* and *esbattesmenten* were rarely discriminated against by the chambers, as few *rederijkers* held them to be inferior to other genres. It is only towards the end of the period that there is any hint of 'an anti-farce trend', as Kramer puts it, and this is by no means widespread.[55] One witness to hostility is the Antwerp *rederijker* Willem van Haecht. Commenting on a festival in 1561, Van Haecht denounces the farce and hopes that it can be dispensed with in future, 'now that all wits are greater and have more knowledge of all arts'.[56] Damning though this remark might be, it is also unprecedented, and hardly represents a large-scale shift away from comic forms: in fact, the very festival Van Haecht

---

Low Countries', *European Medieval Drama* 12 (2008), 185–210.

[52] Reinder P. Meijer, *Literature of the Low Countries. A Short History of Dutch Literature in the Netherlands and Belgium* (The Hague, 1978), 52–3.

[53] 'Het referein kon redeneeren, overtuigen; het lied kon slechts opwekken, ontroeren, aangrijpen': Elslander, *Het refrein*, 9.

[54] 'Nu comd, tRondeel ons te ouerdachtene . . . staett dien zin te pachtene . . . maeckt den zot wisere': Matthijs de Castelein, *De const van rhetoriken* (Oudenaarde, 1986), 54.

[55] Kramer, *Mooi vies, knap lelijk*, 35.

[56] 'Nu als die verstanden kloeker zijn ende alle kunsten in meerder kennisse': W. Waterschoot, *Jan van der Noot: de poeticsche werken* (Ghent, 1975), 115.

is describing here offered a prize of seven drinking bowls for 'playing the best farce, with the fewest faults', and featured fools 'innocently spreading joy, and making foolery in words and deeds'.[57] A measure of the easy acceptance of the farces is the fact that they were predominantly written by the same figures as the openly serious pieces. Each chamber had its own appointed *factor* (maker) who was responsible for composing plays; in some cases, *factors* might even write for several fraternities at once.[58] Despite their title, they were still amateur writers for the most part, with trades and interests outside the chambers. It is clear that they were responsible for farces as well as *spelen van zinne*, simply as an accepted part of their duties. This can be seen in the career of Jacobus Celosse, *factor* of *De Orange Lelie* at Leiden, and author of both the humanist allegory *De konst van redenrijcke* ('The Art of Right-Reasoning') and the comic dialogue *T'vyer en t'water* ('The Fire and the Water').[59] The work of Corneelis Everaert and Jan van den Berghe, who are both represented in the present anthology, provides further examples of this convention. As Ben Stroman notes, the comic was merely part of the *factor*'s repertoire, as 'the rhetorician's need for elaboration' called for 'dynamic variation of seriousness and humour, the mixture of satire and didactics'.[60] The comic was simply one of the modes that *factors* were expected to compose, an accepted part of their activities. Again, there was no inconsistency between the chambers' instructive function and their use of comedy.

What exactly the farces were designed to teach becomes apparent when their particular forms of comedy are considered. At first glance, their chosen style of comedy seems to offer little that might edify the viewer, as the plays are rooted in the brutal strand of ridicule prevalent throughout the Middle Ages. There is certainly little evidence of later, more decorous comic principles in the drama: as Herman Pleij writes, the 'wit or pointed humour' that dominated seventeenth-century drama 'was not a requirement' for the *rederijkers*.[61] Most of the texts involve a central ruse of some kind, which leads to the infliction of pain or embarrassment on another character. Of the texts included here, for instance, *The Beggar* involves a corpse being stolen during a vigil and used to 'haunt' its grieving family, while *Jack Sweet-tooth*

---

[57] 'Wie met minst fauten, spelt dbeste Ebatement . . . wie innocentelyext om svrueghts versterken t'sotteken sal maken in woorden en wercken': J. B. Vander Straelen, 'Geschiedenis der Rederykkamer de Violieren of Violetteblæm, onder zinspreuk: Wt jonsten versaemt, te Antwerpen', *Het taelverbond* 9 (1853), 240.

[58] The office of *factor* is discussed at length in Bart Ramakers, 'Between Aea and Golgotha: The Education and Scholarship of Matthijs de Castelein', in *Education and Learning in the Netherlands*, 179–200, and in Susie Speakman Sutch, 'Dichters van de stad – De Brusselse rederijkers en hun verhouding tot de Franstalige hofliteratuur en het geleerde humanisme (1475–1522)', in *Literatuur in Brussel van de 14de tot de 18de eeuw*, ed. Jozef Janssens and Remco Sleiderink (Leuven, 2003), 141–59.

[59] On Celosse, see Catharina Ypes, *Petrarca in de Nederlandse letterkunde* (Amsterdam, 1934), 40–2.

[60] 'Dynamische afwisseling van ernst en humor, een mengsel van satire en didactiek . . . kan de rederijker zijn behoefte aan stilering ten volle bevredigen': Ben Stroman, *De Nederlandse toneelschrijfkunst: poging tot verklaring van een gemis* (Amsterdam, 1973), 58.

[61] 'Puntige humor ("wit") . . . zoniet een vereiste': Herman Pleij, 'Anna Bijns als pamflettiste? Het refrein van beide Maartens', *Spiegel der letteren* 42 (2000), 187–225 (214).

culminates with two boys being whipped, and *The Barefoot Brothers* includes a protracted fight between a friar and a thief. This focus on trickery and violence is in part
derived from the French fabliau, as a large number of farces take their plots from
fabliaux, albeit without the marked sexual content of the French poems.[62] However,
what makes the *rederijker* plays interesting is that they usually redirect this aggressive form of comedy towards an ethical purpose, forcing it to transmit the values
of their community. It can be noted that the *rederijkers'* humour tends to gravitate
towards the same handful of targets: hunger (*Barefoot Brothers*, *Jack Sweet-tooth*),
death (*Beggar*, *Three Lovers*), poverty (*Fisherman*, *Barefoot Brothers*), rural manners
(*Fisherman*, *Sweet-tooth*), the clergy (*Barefoot Brothers*, *Beggar*, *Three Lovers*), the
nobility (*Three Lovers*), the elderly (*Beggar*), and the young (*Three Lovers*, *Sweet-
tooth*). In other words, two principal categories are mined as sources of comedy:
on the one hand, farces turn causes of anxiety into amusement, making jokes about
privation or mortality; on the other, they ridicule particular social groups. The first
of these is clearly designed to defuse such pressures by means of laughter, along the
lines that Freud described in his theory of comedy, rendering a source of 'frustration'
'small, despicable or comic' in order to 'achieve ... the enjoyment of overcoming' it.[63]
In fact, offering relief of this kind was a conscious part of the *rederijkers'* objectives,
judging from their frequent claims that comedy should spread *vreucht* (joy), an idea
which appears in most of the texts included here.[64]

The second set of targets, however, seems to be a means of defining the urban
spectators as a group in their own right, and even setting up hierarchies within
this group. The people ridiculed are conspicuously outside the social class of the
rederijkers themselves. In most cases they belong to factions beyond the chambers'
core grouping of 'artisans, shopkeepers and merchants', since they are not middle-
class citizens, or are not of working age.[65] The comedy, then, serves to affirm the
audience's membership of the *rederijker's* social group, or presents this group as
desirable, by inviting spectators to mock other groups. This aim often takes a highly
literal form, as the audience-members are often aligned with characters who actively
ridicule others. For instance, in both *The Beggar* and *Three Lovers* there are points
at which the trickster characters stand back to watch the play unfold: that is, rather
than playing a continual role in the action, they merely set its events in motion and
observe the ensuing chaos and humiliation. This has the obvious effect of merging
audience and character, as both equally become witnesses of the *klucht*. The texts
then, with their mocking, savage comedy, spell out where the limits of the urban
community lie, who can be included within this community, and what values and
conduct it should prize.

---

[62] Arjan van Leuvensteijn and Jeanine Stuart, eds., *WD Hooft Door-trapte Meelis en J. Light
Noozeman Klaartje*, Noozeman Lichte Klaartje (Amsterdam, 1999), 37–8.

[63] Sigmund Freud, *Jokes and their Relation to the Unconscious*, trans. James Strachey
(Harmondsworth, 1991), 147.

[64] On this point, see Femke Kramer, 'Rigid Readings of Flexible Texts: The Case of Sixteenth
Century Comic Drama', in *Aspects of Genre and Type in Pre-modern Literary Cultures*, ed. Bert
Roest and Herman L. J. Vanstiphout (Leiden, 1999), 33–46 (42).

[65] Mariët Westermann, *The Amusements of Jan Steen: Comic Painting in the Seventeenth
Century* (Zwolle, 1997), 138.

FIGURE 2. A fool on stage with two allegorical figures. Detail from Pieter Bruegel, *Temperentia*, 1560. Museum Boijmans van Beuningen, Rotterdam.

Outside the farces, the same interest in moral instruction can also be seen in the activities of the fools. It seems that most chambers had an appointed *zotte* or fool to recite comic monologues of the kind represented in the first section of this anthology. They may also have composed such pieces; at least, *The Oath of Master Pawnbroker* seems to have been written by its performer, Jan Colyns.[66] The fools may also have played roles in the formal drama. In *Jack Sweet-tooth*, for instance, it is clear that the foolish character Lippen Loer (Philip Loser) is dressed in motley, the customary clothing of a fool; likewise the title-character of Willam Elias's *Tielebuys* (1541) is derived from 'Tiribus', a traditional 'type of fool who is better off than many serious-minded men', again suggesting that the role was written for a *zotte*.[67] Pieter

[66] See E. Roobaert, 'Jan Welravens, alias Oomken, schilder en rederijker to Brussel', *Bulletin, Musées royaux des beaux-arts* 3–4 (1961), 83–100.

[67] 'De namen Tiribus en Corebus . . . dat van de zot die ondanks of misschien wel dank zij zijn malle streken beter terechtkomt dan menig serieus mens voor zichzelf zou kunnen wensen': W. N. M. Hüsken, '1 augustus 1541: de klucht "Tielebuys" van Willem Vrancx wordt als welkomstspel gespeeld op het landjuweel van Diest. De kluchtentraditie in de Nederlanden', in *Een theatergeschiedenis der Nederlanden. Tien eeuwen drama en theater in Nederland en Vlaanderen*, ed. R. L. Erenstein (Amsterdam, 1996), 106–11 (108).

Bruegel's drawing *Temperentia* (1560) adds further evidence of this, depicting an open-air performance in which a fool shares the stage with two actors dressed as personifications (Fig. 2).[68]

What is important about these figures is that they seem to have been 'artificial' as opposed to 'natural' fools, as such entertainers were classified in the sixteenth century.[69] What this means is that they were not 'innocents', like the entertainers 'unable to function normally because of physical, mental, or emotional conditions' who were found at several medieval courts.[70] They were instead 'fools by art', who imitated or feigned madness, cultivating such a posture ironically. The artificial status of the chambers' fools can be deduced from their stylised appearance. They seem to have worn the traditional fool's costume depicted in several medieval and Renaissance illustrations (Fig. 3). For instance, the famous cap of ass's ears can be witnessed in the opening address of *Master Pawnbroker*, which begins by saluting its speaker's 'four ears'. Similarly the use of the bauble or *marot*, a sceptre carved to resemble the fool's own face, is testified in a number of surviving *tafelspelen* (table-plays).[71] These often consist of little more than an extended dialogue between the fool and his bauble: in *Een marot sot geclap* (*c*.1550s), for example, the fool Goet Geselschap (Good Fellowship) debates the merits of various wild birds with 'een marot, geheten Sot Geclap' ('a *marot*, named Foolish Chattering').[72] In addition to these details, there is some indication that the *zotten* might also have worn blackface on occasion, like the Italian harlequin or some English clowns.[73] At least Lukas Rotgans in his satirical poem *Boerekermis* ('Peasant Festival') describes a foolish actor who 'has thickly smeared his face with chimney-soot'.[74] All of these details show that the chamber *zotten* were artificial fools, wearing conventionalised, even caricatured dress.

All of this allows the fools to play a particular moral and social function. The conspicuously performative nature of the fool, the clear disparity between the unreal costume and the man inhabiting it, creates a powerfully ironic position. The fool is after all artificial, a fantastic posture with no basis in reality: as Robert Hornback has recently written, 'whereas the natural or "innocent" was an unconsciously transgressive social deviant' the 'fool by art' was marked by his 'self-consciousness'.[75] This in turn means that the statements issued by this figure are automatically defined as fictional, lacking any connection to reality. They are, in short, articulated in order

---

[68] Walter Gibson, 'Artists and Rederijkers in the Age of Bruegel', *Art Bulletin* 63 (1981), 426–46.

[69] Enid Welsford, *The Fool: His Social and Literary History* (London, 1968), 119.

[70] Vicki K. Janik, *Fools and Jesters in Literature, Art, and History: A Bio-bibliographical Sourcebook* (Westport, CT, 1998), 1.

[71] The *tafelspel* was typically a comic dialogue with limited action that could be performed by two or three speakers at the dining table itself. See Patricia Pikhaus, *Het tafelspel bij de rederijkers*, 2 vols. (Ghent, 1988–9), 1: 12–15.

[72] Hüsken, Ramakers and Schaars, *Trou moet blijcken*, 8: 207–15.

[73] On English blackface, see Meg Twycross and Sarah Carpenter, *Masks and Masking in Medieval and Early Tudor England* (Aldershot, 2002), 329–33.

[74] 'Hy heeft zyn troni dik met schoorsteenroet bestreeken': Lukas Rotgans, *Boerekermis*, ed. L. Strengholt (Gorinchem, 1968), 58.

[75] Robert Hornback, *The English Clown Tradition from the Middle Ages to Shakespeare* (Cambridge, 2009), 151.

to be rejected as falsehoods. In practice, this circumstance has a plain behavioural dimension, since many of the fool's utterances consist of instructions to the audience, such as 'always drink freely wherever you can' in the *Mock-Sermon on Saint Nobody* (line 21), and 'girls will ripen . . . give them a nudge, they fall on their backs' in the *Wonderful Prognostication* (line 257). By means of these commands, the fool spells out approved forms of conduct to the audience. His calls for idleness, drunkenness and disobedience highlight the necessity of avoiding such behaviour, as his improper position underlines their unacceptability. This could also have a professional as well as moral aspect. *The Blue Barge* and *Master Pawnbroker* each contain specific pieces of advice for particular tradesmen or groups: the former counsels youngsters to seek out 'the best company' while the latter instructs masons not to 'overload their foundations', in either case by seemingly advocating the opposite. The fool again underscores how firmly the chambers integrated the comic into their role as advisors to their communities. Although the monologues might seem less aggressive than the farces, and ostensibly more carnivalesque in their content, they are grounded in much the same educational intent.

FIGURE 3. An artificial fool in traditional costume. Albrecht Dürer, 'Von Vngedult der Straff' ('Of the Impatience of the Wrongdoer'), Sebastian Brant, *Der Narrenschiff* (Basel, Johann Bergmann von Olpe, 1494), fol. 67v.

A final function performed by the chambers was one that is peculiar to the dramatic culture of the Low Countries. By the last decades of the fifteenth century, the chambers had begun to organise events known as *rhetorijckfeesten* in Holland and *landjuwelen* (land-jubilees) in Brabant and Flanders. These were lavish dramatic contests which gathered together several chambers for days, even weeks, of feasting and performance. The *landjuweel* hosted in 1496 by the Antwerp chamber *De Violieren* (The Gillyflower), for instance, included participants from twenty-eight chambers, while the festival at Antwerp in 1561, 'the most spectacular of its kind', lasted for three full weeks and began with a procession of over two-hundred decorated chariots and wagons.[76] Prizes would be awarded under a range of different categories at these events. A typical occasion at Rotterdam in 1561 saw prizes given for 'the best serious play', 'the best fool', 'the best parade in the city', 'the best firework', and 'the best bonfire in front of a tavern'.[77] The chambers also competed to see which could stage the best formal presentation of its *blazoen*.[78] Winning chambers would customarily receive trophies, usually drinking vessels of various kinds, which were probably intended for use during their own feasts. Hence in the accounts of *De Violieren* there is mention of three cups, four silver tankards and a four-ounce silver cup, all won at the Ghent *landjuweel* of 1539; similarly, the prizes offered during the Rotterdam *feest* of 1561 included three wine jars, six tin jugs and an amphora.[79] It seems that these objects were designed to have symbolic rather than monetary value. At least this is the impression given by Richard Clough, an English visitor who witnessed the Antwerp *landjuweel* of 1561. Clough marvelled at the apparent meagreness of the prizes in comparison to the extravagance of the event itself, writing that 'thys was the strangest matter that ever I sawe . . . they shall wyn no more with all but a skalle [drinking bowl] of syllver weying 6 ownsys'.[80]

It was a source of considerable civic pride for a chamber to enter or host these contests; in fact, the main function a chamber possessed outside its own community was to represent its particular city in the competitions. Some of the importance attached to the contests can be seen in the willingness of city *raden* to pay subsidies in order that chambers could compete. In 1532, for example, the council of 's-Hertogenbosch gave an allowance to *Mozes Doorn* (Thorn of Moses) so that its members could travel to a *landjuweel* at Brussels, despite the fact that the *Doorn* already received a generous annual stipend of eighteen guilders.[81] The prestige attached to these events once again underscores the general importance of comedy for the *rederijkers*,

---

[76] E. van Autenboer, 'Een landjuweel te Antwerpen in 1496?', *Jaarboek de Fonteine* 29 (1978–9), 125–50; Anneke Huisman and Johan Koppenol, *Daer compt de Lotery met trommels en trompetten!: loterijen in de Nederlanden tot 1726* (Hilversum, 1991), 53. On the event see Edward van Even, *Het landjuweel van Antwerpen in 1561: eene verhandeling over dezen beroemden wedstrijd tusschen de rederijkkamers van Braband* (Ghent, 1861).

[77] Henk J. Hollaar, *Spelen van sinne vol schoone allegatien, drijderley referyenen – De Rotterdamse spelen van 1561* (Delft, 2006), 14.

[78] See Gerardus J. Steenbergen, *Het landjuweel van de rederijkers* (Leuven, 1951), 222.

[79] Waite, *Reformers on Stage*, 60; *Spelen van sinne vol schoone allegatien*, 14.

[80] John William Burgon, *The Life and Times of Sir Thomas Gresham*, 2 vols. (London, 1839), 1: 388. Clough's 'skalle' is most likely an anglicised version of the Dutch *schaal*, 'bowl'.

[81] P. van der Sluijs, 'Enkele kanttekeningen met betrekking tot de Bossche Rederijkerskamers', *Varia Historica Brabantica* 6–7 (1978), 187–205.

as comic performance invariably had a strong presence at the *landjuwelen*. Prizes were routinely offered for the best farce, the best *refrein int'zotte*, and for the most outstanding fool: at Ghent in 1539, for instance, 'a silver ape of four ounces' was awarded to the fool of *De Violieren* for his clowning.[82] In fact, on occasion comedy could become the exclusive focus of the feasts. In 1551 the fools of several chambers held an entire *landjuweel* of their own at Brussels, participating in days of performance and pageantry.[83]

As a final note, it is worth pointing out that the chambers were strongly affected by new intellectual currents in sixteenth-century Europe. Although their dramas were highly traditional in form, the fact that most *rederijkers* were drawn from the burgher and mercantile classes meant that they were deeply immersed in the political and economic lives of their cities. As a consequence, they could not fail to be influenced by new ideas emerging in the early part of the modern period. One particularly strong influence on their work was humanism. As a number of recent commentators have stressed, the chambers can be considered a vernacular wing of Dutch humanism, as they showed a keen interest in the mythology and philosophy of antiquity, and often strove to communicate this to their audiences.[84] Several of their surviving plays show a marked classical influence, such as the pieces collected in 1553 by Reijer Gheurts of the Amsterdam chamber *De Eglentier* (The Sweet Briar). Gheurts's manuscript includes traditional biblical and allegorical plays, like Ariaen Jacobsz's *Ghepredestineerde blinde* ('The Predestined Blind') and Jan Thönisz's *Sint Jans onthoofdinghe* ('Saint John's Beheading'), but preserves alongside these a number of pieces dealing with Ovidian and Virgilian themes, such as Cornelis van Ghistele's *Eneas end Dido* and Colijn Keyart's *Narcissus ende Echo*.[85] Other classically themed plays include Matthijs de Casteleyn's influential *Historye van Pyramus ende Thisbe* (c.1515), and the anonymous *Pluto Proserpina ontscaect* ('Pluto seizes Proserpina'), a May-play first performed at Dendermonde in 1519.[86] The *rederijkers*, in other words, included knowledge of Greek and Roman mythology among the lessons they sought to impart to their audiences, and used their plays as a channel for this information.

[82] Waite, *Reformers on Stage*, 60.

[83] See W. van Eeghem, 'Rhetores Bruxellenses', *Revue belge de philologie et d'histoire* 15 (1936), 47–78; Herman Pleij, 'Eind juli 1551 – Op het zottenfeest van Brussel wordt Meester Oom als vorst in een massaspel beëdigd – De stedelijke feestviering van bevrijdend ritueel naar gecontroleerd schouwtoneel', in *Een theatergeschiedenis der Nederlanden. Tien eeuwen drama en theater in Nederland en Vlaanderen*, ed. R. L. Erenstein (Amsterdam, 1996), 112–19.

[84] Herman Pleij, *Nederlandse literatuur in de late middeleeuwen* (Utrecht, 1990), 158–91; Anne-Laure van Bruane, 'Sociabiliteit en competitie. De sociaal-institutionele ontwikkeling van de rederijkerskamers in de Zuidelijke Nederlanden (1400–1650)', and Arjan van Dixhoorn, 'Burgers, branies en bollebozen. De sociaal-institutionele ontwikkeling van de rederijkerskamers in de Noordelijke Nederlanden (1400–1650)', in *Conformisten en rebellen – Rederijkerscultuur in de Nederlanden (1400–1650)*, ed. Bart Ramakers (Amsterdam, 2003), 45–64, 65–85.

[85] See the discussion in Mark Meadow, 'Volkscultuur of humanistencultuur? Spreekwoordenverzamelingen in de zestiende-eeuwse Nederlanden', *Volkskundig bulletin* 19 (1993), 208–40.

[86] G. A. van Es, *Piramus en Thisbe. Twee rederijkersspelen uit de zestiende eeuw* (Zwolle, 1965), 157–275; Jozef van Mierlo, *Geschiedenis van de letterkunde der Nederlanden*, 2 vols. (Brussels, 1939–40), 2: 259.

This humanist concern also filters into the comic texts generated by the chambers. There are, for instance, frequent references to the figure of Bacchus, who is adopted as a presiding deity of disorder in many pieces. He is the spirit of carnival itself in the *Sermoen van Bacchus* ('Sermon of Bacchus'), a speaking persona in the *Mandement van Bacchus* ('Commandment of Bacchus'), and is even canonised in the *Mock-Sermon on Saint Nobody*.[87] What is more, many of the plots of *kluchten* are derived from humanist authors. One example is *The Play of Three Lovers* in the present collection, which takes the majority of its narrative from Boccaccio's *Decameron* (*c.*1350).[88] In fact, as Hüsken has found, such sources are used more frequently in *rederijker* drama than folktales or other popular stories.[89] These allusions provide further evidence that the chambers did not isolate comedy from their perceived duty to instruct, as even the most overtly carnivalesque texts could serve as vehicles for learning.

However, alongside these concerns, the chambers were also subject to other, more volatile new ideas. The fact that the chambers consisted of laymen who saw themselves as imparters of religious knowledge seems to have made them a fertile seedbed for Protestantism. While their level of radicalism varied according to region, in the middle decades of the sixteenth century several *spelen* were produced that gave voice to Protestant concerns. The most notorious case of this occurred in 1539 at a *landjuweel* in Ghent. Here the prescribed theme of 'Welc den mensche stervende meesten troost es?' ('What is most comfort to a dying man?') became a lightning-rod for anti-Catholic sentiment: as Erné and Van Dis state in their edition of the Ghent plays, virtually the entire event descended into a 'savage expression of ill-feeling' against Rome, with sixteen out of nineteen plays directly attacking the church and its doctrines.[90] The *landjuweel* was itself followed by several days of rioting, for which the chambers were officially blamed. There were similar controversies both before and after this occurrence: chambers at Amsterdam were implicated in an attempted Anabaptist coup in 1535, and *rederijkers* were executed at Antwerp in 1547 and 1555.[91] However, the most serious flashpoint came in the summer of 1566, with the iconoclastic riots known as the *Beeldenstorm* (Storm of Images), which were directed against the ecclesiastic authorities and Philip II equally. These disturbances sparked a flurry of edicts and prosecutions against the *rederijkers* across the Netherlands, whether or not they were directly involved in the disturbances. In 1566 at Lier, for instance, the *factors* of both of the city's chambers, *De Ongeleerden* (The Unlearned) and *De Groeiende Boom* (The Growing Tree), were arrested and

---

[87] P. de Keyser, 'Het kluchtig sermoen van Bacchus', *Nederlandsch tijdschrift voor volkskunde* 30 (1925), 109–19; Herman Pleij, *Het gilde van de Blauwe Schuit* (Amsterdam, 1979), 253–5.

[88] René van Stipriaan, *Leugens en Vermaak: Boccaccio's novellen in de kluchtcultuur van de Nederlandse Renaissance* (Amsterdam, 1996). See also F. J. Lodder, *Lachen om list en lust. Studies on the Middle Dutch Comic Verse Narratives. Studies over de Middelnederlandse komische versvertellingen* (Ridderkerk, 1997), 219–30.

[89] Wim Hüsken, *Noyt meerder vreucht – compositie en structuur van het komisch toneel in de Nederlanden voor de Renaissance* (Deventer, 1987), 25.

[90] B. H. Erné and L. M. van Dis, *De Gentse spelen van 1539* (The Hague, 1982), 26. See also Anne-Laure van Bruaene 'Printing Plays: The Publication of the Ghent Plays of 1539 and the Reaction of the Authorities', *Dutch Crossing* 24 (2000), 265–84.

[91] Andrew Pettegree, *Reformation and the Culture of Persuasion* (Cambridge, 2005), 94; C. G. N. de Vooys, *Verzamelde letterkundige opstellen* (Antwerp, 1947), 25.

charged with propagating heresy.[92] Similar measures were taken in Mechelen and elsewhere.[93] Along the same lines, in 1567 a proclamation was published at Gouda calling for 'the closure, at least for a time, of all chambers of Meter or Rhetoric, for they are usually conventicles of heretics ... indeed religion is badly damaged by these plays of Rhetoric, and all are gravely offended'.[94]

Again, traces of these concerns can be found in the comedies of the chambers. One of the strangest cases is provided by a text included here, *The Barefoot Brothers*, which managed to spark a round of investigations into *rederijker* activity at Brussels in 1559. Alongside *The Brothers*, two further plays attracted the notice of the authorities, both comic texts, and the inquiry resulted in an official clampdown on all forms of dramatic performance. This case illustrates that comedy could be used as a platform for relatively serious religious issues, or was at least considered a potential vessel for such ideas. Once again, the importance of the comic is underscored, as here it served as a forum for one of the weightiest debates of the period.

To summarise all that has been said so far, while it may be easy to dismiss the comic as a trivial exercise, a form that 'is not meaningful, because its sense and scope hardly inform', it nonetheless possessed a high level of social importance in the early-modern Low Countries.[95] It was clearly valued by the chambers as a means of carrying out their educative functions, and equally capable of transmitting social and religious values. What is more, the fact that the form was deemed suitable for this broad range of concerns allows it to function as a lens through which the culture of the *rederijkers* can be brought into focus. As such, the comic drama of the period is a rewarding topic for study, a point we hope to demonstrate further through the texts collected here.

[92] L. van Boekel, 'Een zestiende-eeuwsche Liersche rederijker, Ambrosius van Molle', *Tijdschrift voor geschiedenis en folklore* 4 (1941), 83–136; L. van Boekel, 'Jeronimus van der Voort. Een zestiende-eeuwsche Liersche rederijker', *Tijdschrift voor geschiedenis en folklore* 6 (1943), 5–80.

[93] Eugeen van Autenboer, *Volksfeesten en rederijkers te Mechelen 1400–1600* (Ghent, 1962), 100.

[94] 'Claudantur simul omnes ad tempus saltem Camere Rhythmicorum sive Rhetoricorum, quia plerumque semper sunt conventicula hereticorum . . . his enim ludis Rhetoricorum potissimum collabitur religio pijque omnes offenduntur gravissime': Van Boheemen and Van der Heijden, *Retoricaal memoriaal*, 273.

[95] 'Komedie is niet zinvol, want inhoud en strekking daarvan refereren vrijwel': Pieter Visser, *Broeders in de geest: de doopsgezinde bijdragen van Dierick en Jan* (Deventer, 1988), 36.

PART I

Dramatic Monologues

This is the Madness

ALTHOUGH ECCENTRIC, fragmentary and difficult to classify, the brief satire *Dit es de frenesie* ('This is the Madness') is a highly significant document. It is in fact the earliest known comic monologue originating from the Netherlands.[1] As such, it warrants inclusion in the present anthology, despite its predating the other pieces collected here by several decades. The text itself has survived in one imperfect and unsigned copy, datable to *c*.1313–25 on the strength of its manuscript context.[2] Its manuscript, the so-called Amsterdamsche handschrift, is now held at the Library of the Royal Academy of Sciences. This seems to have preserved a fragmentary version of the poem. Not only has damage all but deleted two lines of verse, but an unknown amount of text may be missing from the end, since *The Madness* is the last item in the manuscript, and its final page is lost.

The poem itself is anonymous, although there has been some speculation regarding its authorship. The nineteenth-century scholar C. P. Serrure suggested that it might be an early work of Heinric or Hein van Aken, thought to have composed a number of romances and courtesy books at the close of the thirteenth century.[3] Serrure based his attribution on the fact that the Amsterdamsche handschrift also contains an early Dutch translation of the *Roman de la rose*, known as *Die rose* (*c*.1290), which is sometimes assigned to Van Aken. Nonetheless, this evidence aside, Serrure admitted that his theory was based on little more than 'bloote gissing' ('naked conjecture').[4] The attribution of *The Madness* to Van Aken has in fact never gained wide acceptance, and is complicated by the fact that Van Aken's authorship of *Die rose* is itself insecure.[5] It therefore seems unlikely that the composer of the poem can be identified with any certainty.

The Madness itself takes the form of a *biecht* or literary confession.[6] It is delivered by a Dutch student at Paris while he is apparently in bed with a local prostitute. In the space of the poem's ninety-four surviving lines, the student relates the romantic misfortunes that drove him to school, his preference for pies and dice over books, and his difficulty in obtaining a profitable benefice. As the poem concludes he attempts congress with

---

[1] Willy L. Braekman, *Medische en technische Middelnederlandse recepten. Een tweede bijdrage tot de geschiedenis van de vakliteratuur in de Nederlanden* (Ghent, 1975), 9–10.

[2] See Jan Willem Klein, '"Het getal zijner jaren is onnaspeurlijk". Een herijking van de dateringen van de handschriften en fragmenten met Middelnederlandse ridderepiek', *Tijdschrift voor Nederlandse taal- en letterkunde* 111 (1995), 1–23 (7).

[3] See Hein van Aken, *Van den coninc Saladijn ende van Hughen van Tabaryen*, ed. P. de Keyser (Leiden, 1950).

[4] C. P. Serrure, *Vaderlandsch museum voor Nederduitsche letterkunde, oudheid en geschiedenis*, 5 vols. (Ghent, 1855–63), 3: 59.

[5] W. J. A. Jonckbloet, *Geschiedenis der Nederlandsche letterkunde*, 2 vols. (Groningen, 1889), 2: 219; Hein van Aken, *Die rose*, ed. Eelco Verwijs (Utrecht, 1976), xxv; Dieuwke van der Poel, 'The *Romance of the Rose* and I: Narrative Perspective in the *Roman de la Rose* and its Two Middle Dutch Adaptations', in *Courtly Literature: Culture and Context*, ed. Keith Busby and Erik Kooper (Amsterdam, 1990), 573–85.

[6] J. W. Muller, 'Reinaert-studiën. III. Aernout en Willem. B. Het dubbel auteurschap van Reinaert I A en B', *Tijdschrift voor Nederlandsche taal- en letterkunde* 53 (1934), 127–67 (163).

his bedfellow. Judging from the fruitlessness of this coupling, the girl and her client are equally inexperienced, as neither seems to know what to do with their bodies: 'I think she wishes that I should ride/ Now lengthways, and now crosswise' (lines 92–3).

The poem is interesting for revealing the extent to which Dutch comedy was dependent on French at this early stage in its development. It shows a number of fairly strong links to French literature, especially the fabliau. The text seizes on the 'scatology, scattered body parts and sexual explicitness' of the fabliau with consistency and relish, from its concluding episode of unsuccessful sexual acrobatics, to its opening reference to nocturnal 'poets' who 'have their arses gaping wide open' (lines 5–6).[7] What is more, the very persona of its narrator seems to be imported from the fabliaux: his poverty and lechery recall the archetypal *clers escoliers*, the itinerant students who take centre-stage in such texts as *La Borgoise d'Orliens* and *Des trois avugles de compiengne*.[8]

However, away from these fairly straightforward borrowings, the text also displays further traits of the genre. In particular, it shares the fabliau's antagonistic relationship with higher discourses, especially the romance. From the start *The Madness* systematically inverts many romantic conventions. Its narrator complains of love-sickness, bewailing that his love will surely kill him, although the metaphors he selects to describe his suffering are markedly more mundane than elevated. At one point he laments that he has become 'as grey as a cat', a simile that doubly undercuts his extravagant pining, suggesting homeliness on the one hand and animalism on the other (line 15).[9] Moreover, he also allows boredom or self-preservation to overcome the usual 'depression and self-abasement' induced by *amor hereos*.[10] He eventually leaves his mistress for the fleshpots of Paris, reflecting that 'it is not altogether stupid/ If you turn back at halfway' (lines 21–2). Other high discourses are exposed to similar ridicule. The opening section of the text parodies a rhetorical exordium, reading as a sort of distorted *captatio benevolentiae*. The narrator claims that he works all night on his compositions, provided that he is not asleep, before comparing his verse to a *blaest* of nocturnal flatulence, rather than the divine inspiration conventionally evoked by orators.[11] All of this clearly recalls the fabliaux, sharing in its commitment to 'invert the proprieties of official culture'.[12] In fact, the identification between anal expulsion and poetic composition occurs in one of the most famous examples of French *gaîté d'esprit*, Rabelais's *La Vie de Gargantua et de Pantagruel*. At one point in the first book, Grandgousier asks his son 'mon petit couillon, as-tu pris au pot, vu que tu rimes déjà?' ('my little bollock, have you taken to the pot, since you are

---

[7] Jerry Root, 'The Old French Fabliau and the Poetics of Disfiguration', *Medievalia et Humanistica* 24 (1997), 17–32 (17).

[8] *Fabliaux et contes des poètes françois des XI, XII, XIII, XIV et XV siecles*, ed. Etienne Barbazan and Dominique Martin Meon (Paris, 1808), 161–8, 398–408. See Elizabeth Baldwin, 'Chaucer, Medieval Drama and a Newly Discovered Seventeenth-Century Play: The Survival of Medieval Stereotypes?', in *Farce and Farcical Elements*, ed. Wim N. M. Hüsken, Konrad Schoell and Leif Søndergaard (Amsterdam, 2002), 85–102 (89).

[9] On similar metaphors in the fabliaux, see Anne Elizabeth Cobby, *Ambivalent Conventions: Formula and Parody in Old French* (Amsterdam, 1995), 70.

[10] Mary Wack, *Lovesickness in the Middle Ages: The Viaticum and its Commentaries* (Philadelphia, 1990), 162.

[11] Herman Pleij, 'Literatuur als medicijn in de late middeleeuwen', *Literatuur* 2 (1985), 25–34 (30).

[12] Lillian M. Bisson, *Chaucer and the Late Medieval World* (New York, 1998), 257.

already rhyming?').[13] This is a complex pun, hinging on the double-meanings of *pot* and *rimer*: it can mean both 'have you taken a pint-pot, since you are singing', and 'have you used a chamber-pot, since you are smearing shit'. Much like the author of *The Madness*, Rabelais therefore equates poetry with excretion.

As is consistent with its foundation in the fabliau, other aspects of the poem also register further degrees of French influence. Although it is unlikely that the poem simply follows a specific French source directly, since many of its jokes rely on the narrator's poor grasp of the language and would not be possible in a francophone text, its very title suggests some French inspiration. The word *frenesie* is itself taken from French and is not commonly used in Dutch: in fact, to this day some commentators are obliged to render it as the more familiar *waanzin*.[14] When this is added to the Parisian setting of the poem, and the incorporation of French phrases and expressions, it is clear that the piece has firm connections to French comic literature.

Nonetheless French is not the only language to influence the text, as it also contains elements from a range of Latin comic genres.[15] There are a number of episodes within the main narrative that evoke the characteristic idioms of Latin satire. One of the clearest instances of this occurs in the poem's attack on simony, which focuses especially on the use of consistory courts to cheat poorer clerics out of preferment. Complaining that he is likely to be robbed of his stipend once he has secured it, the narrator remarks that 'they will twist my case in such a way/ That I will not keep my benefice' (lines 52–3). He goes on to state that in such hearings 'a florin/ Is better there, believe you me,/ Than a sack full of Latin' (lines 58–60). This brief sequence contains numerous echoes of Latin venality satire which, according to John Yunck, had its heyday in the twelfth and thirteenth centuries, after the expansion of the papal chancery.[16] For instance, the claim that money is superior to Latin resembles the ironic comparisons drawn throughout this literature. The earlier poets speak of 'lucrum Lucam superat, Marco marcam praeponderat' ('lucre overcoming Luke, the mark outweighing Mark') and 'crucis denarii mira potentia' ('the miraculous power of the cross of the coin').[17] In asserting that money has greater power than the language of religious discourse, *The Madness* evokes these claims, similarly asserting that 'money could do miracles', and that 'what official doctrine predicated of God ... was in real life observably true of money'.[18] Further hints of money-satire appear in the narrator's suspicion that his case will be *leecht* (twisted). This term recalls the commonplace that money has the ability to invert and distort, to 'bring about the

[13] François Rabelais, *Gargantua*, ed. R. Calder (Geneva, 1970), 90.

[14] See Pleij, 'Literatuur als medicijn': 30.

[15] For further information on the poem's use of its sources, see Ben Parsons and Bas Jongenelen, 'Better than a Sack Full of Latin: Anticlericalism in the Middle Dutch *Dit es de Frenesie*', *Church History and Religious Culture* 89 (2009), 431–53.

[16] John Yunck, *The Lineage of Lady Meed: The Development of Mediaeval Venality Satire* (Notre Dame, 1963), 85.

[17] 'Song on the Bishops', in *The Political Songs of England: From the Reign of John to that of Edward II*, ed. Thomas Wright (London, 1839), 11; 'De Cruce Denarii', in *Latin Poems Commonly Attributed to Walter Mapes*, ed. Thomas Wright (London, 1841), 223.

[18] Alexander Murray, *Reason and Society in the Middle Ages* (Oxford, 1978), 76. See also Nicholas G. Round, 'Juan Ruiz and Some Versions of *Nummus*', in *The Medieval Mind: Hispanic Studies in Honour of Alan Deyermond*, ed. Ian Macpherson and Ralph Penny (London, 1999), 393.

fraternization of incompatibles', as Marx comments on a sixteenth-century example.[19] The opening lines of one piece show this convention clearly: 'manus ferens munera/ pium facit impium . . . nummus lenit aspera' ('the hand bearing bribes makes the holy scandalous . . . the coin smoothes over sharpness').[20] The suspicions of *The Madness*'s narrator at least resemble the twisting action attributed to money, its reversal of 'proper relations', and conversion of 'values' into their opposites.[21]

The poem also echoes a tradition Kathryn Kerby-Fulton defines as 'reformist apocalypticism'. Examples of this literature include the *Scivias* of Hildegard of Bingen (*c*.1151), Joachim of Fiore's *Expositio in Apocalipsim* (*c*.1184), and Bridget of Sweden's *Tractatus de Summis Pontificibus* (*c*.1370). Broadly speaking, apocalypticism is characterised by its use of prophecy as a means of redressing contemporary abuses. As Kerby-Fulton defines it, 'the state of the Church's religious orders or of one particular order or heretical group is nearly always at the heart of the apocalypticist's concern . . . they handed down judgments on contemporaries, envisioned Church reform by brute force, and reacted indignantly to current political, social, and religious events'.[22] *The Madness* likewise uses visionary language and imagery to criticise and ridicule the church. After a brief conversation with the prostitute character, the narrator breaks off to describe a dream he has had. He claims to have seen 'a calf singing Mass' which later becomes a cardinal at Rome, where it has a lucrative career selling indulgences (line 75). This is followed by a vision of a priest in Kempen, who remains strangely indifferent as a child he is baptising is transformed into a goat in his hands: 'He did not give a fart/ That he did this thing' (lines 86–7).

Aside from the fact that this sequence occurs within the visionary framework of a dream, other details link it to prophetic literature. Like the apocalyptic texts Kerby-Fulton describes, it makes a concerted effort 'to fit the present time and coming periods of time into a pre-eschatological pattern', reworking biblical prophecy to reflect contemporary abuses.[23] The lucrative calf that proves 'most welcome to the pope' not only suggests the idol of Exodus 32.4–35, which leads the Israelites into a 'heinous sin' to be paid for 'in the day of revenge', it also alludes to similar creatures in the prophetic books.[24] The animal also evokes a New Testament account of Christ's sacrifice, and of the future salvation secured by the Passion: 'but Christ, being come an high Priest of the good things to come . . . neither by the blood of goats or of calves, but by his own blood, entered once into the Holies' (Hebrews 9.11–12). The fact that the narrator has witnessed what this passage specifically rules out adds to the sense of catastrophe, as 'things' in the vision drift badly away from the 'good' promised in the Testament. *The Madness* then follows the tactics of apocalyptic complaint, satirising the clergy by generating a vision of grotesque cosmic upheaval. Although its dream sequence seems rather less serious in intent than most medieval apocalypses, it nonetheless applies 'the characteristics that were expected to occur at the end of history' to the

---

[19]   Karl Marx, *Early Writings*, trans. and ed. T. B. Bottomore (New York, 1964), 192.

[20]   'De Nummo', in Wright, *Latin Poems Attributed to Walter Mapes*, 226.

[21]   Andrew Cowell, *At Play in the Tavern: Signs, Coins, and Bodies in the Middle Ages* (Ann Arbor, MI, 1999), 88.

[22]   Kathryn Kerby-Fulton, *Reformist Apocalypticism and Piers Plowman*, Cambridge Studies in Medieval Literature 7 (Cambridge, 1990), 4–5.

[23]   Ibid., 9.

[24]   See for instance Hosea 14.2, Malachi 4.2, and Revelation 4.7.

existing state of the church.[25]

Nevertheless, despite its foundation in these literary or poetic forms, there can be no doubt that the piece is intended for dramatic performance. Piero Boitani's remarks on the English fabliaux are just as appropriate here: like *Dame Sirith* or *De Interludio Clerici ad Puellam*, *The Madness* 'shows the fabliau in the process of becoming theatre'.[26] The text is clearly designed for recital rather than reading. One signal of this is the fact that it has a clearly identifiable, explicitly characterised narrator. Its student is self-evidently a role to be played, suggesting that the piece itself needs to be acted out to achieve its fullest effect. Much the same point is implied by its inclusion of one other brief speaking part. When the student's bedfellow interjects her own voice at one stage in the text, this also calls for active performance, as it would give a player the opportunity to adopt a second persona briefly. In fact, in these respects the text looks forward to later traditions of comic monologue in the Low Countries. Similar features and techniques are no less evident in later pieces, as Arjan van Leuvensteijn and Jeanine Stuart have observed.[27] One piece which bears particularly close comparison is the 1560 text *A Wise and Wonderful Prognostication*, also translated in this volume. This similarly calls for its performer to adopt the role of a well-defined character, in this case the folkloric figure Eulenspiegel, and demands that they parrot and mimic a wide range of other voices.

However, in terms of its place in Dutch drama as a whole, the main conclusion to be drawn about *The Madness* is its immaturity. All told, the text shows how undeveloped the tradition of comic monologue is at this early stage. The very fact that the poem has been driven to take its material from non-dramatic forms such as the fabliau and the Latin satires shows that the piece lacks specifically Dutch models to follow. The writer is clearly working without the benefit of a cohesive tradition to draw from: rather than having a set of exemplars or conventions already in place, he is compelled to look elsewhere for his forms and material. Therefore, while the text is undeniably as 'kostlijk en kostbaar' ('priceless and precious') as Cornelis Kruyskamp describes, being the first extant witness to a rich tradition in Dutch theatre, it also shows the monologue in a relatively inchoate state.[28] Although the text provides early evidence for the monologue in the Low Countries, and may even, as Hüsken and Schoell suggest, have paved the way for the development of the *klucht* itself by including multiple voices, it also shows how little the form is established at this stage in its history.[29]

---

[25] E. Randolph David, 'Abbot Joachim of Fiore: A Reformist Apocalyptic', in *Fearful Hope: Approaching the New Millennium*, ed. Christopher Kleinhenz and Fannie LeMoine (Madison, WI, 1999), 207–14 (207).

[26] Piero Boitani, *English Medieval Narrative in the Thirteenth and Fourteenth Century* (Cambridge, 1982), 29.

[27] Arjan van Leuvensteijn and Jeanine Stuart, eds., *WD Hooft Door-trapte Meelis en J. Light Noozeman Klaartje*, Noozeman Lichte Klaartje, Stichting Neerlandistiek VU Amsterdam (Münster, 1999), 37; Bernadette Rey-Flaud, *La Farce ou la machine a rire: theorie d'un genre dramatique 1450–1550*, Publications romanes et françaises 167 (Geneva, 1984).

[28] Cornelis Kruyskamp, *De Middelnederlandse boerden voor het eerst verzameld* (The Hague, 1957), 10.

[29] Wim Hüsken, *Noyt meerder vreucht – compositie en structuur van het komisch toneel in de Nederlanden voor de Renaissance* (Deventer, 1987), 17; Konrad Schöll, *Das komische Theater des französischen Mittelalters: Wirklichkeit und Spiel* (Munich, 1975).

Dit es de Frenesie

Het dich[t] al dat lepel lect:
waendi dat ic bem vergect,
dat ic oec niet dichte ende make,
des nacht als ic niet en vake?
5   menichgen, als hi slaept,
sijn ers herde wide gaept
ende blaest als ene bosine.
Ay ute vercorne fine!
des es leden menichgen dach,
10   dat mi v minne int herte lach,
ende gine wilt mijns niet ontfarmen.
Dicken hebbedi doen verwarmen
mijn herte ende gemaect cout;
om v bem ic worden out
15   ende graeu als ene catte,
ende gine achtes dit no datte.
ocht v minne mi steruen daede,
wie soude mi betren die scaede?
Lachtijs, maecti v sceren,
20   So willics mi af keren,
want hine dult algader niet
die te haluen wege weder tiet;
anders waric in dole.
Nv liggic te parijs ter scole
25   ende bem daer een studant.
Selden coemt mi boec in die hant,
maer ic lere ontginnen pasteiden;
bem ic dan ter quader weiden,
es een quaet dorp dan parijs?
30   ic wedde sinc contre sijs,
nochtan eysch ic toe twee aes:
die seide dat ic ware .i. dwaes,
hine ware mi niet willecome.
Alsic dan weder thus come,
35   so bem ic meester vander arten
ende wille eten vleesch ende tarten
ende hebbe gewonden den croec.
Ic soude node stoeten een loec,
maer ic songe wel een montet.
40   Int leste hebbic an een net
ende bem een everardijn.

*   The Dutch text is taken from Kruyskamp, *De Middelnederlandse boerden*, 96–9. Used with permission.

This is the Madness

A poet is anyone that can lick a spoon:
Do you think that I am a fool,
That I do not rhyme and compose
At night if I am not asleep?
Many others, as they sleep,
Have their arses gaping wide open,
And blasting away like a trumpet.
Oh you, highest beauty!
Many days have passed
Since love for you lodged in my heart,
But you will not accept it.
Often you have heated up
My heart and made it cold;
Because of you I grow old
And as grey as a cat,
But you don't care one way or another.
Should loving you kill me,
Who would repay the cost?
You laugh, you mock me,
So I am obliged to depart,
Because it is not altogether stupid
If you turn back at halfway;
If I did otherwise I'd be lost.
Now I reside in Paris at school
And I am a student there.
My book seldom comes into my hand,
I learn more about slicing pies;
Am I in the wrong place,
Is there a worse village than Paris?
At dice I bet *cinq contre six*,[1]
Even then I keep back two aces:
Whoever says that I am a fool,
He is not welcome to me.
And when I head back home,
Then I will be master of arts
And I will eat meat and tarts
And I will wear my hair in curls.
I will not have to know how to cook with garlic,
But I might sing a motet well.
At the very least I will wear a net
And will be a mendicant.

[1] 'Five against six' (French).

Ic dronke gerne goeden wijn,
maer ic en weet waermet copen,
dus moet ic achter lande lopen
te minen moyen, te minen maegen,
die mijn ongheual luttel claegen.
so hebbic die prouende met ghewelde
tusscen couden berge ende biestervelde;
so coemt een ander ende wilse mi nemen:
gaet ten biscop van bremen,
hi sal v te rechte houden.
Soe leecht ment in de vouden
dat ic en behoude niet.
Dus es den menichgen gesciet
die sonder recht tsine verloes,
want dat paepscap es al loes.
Ende constu spreken geen latijn?
Ay here, een florijn
es daer beter, geloeft mi des,
dan een sac vol latijns es;
dit coemt al bi symonien.
Nv willic scone vrouwen vrien
ende moet gelt costen mede
al […]
mi bliv[…]
die duuel soude mi bet hebben
want ic bem al sonder goet
ende ligge onder voet
Ki bien fra bien ara.
Waendi dat ic niet en versta?
Hets walsch dat gi spreect.
Gi hebt mi vten slape gewect,
wel leede moete v gescien!
Ic hebbe in minen drome gesien
een calf singen messe
en kende lettren niet sesse,
ende het wert cardinael te rome
ende was den paeus willecome,
want het was sire suster kint –
dus es die werelt nv gescint –

45

50

55

60

65

70

75

80

I drank good wine before,
But I cannot buy that any more,
So I must wander through the whole country
45 And go to my aunts, to my kinsmen,
Who sympathise little with my misfortune.
I would wield my benefice with force
Between Cold Mountain and Waste Land;²
When another comes to take it from me,
50 He must go to the bishop of Bremen,
He will make a reckoning for you.
They will twist my case in such a way
That I will not keep my benefice.
In this way many men have been treated
55 Who lost all they had without justice,
Since the papacy is wholly empty.
But can't you speak any Latin?
Aye, my lord, a florin
Is better there, believe you me,
60 Than a sack full of Latin is;
This all comes about through simony.
Now I want to seduce lovely women
But that will cost me money
All […]³
65 It stays […]
The devil shall swiftly take me
Because I am entirely without goods
And I lie under foot.
*Qui bien fera bien ira.*⁴
70 Do you think I do not understand that?
It's French that you are speaking.
You have woken me from my sleep,
You may well regret doing that!
I saw in my dreams
75 A calf singing mass
It did not know its letters,
And it became cardinal at Rome
And was most welcome to the pope,
Since it was his sister's child –
80 Thus the world is now disgraced –

---

² Biesterveld (Wasteland) and Coudenberge (Coldmount) are the names of actual settlements in North Brabant, leading Jonckbloet and Verwijs to identify this region as the probable origin of the poem; given the context in which they appear, however, and the fact that several regions in the Low Countries contain villages with similar names, these places are more likely to be symbolic: see Jonckbloet, *Geschiedenis der Nederlandsche letterkunde* 2: 219; Van Aken, *Die rose*, xxv.
³ The manuscript is damaged at this point, rendering these two lines unreadable.
⁴ 'Who does good will receive good' (French).

het vercochte om gelt pardoen
Ic sach een kint kerstin doen
van enen pape in kempin lande,
ende onder des papen hande
so wort dat kint een geet.
hine gauer niet omme enen dreet
dattie dinc bet vore.
Wat wijt mi dese hoere?
Si clapt mijn hoeft ontwee!
deus, mi es herde wee!
ende legt mi ouer dander side.
Mi dunct altenen dat ic ride
alse nv langes, alse nv dwers,
op eens graeus moencs ers […]

85

90

It sold pardons for gold.
I saw a child being baptised
By a priest in the land of Kempen,
And under the priest's hands
85 The child changed into a goat.
He did not give a fart
That he did this thing.
What does this whore want from me?
Her chattering splits my head in two!
90 Deuce, I am suffering severely!
She lies over on my other side.
I think she wishes that I should ride
Now lengthways, and now crosswise,
Upon a grey monk's arse […]

The Guild of the Blue Barge

AFTER *This is the Madness*, the earliest Dutch comic monologue to survive is *De Gilde van de Blauwe Scuit* (*c.*1450). Although *The Madness* and *The Blue Barge* are separated by little over a hundred years, there are a number of obvious differences between the two. Whereas the earlier piece is something of an anomaly, being fairly isolated, difficult to classify and seemingly cobbled together from various disparate traditions, *The Blue Barge* shows comic oration in the Netherlands at a much fuller level of development. What is more, it presents the culture of the *rederijkerskamers* as robust, confident and vital, and displays the easy integration of comic performance into the rituals of the groups.

The text itself is preserved in a single manuscript, a 'repertoire book' now kept at the National Library of the Netherlands, which was evidently compiled in the second half of the fifteenth century.[1] Since its rediscovery in the nineteenth century this has sometimes been given the title *Van vrouwen ende van minne* ('On Women and on Love'), after the first few items it contains.[2] Unfortunately, the collection does not provide a very reliable copy of the *The Blue Barge*. In the first place, the text it preserves is clearly corrupt. It contains a number of unaccountable repetitions, as the poem revisits some of the targets already satirised, in a manner at odds with the highly regimented form it is attempting to cultivate. Moreover, a number of lines have obviously been omitted by the scribe, as several couplets are incomplete, and the text as a whole is fragmentary, with anywhere between 36 and 350 lines missing from its opening section.[3] The manuscript also gives little indication of the provenance of the piece. Although *The Blue Barge*'s references to Antwerp and Brabant suggest an origin in one of the southern provinces, it is difficult to fix this with any certainty.

These problems are further exacerbated by the text's own tendency to mask its origins with playfulness and scatology. While on the surface it does seem to disclose some useful information about its production, closer inspection reveals that these references should be treated with caution. The statement of authorship at the end of the piece, for instance, is deeply problematic, as Van Vloten first observed in the

---

[1] The manuscript is described and dated in H. Kienhorst, 'Middelnederlandse verzamelhandschriften als codicologisch object', in *Middeleeuwse verzamelhandschriften uit de Nederlanden*, ed. Gerard Sonnemans (Hilversum, 1996), 39–60 (55).

[2] Eelco Verwijs, *Van vrouwen ende van minne, Middelnederlandsche gedichten uit de 14de en 15de eeuw* (Groningen, 1871). See also Truus van Bueren and Jeanne Verbij-Schillings, 'Een rijkgeschakeerde cultuur: de Hollandse kunstproductie in opdracht van hof, kloosters en steden', in *Geschiedenis van Holland*, ed. Thimo de Nijs and Eelco Beukers, 3 vols. (Hilversum, 2002–3), I: 197–258 (213).

[3] F. van Thijn, 'Blauwe schuit', in *De Nederlandse en Vlaamse auteurs van middeleeuwen tot heden met inbegrip van de Friese auteurs*, ed. G. J. van Bork and P. J. Verkruijsse (Weesp, 1985), 77–8; Herman Pleij, *Het gilde van de Blauwe Schuit: literatuur, volksfeest en burgermoraal in de late middeleeuwen* (Amsterdam, 1979), 243.

late nineteenth century.[4] In the final few lines the author identifies himself with what appears to be a typical Dutch toponym, introducing himself as 'Jacop van Oestvoren'. At first glance this appears to be fairly straightforward: there is indeed a region on the western coast of Holland called Oostvoorne, which could plausibly be the birthplace of the poet. However, the word 'Oestvoren' in fact conceals a number of tacit jokes and allusions. The first of these concerns the village of Maerlant, a settlement located in Oostvoorne. Maerlant is notable for being the workplace of Jacob van Maerlant, the great thirteenth-century vernacular poet, long revered as 'de vader der Hollandsche dichtschool' ('the father of Dutch poetry').[5] Given that Oestvoren is paired with the first name Jacob, *The Blue Barge* appears to be making an oblique reference to Van Maerlant. However, the name includes more meanings than this alone, since *oestvoren* can also be divided into *oest*, from the verb *hoesten* or 'cough', and *voren*, meaning 'forward' or 'in front'. This would suggest that 'dichte van oestvoren' should in fact be read as 'the poet who coughs from the front'.[6] The poet's signature can therefore be seen as a reprisal of a joke used in *The Madness*, which identifies poetic composition and farting, as it insists that this writer's air is expelled forwards, not backwards. Either way, the poet's name is clearly an elaborate fiction. It is either an attempt to claim authority for the text by comparing it to Van Maerlant's work, or a variation on an old comic conceit, or even an obscene pun on the name of the earlier poet. At any rate, it is unlikely to represent the name of an actual *factor*. With this in mind, it is difficult to take seriously any of the other claims the text makes of itself. For instance, its internal date of 1413 is probably a further joke, one that sets the time of the guild's foundation implausibly early.

Nonetheless, despite these problems, it is possible to establish some aspects of the poem's original context with reasonable certainty. The occasion of its performance can be determined from a series of references in the poem. The central symbol of the text, that of the *blauwe schuit* (blue barge) is fundamental here. The *schuit* probably refers to a type of *punt* or carnival float included in the *ommegancken*, processions staged annually by many cities in the Low Countries.[7] The use of ships in such pageants is documented from 1135, when a ship mounted on wheels was apparently drawn through several towns in Brabant.[8] The vessels continued to be used throughout the fifteenth and sixteenth centuries: later examples include the ship of Charles V, which was paraded through Brussels from 1559, and the ship of 'Sint Reynuyt' (Saint Empty) the 'patroon van drinkebroers' ('patron of drinkers'), which is first mentioned in 1520.[9] The blue barge seems to have been one of these *punten*,

---

[4] J. van Vloten, 'Jacob van Oostvoorne (Contribution to Clarification of Several Questions Maerlant) (Bijdrage tot toelichting van verschillende Maerlants-vragen)', *De taal- en letterbode* 1 (1870), 83–93.

[5] John Bowring, *Brieven* (Leeuwarden, 1830), 9.

[6] Pleij, *Het gilde van de Blauwe Schuit*, 82.

[7] See J. Dewolfs, 'Historiek van processies en ommegancken van Onze-Lieve-Vrouw ten Poel-Tienen', *De Brabantse folklore* 26 (1975), 145–55.

[8] Martin W. Walsh, '"Martín y muchos pobres": Grotesque Versions of the Charity of St Martin in the Bosch and Bruegel Schools', *Essays in Medieval Studies* 14 (1997), 107–20.

[9] J. Jacquot, 'Panorama des fetes et ceremonies du regne', in *Les Fêtes de la Renaissance*, ed. J. Jacquot, 2 vols. (Paris, 1958–60), 2: 413–91 (469); Dirk Coigneau, *Refreinen in het zotte bij de rederijkers*, 2 vols. (The Hague, 1982), 2: 392; Gerard Brom, *Schilderkunst en litteratuur in de 16e*

FIGURE 4. The blue barge as a vessel for foolery and carnivalesque debauchery. Print by Pieter van der Heyden after Hieronymus Bosch, *Die blau Schuijte* ('The Blue Barge'), 1559. Collection of the Gemeentemuseum, The Hague.

also drawn through the streets during the *ommegancken*. This is clear from a number of pictorial sources, which invariably link the ship to carnival or *Vastenavond*. In the work of Pieter Bruegel the Elder, for instance, the image appears twice, once in *Dulle Griet* (1562) and once in *De strijd tussen Vastenavond en Vasten* (1559), both times within a riotous carnival landscape.[10] It also makes a significant appearance in a lost painting by Hieronymus Bosch, which survives in an engraved copy by Pieter van der Heyden (Fig. 4). The Van der Heyden imprint includes a quatrain which again links the barge with festivity, connecting it to the clowning, drunkenness and general licentiousness of *Vastenavond*:

> Daer platbroeck speelman is en stierman in de bane
> Daer sien hem de voghelen voer eenen huÿben ane
> En al tiert sijn gheselschap datse moghten sweeten
> Het sullen de sanghers in de blau schuÿte heeten.[11]

en *17e eeuw* (Utrecht, 1957), 122.

[10] See Walter S. Gibson, *Bruegel* (Oxford, 1977), 84.

[11] Dirk Bax, *Ontcijfering van Jeroen Bosch* (The Hague, 1949), 160.

37

(Here the buffoon is a musician and helmsman at once,
Here the birds recognise him as a foolish one,
And although his companions might perspire
They shall be called the singers of the blue barge.)

It also seems that the barge was adopted as a soubriquet for carnival revellers themselves. At Zeeland a popular fraternity of the 'Blauwe Scuten' existed from *c.*1490 to 1597, when it was finally suppressed by the *raad* of Tholen.[12] In fact, the links between the blue barge and popular inversion are so strong that they continued into the twentieth century. In the early 1940s, during the German occupation of the Netherlands, it gave its name to a series of unauthorised prints by F. R. A. Henkels, A. Buning and A. Zuithoff, which were often openly critical of the Nazi-imposed Seyss-Inquart regime.[13] At any rate, it is clear that the central symbol of *The Blue Barge* is firmly connected to medieval civic celebration.

All of this strongly suggests that the poem had similar links to *Vastenavond*. In fact, given its narrator's open praise of carnival in line 282, as a time when certain 'liberties' reign, it can be safely assumed that it participated directly in such festivities, perhaps being recited at the culmination of a procession or during a feast. This setting also explains the text's jarring transition from sharp moral critique to playful ribaldry in its closing section. Like the occasion of carnival itself, which directly precedes Lent, the poem is positioned between sporting revelry and sober penitence, and so reflects this in its tonal shifts. However, for all this, the *Blue Barge* does not seem to have been part of a public celebration. It seems unlikely that the text was designed for recital in the market-place or other open venue, as it is better suited for an exclusive audience of *rederijkers*. One indication of this is the fact that the text addresses most social groups in the third rather than second person. Also telling is its comparative leniency when dealing with merchants and other middle-class professionals, who are in fact the only major social group not to be satirised. The closest the text comes to attacking burghers is a lengthy section on their profligate children, which falls short of directing accusations at the parents themselves. Like many other forms of declamation, therefore, the text was most likely intended to be heard within the confines of the *kamer* itself, during a chamber's private celebrations at carnival-time.

In terms of existing criticism on the piece, the best-known modern reading is probably that of Michel Foucault, whose *Histoire de la folie* (1961) opens with a lengthy and detailed discussion of the Ship of Fools motif in medieval and Renaissance art. In the course of this discussion, *The Blue Barge* is evoked at a number of points, as Foucault considers it the earliest witness to a pre-Enlightenment view of madness: according to Foucault, the poem conceives insanity as 'a dramatic debate

---

[12] J. L. de Jager, *Volksgebruiken in Nederland: een nieuwe kijk op tradities* (Utrecht, 1981), 92–4; W. M. H. Hummelen, *Repertorium van het rederijkersdrama 1500–ca.1620* (Assen, 1968), 250; J. F. M. Sterck, 'Onder Amsterdamsche humanisten', *Het boek* 9 (1920), 161–74; P. J. Meertens, *Letterkundig leven in Zeeland in de zestiende en de eerste helft der zeventiende eeuw* (Amsterdam, 1943), 152.

[13] Sigrid Pohl Perry, 'The Secret Voice: Clandestine Fine Printing in the Netherlands, 1940–1945', in *The Holocaust and the Book: Destruction and Preservation*, ed. Jonathan Rose (Boston, MA, 2001), 107–27; Alston W. Purvis, *H. N. Werkman* (London, 2004), 79–108.

in which . . . the secret powers of the world' are laid bare.[14] While it would be inappropriate to discuss these ideas at length here, since the *Histoire* has a much broader focus than this text alone, it is worth noting that there are a number of drawbacks to Foucault's treatment of the poem. Firstly, the framework in which he interprets the text is problematic, as it obscures the poem's roots in Dutch-language culture. Foucault subsumes the text into a pan-European attitude towards madness, his focus being 'the Western world' as a whole, 'the entire face of Europe'.[15] This breadth of scope obscures the important ways in which the poem engages with the activities of the *rederijkers* themselves. The text is organised as a parody of the charters granted to the chambers by municipal authorities, with their various stipulations on the expected conduct of prospective members. Knuvelder in fact compares it to a half-serious charter granted by Philip the Good to a real *narrengezelschap* (fool's brotherhood) at Dijon in 1454.[16] This ironic imitation extends to the symbol of the barge itself. The text uses the barge as a *blazoen*, an emblem by which the mock-guild may be known. The joke gains added force from the fact that many chambers emphasised the colour blue in their chosen symbols, presumably for its associations with the Virgin Mary: examples include the *Blauwe Acoleyen* (Blue Columbine) at Rotterdam and the *Blauwe Lavendelbloem* (Blue Lavender-Flower) at Ter Heide.[17] *The Blue Barge*, in short, closely mimics the forms used by chambers to define themselves.

This play with symbolism is important because it underpins much of the satire of the piece, enabling it to use a number of peculiar tactics. The use of this emblem highlights a comic contrast between the guild and the actual conduct of the chambers. The emphasis throughout the poem is on the openness of the mock-chamber, as it will happily admit every social rank as *ghildebroeder*, from the knight to the monk, to the 'young wife' and the beguine. The text therefore replaces the carefully guarded, exclusive membership of the chambers with an acceptance of all-comers, and even extends this hospitality to those who would normally be barred from joining, such as women, children and the poor. This point is further reinforced by the use of a mascot from the world of misrule, with its connotations of public display and communal participation. The guild is as open to all as a carnival procession, and as widely accessible as drunken celebration. The privileges usually conferred by belonging to a guild thus becomes no privilege at all, since membership is indiscriminate. There is no prestige to be derived from joining this guild, only disgrace. This in turn serves to mark the statements of the text as satirical: the mere inclusion of an object within this parodic, valueless guild effectively becomes an attack on it.

What is more, there is also a clear moral dimension to this mockery. Given that many of the titles adopted by the chambers had clear biblical resonances, such as *Die*

---

[14] Michel Foucault, *Madness and Civilization: A History of Insanity in the Age of Reason*, trans. Richard Howard (London, 1989), xiv.

[15] Ibid., 3.

[16] G. P. M. Knuvelder, *Handboek tot de geschiedenis der Nederlandse letterkunde*, 4 vols. (Malmberg, 1948–53), 1: 412.

[17] F. C. van Boheemen and T. C. J. van der Heijden, *Retoricaal memoriaal: bronnen voor de geschiedenis van de Hollandse rederijkerskamers van de middeleeuwen tot het begin van de achttiende eeuw* (Delft, 1999), 464, 750–1.

Jesus Oogen (The Eyes of Jesus) at Voorburg or *Het Bloemken Jesse* (The Root of Jesse) at Middelburg, it is tempting to connect the barge to Noah's ark, the most famous vessel in Christian iconography.[18] Since the ark was widely thought to foreshadow the Christian church, which would weather the coming storm of Judgement Day, this figuration would add a further level of meaning to the barge, and to the mock-guild that bears its name.[19] Through this association the guild becomes a kind of anti-church, a refuge for the sinful and damned. Again this drives home an implicit moral point, as it hints that the groups placed within the guild are venal, even corrupt. Consequently, much of the satire of the text works by caricaturing the conventions of the chambers. Foucault's handling of the poem therefore distracts attention away from the important ways in which it plays with the culture of the *rederijkerskamers*.

A further problem with Foucault's commentary is his claim that the piece might have some basis in actual practices. Foucault argues that the text and similar accounts of the ships of fools, such as Sebastian Brant's popular *Narrenschiff* (1494), might reflect real-life treatment of the mentally ill. He insists that the ships 'had a real existence . . . for they did exist, these boats that conveyed their insane cargo from town to town'.[20] Not only has this claim been directly challenged by a number of subsequent commentators, but it overlooks *The Blue Barge*'s foundation in literary convention rather than concrete reality.[21] The text is in fact an interesting variation on the estates satire, a form with a long history in medieval literature. Like *The Blue Barge*, estates satire typically consists of a series of caricatures and moral criticisms, directed at individual classes, and working gradually down the social scale: as James Simpson summarises, it 'both surveys and implicitly addresses the whole nation, conceived as a set of occupations or estates'.[22] There are examples in most European literatures: among the most famous are Chaucer's *General Prologue* to *The Canterbury Tales* (c.1387), with its regimented description of 'nyne and twenty' pilgrims and 'the condicioun of ech of hem', and the fifteenth-century *danse macabre*, in which the figure of Death calls each occupation to join his irresistible dance.[23] Estates satire was well established in the vernacular literature of the Low Countries by the time *The Blue Barge* was composed. As early as the 1290s Dutch poets were making use of the form, as it appears in portions of Van

---

[18] Van Boheemen and Van der Heijden, *Retoricaal memoriaal*, 806–7; M. G. A. de Man, 'De voormalige Middelburgsche rederijkerskamer het Bloemken Jesse onder de kenspreuk In minnen groeyende, en hare gildepenningen', *Jaarboek van het Kon. Ned. genootschap voor munt- en penningkunde* (1917), 1–40.

[19] Richard W. Unger, *The Art of Medieval Technology: Images of Noah the Shipbuilder* (New Brunswick, NJ, 1991), 63.

[20] Foucault, *Madness and Civilization*, p. 8.

[21] W. B. Maher and B. Maher, 'The Ship of Fools: *Stultifera navis* or *Ignis fatuus*', *American Psychologist* 37 (1982), 756–61; H. C. Erik Midelfort, 'Madness and Civilisation in Early Modern Europe: A Reappraisal of Michel Foucault', in *Michel Foucault: Critical Assessments*, ed. Barry Smart (London, 1998), 117–33; H. C. Erik Midelfort, 'Reading and Believing: On the Reappraisal of Michel Foucault', in *Rewriting the history of madness: studies in Foucault's Histoire de la folie*, ed. Arthur Still and Irving Velody (London, 1992), 105–10.

[22] James Simspon, *Reform and Cultural Revolution, 1350–1547*, Oxford English Literary History 2 (Oxford, 2004), 246.

[23] *The Riverside Chaucer*, gen. ed. Larry D. Benson (Oxford, 1990).

Maerlant's *Van den lande van oversee* ('Of the Land over the Sea').[24]

While *The Blue Barge* is slightly unusual in adapting this poetic framework for performance, its modifications are not without precedent. There are other instances of the form crossing into drama. This does not only occur in other Dutch texts, such as the comparable monologue *The Oath of Master Pawnbroker*, but also in other languages and traditions. One example in English is *The Judgement* from the Chester mystery cycle: this presents various social groups descending to hell, including a 'Rex Damnatus' (Damned King), 'Justicarius Damnatus' (Damned Magistrate), and 'Mercator Damnatus' (Damned Merchant).[25] The troupe of actors encountered by Don Quixote suggests a similar usage in Spain, as the players are variously dressed as an emperor, a queen, a soldier and a knight, and appear to be performing a stage version of the *danse macabre*.[26]

What makes *The Blue Barge* particularly unusual in this context, however, is the code which underpins its satire. Herman Pleij has dubbed this a *nieuwe burgermoraal* ('new bourgeois morality').[27] Conventional estates satire tends to be governed by a single set of moral and political assumptions, which are derived in turn from medieval social theory. Such work tended to emphasise above all the corporate and interrelated nature of human society, and the necessity of each group carrying out its designated function within this order. In Morton Bloomfield's summary, medieval political philosophy conceived 'society as a precisely articulated institution with each part performing its proper function and thereby realising its perfection'.[28] Society is therefore understood as a sort of mechanism, which can only achieve its optimal form when its components enter into their proper relationships. As the influential homilist Aelfric of Eynsham puts it, each group within society is really the servant of its counterparts: 'In this world three orders are established . . . the farmer labours for our food, the warrior must fight against our enemies, and the servant of God must continually pray for us and spiritually fight against unseen foes'.[29] Reciprocity, duty and harmony are thus the fundamental ideals of this social formation.[30]

---

[24] Jacob van Maerlant, *Van den lande van ouer zee*, ed. Garmt Stuiveling (Amsterdam, 1967).

[25] *The Chester Mystery Cycle*, ed. R. M. Lumiansky and David Mills, Early English Text Society, ss 3, 2 vols. (London, 1974), 1: 467–83. See Eva M. Campbell, *Satire in the Early English Drama* (Columbus, OH, 1914), 18–19.

[26] Miguel de Cervantes Saavedra, *El ingenioso hidalgo Don Quijote de la Mancha*, ed. Francisco Rodríguez Marín (Santiago, 2005), 524–9. See Víctor Infantes, *Las danzas de la muerte: génesis y desarrollo de un género medieval* (Salamanca, 1997), 339–40.

[27] Pleij, *Het gilde van de Blauwe Schuit*, 209. See also the work of Menno ter Braak, which postulates the existence of a *carnavalsmoraal*, which he terms an 'inhalig burgerlijk' ('acquisitive burgher') morality: Menno ter Braak, *Verzameld werk.*, ed. M. van Crevel, H. A. Gomperts and G. H. 's-Gravesande, 5 vols. (Amsterdam, 1950–80), 1: 132–58. See also the study by Johannes Melters, which considers the *Schuit* as a reappropriation of the *Narrenfigure* (fool-narrator) for didactic ends: Johannes Melter, *Ein frölich Gemüt zu machen in schweren Zeiten: der Schwankroman in Mittelalter und Früher Neuzeit* (Berlin, 2004), 250–4.

[28] Morton Bloomfield, *Piers Plowman as Fourteenth-Century Apocalypse* (New Brunswick, NJ, 1961), 102–3.

[29] Ælfric, *Lives of the Saints*, ed. W. W. Skeat, Early English Text Society, 2 vols. (London, 1881), 1: 120–2.

[30] For a concise review of this model, its history and its dissemination, see J. H. Burns, *The*

This idea of society as a system of mutually dependent classes informs traditional estates satire. The genre takes this conception and develops it into a firm criterion by which satiric judgements can be made, turning it into a standard against which the conduct of individual estates can be measured and condemned. One important example of this process is the widely disseminated *De Duodecim Abusivis Saeculi* ('Twelve Abuses of the Age'), known in various forms across Europe from the seventh century onwards.[31] The *Duodecim* unequivocally contrasts the behaviour of figures or groups against the ideal functions they should carry out: one fourteenth-century version consists entirely of such gnomic statements as 'rex sine sapiencia / episcopus sine doctrina' ('king without wisdom, bishop without learning'), and 'miles sine probitate ... populus sine lege' ('knight without honour, commons without law').[32] The text therefore understands each object of attack as a transgressor against its proper place and purpose. The structural model of society outlined by Aelfric, in other words, forms the entire basis of its satire. This condition recurs throughout the estates genre as a whole: as Jill Mann writes, 'estates literature is governed by the notion of function ... the idea of a total society in which all have their allotted place and relation to each other'.[33]

The Blue Barge, however, departs radically from this traditional means of critique. Throughout the text, the judgements operate along new lines, as its satire seems to be founded on a different set of ideals. This can be witnessed most closely in the section addressing knights. Here the text avoids mentioning any of the usual criteria by which the worth of knights is assessed: instead of referring to their honour, courage or ability to repel threats to society itself, the text is merely interested in their management of capital. In the opening section of the monologue, 'knights or squires' are criticised for 'wasting twice their income' (line 31) and 'allowing their debt to pile up' (line 21). This pattern is sustained throughout the poem. Time and again money supplies the poem with the basis for its complaints. Thus abbots and other members of the high clergy are upbraided for squandering their wealth, while monks are rebuked for overspending, and the children of burghers are derided for wasting their inheritances. Rather than allocating each group its own function within society as a whole, *The Blue Barge* reduces all estates to the same basic demand. Its ruling ideal is the proper management of finance, and the related virtues of thrift, prudence and living within one's means. These are the standards against which the poem appraises its targets, and in the name of which it rebukes them. The poem then subsumes all classes into the same role. It does not regard society as a system of interdependent and interrelated elements, but recognises only one ideal function governing all. The shrewd treatment of money has become the sole standard by which virtue is to be assessed.

Cambridge History of Medieval Political Thought c.350–c.1450 (Cambridge, 1988), 520–72.

[31] M. L. W. Maistner, *Thought and Letters in Western Europe, AD 500–900*, rev. edn (London, 1957), 143–6; Ruth Mohl, *The Three Estates in Medieval and Renaissance Satire* (New York, 1933). On this convention in the Low Countries, see Ter Braak, *Verzameld werk*, 1: 440.

[32] *Historical Poems of the XIVth and XVth Centuries*, ed. Rossell Hope Robbins (London, 1959), 232.

[33] Jill Mann, *Chaucer and Medieval Estates Satire: The Literature of Social Class and The General Prologue to the Canterbury Tales* (Cambridge, 1973), 7.

This play with conventional values and ideals is of course not without analogues, especially in medieval comic literature. It recalls the 'materialist, hedonistic ethos' Charles Muscatine detects in the fabliaux, or Bakhtin's 'logic of the carnival world', in that it puts forward a system of values that is markedly at odds with conventional morality.[34] It also resembles venality satire, which similarly constructs an alternative morality around cash: as Laura Kendrick writes, this tradition achieves its point by 'blatantly imitating the outward forms of familiar Latin biblical and liturgical texts, but replacing their idealizing spiritual message with a grossly materialistic one', again using money as a standard for moral judgement.[35] Nonetheless, *The Blue Barge* does not follow such examples in every respect. Unlike these traditions, there is little suggestion that its proposed code is to be taken ironically, or as a means of 'reminding us of the existence of the rule'.[36] Crucially, the text does not highlight the disparities between its own method of judgement and ordinary moral standards, but seems to regard its system as wholly consistent with accepted ideas on conduct. In other words, the text is entirely sincere in using money as a means of formulating its evaluations. Given its probable origins in the chambers of rhetoric, this point is interesting. It might be said that the text is giving voice to the value system of the mercantile culture from which the chambers emerged. The position in which it is based may simply be that of its creators, a monetary, middle-class ethos which treats wise investment and frugality as moral imperatives. The text can be seen, in short, as a confident statement of Pleij's *burgermoraal*. By raising profit and prudence into a universal code, and by letting them overshadow all other social duties, it shows the mercantile, artisinal *rederijkers* at their most self-assured.

---

[34] Charles Muscatine, *Medieval Literature, Style and Culture* (Columbia, 1999), 166; Mikhail M. Bakhtin, *Problems of Dostoevsky's Poetics*, trans. Caryl Emerson (Minneapolis, MA, 1984), 125.

[35] Laura Kendrick, 'Medieval Satire', in *A Companion to Satire*, ed. Ruben Quintero (Oxford, 2007), 56.

[36] Umberto Eco, 'Frames of Comic "Freedom"', in *Carnival!*, ed. Thomas A. Sebeok and Marcia E. Erikson (Berlin, 1984), 6.

Het gilde van de Blauwe Schuit

Ende alle ghesellen van wilde manieren
Ontbieden wi gruet ende saluut,
Te comen in die Blauwe Scuut
Ende in der Blauwer Scuten ghilde.
5 Sijn si onedel of van den scilde,
Hem allen gaern men ontfaet,
Opdat si leven als hierna staet
Ende werken mit al haer vermoghen.
Nu hoert, ic sal haer leven toghen,
10 Die onser Scuten toebehoert.
Ende eerst van den heren voert,
Ridders of knechts, die lien of lant
Versetten om ghelt in anders hant.
Of die ter lomberde gaen
15 Ende laten daer hoer pande verstaen
Doer groten commer, suldi weten.
Ende die hoer coren groen eten,
Ende die hoer renten niet en moghen verbeijden,
Ende garen groten staet leijden,
20 Ende die alle jaers wat lants vercopen,
Ende haer schult laten hopen,
Ende die fyolen laten sorghen,
Ende die copen al dat men wil borghen
Ende haren staet niet en minderen:
25 Dat sijn onse verloren kinderen.
Ende die gheringhe sijn ter hant

* The Dutch text is taken from Pleij, *Het gilde van de Blauwe Schuit*, 237–44. Used with permission.

The Guild of the Blue Barge

And all fellows of wild habits[1]
We bid, with greetings and salutations,
To come into the Blue Barge
And enter the Blue Barge guild.
5 Be they commoners or with a coat of arms,
All of them are invited,
On condition that they live as stated here
And work with all their effort.
Now hear this, I will show the way of life
10 Of those who belong on our Barge.
And firstly I speak of the lords,
Knights or squires, who pawn fief or land
To get money into their hand.
Or else they go to the pawnbroker
15 And yield there their property for ever
Owing to their great trouble, you should know.
And they eat their corn while it is green,
And they can never wait for their rents,
And need more than their estate yields,
20 And every year they peddle some lands,
And allow their debt to pile up,
And they let the bottles fret,[2]
And they buy as long as others will loan,
And they will not reduce their household:
25 These are our lost children.[3]
And they seldom put a hand

[1] The text uses *ghesellen* (fellows) throughout to describe the members of the guild, and at points refers to their *gheselscop* (fellowship, company, society). The term covers a range of meanings. Two in particular seem to be evoked here. On the one hand, the text uses *ghesel* in the sense of a journeyman, a member of a craft guild who has completed his apprenticeship; on the other, the word is also used in the sense of a companion or acquaintance, with connotations of dissoluteness, somewhat like the modern *drinkgenoot* (drinking mate) or *bargenoot* (bar mate). *Ghesellen* therefore means both 'guild brothers' and 'drunkards', 'layabouts'. The term also has further significance for the *rederijkers*, who would occasionally style themselves 'ghesellen van der Retoryke' or 'den gheselscipe van den Rethorijken', especially in Flanders: see B. Ouvry, 'Officieel ceremonieel te Oudenaarde, 1450–1600', *Handelingen van de Geschied- en oudheidkundige kring van Oudenaarde* 22 (1985), 25–64; Meertens, *Letterkundig leven in Zeeland*, 122; Van Boheemen and Van der Heijden, *Retoricaal memoriaal*, 185, 226.

[2] That is, they do not worry themselves, they are recklessly carefree. This is the first documented example of this colourful proverb, which has a long history in *rederijker* literature, appearing in the work of Cornelis Everaert and several other sources: see F. A. Stoett, *Nederlandsche spreekwoorden, spreekwijzen, uitdrukkingen en gezegden*, 2 vols. (Zutphen, 1923–5), 1: 224–5.

[3] According to Johannes Kat, this may be a reference to the Parable of the Prodigal Son, from Luke 15.11–32: see J. F. Kat, *De verloren zoon als letterkundig motief* (Amsterdam, 1952), 28.

Te slaen voer hoeft of mont of tant,
Ende die dor dobbelen of drincken,
Singhen, springhen ende clincken,
30 Ende die wildelic ghebaren,
Ende die haer renten dubbelt vertaren,
Ende altoes liever vertrecken willen
Dan si thuus bleven stille,
Ende die ghaerne belleren mil sconen vrouwen,
35 Die sullen dat ghilde ophouwen.
Voert van den gheestliken heren,
Die willen wi in onse ghilde eeren,
Apten ende grote prelaten,
Die haer cloester t'achter saten,
40 Ende versetten ende vercopen
Des cloosters renten bi groten hopen,
Ende die na hoer ghenuchte leven
Ende niet veel daer om en gheven
Om den kommer ende lachter,
45 Dat haer cloester soe gaet t'achter,
Ende des nachts brassen ende hoveren,
Ende onnutlic haer goet verteren,
Ende die voecken mit sconen wiven,
Die sullen in onse ghilde bliven.
50 Hoert, gi papen ende gi clercken,
Die gaern mit der lenden werken
Ende gaerne haer ghenuuchte driven
Mit maechden of mit mannenwiven,
Of die gaerne drincken wijn
55 Ende meer in 't gheselscap sijn
Dan haer renten moghen draghen
Ende bi nachten ende bi daghen
Boeven, spelen, dobbelen ende drincken
Ende niet veel daerop en dincken,
60 Of haer guet mit groten hopen,
Ende dan te Rome lopen
Om ander goet, ende dan verteren
Al haer goet ende cleyder mede,
Ende comen weder naect thuus

46

Before their head or mouth or teeth,[4]
And they constantly dice or drink,
Sing, leap and carouse,
30   And they gesture wildly,
And they waste twice their income,
And will always prefer to go out
Than to stay quietly at home,
And they yearn to parade with beautiful women:
35   They shall found the guild.
Next of the spiritual gentlemen:
We will honour them in our guild,
Abbots and grand prelates,
They cause their cloister to decline,
40   And they pawn and peddle
The cloister's assets in great heaps,
And they live by their desires
And do not care very much
About the distress and ridicule
45   As their cloister goes under,
And at night they revel and squander,
And uselessly eat up their goods,
And they sport with lovely women:[5]
They shall remain in our guild.
50   Hear this, you priests and you clerks,
Who yearn to work with your loins
And long to fulfil your desires
With maidens or with housewives,
Or desire to drink wine
55   And more, in a fellowship,
Than their assets might sustain,
And at night and by day
Frolic, play, gamble and drink,
And do not think much of it,
60   Or waste their goods in great heaps,[6]
And then run to Rome
For more property, only to devour
All their goods and clothes as well,
And come home again naked

[4] That is, they do not work to earn their pleasure or food.

[5] The text has *voecken*, the Middle Dutch form of *fokken*, which the *Oxford English Dictionary* gives as a probable cognate for the English 'fuck'. The term is not obscene in Dutch, however, and is in fact closer in meaning to 'breed', 'cultivate', 'raise' or 'sire'.

[6] The original is missing a verb here. We follow Pleij and Verwijs in inserting a form of *gaeten* (fritter) or *verbrassen* (squander): Verwijs, *Van vrouwen ende van minne*, 96; Pleij, *Het gilde van de Blauwe Schuit*, 243.

65   Sonder proven seer confuus;
Of die papen ende provende heren,
Die haer proven permuteren
Om ander proven die arger sijn,
Ende nemen daerof dat gheldekijn
70   Ende brenghen't over mitten ghesellen:
Dese mach men in der Scuten tellen.
Hoert, moniken ende beghinen lude,
Die en willen wi niet vertruden,
Die sielmissenghelt ende steecpenninghen
75   Mitten ghesellen overbrenghen,
Ende al haer baet van haer termijn
Verminnen of verdrincken in wijn,
Of die 't mit gueden ghesellen verteren
Ende lichtelic absolveren
80   Van al dat een heeft misdaen,
Opdat si daerof ghelt ontfaen,
Ende die crancke rekeninghen
Haren clooster daerof bringhen,
Wat si winnen in haer termijn:
85   Dese sullen in 't ghilde bliven.
Voert die poorters in die stede

65 Without benefice, greatly confused;[7]
   Or those priests and beneficed clerics,
   Who switch around their prebends
   For other benefices: they are the worst.
   They take money from this
70 And carry it over to their drinking fellows:
   These you may include within the Barge.
   Hear this, noisy monks and beguines[8]
   Whom we will not turn away,
   Chantry money and alms pennies[9]
75 They bring over to their drinking companions
   And spend all the profit from their begging patches
   On whoring or drinking up wine,
   Or they squander it with good fellows
   And easily give absolution
80 For all that one has done wrong,
   Because they take money for that,
   And they bring crooked tallies
   To their cloister
   Of what they collect in their begging rounds:[10]
85 These shall remain in the guild.
   Next the freemen of the town

[7] These and the following lines are comparable to *The Madness*, lines 49–56.

[8] The text is confused here, since the description that follows seems more appropriate to friars than monks, or at least borrows more freely from conventional anti-fraternal satire. The specific charge that begging produces only material rewards is a commonplace in medieval complaints against the mendicants, as is the truism that they 'easily give absolution'. In 1357, for instance, Archbishop Fitzralph of Armagh complained that two thousand 'murderers, thieves, incendiaries and open evildoers' in his diocese, who had previously been excommunicated, had all been absolved by friars: see *Dialogus inter Militem et Clericum*, ed. Jenkins Perry (London, 1925), 44–5; Penn R. Szittya, *The Antifraternal Tradition in Medieval Literature* (Princeton, 1986), 24–52. In fact, monks would not be involved in begging or pastoral work at all, further implying that the text has friars in mind here. Likewise, the poem could well intend beghards in this section rather than the beguines, since 'whoring' and begging do not sit easily with the female lay communities. The fact that the text devotes a later section to *minliken beghinen* might further signal that beghards are the real target, as might the parallels between this passage and other satires on the beghards: see J. W. Muller, 'Ze(e)rden, scheren, sarren', *Tijdschrift voor Nederlandse taal- en letterkunde* 45 (1926), 15–22; Ernest W. McDonnell, *The Beguines and Beghards in Medieval Culture* (New York, 1969), 465; Robert Lerner, *The Heresy of the Free Spirit in the Later Middle Ages* (Berkeley, CA, 1972), 39.

[9] The text has 'sielmissenghelt' and 'steecpennighen', literally 'soul-mass money' and 'stickpennies'. This latter phrase has come to mean 'bribe' in modern Dutch, and probably has mildly pejorative connotations here. A parallel term has also been noted in Elizabethan English, apparently peculiar to the Norfolk dialect: see James Hooper, 'Stickpenny', *Notes and Queries* 10 (1905), 70; Johan Bense, *A Dictionary of Low Dutch Elements in the English Vocabulary* (The Hague, 1939), 469.

[10] That is, they extort money from their communities, concealing the true amounts they gain by submitting bogus reports.

Ende gueder luden kinder mede,
Die niet en sorghen noch en sparen
Ende grof en grotelic vertaren
90   Dat hem van haer ouders is bleven,
Ende niet veel daerom en gheven
Hoe onnuttelic sij 't overbringhen,
Ende dobbelen, spelen ende singhen
Sonder sorghen, wilder dan wilt,
95   Hi en dochte niet dat hi een mite hilt:
'God onse Heer is rijc ghenoech;
Laet ons nemen onse ghenoech
Van den onsen sonder sorghen;
Laet si sorghen die ons borghen.'
100   Ende die niet en sorghen nacht noch dach
Voer al haer goet is wechghebract
Mit vrouwekyns of mit lichten wiven,
Of mit buverien te driven,
Ende die slapen toter noen,
105   Voert dan niet en moghen doen,
Ende die nachts waken ende braken,
Want si in 't gheselscop raken,
Ende die niet en moghen doen of werken,
Ende die harde nauwe merken
110   Wat die beste ghesellen sijn,
Is 't in bier of in wijn;
Ende die renten noch lant en copen,
Noch ghelt in hare kisten hopen,
Ende die meer verteren in een jaer
115   Dan drie jaer renten belopen voerwaer,
Ende die dus gaen desen ganc,
Al souden si daerna drie jaer lane
Buten lande dienen ende varen,
Nochtan en soude si niet sparen:
120   Dus gherecht sijn si ende fijn;
Dese moghen wael in 't ghilde sijn,
Want si meest meesten ende groyen,
Als si die Blauwe Scuut sien royen.
Voert van den gueden vroukijns fijn,
125   Die gaern bi die guede ghesellen sijn
Ende die Venus dwinghet, die goddinne,

And the good people with their children too
Who neither care nor save,
And grossly and greatly consume
90   That which their parents left them,
And do not give much thought
To how uselessly they spend it,
And dice, play and sing
Without concern, wilder than wild.
95   He does not fear that he only has one penny:[11]
'God our Lord is rich enough;
Let us take our fill
For ourselves without concern;
Let those that worry about us pay'.
100   And they do not care night or day
Until all their goods are squandered
With young girls or loose women,
Or with funding debauches,
And they sleep until noon,
105   Even then they will not do anything,
And they stay awake at night and frolic,
As they cling together in fellowship,
And they will not do any duty or work,
And they barely give a thought
110   To who is the best company,
Whether it is found in beer or in wine;
And they do not buy assets or land,
Or pile money into their chests,
And they waste more in a year
115   Than three years of interest amounts to,
And they go about in this manner;
Even if they should serve and travel
For three years outside the country
They still will not save anything:
120   Thus they are proper and fine,
They ought to be in the guild,
For they will increase and multiply,
As they see the Blue Barge rowed.
Next are good and fine women,
125   Who wish to be with the good fellows
And whom Venus controls, the goddess,

---

[11] The text here has 'mite', the smallest denomination of currency in the Low Countries: in Flanders there were forty-eight *mijten* to a *stuiver*; in Brabant seventy-two. *Mijten* became notorious for their poor quality, since mints would often strike them from pure copper rather than silver alloy, owing to the prohibitive cost of silver. For this reason they were often known as *monnaie noire* or 'black money', as opposed to *monnaie blanche*, 'silver money': see Peter Spufford, *Money and its Use in Medieval Europe* (Cambridge, 1989), 328–9.

Ende gernen draghen verholen minne,
Is 't abdisse of nonne,
Die d'een bet dan d'ander gunne,
130 Ende mit Sinte Jorys vissop sijn begoten:
Dese moghen den Scuten ghenoten
Want si guede ghesellen beraden,
Als si mit commer sijn beladen.
Voert van den minliken beghinen,
135 Die so heilich sijn van scinen,
Ende so minlic oechkijns draghen,
Dat een dat herte duncke waghen
Ende vergaren mit haren aensien,
Ende gaerne gueder minnen plien
140 Ende in rechter caritaet:
Hiermede is 't dat men die Scuut laed.
Oec maechden die men te langhe hout,
Ende groet worden ende out
XXV jaer of meer;
145 Dese maechden torentet al te seer,
Dat si alleijn bliven.
Hoert van den mannenwiven,
Die gaerne goet gheselscop driven,
Waer 't dat hem tevoren quaem,
150 Die hebben oude mannen,
Die hem gheen solaes en gannen,
Noch een doen noch en driven.
Dese vrouwen ende dese wiven
Gaerne na guede ghesellen vraghen,
155 Die hern haer leet helpen draghen
Ende mit vroechden willen leven,
Mer dese moeten dicke gheven:
Hierom sullen si in die Scuut
Die vracht wesen uut ende uyt.
160 Voert van al den gueden ghesellen,
Die willen wi in onse ghilde tellen
Ende eeren ende minnen,
Ende gaerne haer broet winnen
Mit ambocht of mit comenscop,
165 Ende dat weder mit gheselscop
Bi brenghen mit groten hopen,
Ende gheen lant daermede copen;

And who long to harbour a secret love.
If it is an abbess or nun
That gives her favours to one more than another,
130 And is soaked with Saint George's fish-oil,[12]
These may enjoy the Barge,
For they give comfort to good fellows
When they are laden with sorrow.
Next are the love-loving beguines,
135 Who are so holy to look upon,
And have such romantic eyes
That one's heart seems to tremble,
And be trapped by the sight of them,
And they yield to good love
140 Out of true charity:
It is for this that they are loaded on to the Barge.
Also maidens that are kept for too long,
And grow ripe and old
For twenty-five years or more,
145 These maidens rage all too severely,
Because they remain alone.
Hear this, about married women,
Who long to go around with good company,
If only some should come before them;
150 They have old husbands
Who will not offer them comfort,
Either in deed or in intent.
These women and these wives
Yearn to ask the good fellows
155 To help them bear their misery
And to live with joy,
And they must give plentifully:
For this they shall be in the Barge
As the freight, undoubtedly.
160 Next come all the good fellows
That we wish to count amongst our guild
And to honour and to love,
And who want to earn their crust
With craft or with trade,
165 And always bring it to their company
In great heaps,
And therefore purchase no land;

---

[12] This is one of many proverbial innuendos relating to Saint George. It is not known why sexual connotations should be attached to this particular saint, although the literature of the period contains numerous similar references: see Eric de Bruyn, *Symboliek van de Hooiwagen-triptiek en de Rotterdamse Marskramer-tondo verklaard vanuit Middelnederlandse teksten* ('s-Hertogenbosch, 2004), 98.

Ende die dienres ende knapen
Willen wi in onse ghilde rapen,
170   Die al haer winninghe ende baten
Des sonnendaechs in die taverne laten,
Ende verteren drie weken t'achter
Of een maent, dat en is gheen lachter,
Of die op een dach verspelen
175   Haer somerhuer of soveel
Als si winnen binnen den jaer,
Ende hem dat weder suer ende swaer
Laten worden vro und spaed:
Dese nemen wi in ghenaed.
180   Ende die joncwiven in die steden
Ende opten landen oec mede,
Die haren sin legghen of stellen
An een of an tween goeden ghesellen,
Ende liever gaen dansen ende spelen
185   Dan si te huus deden vele,
Ende des nachts mitten ghesellen waken,
Al souden si sterven van vake,
Die nochtan niet en souden laten,
Si en souden haren buel inlaten:
190   Deze sijn in der Scuten ghilde.
Nu mocht een vraghen of hi wilde,
Die in dit ghilde comen woude,
Of hi aldese punten soude
Moeten doen die sijn voerscreven.
195   Hierop willen wi antwoert gheven:
Een mensche sal in hemselven gaen
Ende sien sijn regiment aen
Van sinen leven ende wandelinghen,
Van seden ende van allen dinghen,
200   Die hi daghelix plecht te hantieren.
Vint hi meer punten van manieren
Dan hem meer ter wijsheit trecken,
Dan wijsheit die ter dwaesheit trecken,
So en is hi in onse ghilde niet.
205   Mer die in hemselven siet
Meer punten dan hier staen voerscreven,
Dan wijselike mede te leven,
Die sinen staet meest regeren
Ende sinen goede meest deeren,
210   Dese sullen in onse Scute gaen
Ende onse ghilde nemen aen.
Oec soe willen wi een except maken
Dat onse ghilde en sal niement ghenaken
Noch in onse ghilde wesen

And the servants and hirelings
We wish to harvest for our guild,
170 That leave all their earnings and profits
In the tavern on Sundays,
And consume everything after three weeks
Or a month, that is no joke,
Or else in one day gamble away
175 Their summer wages, or as much
As they earn within a year,
And from this they grow sour and heavy,
They are made to become so, sooner or later:
These we take in, with mercy.
180 And the young girls in the towns
And from farmland as well
Who should fix or settle their mind
On one or on two good fellows,
And who would rather go dancing and playing
185 Than do their housework well,
And at night lie awake with fellows,
Although they might die from fatigue,
All the same they cannot leave off
Welcoming their lovers in:
190 These are in the guild of the Barge.
Now, should anyone ask or desire,
How he might come into the guild,
If he might do so, all these points
He must perform as written here.
195 We wish him to give an answer to this:
If a man shall come for his own good,
And watch his behaviour,
His life and deportment,
With virtue, and with all the true things
200 That he pledges to pursue daily;
If he follows more points of conduct
That will lead him closer to wisdom
Than advice that leads to foolishness,
Then he is not one for our guild.
205 But he that sees himself
In more points written here
Than in those by which one may live wisely,
He that will ruin most of his estate,
And will bankrupt his loved ones,
210 These men shall go into our Barge
And be taken for our guild.
Also we will make a regulation
That no man will approach our guild
Or be in our guild

215 Die een punt heeft van desen,
Als moerdbranders, dief of moerdenaer,
Zerovers of verraders swaer,
Boerssniders ende alle lodders meede,
Die quade fauten hebben onder haer leden:
220 Dese sijn al uutghenomen
Ende die en moghen in onse ghilde niet comen.
Mer het wait veel overal,
Dat een mit groten ongheval
Dootsclach doet in toornre heet,
225 Dat hem na is harde leet,
Of die sijn lijf moet verweren:
Dese nemen wi op mit eeren.
Of die rulers opter straten
[…]
230 Ende niet en roven op ghene vaert,
Si en sijn daer jeghens bewaert,
Of viant des lants heren,
Daer si roef of rovers gheren,
Sijn si scout of van den scilde,
Soe nemen wi se in onse ghilde.
235 Voert maec ic u een bediet,
Dat wi en willen die wiven niet,
Die sijn van sulken leven,
Dat si daer niet om en gheven
Mit wien si sijn of mit hoeveel,
240 Of die't al in laten gaen,
[…]
Maghen, swagheren suldi verstaen,
Of die quaet sijn van wanderinghe
En willen wi om ghene dinghe.
245 Mer een wijf die moet wel minnen
Eenen ende oec den anderen sinnen
Ende toghen hem haer ontfarmhede,
Mer al mit besceijdenhede,
Dat's te segghen, soe ic meen,
250 Dat si niet en gaet ghemeen
Boven een of twe.
Anders en doech si min noch meer

215   That has a mark against him,
       Such as arsonists, thieves or murderers,
       Pirates or high traitors,[13]
       Cut-purses, or all spongers besides:
       They have wretched faults, preventing their entry;
220   These are all excluded
       And must not come into our guild.
       But it often occurs, generally speaking,
       That one with great misfortune
       Commits murder in the heat of anger;
225   For him that is a hard sorrow,
       Or that one must defend his life:
       These we will take in with honour.
       Or the mercenaries on the streets
       […][14]
230   And do not steal under any circumstances,
       Unless it be from those who oppose them,
       Or from enemies of the lord of the land,
       When they search for loot or robbers:
       Whether they are foot-soldiers or with a coat of arms,
       We take them into our guild.
235   Next I will make a declaration for you,
       That we do not want those women
       Who live their lives in such a way
       That they do not care
       With whom they consort, or with how many,
240   Or to whom they give themselves,
       Blood relatives, in-laws, as you know,
       […]
       Or who are cruel of character,
       We do not want them by any means.
245   But a woman must love
       One man well, and be courteous to other men,
       And show them her compassion,
       But wholly with discretion,
       That is to say, I mean,
250   That she should not take on
       More than one or two.
       Otherwise she will be reckoned

---

[13]   As the careers of the Baltazar de Cordes, Siemen Danziger and Murat Reis serve to illustrate, pirates and corsairs became increasingly active around the Low Countries during the sixteenth century. Their numbers grew still further after the Dutch Revolt in the latter half of the century, as the *Westindische Compagnie* set its designs on Spanish territories in the New World, and exploited the *zeerooveren* to further this end: see Virginia W. Lunsford, *Piracy and Privateering in the Golden Age Netherlands* (Aldershot, 2005).

[14]   The text seems to be missing a line here.

Dan dat men rekent voer een hoer,
Die om cleijn ghelt dat dinc doen.
255 Dese previlegien ende desen punten voerscreven
Hebben wi onse ghilde ghegeven
Ende onse ghildebroeders mede,
Ende sal dueren in ewichede,
Totdat si hem anders saten,
260 Dat si onse ghilde moghen laten
In wijsheit of in huwelic,
Of dat si werden te rijc.
Mer die leven bi onsen raed
Houden wi vast ende ghestaed
265 Alle previlegien ende virtuut,
Die toebehoren die Blauwe Scuut,
Also langhe als si t'onswaert keeren
Ende iet hebben te verteren
Ende onse ghilde willen hantieren.
270 Ende omdat wi willen in allen manieren
Onse privilegien houden in staden,
So hebben wi bi onsen raden
Ende mit raden onser kinder mede,
Die wi heten van den quaden beleden,
275 Binnen onsen leven dit bezeghelt.
Dat sulver is vercoft ende ghelt,
Daer die seghel of was ghewracht
Ende dat ghelt is overghebracht,
Also den menighen wel is bekent,
280 Die kennen onse quade regiment.
Ghegeven in Ons Heren jaer
MCCCC ende XIII voerwaer,
Opten rechten vastelavont
Als die van Brabant wel is cont,
285 Doe si in Oestpolre staken
Ende die speren in die eer van vrouwen braken
Jeghens die van Oedekiinskerke.
Hierbi so mach men merken,
Doe dit ghilde in Brabant quam
290 Ende men dit ghilt annam,
Mer dit ghilt was langhe tevoren

58

A whore, no more and no less,
Who does the thing they do for small change.
255   These privileges and these points written here
We have given to our guild
And to our guild-brothers as well,
And they shall endure for eternity,
Until they conduct themselves differently,
260   So that they must leave our guild
In wisdom or in wedlock,
Or until they become rich.
But those who live by our counsel,
We hold them fast and steady,
265   With all privileges and statutes
That pertain to the Blue Barge,
For as long as they turn to us
And have something to squander,
And wish to take part in our guild.
270   And because we wish in every way
To hold our privileges firm,
We have by our own counsel
And with the counsel of our children too,
Whom we accuse of poor governance,
275   Sealed this document with our lives.
The silver has been sold and melted down
From which the seal was made,
And the money has been carried off
As many know well:
280   They know the evil way we handle things.
Given in the year of Our Lord
MCCCC and XIII, in truth,
By the liberties of carnival
As those from Brabant know well,
285   When they were in the lists at Fartpolder[15]
And broke spears in honour of women,[16]
Close to Smallbollockschurch.[17]
From this one can tell
The date this guild came into Brabant,
290   As this guild was recorded there;
But a guild had long before

---

[15] A travesty of *Oostpolder*, literally 'East polder'. There are several areas with this name across the Netherlands, two examples being found at Groningen and Wester Gouwe.

[16] That is, participated in a tournament. Corstius assumes that this line refers to an actual *toernooi*, although it is more likely to be a parodic fantasy, involving peasants rather than knights: J. C. Brandt Corstius, *Geschiedenis van de Nederlandse literatuur* (Utrecht, 1959), 89.

[17] Or *Oudekinkerk*, 'Old-children's-church'. The name is a burlesque of Hoedekenskerke, a village in Zeeland.

t'Anwerpe verheven ende vercoren,
Eer 't die van Brabant ophieven.
Mer t'Anwerpen en sijn ghien brieven
Noch gheen hantvesten, hoe si souden leven.
Si en worden hem hierna ghegeven
Uten hantvesten ende uuten coren,
Die Jacop dichte van Oestvoren.
Salus Regina Miseris

295

Been exalted and blessed at Antwerp,
Before one was founded in Brabant.
But at Antwerp there are no letters,
295 And no charters, showing how the brothers should live.
The rules stated here are given to them
Out of charters and out of documents,
Written by Jacob van Frontcough.
Salus Regina Miseris[18]

[18] 'Hail, queen of the wretched': probably adapted from the antiphon traditionally sung between Trinity Sunday and Advent in the liturgical calendar: 'Salve, Regina, Mater misericordiae/ vita, dulcedo, et spes nostra, salve' ('Hail, queen, mother of mercy, our life, sweetness and hope, hail'). On the use of the *afrondingsformule* (conclusion-formula) in Middle Dutch literature, see Gerard Sonnemans, 'What's in a name? Het belang van opschrifen in verzamelhandschriften', *Middeleeuwse verzamelhandschriften*, 61–78.

A Mock-Sermon on Saint Nobody

THE *Spotsermoen over Sint Niemand* is preserved in a single manuscript, now held at the Royal Library of Brussels. According to Leendertz, who gives a full description of the manuscript and its contents, the text may originate from Ghent, since it is bound with several letters, lists of parishes and other documents relating to the city.[1] On the basis of the handwriting style, the manuscript seems to have been compiled in about 1550. However, this reveals comparatively little about the date of *Saint Nobody*, since it is impossible to gauge how much time elapsed between the composition of the text and its transcription. The other pieces in the manuscript offer little help in dating the piece, since they reflect a very wide range of dates. For example, a poem commemorating the Peace of Cadzand was evidently written shortly after 1492, whereas some of the *refreins* and *liedekens* appear to be almost contemporary with the manuscript itself.[2] The actual text of *Saint Nobody* also offers few clues. It contains little topical material, and the details that might reflect context are difficult to interpret. For instance, while it is tempting to view its mocking references to indulgences, excommunication and the cults of the saints in light of the debate on such issues during the Reformation, it is not easy to establish whether these practices are being parodied as long-accepted habits, or satirised as corruptive traditions that should be curtailed. The former is more plausible, but the latter cannot be ruled out entirely: as Sander Gilman has noted, such customs were targeted by parodists with equal vehemence both before and after the Reformation.[3]

As its name might suggest, *Saint Nobody* belongs to an extremely popular subgenre of festive parody, the mock-sermon or *sermon joyeux*. This form was evidently a common one in the Low Countries: nine other Middle Dutch examples are still extant.[4] However, its popularity was not confined to the Netherlands alone, since the *sermon joyeux* was one of the most fruitful traditions in European popular culture more widely. In French there are thirty-one surviving examples of the form, most dating from the last half of the fifteenth century, and further specimens are found in Latin, Portuguese, Spanish and German.[5] There are also two surviving

---

[1] P. Leendertz, 'Eenige geneuchlijcke dichten', *Tijdschrift voor Nederlandse taal- en letterkunde* 20 (1901), 59–80 (59).

[2] See Jacoba van Leeuwen, 'Praise the Lord for this Peace!: The Contribution of Religious Institutions to the Ceremonial Peace-Proclamations in Late Medieval Flanders', in *The Use and Abuse of Sacred Places in Late Medieval Towns*, ed. Paul Trio and Marjan de Smet (Leuven, 2006), 50.

[3] Sander Gilman, *Parodic Sermon in European Perspective: Aspects of Liturgical Parody from the Middle Ages to the Twentieth Century* (Philadelphia, 1974), 31–50.

[4] See Dick Kaijser, 'Het laatmiddeleeuwse spotsermoen', *Spektator* 13 (1983), 105–27.

[5] Jelle Koopmans, *Recueil de sermons joyeux: édition critique avec introduction, notes et glossaire* (Geneva, 1988); Paul Meyer, 'Mélanges de poesie française, iv: Plaidoyer en faveur des femmes', *Romania* 6 (1877), 499–503; I. S. Revah, *Les Sermons de Gil Vicente. En marge d'un opuscule du professeur Joaquim de Carvalho* (Lisbon, 1949), 19–21; Otis Howard Green, *Spain and the Western Tradition: The Castilian Mind in Literature from El Cid to Calderón* (Madison,

examples from medieval England, one in Middle English dating from *c.*1500, and the other in Anglo-Norman, composed in the first quarter of the fourteenth century.[6] In fact, the form was so pervasive that it had direct influence on poetry and drama throughout the Middle Ages and early-modern period. Echoes of the form have been detected in a number of key texts, such as Jean de Meun's section of the *Roman de la rose*, Chaucer's *Prologue of the Wife of Bath*, Shakespeare's *Twelfth Night* and Molière's *Dom Juan*.[7] It had no less an impact on the literature of the Netherlands, as Erasmus's *Praise of Folly* also partly recalls the form.[8]

Saint Nobody typifies this important tradition in a number of respects. In the first place, it carries out the central tactic of mock-sermons, systematically inserting images of the lower body into aspects of religious practice. Thus it recounts a funeral procession in which the dead man is carried on a muck-cart and buried in a pig-sty, and treats drinking and sex as alternative sacraments, advising the audience that 'drinking to drunkenness' will give them access to heaven (lines 16–17), and assigning particular duties to the women in the crowd: 'you women and young daughters as well . . . tip this water into your body,/ Even if you should lose your maidenhead along the way' (lines 156–9). There are also repeated references to the anus in the context of devotion, as the speaker fears that his hearers will lose their memory of the sermon through this orifice (line 12). These types of reversal are quite typical of the *sermon joyeux* as a genre, as it often serves to 'transfer every high ceremonial gesture . . . to the life of the belly and the reproductive organs', as Bakhtin puts it.[9] For instance, *Saint Nobody*'s central techniques are mirrored in the French *Sermon du ménage et des charges de mariage* ('Sermon on the household and the cost of marriage'), in which the preacher refers to his 'scripture' in similarly alimentary terms:

> Ces parolles on trouvera
> Au livre des tripes d'un veau . . .
> Capitulo plein d'herbe verde,
> Folio illuminé de merde.[10]

WI, 1968), 45–7; Paul Lehmann, *Die Parodie im Mittelalter* (Munich, 1922), 231–2; Johannes Bolte, 'Georg Schans Gedichte vom Niemand', *Zeitschrift für vergleichende Litteraturgeschichte* 9 (1896), 73–88.

[6] Malcolm Jones, 'The Parodic Sermon in Medieval and Early Modern England', *Medium Ævum* 66 (1997), 95–114; Thomas Wright and James Halliwell, *Reliquae Antiquae* (London, 1841–3), 2: 218–23.

[7] See Lee Patterson, 'Feminine Rhetoric and the Politics of Subjectivity: La Vielle and the Wife of Bath', in *Rethinking the Romance of the Rose: Text, Image, Reception*, ed. Sylvia Huot and Kevin Brownlee (University Park, PA, 1992), 316–58 (331–3); Lee Patterson, *Chaucer and the Subject of History* (Madison, WI, 1991), 304–7; John Astington, 'Malvolio and the Eunuchs', *Shakespeare Survey* 46 (1994), 23–35; Claude Bourqui, *Polémique et stratégies dans le Dom Juan de Molière* (Paris, 1992), p. 78.

[8] A. H. T. Levi, 'Introduction', in *Collected Works of Erasmus*, gen. ed. Ron Schoeffel, 89 vols. (Toronto, 1974–), 27: xx.

[9] Mikhail M. Bakhtin, *Rabelais and his World*, trans. Helene Iswolsky (Bloomington, IN, 1984), 20–1.

[10] Koopmans, *Recueil de sermons joyeux*, 368.

> (These words can be found
> In the Book of Calf's Tripe . . .
> In the chapter full of green grass,
> On the page illuminated with shit.)

This form of humour also occurs in the other Dutch *spotsermoenen*. The same pattern appears in the earliest surviving Dutch example, the fragment *Dit es van den scijtstoel* ('This is from the shitting-stool'), dating from *c*.1500. This likewise identifies elements of religious practice with faeces: its title alone substitutes *preekstoel* (preaching stool) for a more excremental equivalent. By drawing dirt and drunkenness into a devotional context, *Saint Nobody* is simply following a key strategem of the *sermon joyeux* as a genre.

Nonetheless, however much it may debase the idioms and techniques of homilies, the structure of *Saint Nobody* closely follows late-medieval preaching convention. By the later Middle Ages sermons came to be governed by a strict framework, largely in response to the 'scholastic discipline' of the universities, with its emphasis on 'systematic analysis' and 'definitions and marshalling'.[11] Hugh Oliphant Old provides a useful summary of the usual form:

> The convention of the thema and prothema became characteristic . . . . Together the two served to introduce the sermon: the thema announced the text, and the prothema, by means of introducing a second text, spoke of the significance of the text for the listener. The prothema then moved on to an invocation of divine help for the preacher and the congregation, frequently asking the congregation to recite the Ave Maria or the Pater Noster . . . a peroration concluded the message.[12]

Saint Nobody faithfully maintains this sequence. The gibberish Latin with which the piece commences (lines 1–6) provides it with a thema. A vernacular 'translation' of this is supplied later on, even though it does nothing to disclose the contents of the Latin (line 15). The prothema is then invoked, as the preacher recounts the story of a man who 'drank so much he burst', an anecdote allegedly taken from 'capito nullo' ('chapter nothing', lines 23–4). This has the purpose of moving the 'message' of the sermon from general to specific terms, as the unfortunate drinker comes to stand as a direct 'example' for the congregation to follow: they are invited to 'think what bliss' he attained (lines 29–30). There are also intermittent calls for prayer, albeit with a clear abusive intent: 'help me pray for the spiritual or worldly/ That they may live long, and do so painfully' (lines 103–4). The final lines give a compact instruction to the hearers, which effectively summarises the preceding arguments, and returns to the theme and central 'authorities' of the sermon. In spite of its stylistic excesses, therefore, the text remains firmly within the overall schema of the late-medieval *ars praedicandi*. Its formal aspects are tightly regimented, in contrast to the boisterous and unbridled subject matter it contains. This close imitation is once again typical of the mock-sermon. As Gilman notes, the entire 'basis for parody' in the form lies

---

[11] C. H. Lawrence, *The Friars: The Impact of the Early Mendicant Movement on Western Society* (London, 1994), 120–1.

[12] Hugh Oliphant Old, *The Reading and the Preaching of the Scriptures in the Worship of the Christian Church* (Grand Rapids, MI, 1998–2004), 3: 299.

in creating a 'contrast between the idealized sermon form and the actual sermon, between the literary and rhetorical structure'.[13] Eli Rozik gives a similar generalisation, noting that 'the mock sermon parodies its model' by rigorously upholding 'its way of reasoning'.[14]

Saint Nobody is no less typical in its actual content. The undoubted centre-piece of the text is its description of the 'holy man' Saint Drincatibus, who is in reality little more than a drunken derelict. The text describes in great detail how Drincatibus would drink until he became incontinent, presenting such habits in terms borrowed from martyrology (lines 82–8):

> He drank so much, as many know well,
> That all day his breeches were filled with shit.
> Think what he must have suffered from that . . .
> Was this not a miraculous mystery?

This again follows the usual course of mock-sermons, both before and after the Reformation. Many of the surviving texts make the lives of saints particular targets for ridicule, with nine of the thirty-one French texts incorporating some form of parodic hagiography. These are usually constructed around such fanciful or suggestive figures as 'Saint Fausset' (Saint Falsehood), 'Sainct Oignon' (Saint Onion), 'Sainct Frappecul' (Saint Slap-arse), 'Saint Pou' (Saint Flea), 'Saint Velu' (Saint Hairy), or 'Saincte Caquette' (Saint Chatterer).[15] The Dutch examples also follow suit: alongside the saints Drincatibus and Bacchus, there are references to 'Sint Snottolf' (Saint Snot-Nose), 'Sinte Heb-niet' (Saint Have-not), 'Sint Aelwaere' (Saint Punch-Up), and 'Sint Raspinus' (Saint Prison).[16] In fact, such is the prevalence of mock-saints in the *sermon joyeux* that Livingston characterises the form as a whole as an 'irrévérentieuse caricature d'une vie de saint', while Koopmans and Verhuyck list parodic hagiography among the 'principaux thèmes' of the literature.[17]

Saint Nobody openly ties itself to these precedents by claiming to recount the life of its titular saint. Although 'sint Niemand' only appears in the title of the piece and

---

[13] Gilman, *Parodic Sermon in European Perspective*, 9.

[14] Eli Rozik, *The Roots of Theatre: Rethinking Ritual and Other Theories of Origin* (Iowa City, 2002), 220.

[15] Jacques E. Merceron, 'Obscenity and Hagiography in Three Anonymous *Sermons Joyeux* and in Jean Molinet's *Saint Billouart*', in *Obscenity: Social Control and Artistic Creation in the European Middle Ages*, ed. Jan M. Ziolkowski (Leiden, 1998), 335–6; Koopmans, *Recueil de sermons joyeux*, 215–18, 443–55, 529–31; Jelle Koopmans, *Quatre sermons joyeux* (Geneva, 1984), 79–87. See also Jacques E. Merceron, *Dictionnaire thématique et géographique des saints imaginaires, facetieux et substitutes en France et en Belgique francophone* (Paris, 2002). Also useful is Tania van Hemelryck, 'Classé X en moyen français . . . Des saints facétieux', *Le Moyen Français* 50 (2003), 93–114.

[16] Jos Biemans, Hans Kienhorst, Willem Kuiper and Rob Resoort, *Het Handschrift-Borgloon* (Hilversum, 2000), 162–4; Eugénie Droz and H. Lewicka, *Le Recueil Trepperel*, 2 vols. (Geneva, 1961), 2: 81–96; Marius Meeus, *Wat betekent arbeid?: over het ontstaan de westerse arbeidsmoraal* (Assen, 1989), 91.

[17] Charles Harold Livingston, *Le Jongleur Gautier le Leu: étude sur les fabliaux* (London, 1951), 130; Jelle Koopmans and Paul Verhuyck, *Sermons joyeux et Truanderie* (Amsterdam, 1987), 14.

nowhere else, the mere fact that his name is invoked is significant. Saint Nobody first appears in the *Historia de Nemine* (thirteenth century), which is in many respects the prototype of all later mock-hagiography. The *Historia* is not in fact a mock-sermon in the strict sense, but more of an academic exercise: as Martha Bayless writes, it is deeply rooted in medieval intellectual life, satirising contemporary exegetic practices.[18] The *Historia* gathers together instances of the word *nemo* (nobody) from scripture and patristic sources, and assembles them to form a biography for this holy man.[19] It thus reports that Nemo was honoured by Jesus, who ordered his followers to 'salute Nobody by the way' (Luke 10.4), and declares that he is immortal, since Ecclesiastes 9.4 attests that 'Nobody liveth forever'.[20] Even though such learned word-games are quite far removed from the vernacular mock-sermons, as Ian Russell in particular has observed, Nemo was drawn into the *sermons joyeux* at an early date.[21] Here he serves to ridicule saints' lives in general, as further improbable deeds are attributed to him.[22] The Dutch sermon's allusion to Nemo, even though Drincatibus is its real focus, situates it squarely in this tradition. In fact the piece seems to use Saint Nobody purely to signal its membership of this literature, as it claims entry into this group of texts by quoting his name.[23]

In terms of its performance, the actual occasion of *Saint Nobody* is fairly easy to establish. Internal evidence suggests that the text would have been recited at Shrovetide or *Vastenavond*, like *The Blue Barge* before it. This is apparent from the prayer its speaker offers to unfortunate captives, who allegedly 'will be slain' in a few weeks' time (line 107). Urging the congregation to pray for these wretched prisoners, he goes on to name them as 'Peter Ox, Gerald Goose,/ Giles Rabbit, John Capon, Peter Sheep' (line 108–10). In other words, the prayer is an ironic tribute to a series of foodstuffs. What makes this litany significant is its clear seasonal implications. As Herman Pleij states, this 'ludicrous list of personifications of food' refers to meat proscribed during Lent, since 'some . . . would not appear on the table till Easter', while others 'either should or should not be served during the coming Lenten fast'.[24] Since the sermon is anticipating the 'banning' of these figures, and their eventual devouring at Easter, it was evidently composed for Shrovetide celebrations. The overall emphasis on penance and confession, albeit with such impious recommendations as 'whoever drinks so that his eyes race . . . delivers at every turn a soul out of purgatory', would also be consistent with this point in the festive calendar (line

---

[18] Martha Bayless, *Parody in the Middle Ages: The Latin Tradition* (Anne Arbor, MI, 1996), 79.

[19] Lehmann, *Die Parodie im Mittelalter*, 240.

[20] H. Denifle, 'Ursprung der Historia des Nemo', *Archiv für Literatur- und Kirchen- Geschichte des Mittelalters* 4 (1988), 330–48 (345–6).

[21] Russell's remarks on popular sermons are unpublished, but summarised in Diane Dugaw, *Deep Play: John Gay and the Invention of Modernity* (Cranbury, NJ, 1991), 307.

[22] Gerta Calmann, 'The Picture of Nobody: An Iconographical Study', *Journal of the Warburg and Courtauld Institutes* 23 (1960), 61.

[23] The *Historia de Nemine* was evidently well known in the Netherlands, as a Dutch version was produced with the title 'Van sinte Niemant, ende van zijn, wonderlijc leven, groote macht ende heerlijckheyt' ('Of Saint Nobody, and of his miraculous life, great deeds and holiness'): T. J. I. Arnold, *Veelderhande geneuchlijcke dichten, tafelspelen ende refereynen* (Utrecht, 1977), 150–6.

[24] Herman Pleij, *Dreaming of Cockaigne*, trans. Diane Webb (New York, 2001), 148.

48–9). This setting is not unusual for mock-sermons.[25] Another Dutch text, the *Mandement van Bacchus* ('Commandment of Bacchus'), explicitly attaches itself to Shrovetide: it parodies both the language of sermons and official proclamations, and specifies that its narrator Bacchus is overlord until mid-February, the date at which Lent commences.[26] The device of offering prayers to prohibited food is also common. One French example, *Le Sermon joyeux de Saint Jambon et de Sainte Andouille* ('The Sermon of Saint Ham and of Saint Sausage'), develops this even further, describing the 'martyrdoms' of its featured 'saints', as they are 'salted, hung, boiled or roasted, cut into slices and finally eaten'.[27] The same idea also occurs in the Middle Dutch *Legende van Sinte Haryngus*, which similarly recounts the passion of the eponymous 'Saint Herring'.[28] Several *sermons joyeux* therefore share *Saint Nobody*'s pre-Lenten context, and its focus on proscribed meats.

Just as it is clear when *Saint Nobody* was performed, the actual manner of its performance can also be pieced together, as external sources shed some light on its probable staging. In the first place, it is possible to speculate with reasonable confidence on the costume worn by its speaker. Accounts from other parts of Europe repeatedly associate mock-preachers with particular types of dress. Perhaps the fullest of these sources is Thomas More's *Confutation of Tyndale's Answer* (1532), which at one stage ridicules Protestant preachers by comparing them to 'a sort of freres folowynge an abbote of mysrule in a Christemas game'. More then goes on to give a detailed description of how such figures customarily behave: 'that were prykked in blankettes, and then sholde stande vp and preche vppon a stole and make a mowynge sermon . . . fyrst gapeth & then blesseth, and loketh holily and precheth ribauldrye to the people that stand about'.[29] It is clear from this account that the costume of a mock-preacher has a clear deflationary function, replacing the trappings of priestly office with mundane domestic equivalents: a blanket rather than a vestment or habit, a stool rather than a pulpit. The same usage of deliberately ramshackle props is testified elsewhere. Samuel Pepys records seeing a similar performance in May 1669 at Lambeth Palace, 'a mockery by one Cornet Bolton . . . that behind a chair did pray and preach like a Presbyter Scot that ever I heard in my life . . . till it made us all burst'.[30] The use of a chair rather than a pulpit serves much the same purpose as the 'blankettes' of More's figure, transplanting the everyday into the sphere of devotion. Outside England, an account from a sixteenth-century German chronicle makes much the same point, as well as showing how elaborate such performances might be. In 1524 at Buchholz an entire parodic procession was staged around a sermon, in which various clerical accoutrements were burlesqued: the congregation carried 'banners made of rags', 'gaming boards for songbooks', 'dung forks for candles', and

---

[25]   Gilman, *Parodic Sermon in European Perspective*, 24–5.

[26]   Herman Pleij, *Het gilde van de Blauwe Schuit* (Amsterdam, 1979), 253–5.

[27]   Koopmans, *Quatre sermons joyeux*, 47–56; Michel Jeanneret, *A Feast of Words: Banquets and Table Talk in the Renaissance*, trans. Jeremy Whiteley and Emma Hughes (Chicago, 1991), 205.

[28]   Willem De Vreese, 'De legende van Sint-Haringus', *Het boek* 11 (1922), 299–304.

[29]   Thomas More, *The Confutation of Tyndale's Answer*, ed. Louis A. Schuster, in *Complete Works*, 14 vols. (New Haven, 1963–97), 8: 919.

[30]   Samuel Pepys, *The Shorter Pepys*, ed. Robert Latham (London, 1993), 1020.

wore 'sieves and bathing caps in parody of canon's berets', while the preacher himself took the form of 'a mock-bishop dressed in a straw cloak, with a fish basket for a mitre'.[31] Given the general pattern of mock-preachers dressing themselves in humdrum versions of clerical robes, it seems fair to assume that the actor reciting *Saint Nobody* wore similar apparel.

Alongside the costume, it is also possible to deduce what props might have accompanied the performance. The reference to 'indulgences' in line 149 is interesting. There is a possibility that this simply refers to ale, in keeping with the general characterisation of drinking as a form of sacrament: earlier the poem does suggest that alcohol can function as an indulgence, asserting that 'He that drinks until he dishonours his trousers,/ He should have for starters/ Forty days indulgence' (lines 51–3). However, what makes this reading problematic is the fact that the congregation is specifically warned against 'disturbing the pardons' (line 149). This contradicts the general thrust of the piece, with its counsel to 'drink yourself to drunkenness' (line 17). It may therefore be possible that the preacher has some actual mock-indulgences to distribute to his listeners. Such behaviour is certainly not without parallel, as there are numerous references to mock-preachers carrying indulgences or handing out similar gifts to the crowd. The speakers of French *sermons joyeux* often advertise the fact that they have *pardons generaux* with them, using this as a pretext for lurid 'enumeration of categories pardoned for their sexual misdemeanours'.[32] Likewise, other mock-preachers seem to have given items to the revellers, such as the character Foly in Sir David Lindsay's play *Ane Satyre of the Thrie Estaitis* (1552), who hands out 'meat' and 'folie hattis' before delivering a satirical sermon on the theme 'Stultorum numerus infinitus' ('the number of fools is infinite').[33] It seems at least possible that the performer of *Saint Nobody* had a stock of parodic pardons with him, to issue to the audience at the conclusion of his speech.

A further possibility is also suggested by the frequent references to 'this water', meaning ale. As other sources make clear, drink could be incorporated directly into the performance of sermons. A description of a Lincolnshire mock-preacher in 1601, for instance, notes that the figure kept a 'pott of ale or beare' by him 'in steade of an hower glasse'. This last item was apparently used to demarcate the sections of his sermon, as the preacher 'did Drinke at the concluding of any poynte or parte of his speech'.[34] The fact that *Saint Nobody* refers to ale in such direct, immediate terms implies that the speaker also has a drink before him, which might be put to similar use.

But beyond these pieces of evidence, perhaps the most important thing that the text reveals is the deep-rooted conservatism of the mock-sermon. Although the great nineteenth-century scholar Gaston Paris may have been 'astonished' by the

---

[31] Robert W. Scribner, *Popular Culture and Popular Movements in Reformation Germany* (London, 1987), 74.

[32] Daron Lee Burrows, *Two Old French Satires on the Power of the Keys: L'Escommeniement au lecheor and Le Pardon de foutre* (London, 2005), 97.

[33] David Lindsay, *Ane Satyre of the Thrie Estaitis*, ed. Roderick Lyall (Edinburgh, 1989), 155–7.

[34] Norreys Jephson O'Conor, *Godes Peace and the Queenes: Vicissitudes of a House, 1539–1615* (London, 1934), 120.

'audacity and freedom' of the *sermons joyeux*, *Saint Nobody* demonstrates that a conventional, even didactic element is at the heart of these works.[35] Beneath the surface ribaldry and disorder of the piece, with its copious allusions to faeces and dissipation, there is an instructive intent at work. This can be readily seen in the inversions that *Saint Nobody* carries out. These in fact have a clear moral purpose. The text is not content to confuse the transcendent and earthly, but also extends this practice to good and evil. Throughout the piece virtue and sin are made to exchange places: hence at one stage the text describes the spirit of a dead glutton 'clothed in black' and sent to dwell 'where it was all dark', although it insists that the man was an angel, and promotes him as a model for devotion (line 26). The system of divine punishments and rewards is also reversed: the hearers are promised that 'the kingdom of heaven is to be won/ By drinking to drunkenness' (lines 21–2). Even the motives of the preacher himself are implicated in this inversion. At one stage he pleads for money from those assembled, although he reveals that this is not for charitable ends, but to pay off a prostitute who 'pestered me outside' (line 125). The sermon not only inverts the usual hierarchy between souls and bowels, but extends this programme to behavioural codes as well, placing immorality in the place of goodness. In other words, it does not merely overturn the gestures and symbols of the sermon, but capsizes the values at its centre, giving the logic of carnival a moral dimension.

Nonetheless, these new values are not permitted to challenge the standing of conventional morality. This moral reversal in fact serves to disown and undermine the debauchery that the preacher appears to advocate. This is particularly apparent in the text's continual play with nothingness. Not only does it make repeated references to 'empty churches', but the 'scriptures' it evokes are all similarly negated: it refers to 'chapter nothing' and the 'Book of Nothing' (lines 1 and 23), and bases its arguments on texts that 'have not been written' (line 14). Needless to say, this is quite at odds with the carnival imagery Bakhtin outlines, which always 'has a positive, assertive character', and bases itself in 'fertility, growth, and a brimming-over abundance'.[36] Against this conception, *Saint Nobody* roots itself in absence rather than substance, and in non-existence rather than plenitude. This in turn has the result of stifling any sense of real upheaval, cancelling the 'unofficial point of view' that Bakhtin describes.[37] The text instead manages to enshrine accepted morality, dispelling the sermon's message even as it is issued. By identifying its voice with emptiness and defining its authorities in negative terms, the sermon is presenting itself as a fiction devoid of any real content. It characterises itself as something fundamentally hollow, as its speaker and his discourse have literally no underlying essence, disclosing and offering nothing. This means that the alternative morality the sermon seems to proclaim is granted no real being of its own. What appears to be a possibility beyond common standards is presented only as a lack.

The sermon thus refers its audience back to the normality it seems to attack. There is literally nothing beyond accepted convention, as even this apparent break with the status quo turns out not to exist, having no being of its own. Ultimately, then, although *Saint Nobody* pretends to support hedonistic excess, it only serves

---

[35] Gaston Paris, *Mediaeval French Literature*, trans. Hannah Lynch (London, 1903), 160.
[36] Bakhtin, *Rabelais and his World*, 19.
[37] Ibid., 41.

to discredit the code it describes. It follows Peter Dronke's general description of medieval parodic literature, as its 'mocking fantasy . . . is teased out in detail as though it were reality . . . and yet – this is essential to the fantasy – the Christian God and his cult remain'.[38] In spite of its scurrilous and often repulsive subject-matter, therefore, the *spotsermoen* retains at all times a deep-seated moral sensibility. It actively emphasises the validity of the framework it seems to uproot and destroy. Just as it was probably staged 'upon a scaffold near the church door', so it is attached firmly to the religious structures it seems to deride.[39] The text again foregrounds the instructive intent of the *rederijkers*, their status as self-appointed educators of their communities.

---

[38] Peter Dronke, 'Profane Elements in Literature', in *Renaissance and Renewal in the Twelfth Century*, ed. Robert L. Benson, Giles Constable and Carol D. Lanham (Cambridge, MA, 1982), 569–92 (584).

[39] E. K. Chambers, *The Medieval Stage*, 2 vols. (Oxford, 1903), I: 381.

Spotsermoen over Sint-Niemand

Non scriptum est in libro Nullorum
De uno Nullo Willecommorum
Capitulorum nullo decimo sexto.
Ille Nullus non fuit curatus
5 *Nec etiam magistratus*
In nullo prolegeorum.
Ongheminde vriendekens overal,
Verstaet u doch wat ic hier segghen zal.
Dees woordekens ghenomen uuten Latine
10 Behooren hier wel ghenoteert te zijne.
Ende ontfanc se doch in hulier hert met allen,
Al sauden zij u wederom ten eersgate uutvallen,
Want het bescrijft den abelsten die men vint
Sonder papier, penne ofte int,
15 Ende seit: pijnt doch wel te verstane,
Dat hemelrijcke es te winnene
Met droncken te drinckene, ic moet verclaren.
Dus mijn beminde, wilt doch hulieder ziele bewaren
Ende en sparen goet noch eerve,
20 Al sauden u kinderen van hongher sterven,
Drijnct vrij altijts waer gij muecht,
Dat daerbij u ziele mach commen ter onderster vruecht.
Wij vinden in *capito nullo* van eenen gast,
Die eens zo vele dranc dat hij barst;
25 Hoe voer hij? Hij was zeer fierlijc gheleet
Van veel inghelen, al in 't swart ghecleet,
Ende trocken metier ziele, zo ic las,
Onder hemelrijcke, daer 't alderdonckerst was.
Peijnst wat blijscepe dat men daer mochte maken.
30 Kinderen, bidt ooc dat ghij er alle muecht gheraken,
Zo werdij bevrijt van allen lichten claer.
Nu wel, dat latic daer.
Non scriptum est in libro Nullorum
De uno Nullo Willecommorum
35 *Capitulorum nullo decimo sexto.*
Sanctus Drincatibus bescrijft ons van eender tombe,

---

* The Dutch text has been reproduced from Pleij, *Het gilde van de Blauwe Schuit*, 256–9. Used with permission.

A Mock-Sermon on Saint Nobody

Non scriptum est in libro Nullorum
De uno Nullo Willecommorum
Capitulorum nullo decimo sexto.
Ille Nullus non fuit curates
     Nec etiam magistratus
     In nullo prolegeorum.[1]
Unbeloved friends everywhere,
You must hear what I will say here.
These words are taken from the Latin,
It is right that they are carefully considered.
And so take them into your heart, all of you,
Although they might fall out of your arsehole again,
For they describe the noblest man that one may find
Without paper, pen or ink,
And they say: Think, and understand well,
That the kingdom of heaven is to be won
By drinking to drunkenness. I must explain.
Thus, my beloved, if you would save your soul,
And not hoard your goods or inheritance,
Although your children might die from hunger,
Always drink freely wherever you can,
So that through this your soul might reach the lowest joy.
We read in *capito nullo* about a man,[2]
Who once drank so much he burst;
How did he look? He was very finely dressed
As many angels are, all clothed in black.
And then his soul went, so I read,
Beneath heaven's kingdom, where it was all dark.
Think what bliss one may find there.
Children, pray that you all might fly there too,
So that you will be freed from all clear lights.
Well now, I leave that there.
Non scriptum est in libro Nullorum
De uno Nullo Willecommorum
Capitulorum nullo decimo sexto.
Saint Drincatibus informs us of a tomb,

Line numbers in margin: 5, 10, 15, 20, 25, 30, 35

---

[1] This section parodies the *thema* of the conventional sermon, or the scripture on which the sermon will be based. The text consists of garbled Latin, interspersed with snippets of Latinised Dutch. Its meaning approximates to: 'It is unwritten in the Book of Nothing of one Nullo Willecommorum (i.e. Welcome-to-Nobody), in the nothing-and-sixteenth chapter. This Nullo was not a priest, nor was he a teacher, in nothing of a prologue'. This recalls More's description of the mock-preacher basing his 'mowynge sermon' on 'some fonde textes of his own hed', rather than 'medl[ing] wyth ye very scrypture yt selfe': *Confutation of Tyndale's Answer*, 919.

[2] That is, 'chapter nothing'.

Daerin begraven licht Nullus Willecomme,
Die zo ghemindt was voor zijn doot,
Dat men hem alomme de duere vuer den nuese sloot.
40 Elc placht hem met niet te bescijnkene.
Kinderen, dit verdiendi met grooten tueghen te drinckene.
Hij pijnde daeraf zeer selden te falene.
An zijn tombe zijn ooc veel schoone pardoenen te halene,
Plena culpa esser te ghecrijghene.
45 Wel, hieraf willic noch wat pijnen te swijghene
Ende commen weder te mijre cameren binnen,
Dat men hemelrijcke met drijnckene mach winnen.
Want wie drijnct dat hem die ooghen loopen, in wijne of in biere,
Die verlost telcken een ziele uuten vaviere.
50 Hoort wat ons Sanctus Drincatibus bescrijft:
Zo wie drijnct, dat hij zijn brouc onnheert,
Die zoude hebben voor zijn beghin
XL daghen aflaets tweewaerf XX min,
Ende ooc zoveel carinen daeran.
55 Diets niet en ghelooft es onder 's paus ban.
Dus pijnt u doch gheen tueghen te vermijnckene,
Maer desen zomere zeer stijf te drijnckene,
Al mueghdij somtijds wat zijn sonder ghelt,
Ghij en zult van den kachielen niet zijn ghequelt.
60 Hoort doch, wies ic hulieden vermane,
Dat's dees goe weke om hulieder pardoen te gane,
Want ic zegghe ulieden sonder eenighe fute,
Van t'avent in acht daghen gaen zij ute.
Voort verman' ick ulieden, om ulieder zinnen te verclouckene,
65 Alle drie dees kercken te besouckene,
Want het zijn zeer ledeghe plaetsen, zo ic hebbe verstaen.

Where Nullus Willecomme lies buried,
Who was so loved before his death
That men always slammed the door before his nose.
40 Everyone plied him with nothing to drink.
Children, this you can earn by drinking great drafts
He gave very little thought to failing in this.
At his tomb there are very fine pardons to be had,
Plena culpa is there to be seized.[3]
45 Well, from here I will take pains to be silent
And to come back within my chamber,[4]
So that men may win heaven's kingdom with drinking.
For whoever drinks until his eyes race, in wine or in beer,
He delivers at every turn a soul out of purgatory.
50 Hear what our Saint Drincatibus writes:
He that drinks until he dishonours his trousers,
He should have for starters
Forty days indulgence minus two times twenty,
And just as much penance from that.
55 He that does not believe this falls under the pope's curse.
Thus take care that you do not mess up your drafts,
But try this summer to drink very stiffly,
Although you may sometimes be without money,
You shall not be free from those cowards.[5]
60 Listen, though, I caution you against something,
That is, working for your absolution this holy week,
For I say this to you without any artifice,
From this evening go out for eight days.
Therefore I urge you, in order to lighten your moods,
65 To seek out all three of these churches,
For they are very empty places, so I have heard.[6]

---

[3] This line contains a pun on the standard confessional formula, taken from the penitential prayer the *Confiteor*, replacing *mea culpa* ('my own fault') with *plena culpa* ('full of fault').

[4] That is, to return to my original point.

[5] These lines seem to parody Juvenal, *Satires*, 10.22, 'Cantabit vacuus coram latrone viator' ('the empty-handed traveller can rejoice in the presence of the robber'): *Persi et Juvenalis Saturae*, ed. W. V. Clausen (London, 1992). Since the phrase had become a common moral proverb during the Middle Ages, it is an obvious target for ridicule in this deliberately amoral text: see Barlett J. Whiting and Helen W. Whiting, *Proverbs, Sentences and Proverbial Phrases from English Writings Mainly before 1500* (Cambridge, MA, 1968), 266. In fact, Gilman specifically notes that traditional adages were often lampooned in mock-sermons, especially those performed at Shrovetide: Gilman, *Parodic Sermon in European Perspective*, 25.

[6] This and later references to *ledegher kercken*, meaning 'empty churches' in the sense of 'frivolous' or 'vain', probably alludes to local taverns. The idea that the tavern was a sort of anti-church is a common medieval conceit. As one fifteenth-century English author puts it, 'þe tauerne is welle of glotonye, for it may be clepyd þe develys scolehous & þe deuelys chapel, for þere his dyscyples stodyen and syngyn, bothe day & nyht, & þere þe deuyl doth meraclys to his seruauntys': Arthur Brandeis, *Jacob's Well, an Englisht Treatise on the Cleansing of Man's*

Voort zo saud' ic ulieden allen raen
Van dien waterken te drijnckene, hetzij in III of IV stopen,
Al sauden zij ulieden onder ten eersgate uutloopen.
70 Ende en spares niet, ghiet 'et vrij in u rebben,
Al saudi er 's morghen den keldercurts of alle hebben.
't Es zeer precieus in zijn bestier,
Want men halet wel zeven milen van hier.
Sanctus Drincatibus, desen heleghen sanct,
75 Was d'eerst, die dees groote tueghen vant,
Want hij woonde met Bacchus, den heleghen man,
Die hem altoos leerde drijncken dotan,
Want hij dranc zo zeere om te comen t'zijnen lotte,
Dat hij laestent versmierde in zijn snotte.
80 Daer starf hij, zo die scriftuer zeit in 't clare,
Gheen sant, maer ledich maertelare.
Want hij dranc vele, zo menich wel weet,
Dat hij alle daghe zijn brouc vul sceet.
Peijnst wat hij dan lijden moeste om dat,
85 Want hij hadde den dicxsten tijt d'heersgat nat.
Hij was dicwilt begaet daer hij lach en sliep,
Dat hem onder te zijnen scoen uutliep.
Was ditte niet een wonderlic misterie?
O laes, doen drouch men te grave up een berie.
90 Niemant en wilde 'm ontcleeden up dat pas,
Omdat hij zo dicht besceten was.
En worpen zij hem neder, elc mocht anscauwen,
Besnot, besceet ende zo jammerlic bespauwen,
Datten de vraukens sleepten in eender houc.
95 Daer trocken zij hem zijn dwael uutter brouc
Ende liet' er de honden en catten an cnaghen.
O vraukens, ontsiedij niet de plaghen,
Dijnct doch wat ghij hebt ghemaect.
Dien haermen Sanct lach er mesmaect,
100 Alsof hij uut een scijtleij ghecommen hade.
Zo steerfde hij martelare, alzo hij dede.
Nu wel, ghijlieden zult alle vallen in knieghebede
Ende helpen mij bidden voor gheestelic of weerlic,
Dat zij langhe leven, dat's deerlic.
105 Voort zo zuldij ooc bidden up dit termijn

Afterwards I should so advise you all
To drink of this water, take three or four tankards,
Though it should run out below, through your arsehole.

70 Yet do not spare it, pour it freely into your ribs,
Although you could all have cellar fever in the morning.
It is very valuable in its effects,
For men carry it a good seven miles from here.
Saint Drincatibus, this holy saint,

75 Was the first that took these great drafts,
For he lived with Bacchus, the holy man,
Who taught him to devote himself always to drinking,
Thus he drank so much that his fate came to pass,
And in the end he was smothered in his snot.

80 Then he died, so the scripture clearly says,
No holy man, but an empty martyr.
For he drank so much, as many know well,
That all day his breeches were filled with shit.
Think what he must have suffered from that,

85 For he had a soggy arsehole for most of the time.
He was often befouled where he lay and slept,
So that it ran out of his shoes.
Was this not a miraculous mystery?
Alas, men drew him to his grave upon a muck cart.[7]

90 But nobody would undress him up to that point,[8]
Because he was so thickly caked in shit.
And they threw him down, so all might see,
Snotty, shitty and so pitifully spat on
That the women dragged him into a pigsty.

95 There they took a cloth from him, out of his breeches,[9]
And let the dogs and cats gnaw on it.
Oh women, do you not see these torments,
Think now what you have done.
That poor saint lies there undone

100 As though he had come out of a cesspit.
Thus he died a martyr, so he did.
Well now, you should all fall to your knees
And help me pray for the spiritual or worldly
That they may live long, and do so painfully.

105 Next you should also pray at this time

Conscience, Early English Text Society, os 115 (London, 1900), 147.
   [7] There is an untranslatable pun here, as the Middle Dutch is *berie*, which closely resembles *baar*, 'bier'.
   [8] Possibly a blasphemous reversal of the mocking of Christ, in which Jesus is stripped by his captors prior to crucifixion. See Matthew 27.28–31.
   [9] The term *dwaal* ('cloth'), although it seems to mean a handkerchief here, also has religious connotations, since it might refer to the covering of an altar.

Voor die te Pamel ende elder ghevanghen zijn,
Want zij en cuenen in gheener maniere verwerven,
Zij en moeten alle dees verre sterven.
Hoort wie zij zijn: daer es Pieter Osse, Gheert Coen,
110   Gille Conins, Pieter Scaep, Jan Capoen;
Die mueghen nu wel zijn in grooten truere,
Want zij trecken dees weke alle duere.
Ende voort die van den gheslachte zijn, 't zij quae of goe,
Zij ghebannen te Pamel tot Paesschen toe.
115   Dus bidt doch dat dees pacienten sonder sparen
In hongierighe buucken mueghen varen.
Voort bidd' ic om een cleen aelemoesen van uwen ghelde
Om eenen haermen ziecke, dat's Miesken van der Velde.
Daer es zo groot ghebreck in huus,
120   Want zijn joncwijf vant lestent een muijs
In scaeprae van hongher ghestorven.
Wel, hier es noch een bede an mij verworven,
Maer ic scaem mij: hier zijn zo vele clappers.
Nochtans ic recommandeer se ulieden, 't es Gillucken Slappers.
125   Zou heeft mij daerbuuten zozeer staen quellen
Ende zou es zo ontfaermartich onder die ghesellen,
Wilt hier doch wat toesteken,
Want zou lijdt heijmelicke ghebreken.
Wel, mij es ghelast, dat ic ulieden saude verclaren,
130   Dat alle die te Paesschen ghebannen waren,
Muechdy weder huusen ende hoven t'elcker ure.
Ic sal se u alle noemen bij aventuere:
Daer es Jan Cabeljau, Pieter Scelvis, Jan Looc,
Gheert Roche, Gille Vloote ooc,
135   Pieter Pladijs, Jan But, Tijs Muecke,
Men saud se herberghen bij den ruecke.

For those who are captive at Pamel and elsewhere,[10]
Because they can be recruited in no other way,
They must all of them die far away.
Hear who they are: there is Peter Ox, Gerald Goose,
110   Giles Rabbit, Peter Sheep, John Capon;[11]
They might well now be in great distress,
As they try to open every door.
And those that will be slain, for good or ill,
Are forbidden from Ash Wednesday till Easter.[12]
115   Thus pray that these sufferers, without exception,
Might travel into hungry bellies.
Next I pray for a small alms donation, from your money
For a poor sick boy, that is Michael of the Field.
There is such great lack in his house,
120   That all his serving girl found yesterday
Was a mouse in the cupboard, dead from hunger.
Well, here is another plea I have been given,
But I shame myself to say it, there are so many chatterers here.
Nonetheless, I commend someone to you, that is, Gillian Trollop.[13]
125   She has pestered me outside so very stubbornly
And she is popular among the young fellows;
Will you hand over something here,
For she secretly leads a deprived life.
Well, it falls to me that I should recount to you,
130   All of those that are in hiding until Easter,
They are in every house and courtyard at every hour.
I shall name them all for you, with great effort:[14]
There is John Cod, Peter Haddock, John Lox,
Gerald Ray, Giles Skate as well,
135   Peter Plaice, John Flounder, Matthew Mackerel,
Men should harbour them by the hearth.[15]

---

[10] Pamel was a town in eastern Flanders, on the river Scheldt. It is most famous for being the birthplace of the poet Matthijs de Castelein, a key theoretician of the *rederijkers*. It is now part of the city of Oudenaarde.

[11] The various figures listed here are personifications of foodstuffs prohibited during Lent: hence 'from Ash Wednesday to Easter' they are 'forbidden' (line 114).

[12] That is, from the first day of Lent until its conclusion.

[13] Despite the coincidence in meaning, the Dutch *slapper* is probably not related to the British slang term 'slapper', in the sense of 'a prostitute or slut'. According to Thorne, the British 'slapper' is 'probably a corruption of *shlepper* or *schlepper*, a word of Yiddish origin, one of whose meanings is a slovenly or immoral woman': Tony Thorne, *Dictionary of Contemporary Slang* (New York, 1990), p. 468. The Yiddish term is in turn derived from Middle High German *schleppen*, 'drag', whereas the Dutch *slapte* originally means 'slack', 'loose', or 'slow'.

[14] Unlike the previous list, this roll call of fish and vegetable personifications is part of the acceptable diet during Lent. Thus 'these you must shelter' (line 140), since no other food will be available during the fast.

[15] That is, in order to smoke them.

79

Dan esser Lans Caerper ende Feijnse Bliec,
Joos Sallems, Jan Vetvis, al zijn zij ziec,
Dees mueghdij herberghen, tzij quae of goe,
140   Van nu voortan tot Paesschen toe.
Nu zijnder ooc vraukens mede in 't rabot:
Dat's Calle Olive ende Griete Olipot,
Trijn Fijghen, Calleke Appel, Beelke Rosijns,
Ende daer wasser noch vele meer in den ban,
145   Die ic niet alle ghenoemen en can.
Hoort naer de gheboden van deser ledegher kercken:
Hier commen IV daghen dat ghij niet veel en zult wercken,
Dan moettij dees ledeghe plaetsen visenteren.
Ende en wilt dees aflaten niet perturberen,
150   Want zij en zijn niet zeer goet noch affect.
En dat ghij er ooc niet mede en ghect,
Want 't en es gheen cleen sake van desen,
Ghij sautere om verwaten wesen.
Dus versouct dees kercken meesters ende cnapen,
155   Al saudi er 's nachts in scuere om slapen.
Ende ghij vraukens en jonghe dochterkens mede,
Besouct ooc dese ledeghe stede
Ende wilt van den waterken in u lichaem driven,
Al saude d'maechdom onderweghe bliven.
160   *Absolvat vulgat*, dat 's 't avont 't heersgat nat,
Dat verleen u Drincatibus, den ledeghe Sant,
Dat ghij alle muecht commen daer hij hemselven vant.
't Selve aflaet dat Bacchus Drincatibus gaf –
Daer zo willic nu swijghen af –
165   Moet u toecommen, ic zegh 't u plat,
Dat's altijts 't hemdeken vooren ende bachten nat.
Amen.

Then there is Lance Carp and Vincent Bream,
Joseph Salmon, John Blubber,[16] although they may be ill,
These you must shelter, be it bad or good,
140   From now on until Easter.
Now there are also women in this register:
There is Cal Olive, and Gretchen Oilpot,
Trudy Fig, Caley Apple, Beverley Raisin,
And there are many more in exile,
145   So many that I cannot name them all.
Hear the rulings of these empty churches:
There come four days in which you should not work hard,
Then must you visit these empty places,
And you will not disturb these indulgences:
150   They are not very good or effective,
But nonetheless you must not touch them here,
As it is no small thing to do so,
You shall be cursed for it.
Thus seek out these churches, you masters and lads,
155   Even if you should sleep in a barn at night.
And you women and young daughters as well
Should also visit these empty places,
And desire to tip this water into your body,
Even though you should lose your maidenhead along the way.
160   *Absolvat vulgat*, that is, 'tonight your arsehole is wet',[17]
May Drincatibus, the empty saint, grant you this,
That you all might reach where he himself went.
So the same blessing that Bacchus gave Drincatibus –
On this matter I will I now be silent –
165   Might come to you, I speak it to you plainly:
That is, may your shirt always be wet before and behind.
Amen.

[16] Lambrecht's glossary of Dutch terms, compiled in 1562, defines *vetvisch* as 'poisson gras *ou* lard de poisson' ('fish grease or fat of fish'): Joos Lambrecht, *Het naembouck van 1562. Tweede druk van het Nederlands–Frans woordenboek*, ed. René Verdeyen (Paris, 1945), 211.

[17] The garbled Latin of this line combines two well-known words, *absolvo* ('I absolve'), from the formula recited by priests after confession, and *Vulgate*, Jerome's Latin version of Scripture. There also is an untranslatable pun here, which relies on the phonic similarity between *vulgate* and the Middle Dutch *vul gat* ('full arsehole').

The Oath of Master Pawnbroker

THE *Eedt van Meester Oom* originates from Brussels, and dates from 1551. The text survives in a printed booklet of 1552, produced by the Leuven printer Reynier van Velpen, perhaps better known by his Latinised signature Reinerus Velpius. Van Velpen was one of the most significant Flemish printers of the late sixteenth century: his career lasted for nearly two decades and gave rise to an entire dynasty of printers, as two sons and a granddaughter followed him into the business.[1] Nevertheless, *The Oath* is curiously out of step with the bulk of his work. Most of the books Van Velpen produced are lengthy volumes of academic theology, evidently intended for Leuven's university. Typical examples include Pierre Cousturier's *De Vita Cartusiana* (1572), Stephen Gardiner's *Confutatio Cavilationum* (1554) and Giovanni of Bologna's *De Aeterna Dei Praedestinatione* (1555).[2] In fact, after 1558 Van Velpen developed close links to a number of English Catholic intellectuals resident at Leuven, such as John Fowler and Nicholas Sanders, whose *De Visibili Monarchia Ecclesiae* he printed in 1571.[3] *The Oath*, with its vernacular content and boisterous subject-matter, seems to be an early attempt by Van Velpen to tap into a more popular market. Since it was printed in the same year Van Velpen obtained his *drukkersoctrooi* (printing licence), it is most likely an experiment by a printer who has yet to establish himself or his reputation.

In many respects *The Oath* follows the same course as several other festive monologues, reproducing their general formula closely. Much like *Saint Nobody*, it parodies official discourse by inserting episodes of inversion and scatology into an authoritative form of speech. Although it is often classified as a *spotmandement* (mock-proclamation), the specific genre it mimics is the coronation oath.[4] As the text progresses, its speaker, who styles himself an official clerk or registrar, leads Meester Oom the 'King of Fools' through various promises to his 'people'. As is consistent with this sort of burlesque, the text preserves the conventions it is imitating with reasonable fidelity. In fact, a number of lines seem to recall specific promises included in the oath of Charles V to his Burgundian territories. For instance, just as Charles swore to 'keep and maintain our said lands in good peace, tranquility and repose', so the King of Fools vows to outlaw work and 'show all a good example' by sleeping until noon and drinking until midnight (line 109). Likewise Charles's vow that 'everyone should know the love that we bear them' finds an ironic counterpart in the king's desire to 'gain praise and love everywhere' by being 'a faithful one in the

---

[1] Pierre Delsaerdt, *Suam quisque Bibliothecam* (Leuven, 2001), 90, 417.

[2] G. Glourieux and A. Rouzet, 'Les Velpuis á Louvain. Formation d'un atelier', in *Ornamentation typographique et bibliographie historique*, ed. Marie-Thérèse Isaac (Brussels, 1988), 67–85 (67–8).

[3] Christian Coppens, *Reading in Exile: The Libraries of John Ramridge, Thomas Harding, Henry Joliffe, Recusants in Louvain* (Cambridge, 1993), 32–3.

[4] See for instance F. Van Thijn, 'Eedt van Meester Oom', in *De Nederlandse en Vlaamse auteurs van middeleeuwen tot heden met inbegrip van de Friese auteurs*, ed. G. J. van Bork and P. J. Verkruijsse (Weesp, 1985), 188.

tavern' (lines 125, 117).[5] The text even culminates with a travesty of the well-known 'slogan of legalistic and dynastic continuity' first used at the coronation of Charles VII in 1422, as its audience is required to shout 'Vive le roi, stultus stultorum!' (line 155).[6] Also like a genuine oath, the audience are not treated as passive observers. They actively collude with the proceedings, as they are called on to voice their support for the speech at various points. As recent commentators have noted, the text effectively 'allocates a third speaking role to the public, who speak throughout as citizens of the new kingdom, and at the end must also affirm that the new laws will be maintained'.[7]

While the text typifies the comic monologue in its overall form, it also has an especially close resemblance to one text in particular. It is comparable in content and execution to *The Guild of the Blue Barge*. Like the earlier text, it incorporates a great deal of material from the tradition of the estates satire, as its middle section includes a far-ranging critique of numerous trades and social groups. In fewer than two hundred lines it mocks priests who gamble away their clothes, young lords who 'rent horses to attain their knighthood', braggart soldiers, and a wide range of further classes and professions (line 22). While the range of groups ridiculed is larger than that found in *The Blue Barge*, the basic joke is much the same. It is the absurd, impetuous or wasteful behaviour of these figures that qualifies them to enter the foolish kingdom, as their current habits bestow this dubious accord upon them. The text therefore uses the same central device that occurs in *The Blue Barge*: it denounces its targets by giving them a hollow reward, granting them entry into a company of fools and idiots. There is also a further echo of *The Blue Barge* in the text's easy vacillation between moral satire and rich vulgarity. Despite its far-ranging criticisms, the text concludes on a lavatorial note, instructing its listeners 'now stick all your fingers in your hole and then kiss them' (line 169). As Walter Gibson reflects, 'we may doubt the people present on this occasion were much edified', given its culmination with this 'particularly obscene gesture'.[8] *The Oath*, in other words, follows the form of the earlier monologue, despite casting itself in a different genre. It also shuttles between the didactic and grotesque, showing both a concern for social order and a fascination with images of excretion.

Alongside these echoes, the text is also reminiscent of the tradition of Luilekkerland or Cockaigne, an imaginary 'land of plenty' that features in several European literatures.[9] According to its earliest description in the *Fabliau de Cocagne* (c.1250),

---

[5] Steven Gunn, David Grummitt and Hans Cools, *War, State, and Society in England and the Netherlands 1477–1559* (Oxford, 2007), 245.

[6] Ernst H. Kantorowicz, *The King's Two Bodies: A Study in Mediaeval Political Theology* (Princeton, NJ, 1957), 410.

[7] 'De derde rol is het publiek opgedrongen, dat steeds als onderdanen van het nieuwe rijk wordt toegesproken, en aan het slot eveneens moet antwoorden of het de nieuwe wetten zal onderhouden': Hinke van Kampen, Herman Pleij, Bob Stumpel, Annebel Venmans and Paul Vriesema, *Het zal koud zijn in 't water als 't vriest* (The Hague, 1980), 38. See also Clifford Davidson, *Fools and Folly* (Kalamazoo, MI, 1996), 123.

[8] Walter Gibson, *Pieter Brueghel and the Art of Laughter* (Berkeley, CA, 2006), 27.

[9] On analogues in Middle English, German, Italian and French, see 'The Land of Cokaygne', in *Old and Middle English, c.890–c.1400: An Anthology*, ed. Elaine Treharne, 2nd edn (Oxford, 2004), 431–5; Wim Tigges, 'The Land of Cokaygne: sophisticated mirth', in *A Companion to Early English Literature*, ed. N. H. G. E. Veldhoen and Henk Aertsen (Amsterdam, 1988), 97–104;

this country boasts several unique geographic features, such as rivers of red wine, showers of hot puddings, fence-posts made of sausage, and a fountain of youth.[10] The story of Cockaigne clearly had some currency in the Netherlands from an early date, as a number of villages in the Low Countries were apparently named in its honour, such as Kockengen in Utrecht and Koekange in Drenthe.[11] It is also the subject of three fifteenth- and sixteenth-century Dutch accounts, and appears in a well-known painting by Pieter Bruegel the Elder, itself adapted into an engraving by Pieter van der Heyden.[12] The tradition was still widely known in Holland in the seventeenth and eighteenth centuries: popular songs and prints about the land circulated throughout this period, and the famous buccaneer Exquemelin was evidently familiar with the myth, speculating that 'the old story ... of the land where the houses were covered with pancakes' may stem from the Caribbean practice of placing cakes 'on the roof-tops to dry'.[13] Although *The Oath* lacks some of the more elaborate or grotesque elements of Cockaigne texts, such as its jugs made of beer, its roof-beams of eels and butter, or its four Christmases a year, it does seem to be grounded in the same set of ideas. By envisioning an entire 'foolish kingdom' in which indolence, rapacity and promiscuity are obligatory, where work is illegal and 'all days are amorous' (line 128), it reproduces many of the key themes of the popular utopia: like depictions of Cockaigne, it projects a 'world of instant gratification ... wishing away all physical and sensual limitation'.[14] The only distinction is that this state is brought about by legislation and policy, rather than from the landscape itself, a change which perhaps reflects the urban rather than rural origins of *The Oath*. In other respects, however, the conventions remain largely intact.

Nonetheless, despite treading some familiar ground, *The Oath* does demand attention in its own right. The piece is notable for the central role it played in one of the most elaborate and well-documented comedic performances of the *rederijkers*. This setting in turn shows the important status that the chambers awarded to foolery in general. *The Oath* was originally performed at Brussels in July 1551, when it appeared as part of a spectacular and singular *zottenfeest* or Feast of Fools. The Feast was a long-established annual tradition in the southern Netherlands and northern France, and had grown ever more elaborate throughout the fifteenth century, after ecclesiastic attempts to suppress it only transferred it into secular hands.[15]

Elfriede Marie Ackermann, *Das Schlaraffenland in German literature and folksong: social aspects of an earthly paradise* (Chicago, 1944); Carlo Ginzburg, *The Cheese and the Worms: the cosmos of a sixteenth-century miller*, trans. John Tedeschi and Anne Tedeschi (Baltimore, 1980), 82–6.

[10] Veikko Vaananen, 'Le "fabliau" de Cocagne', *Neuphilologische Mitteilungen* 48 (1947), 3–36 (22–7).

[11] On onomastic references to Cockaigne across Europe, see Malcolm Jones, *The Secret Middle Ages* (Stroud, 2002), 145–6.

[12] All three texts are translated and discussed in Herman Pleij, *Dreaming of Cockaigne*, trans. Diane Webb (New York, 2001), 33–44.

[13] G. Kalff, *Het lied in de middeleeuwen* (Arnhem, 1972), pp. 490–3; Nicolaas Boerma, 'Mit dem Schiff nach Schlaraffenland', *Arbeitskreis Bild Druck Papier* 8 (2003), 37–49; Alexandre Exquemelin, *The Buccaneers of America*, trans. Alexis Brown (Harmondsworth, 1969), 61.

[14] J. C. Davies, 'The History of Utopia: A Chronology of Nowhere', in *Utopias*, ed. Peter Alexander and Roger Gill (London, 1984), 8.

[15] On the history development of the feast, see Natalie Zemon Davis's essay 'The Reasons of

Nonetheless, the Brussels *feest* was still an event of almost unparalleled scale. It was organised along the same lines as a *landjuweel*, in that it called on the participation of fools from a range of chambers across the Low Countries: it was, in effect, a *rederijkerfeest* in which each chamber and city would be represented by its fool rather than its *factor*. As Pleij observes, participation in this event was considered no less prestigious than attendance at a standard festival, since the chambers regarded 'a fool as a status symbol', even something 'appropriate to their proper equipment' as a chamber.[16] The chambers and civic authorities were evidently eager for their fools to take part, as they granted generous allowances for this purpose: for instance 'Langhen Caesken' (Long Nick) of 's-Hertogenbosch was given twelve guilders by the city 'to win the prize of the fools' at Brussels.[17]

The event itself is outlined in a contemporary chronicle, and has been further discussed by Van Eeghen, Marijnissen, Pleij and Moser, amongst others.[18] It lasted for several days, and incorporated a broad range of different set-pieces. The entire feast began with a formal entry of the fools, led by Meester Oom himself, their supposed 'Prince', mounted on a donkey. The procession terminated at one of the city's churches, which became the setting of a *zottenmis* (Fool's Mass), recited in traditional piping voices. After the mass was concluded, a mock-court was held, at which 'justice was served, to reprove any offences the fools might have done', and at which Oom formulated verdicts and handed down pronouncements.[19] It seems that *The Oath* was recited at this stage in the proceedings, as one of Oom's judgements dealing with currency and trade is also preserved in Van Velpen's edition.[20] The court was followed by a large banquet. Later in the festival the fools were given free rein of Brussels for an entire day, and were licensed to indulge in pranks and stunts in the streets for the entertainment of the citizenry. The most spectacular event, however, seems to have been a tournament held in the Grote Markt, the central square of the city. This included such sights as contenders battling one another on *huppelpaardjes*

Misrule', in her *Society and Culture in Early Modern France* (Stanford, 1987), 97–123.

[16] 'Een zot als status-symbool . . . behoort ook tot de uitrusting van de rederijkerskamers': Herman Pleij, 'De zot als maatschappelijk houvast in de overgang van middeleeuwen naar moderne tijd', *Groniek* 23 (1990), 19–39 (23).

[17] 'Item ter ordinantie . . . gereyst ende betaelt Langh Claesken tot behulp van zynre reysen tot Brussel, bescreven omme te scinne den pryse vanden sotten 12 car. gul.': Rogier Adriaan van Zuylen, *Inventaris der archieven van de stad 's Hertogenbosch* ('s-Hertogenbosch, 1863–76), 1: 670.

[18] W. van Eeghem, 'Rhetores Bruxellenses', *Revue belge de philologie et d'histoire* 15 (1936), 47–78; R. Marijnissen, 'De eed van Meester Oom. Een voorbeeld van Brabantse jokkernij uit Bruegels tijd', in *Pieter Bruegel und seine Welt*, ed. O. von Simson and M. Winner (Berlin, 1979), 51–61; Herman Pleij, 'Eind juli 1551 – Op het zottenfeest van Brussel wordt Meester Oom als vorst in een massaspel beëdigd – De stedelijke feestviering van bevrijdend ritueel naar gecontroleerd schouwtoneel', in *Een theatergeschiedenis der Nederlanden. Tien eeuwen drama en theater in Nederland en Vlaanderen*, ed. R. L. Erenstein (Amsterdam, 1996), 112–19; Dietz-Rüdiger Moser, *Fastnacht–Fasching–Karneval: das Fest der 'Verkehrten Welt'* (Cologne, 1986). An English account is given in Keith P. F. Moxey, 'Pieter Bruegel and the Feast of Fools', *The Art Bulletin* 64 (1982), 640–6.

[19] 'Gemaect was justicie ende dat naden delicten dwelck de sotten mochten mesdaen hebben': Van Eeghem, 'Rhetores Bruxellenses', 75.

[20] Marijnissen, 'De eed van Meester Oom', 51–61.

(hobby-horses), armed with *marots* and inflated bladders. Finally the festivities were concluded by an emphatic restoration of proper order, as the *raad* of Brussels hosted a lavish open-air banquet, accompanied by instructive *zinnespelen*, and conspicuously attended by the city's magistracy and most prominent ecclesiastics. Despite its surface upheaval, therefore, the event as a whole served to confirm the given power-structure of the city: 'the chaos it created also showed the necessity of the existing order, which it was a relief to bring back again at the end of the festivities'.[21]

This purpose inevitably makes its way into *The Oath* itself. It can be clearly seen in the structure of the text, with its pauses to involve the audience. By allowing the spectators to participate, and in such a carefully prescribed manner, the text is asking them to confirm their membership of a community; what is more, it also asks them to acknowledge that they recognise the shared values of this group, that the profligate or inefficient behaviour the registrar describes is indeed *sotter* (foolish) or *onghestapelde* (unreasonable). The text might therefore be classified as a further example of *burgermoraal*, motivated by the values of the urban economy which the *rederijkers* and their audience inhabited.[22]

Such values can also be detected in the overriding concern with money. The central figure of Meester Oom has strong links with currency, as his name is a euphemism for 'pawnbroker': it literally translates as 'Master Uncle', playing with the superficially benevolent, avuncular character of this profession. While installing such a disreputable figure as monarch is ironic on the one hand, being part of *The Oath*'s programme of inversion, it is also a statement of the power of money. The pawnbroker is a concrete manifestation of the dangers of debt. He is a reminder of the consequences of recklessness, as his shop is the eventual destination for profligates, wastrels and spendthrifts. With this in mind, it in fact becomes entirely logical that he is placed in a position of authority in the pointedly inverted world of the carnival. He is something to be strenuously avoided by the spectators in their normal life, a possibility they must work to bypass, but in this unreal world his power is both accepted and celebrated. As a result of this, just as Oom leads the spectators to swear that 'reckoning yourself into loss' (line 63) and 'making today and breaking again tomorrow' are idiotic practices (line 65), he also leads them to confirm the importance of careful financial management. As they submit to his rule in jest, sarcastically swearing loyalty to him, they acknowledge the importance of regulating their spending in actuality, as nobody would wish to be a subject of the pawnbroker in real life. The *zottenfeest* is therefore a product of its society, a further mouthpiece for the capitalistic ethos cultivated in the urban, middle-class milieu of the chambers. In essence, *The Oath* confirms that money is always on the throne as it pays ironic tribute to Meester Oom. The economic associations of the figure are in fact spelled out even more explicitly in his other festival appearances. For instance, in the *landjuweel* at Antwerp in 1561, he apparently rode through the city 'seated in

---

[21] 'In de aldus geschapen chaos wordt tevens duidelijk gemaakt hoe noodzakelijk de bestaande orde wel is, waarin men na afloop van de feestelijkheden weer opgelucht kan terugkeren': Pleij, 'De zot als aaatschappelijk houvast', 24.

[22] See Herman Pleij, *Het gilde van de Blauwe Schuit: literatuur, volksfeest en burgermoraal in de late middeleeuwen* (Amsterdam, 1979), 209; Menno ter Braak, *Verzameld werk*, ed. M. van Crevel, H. A. Gomperts and G. H. 's-Gravesande, 5 vols. (Amsterdam, 1950–80), I: 132–58.

a chariot lavishly decorated with greenery, draped all around with playing cards'.[23] This last detail neatly encapsulates the links with playfulness, cash and rash expenditure that the figure displays in *The Oath*.

One final point of interest about *The Oath* is the insight it gives into the men who occupied the role of fool, and were thus responsible for delivering these monologues. The name of the mock-king himself has been recorded along with the other details of the *feest*. Meester Oom was apparently played by one Jan Colyns, also known as Jan Walravens. Colyns was by profession a painter, and was a longstanding member of the chamber of *De Corenbloem* (The Cornflower) at Brussels.[24] In his life outside the *zottenfeest*, Colyns seems to have been a prominent and respectable citizen of the city. His family was mostly comprised of merchants and tanners, and at least one Colyns appears as a free master of the Guild of Saint Luke, the professional association of painters.[25] He had a bronze medal cast for him by Jacques Jonghelinck in 1563, which is now held at the Rijksmuseum in Amsterdam.[26] There is, in short, little to suggest that he was anything but a prosperous craftsman at Brussels. All told, Colyns shows that there was little distinction between the fools and other high-ranking *rederijkers*. Despite dealing in inversion and the suspension of normal standards, the chamber fools were no less part of the wealthy, professional class than the other chamber members. The position of fool therefore seems to have been just another honorary office to the *rederijkers*, of much the same value as *factor*, *keiser* or *cnape*.

[23] Davidson, *Fools and Folly*, 125.
[24] See E. Roobaert, 'Jan Welravens, alias Oomken, schilder en rederijker to Brussel', *Bulletin, Musées royaux des beaux-arts* 3–4 (1961), 83–100.
[25] Alejandro Vergara, *Patinir: Essays and Critical Catalogue* (Madrid, 2007), 56–7.
[26] Jan van der Stock and Hans Nieuwdorp, 'Het Christusbeeld van de Meir te Antwerpen. Een meesterwerk van de gebroeders De Nole uit de vergeetboek', *Revue belge d'archéologie et d'histoire de l'art* 55 (1986), 69–96 (76).

Eedt van Meester Oom

Dit is den Eedt van Meester Oom met vier ooren, Prince der dooren.

Die Ghrijpier:
Hoort ende swijcht die hun in der sotten rijck generen al,
Wat die Coninck der dooren hier gheloven en sweren sal.
Heer Coninck, hier sittende in u Malvesteijt,
Den Eet te doene suldij sijn bereijt,
5   En opdat ghi weten moecht, dwelc u noot is,
't Rijck der sotten dat zeer wijt en groot is
Wel te regerene buten en binnen
Met onbedachte, onghestapelde sinnen,
Soo moet ghi met mallen rade onverbolgen
10   Dese punten onderhouden die hierna volgen.
In den eersten moetij alle geestelicke personen
Die gheern onder d'oude cleermerct woonen
En gheern in den boec lesen tot hunder schade
Die men open slaet niet wijs van rade,
15   Die wijn en bier niet en laten verscalen
En veel meer borghen dan si connen betalen,
Nonnen die uutlopen en gaen hun gangen,
Munneken die de cappe op den tuyn hangen,
Dese moetij al scutten en schermen
20   Als si van aermoede claghen en kermen.
Voordt moetij allen eesel vassallen

---

*   The Dutch text has been reproduced from Pleij, *Het gilde van de Blauwe Schuit*, 248–52. Used with permission.

The Oath of Master Pawnbroker

This is the oath of Master Pawnbroker with four ears, the Prince of Fools.[1]

The seizecretary:[2]
Listen and be silent, all those who live in the kingdom of fools,
To what the king of fools declares and promises here.
Lord king, sitting here in your malusty,[3]
You should be ready to perform the oath,

5 And in order that you might know, as you need to,
How to govern well the Kingdom of Fools,
Which is very wide and great, without and within,
With thoughtless, unreasoned habits,
So you must with ridiculous counsel

10 Calmly maintain these points that follow here.
In the first place you have responsibility for all churchmen
Who yearn to dwell in the old clothes' market,[4]
And crave to read those books to their shame
That men do not open to learn from their counsel;

15 Who do not leave wine and beer to mature,
And spend on credit much more than they can pay.
Nuns who head out and wander as they please,
Monks who hang their copes in the garden:[5]
All of these you must shelter and shield

20 When they complain and moan from poverty.
Next you have all the asstocratic retainers,[6]

---

[1] The four ears are a reference to the cap of donkey's ears traditionally worn by fools.

[2] The original text names its speaker *ghrijpier*, a portmanteau formed from *griffier* (registrar) and *grijpen* ('to grasp' or 'to snatch').

[3] The text's *Malvesteijt* combines *majesteit* (majesty) and *mal* (ridiculous).

[4] The market itself is probably a topical reference to the Oude Kleermarkt (Old Clothes' Market) at Brussels, which used to stand next to Sint-Niklaaskerk, and is first mentioned in the 1520s; it was later moved to Korte Ridderstraat and renamed 'Kleerkopersstraat' or 'Rue des Fripiers', both meaning 'Clothes-Seller Street'. As Janssens notes, the epithet *oude* referred to the quality of the clothes sold, rather than the market itself: see Frederik Janssens, 'Straatnaamgeving' (Catholic University of Leuven: unpublished Ph.D. thesis, 1983), 107. The trope of clerics pawning their clothes, usually to fund gambling, is a commonplace in medieval literature, dating back at least as far as the *Carmina Burana* (twelfth century), in which the 'abbas Cucaniensis' ('abbot of Cockaigne') boasts that 'qui mane me quaesierit in taberna/ post vesperam nudus egredietur' ('whoever follows me into the tavern after vespers leaves naked'): Edwin Hermann Zeydel, *Vagabond Verse: Secular Latin Poems of the Middle Ages* (Detroit, 1966), 86. Much the same joke occurs in a refrein of 1524: see C. G. N. De Vooys, 'Een ongedrukte bundel refereinen van 1524', *Tijdschrift voor Nederlandse taal- en letterkunde* 21 (1902), 66–117 (102).

[5] That is, they abandon their order and Rule, or even strip naked to fornicate, an activity traditionally associated with a garden setting. See for instance the fifteenth-century song 'Ic sach in enen rozengaerde' ('I saw in a rosegarden'): K. Heeroma, *Liederen en gedichten uit het Gruuthuse-handschrift* (Leiden, 1966), 329.

[6] The text has *eesel*, a composite of *edel* (noble) and *ezel* (ass).

Die met gehuerde peerden hun ridderscap halen,
Alle groote pochhansen sender moet,
Alle groote braggheerders sonder goet,
Alle Cappiteynen, ruters en knechten,
Die liever moeskoppen dan op di vianden vechten,
Die 't al metter tonghen connen vernielen
Maer laten di lappen sien, oft keeren di hielen,
Dese moetij in sotter ordinancien leijen,
Soo lang totdat si ghesneden sijn van der keijen.
Oock moetij alle leepe, loose gheesen,
Oude coppelerssen, jonge gescuerde weesen,
Camercatten, sluypsielen met hoppen,
Meijskens die de knechtkens naloopen,
Vroukens die meer dan met eender spoelen weven,
Heijmelijc nootturft soeken en gelt toegeven,
Alle laudaten, alle vrou vuylen,
Alle scieloosen, alle afgereden guylen,
Dese en dierghelicke vrouwen
Moetij in hun oude previlegie houwen,
Di hun noit van gheenen heeren en zijn genomen,
Voordat si Sint Jops of in 't Gasthuys comen.
Oock moetij die edel ghilde, licht van sinnen,
Die 't heden verteren dat sij morghen winnen,
Die geldeloos slempen met genuchten
En hun panden tot mijns oomkens vluchten,
't Ghelach met rock oft mantel betalen,
Alle mulders die sonder muelen malen,

25

30

35

40

45

Who by renting horses attain their knighthood;
All great Jack-a-dandies without courage,
All great good-timers without any goods,
25 All captains, lieutenants and knights,
Who prefer to pillage than to fight their foes,
Who can all triumph with their tongues,
But let them see the enemy, and they turn their heels:
These you must lead with foolish ordinances,
30 Until the stones are drawn from their heads.[7]
Also you must lead all flighty, false women,
Old bawds, young debauched orphans,
Concubines,[8] secret whores with ambitions,
Girls who trail after servants,
35 Women who weave with more than one spool,
Furtively seeking fulfilment and paying money,
All trollops, all foul women,
All reckless, all jaded sluts,
These and suchlike women,
40 You must defend through your old privilege:
They had never been taken by young sirs
Until they came to Saint Job's or to the Guesthouse.[9]
Also must you protect the noble guild, light of scruples,
Who eat up today what they earn tomorrow,
45 Who carouse moneyless with madness,
And run their goods to my uncle,[10]
To pay the tab with their tunic or robe:
All millers who grind without meal,

---

[7] An allusion to the tradition that madness stems from a stone lodged in the brain, the so-called *pierre de la folie*. The operation to extract this stone is the subject of numerous paintings and engravings throughout the late-medieval and early-modern period, of which the earliest is Bosch's piece *De keisnijding* ('The Stone-Cutting'), *c.*1480. Other treatments of the same theme include those of Jan van Hermessen, Theodor de Bry, Pieter Bruegel the Elder and Carolin Allardt: see Sander Gilman, *Seeing the Insane* (Lincoln, NE, 1996), 36–40.

[8] The text has 'camercatten', literally 'chamber-cats'. There is an interesting parallel between this stanza and the well-known miracle play *Mariken van Nieumeghen* (*c.*1518). *Camercatten* and a number of other terms used here are also listed in the earlier text, as its narrative describes the various shady figures Mariken and her demonic lover Moenen live amongst at Antwerp. See Dirk Coigneau, *Mariken van Nieumeghen* (Hilversum, 1996), 98.

[9] This line refers to the Saint Jobsgasthuis at Utrecht, a hospital founded in 1504 by Willem van Heusden for the treatment of venereal disease, especially syphilis. According to Van der Wurf-Bodt, this had enough beds for eighteen patients by the 1550s: Coby van der Wurf-Bodt, *Van lichte wiven tot gevallen vrouwen: prostitutie in Utrecht vanaf de late middeleeuwen tot het eind van de negentiende eeuw* (Utrecht, 1988), 25. The Old Testament figure Job was linked with disease throughout the Middle Ages, and his name was evoked as a charm for various dermatological complaints, owing to the afflictions documented in Job 2.7: see Willy L. Braekman, *Middeleeuwse witte en zwarte magie in het Nederlands taalgebied* (Ghent, 1997), 244–6.

[10] That is, to the pawnbroker.

Alle die hun selfs scande vermanen,
50 Alle die liegen dat sij selver waers wanen,
Alle die butenshuys vruecht bedrijven
En binnen huyse vechten en kijven,
Desen moet hun privilegie ooc houden stadt
So lang dat si comen daer Valetijn meester sadt.
55 Oick moetij met save-comt-uut bewaren
Alle cooplieden die naer Sinte Reynuuts varen,
Alle die sonder verstant coopen en vercoopen,
Alle die met ijdelen meyrsen loopen,
Alle quacsalvers die hun laten verdullen,
60 Alle spesiers die hun sacken met hoy vullen,
Alle die den grooten sack in den cleijnen lappen,
Alle wijncoopers die achter uuttappen,
Alle die naer haer selfs schade reijcken,
Alle brouwers die de catten laten in d'mout seijken,
65 Alle die 't heden maeckt en morgen weer breckt,
Alle taverniers daer di soch den tap uuttrect,
Alle die hun goet hoeren en boeven deijlen,
Alle sceppers die met ghescuerde seijlen seijlen,
Alle boeren di hun saet in bedorven ackers sayen,
70 Alle cleermakers di met gebroken naelden nayen,
Lakensnijers die hun goet vermeten,
Scoenmakers die den haen laten d'leer eeten.
Timmerlieden die qualijc wachten hun screven
En wevers die met ijdelen spoelen weven,
75 Alle smeden die hun ijser verbranden,
Alle berbiers die hun sceeren tot scanden,
Alle metsers die haer fondament beswaren,
Alle goutsmeden die de souduere sparen,
Beeltsnijders die van consten rasen,
80 Alcumisten die hun goet in d'asschen blasen,
Ghelaesmakers die hun gelas verlasten,
Cupers die overal naer d'bomgat tasten,
Tengieters die hun tin verloren gieten,
Beckers die altoos een broot te cort scieten,
85 Vleeschhouwers di mager laten werden 't vet,

92

All men that warn others against their own shame,
50   All that lie so much that they think themselves true,
All that pursue joy outdoors
And in the house fight and bicker:
These must also stand firm by their privilege,
As long as they go where Valentine holds court.[11]
55   Also you must protect with a safe-to-go-out[12]
All merchants who travel to Saint Empty,[13]
All who buy and sell without understanding,
All who tout with useless merchandise,
All quacksalvers who let themselves be duped,
60   All spice-dealers who fill their sacks with hay,
All who patch up their small sacks with their biggest,
All the vintners that draw wine from behind,
All who reckon themselves into loss,
All brewers who let cats piss in the malt,
65   All that make today and break again tomorrow,
All innkeepers that suck from the tap spout,
All who share their goods with whores and swindlers,
All shipmen that sail with shredded sails,
All farmers that sow their seed in rotten fields,
70   All clothiers who sew with broken needles,
Drapers who poorly measure their goods,
Shoemakers that let hens peck the leather.
Carpenters that never wait for the plans,
And weavers that weave with empty spindles,
75   All smiths that incinerate their iron,
All barbers that shear a man into humiliation,
All masons that overload their foundations,
All goldsmiths that spare the solder,
Stonecutters that jabber about their art,
80   Alchemists that burn their goods to ashes,
Glassblowers who smash their glass,
Coopers who botch all near the bunghole,
Whitesmiths that pour away their tin,
Bakers that always fire the loaf too little,
85   Butchers who let the fat become meagre,

---

[11] As Pleij notes, Valentine is probably being evoked here as patron saint of epilepsy rather than lovers, since this condition was regarded as a type of madness in the Middle Ages: Pleij, *Het gilde van de Blauwe Schuit*, 252.

[12] A deliberate corruption of *sauf-conduit*, the 'officially granted privilege of passing through an overlord's domain undisturbed or under escort': Hans Kurath and Sherman M. Kuhn (gen. eds.), *Middle English Dictionary* (Ann Arbor, MI, 2001), C.4: 496.

[13] The fictional *patroon van drinkebroers* ('patron saint of drinkers'): see the *Guild of the Blue Barge* in the present anthology, n.9.

Visschers die altoos visschen achter d'net,
Schilders die hun aensichten bederven,
Legwerckers die't saterdaechs qualic kerven,
Alle ambachtslien en alle hantwercken,
90 Die aldus u Rijcke verstercken,
Dees moetij hun previlegie nu vermeeren fijn,
Totdat si S. Reynuuts naect uuten cleeren sijn.
Item alle Rethorisienen en Musisienen
Die haren tijt verquisten en lutter danx verdienen,
95 Elcken doen lachghen, en selfs druc insluyten,
Alle spelien, ghescuerde fluyten,
Alle die niet en connen helen noch swijgen,
Alle die een roye tot haer selfs eyrse crijgen,
Alle sophisten, artisten, juristen,
100 Mercurialisten, die hun wijsheijt verquisten,
Alle die hun groote dinghen vermeten
En gheen bescheet daeraf en weten,
Alle wilde gheesten, quaet om temmen,
Di huys en erve duer 't keelgat laten swemmen,
105 Alle die hun selven in d'nette breijen,
Allen die levende van eertrijck scheijen,
Dese en dierghelijcke ghesellen
Suldi als regenten over u Rijcke stellen.
Oock moetij elcken goet exempel bewijsen
110 Dat men u Malevesteijt mach prijsen.
Ghi suit totter middernacht gieten en gapen
En 's morgens suldi langhe slapen
En eer ghi half aen oft ghecleet sijt fijn,
So moetij wederom aen den ontbijt sijn
115 En nummermeer veel swaers drooms hebben
En altoos den besten pant mijns ooms hebben
En waer een in die taverne is bij desen
So moetij altoos die ander wesen
En uut u Rijc bannen die u seggen van wercken,
120 Maer liver in 't vrouwenhuys dan in der kercken.
En wie u claecht sijn vleeschelicke nootsaken
Die moetij helpen sijn houwelijck maken,

Fishermen that always fish behind the net,[14]
Painters who smear their faces,[15]
Tapestry-workers who never work on Saturdays,
All craftsmen and all their artisans,
90   Who thus strengthen your kingdom:
These are the ones whose privileges you must now increase,
Until Saint Empty's Night they are without clothes.
Likewise all rhetoricians and musicians,
Who waste their time and earn little thanks,
95   Each makes laughter, and causes himself anxiety,
All players with blocked flutes,
All that can neither speak up nor keep quiet,
All who draw a rod to their own arse,
All sophists, masters and jurors,
100   Rhetoricians who squander their knowledge,
All who assume great things about themselves,
Yet do not know one opinion about them,
All wild spirits, hard to tame,
That let their house and grounds swim down their throats,
105   All that weave a net for themselves,
All that live separated from the kingdom of earth,
These and suchlike fellows
You shall appoint as regents over your kingdom.
Also you must show all a good example
110   That men might praise your malusty.
You should sit and drink until midnight
And in the morning you should sleep a long time
And before you are half or fully dressed
You must have breakfast again
115   And never again have bad dreams
And always have the best pledges for my uncle
And be a faithful one in the tavern from now on.
Likewise you must always be contrary
And ban from your kingdom those telling you to work,
120   And prefer to be in the cathouse than in church.
Whoever complains to you about bodily needs
You should help him to make a marriage,

[14] 'Achter het net vissen' remains a common proverb in the Netherlands, meaning 'to come too late', or 'to waste one's effort at a fruitless task': see F. A. Stoett, *Nederlandse spreekwoorden en gezegden: verklaard en vergeleken met die in het Frans, Duits en Engels*, 2 vols. (Zutphen, 1923–5), 2: 73. It is also one of many popular sayings depicted in Pieter Bruegel's *Nederlandse spreekwoorden* (1559): see Jan Grauls, *Volkstaal en volksleven in het werk van Pieter Bruegel* (Brussels, 1957), 106. In fact, by reconceiving the city in this way, as a landscape populated by proverbial figures, the text bears comparison to the Bruegel piece; it also recalls Rabelais's similar 'land of proverbs', the 'isle d'Ennasin', in *Gargantua et Pantagruel* 4: 9.
[15] A possible reference to the profession of Colyns, the fool playing Meester Oom.

Opdat hij mach geraken uuter pijne,
Te bedde wijsen oft achter die gordijne,
125 So crijchdij prijs en lof van alle beijen.
Helpt den naecten blinden in huys leijen,
Want een coninck moet compassieus sijn
Alle daghe amorues, niet te amorues, sijn,
Al ees't dat men bi eender vrouwen zeer gequelt leeft.
130 Ooc moetij elcken betalen als ghi gelt gheeft,
Alle woorden nauw vangen waer gij se betraept
En van niemant quaet seggen als ghij slaept,
Maer 't volck overal verblijden alteenen
Al soud' er wijf en kinderen om weenen.
135 En wouw ymant u Malevesteijt befamen,
Ghi en muecht niet root worden noch schamen.
Dus comt ghi eeselheeren die besidt sijn leen,
Wat di Coninck hiertoe seijdt, jae oft neen.

Die Coninck seijdt:
Jae, jae, neen, neen.

Die Grijpier:
140 Nu heer Coninck, legt u vingheren beije,
Segt mij naer en sweert op dees keije:
'Dat sweer ick bij den pispot en bij di provate
En bij den bril met den openen gate
En so warachtich als di drengere die 'r op sat,
145 Die so uutermaten veel drone en at
Alsoo 't in't vuyl boeck ghescreven steet,
Dat hij hem van achter en van vuere bedreet,
Dat ick 't voorgenoemde met alder trouwen
Naer mijn vermuegen sal van boven onder inhouwen
150 En dat selve helpen stercken en vermeeren.

Die Grijpier:
Hoordij dat wel, ghij eselheeren,
Wat die Coninck hier sweert en ghelooft?
Salft hem en sedt hem die croone op 't hooft
En roept al tesamen in een populorum:
155 'Vive le Roy, stultus stultorum.'

So that he may gain absolution through pain.
Send him to a bed or behind the curtains,
125 In this way you will gain praise and love everywhere.
Help the naked blind to lie at home,
For a king must have compassion,
All days should be amorous, but not too amorous,
Even though a man may be tormented by having a woman in his life.
130 Also you must pay everyone when you hand out money,
Catch hold of all words when you trap them,
Speak evil of no man while you sleep
But delight the people everywhere and always,
Although women and children might weep from it.
135 And when any man defames your malusty,
You must not turn red or be ashamed.
So come all you donkey-lords that hold loans,
Hear what the king says to this, yes or no:

The king says:
Yes, yes, no, no.

The seizecretary:
140 Now listen, king, spread your fingers out,
Say this after me, and swear it on this key:
'This I swear by the piss-pot and by the privy,
And by the seat with the open hole
And as truly as the strainer who sat upon it
145 Who drank and ate so tremendously much,
Just as it is written in the foul book
That he befouled himself behind and before,
So I shall undermine the aforementioned with all faith
According to my abilities, from top to bottom,
150 And will help to strengthen and increase it'.

The seizecretary:
Do you hear well, you donkey-lords,
What the king here swears and promises?
Anoint him and set the crown on his head
And shout out together in a *populorum*:[16]
155 'Vive le roy, stultus stultorum!'[17]

---

[16] That is, in one voice.

[17] 'Long live the king, Fool of Fools'. The French portion of this line is of course derived from the established proclamation made at the end of a coronation, 'Le roi est mort, vive le roi'. The Latin term that follows it occurs in several early modern comic and parodic texts, such as the English 'Epitaph for Lobbe, the King's Fool' (*c.*1526): see Wolf Wolfensburger, 'Eulogy for a Mentally Retarded Jester', *Mental Retardation* 20 (1982), 269–70. In this context the phrase may have blasphemous connotations, since its pairing with *roi* recalls the biblical epithet *rex regum*, in Rev. 17.14 *et passim*.

Die Grijpier:
Hoort nu, ghi ondersaten, ghij moet ooc manschap sweeren
Den Coninck, en helpen hem tsijne verteren
En hem altijt bijstaen, nacht en dach,
So lang als hij slach verdragen mach,
So lang als hi wijn oft bier heeft in di flessche,
So lang als hi cruys oft munt heeft in di tessche,
So lang als hij eenen pant heeft te raeye,
So lang als hij t'eten heeft in di scappraeye,
Dat ghij hem daerin suit bijstaen alteenen
En daertoe dapperlijc hant en mont leenen,
Opdat hij 't ghequel des rijcdoms werde quyte,
So lang dat hi veriest es van niet een myte:
Dat sweerdi, segt ja, neen, elck man voor man,
Steckt nu al u vingeren in 't gat en cust se dan.

160

165

The seizecretary:
Hear now, you subjects, you must also swear fealty
To the king, and help him in his consuming
And always stand by him, night and day,
As long as he can endure a beating,
As long as he has wine or beer in the bottle,
As long as he has coins or change in his wallet,
As long as he has a pledge available,
As long as he has tuck in the larder,
So you shall stand by him forever in all this,
And doughtily lend him your hand and mouth,
So that he becomes free from the torment of wealth,
Until he is liberated from his last penny:
This you swear, say yes, no, every man before a man:
Now stick all your fingers into your hole and then kiss them.

160

165

A Wise and Wonderful Prognostication

*E*EN SCHOONE *ende wonderlijcke prognosticatie* was first printed in 1560 by Marie Ancxt, widow of the publisher Jacob van Liesveldt.[1] It survives in one copy, now held at the Royal Library of Brussels. Little is known for certain about the text, as Ancxt reveals almost nothing about its provenance. Her edition includes none of the devices that usually accompany printed editions of *rederijker* drama, such as the emblem or motto of its chamber, or a note recording the circumstances of its original performance. Nonetheless the text's allusions to the so-called *Gelderse oorlogen*, a series of wars between the duchies of Burgundy and Guelders in the first half of the sixteenth century, suggest that it was composed about twenty years before it was published (see lines 164–6). Likewise, there is reason to connect the piece with one of the larger commercial centres of Flanders or Brabant. The cities listed at the end of the poem would certainly place it in the southern Netherlands, as would its unflattering reference to a Walloon, a French-speaking Fleming (line 250).

Although it has survived in a printed text designed for reading, *A Prognostication* was clearly designed for performance by a fool. There are hints of this throughout the text, as certain passages are evidently written with a particular type of routine in mind. For example, lines 248–9 contain a compressed dialogue: 'If you are in Ghent with a girl alone in her room,/ What should you do? Embrace! Should you? Yes, I would!' As the most recent editors of the text point out, this can only be satisfactorily read as an exchange between an actor and his *marot*, the sceptre or bauble traditionally carried by professional fools.[2] Since the *marot* is typically 'responsible' for the most scurrilous or indecent remarks, the passage may be rewritten as follows:

OWLGLASS:	If you are in Ghent with a girl alone in her room, what should you do?
MAROT:	Embrace!
OWLGLASS:	Should you?
MAROT:	Yes, I would!

Traces of these two roles can be glimpsed throughout the rest of the poem. Their presence explains, for instance, the curious *non sequiturs* that litter the piece. Such incongruous remarks as 'catch that, said the devil, and he let out a fart' may function as interjections by the *marot* into the speech of the main narrator (line 155). Beyond the words of the *marot*, other voices also make similar intrusions into the monologue. The text as a whole is characterised by its extreme polyphony: there are numerous quotations, parodies, fragments, and imitations of everyday speech

---

[1] Lessing J. Rosenwald and Frederick Richmond Goff, *Early Printed Books of the Low Countries: The Lessing J. Rosenwald Collection* (Washington, DC, 1958).

[2] Hinke van Kampen, Herman Pleij, Bob Stumpel, Annebel Venmans and Paul Vriesema, *Het zal koud zijn in 't water als 't vriest: zestiende-eeuwse parodieen op gedrukte jaarvoorspellingen tekstuitg. met inleiding en commentaar* (The Hague, 1980), 58. On the *marot*, see John Southworth, *Fools and Jesters* (Stroud, 2000), 207–9.

scattered throughout the piece, as it incorporates proverbs, instructions from old women to their servants, cries of street vendors, oaths sworn by young lovers and the sales-patter of prostitutes. These scraps of borrowed speech would allow the performer to show off his skills at mimicry, as he could adopt comic voices or even personae to suit the words being uttered. There is also scope for physical comedy in the text: for example, the narrator's reference to 'fine games of Kiss-my-arse' could be accompanied by a brief mime to make its meaning more intelligible to the audience (line 216).

It is also possible to deduce the occasion on which the piece was staged. The text draws its framework from the genre of the *spotprognosticatie* (mock-prophecy), as its narrator offers a series of deliberately absurd and facile forecasts for the following twelve months. Since genuine almanacs and prophecies sold in greatest numbers at the year's end, as they claimed to reveal what the coming year would bring, the text's parody would have most relevance during *Kerstmis* or Yuletide.[3] As such, it seems likely that the poem was performed as part of Christmas celebrations. Given that its geographical references place it in the southern Netherlands, it was most likely played at the revels hosted by one of the Flemish or Brabantine chambers at this point in the festive calendar.

In terms of its overall content, the poem belongs to the general tradition of Eulenspiegel texts.[4] Like the best-known example of Eulenspiegel literature, the collection of stories compiled by Hermann Bote in *c.*1510, it focuses on the folkloric figure Till Eulenspiegel, known in English as 'Owlglass'.[5] In essence, Eulenspiegel is 'an archetypal jester-trickster': as Derek Brewer aptly summarises, he is an 'awkward, upsetting, malicious, deceitful person who usually gets away with the unpleasant tricks he plays' throughout the stories in which he features.[6] *A Prognostication* is in fact one of several Eulenspiegel tales in Dutch. While the figure may be more readily associated with Saxony, he was no less popular in the Low Countries during the medieval period. The site of his burial is still alleged to be in Belgium, and the first English version of his adventures was printed at Antwerp, predating Robert Copland's *Howleglas* (1560) by some four decades.[7] Moreover, in 1525 a widely read anthology of Dutch Eulenspiegel tales was compiled and printed in Brabant by Michiel Hillen van Hoochstraten.[8] Indeed, the attribution of *A Prognostication* to

---

[3] On the popularity of almanacs in the early modern period, see J. Salman, *Een handdruk van de tijd: de almanak en het dagelijks leven in de Nederlanden 1500–1700* (Zwolle, 1997).

[4] Overviews of the tradition can be found in Priscilla Hayden-Roy, 'Till Eulenspiegel – Transgressions against Convention: Interpreting the Parasite', *Daphnis* 20 (1991), 7–31; Alison Williams, *Tricksters and Pranksters: Roguery in French and German Literature of the Middle Ages and the Renaissance* (Amsterdam, 2000), 143–76.

[5] The most comprehensive collection of Eulenspiegel stories remains Wolfgang Lindow, *Ein kurtzweilig Lesen von Dil Ulenspiegel* (Stuttgart, 1978). English translations can be found in Stanley Appelbaum, *Medieval Tales and Stories* (Toronto, 2000); Hermann Bote, *Till Eulenspiegel: His Adventures*, trans. and ed. Paul Oppenheimer (London, 2001).

[6] Beatrice K. Otto, *Fools are Everywhere* (Chicago, 2001), 99; Derek Brewer, ed., *Medieval Comic Tales* (Cambridge, 2008), xxvi.

[7] See Robert Collier Proctor, *Jan van Doesborgh: Printer at Antwerp* (London, 1894); G. J. van Bork and P. J. Verkruijsse, *De Nederlandse en Vlaamse auteurs* (Weesp, 1985), 174.

[8] Loek Geeraedts, *Het volksboek van Ulenspieghel* (Antwerp, 1948).

Eulenspiegel may be an attempt to capitalise on the success of Van Hoochstraten's collection. It is certainly suspicious that a similar woodcut appears on the frontispiece of both texts, as both depict the protagonist clinging to his father's donkey, and revealing his buttocks to two peasants behind him. If this was a marketing ruse, it was evidently fruitful: *A Prognostication* sold sufficiently well to be reprinted some forty years later, as a second edition appeared in 1606.

However, *A Prognostication* is also distinguished from other Eulenspiegel texts by its narrative framework. It does not simply recount Eulenspiegel's swindles and exploits, like Bote's and Van Hoochstraten's anthologies, but instead uses him as a dramatic persona. Rather than being narrated, Eulenspiegel is himself the narrator of the piece. From the outset, his voice governs the text, as he begins with a gloating celebration of his escapades. During this tribute to his cunning, Eulenspiegel even claims to be immortal: 'Many also believe that I am dead and gone,/ But Owlglass lives on up to this very day' (lines 21–2).[9] After this boastful prologue, the real business of the text begins, as Eulenspiegel puts forward his 'prophecies' for the coming year. As might be expected, these forecasts are clearly fraudulent. Not only are they absurd in themselves, but Eulenspiegel admits that he has no idea 'how to write this prognostothingummy', although cannot stand idly by while others are growing rich (line 30). The text itself is the swindle here, the trick that Eulenspiegel is playing. In effect, the buyer of the volume becomes a willing dupe of the lord of cheats.

It is important to note that the poem is a full-blooded Eulenspiegel text, in spite of its unconventional approach. Although Van Kampen and his co-writers hold that the Owlglass references were merely tacked on by an enterprising printer, the text's use of the figure is more subtle than this reading allows.[10] The poem demonstrates a profound and sensitive connection to the Eulenspiegel tradition. Most obviously, the powerful strand of satire found in the folk-stories also appears in the poem. The same range of targets is ridiculed, as the poem mocks students, women and merchants.[11] But there is also a similarity of even greater importance here. *A Prognostication* does not merely echo Eulenspiegel's mockery, but also makes use of his specific techniques. The key strategies of the text mirror those of Eulenspiegel the trickster. Readers of the Eulenspiegel stories have long noted that the trickster employs one tactic with great regularity, as he invariably chooses to understand the speech of his victims in its most immediate sense. Hence Goethe writes that 'all the main jokes of the book are based on the fact that everybody talks in figures of speech and Eulenspiegel understands all this literally'.[12] A clear example of this tendency occurs in Tale 33, when an innkeeper informs the trickster that 'at this table one eats for 24 pfennigs'. In response, Eulenspiegel orders a meal, eats heartily, and demands that his host hands over the stipulated sum 'as my wage'.[13]

---

[9] This anticipates his death and resurrection in Charles de Coster's nationalist reworking of the folktales: see Charles de Coster, *La Légende et les aventures héroiques, joyeuses et glorieuses d'Ulenspiegel et de Lamme Goedzak au pays de Flandres et ailleurs* (Paris, 1869), 445–78.

[10] Van Kampen, *Het zal koud zijn in 't water als 't vriest*, 57.

[11] George Test, *Satire: Spirit and Art* (Gainesville, FL, 1991), 54.

[12] Johann Wolfgang von Goethe, *Maxims and Reflections*, trans. Elisabeth Stopp, ed. Peter Hutchinson (Harmondsworth, 1991), 133.

[13] Bote, *Till Eulenspiegel*, 65–6.

In certain contexts, this strategy gains a firmly satirical edge. When Eulenspiegel 'exasperates his contemporaries by interpreting everything literally', he is demonstrating that all language can be successfully understood in its most obvious sense.[14] He is disregarding subtle or obscure meanings, and following those that are most readily accessible. The fact that he prospers from this approach suggests that these surface meanings are in fact superior to the esoteric, or at least of greater practical value. Eulenspiegel thus succeeds in championing sense that can be grasped by anyone. In other words, he is egalitarian in his attitude to language, privileging common forms of knowledge over hidden meanings. When this is applied to the language of professionals, such as the craftsmen, scholars and priests that Eulenspiegel confronts, it serves to denigrate them. Since he devalues the arcane, exclusive knowledge on which their positions rest, he deflates their prestige. According to him, the best that can be known can be known by anyone: specialist information is of no importance, and neither is any vocation based on it. Eulenspiegel's extreme literal-mindedness becomes an attack on elitism.

A Prognostication extends this logic to prophecy. The principal joke of the text is that Eulenspiegel 'forecasts' events that are clearly inevitable. At one stage he states that 'he that is most often in the kitchen catches the best morsels' (line 54), while elsewhere he announces: 'The husband will often be angry with the wife./ The wife will comb her husband's hair with a stool' (lines 162–3). His prediction for the winter months consists of little more than 'it will be cold' (line 144). Eulenspiegel's prophecies only consider what is already obvious. Once again, Eulenspiegel turns away from concealed or obscure knowledge, replacing secrecy with blatancy. Everything he reports is, in the words of Jacob Burckhardt, 'general and intelligible to all'.[15] It can thus be seen that the behaviour of 'Drunktor Owlglass' mirrors the habits of Eulenspiegel the trickster. The text undermines the claimed insights of prophecy in the same way that the trickster debunks pretensions of wisdom. While *A Prognostication* is not anecdotal, it has fully adopted this figure as its mouthpiece, leaving his basic nature intact. In other words, the appropriation of Eulenspiegel as a speaking persona may not have been the work of the printer, but may have originated with the fool who initially performed it. Ultimately, what *A Prognostication* highlights is the importance of popular tradition in the comedy of the chambers. Despite their humanist ambitions, the *rederijkers* owed a significant debt to demotic sources: here a fool turns to folklore to construct the role he plays, rather than to a learned authority such as Boccaccio or Terence.

---

[14] Rudi Keller, *A Theory of Linguistic Signs* (Oxford, 1998), viii.

[15] Jacob Burckhardt, *The Civilization of the Renaissance in Italy*, trans. S. G. C. Middlemore, ed. Peter Burke and Peter Murray (Harmondsworth, 1990), 112.

Een schoone ende wonderlijcke prognosticatie

Een schoone ende wonderlijcke prognosticatie
van sloctoors Ulenspieghels calculatie,
in beede boeverijen seer hooghe gheleert,
daeromme wort hi van groote hanssen gheëert.
5   Naer d'ezele conste ghepractiseert sonder abuys
op den meridiaen van 't verrevermaerde gasthuys.
Coopt, leest, lacht ende wilt wel verstaen,
daer en cleeft gheen dertichhondert guldens aen.

Gheprint t'Antwerpen met consente van den Hove, op die Camerpoortbrugghe, in den Schilt van Artoys, by die Weduwe van Jacob van Liesveldt. Anno MDLX.
Onderteekent, P. de Lens

Ulespieghel spreect
Eens was ick gheboren en dickmael genoopt.
10   Mijn ouders hebben tevergeefs op mi ghehoopt,
want ick en wilde noyt mijn leven niet veel dueghen,
Nochtans en looch ick noyt cleene lueghen.
Al was uutermaten avontuerlijc mijn beghin,
't Vervolch en was niet avontuerlijcker te min.
15   En al meent eenyegelijck mijn guychelspel te weten,
Ick en hebber nochtans noyt maer drie bescheten,
Maer ick hebber veel beveesten ende bedroghen;
Segdy contrarie, soo hebdy seer gheloghen.
Veel hoopten en baden dickwils om mijn sterven,
20   Maer quaet cruyt can al te qualijck bederven.
Veel meenen oock dat ick doot ben en overleden,
Maer Ulespieghel leeft noch op den dach van heden.
Al sijn die menighe seer herdt van opsette,
Sy draghen nochtans Ulenspieghel onder die bonette.
25   Al sterft er een Ulenspieghel, oft al wort hi verloren,
Daer wordtter wel seven daerteghen gheboren.
Aldus en can ick my tot sterven niet begheven,
Want Ulenspieghel sal eewelijck blijven leven.
't Is een fray constenaer die my heeft gheweven.

Die Bachtenloghe
30   Ick en weet wat van dees pronselinghe scrijven,
Nochtans waer 't jammer dattet achter soude blijven.
Aldus wil ick myselven daertoe gaen stouwen
Om een cleen prognosticatiken te brouwen.
Ende eerst voor de protelloghe suldy weten,

* The Dutch text has been reproduced from the 1560 edition, published in Van Kampen *et al.*, *Het zal koud zijn in 't water als 't vriest*, 59–79. Used with permission.

A Wise and Wonderful Prognostication

A wise and wonderful prognostication
From Drunktor Owlglass's calculation,
Very highly learned in all deceptions,
For this he is honoured by great beer-mugs.
5   It is practised after the assteemed[1] art, without mistakes,
Made on the meridian of the most revered hospital.
Buy, read, laugh and understand it well,
It will not cost you thirteen hundred guilders.

Printed in Antwerp, with license from the court, in the Camerpoortbrugghe, in the Shield of Artois, by the widow of Jacob van Liesveldt. Anno MDLX.

Undersigned, P. de Lens.

Owlglass speaks
I was born once, and often punished.
10   My parents have hoped in vain for me,
For I have not led my life with much virtue,
Nonetheless when lying my lies were not small.
While my beginning was very auspicious,
All that followed was no less eventful.
15   And everyone seems to know my games,
I have never yet shat on only three men,
But I have often farted and deceived;
If you say the contrary, then you have lied grossly.
Many hoped and often prayed for me to die,
20   But a bad weed can be difficult to root out.[2]
Many also believe that I am dead and gone,
But Owlglass lives on up to this very day.
Although very many have heard the opposite,
They all carry some Owlglass under their hats.
25   Although an Owlglass may die, or else may be lost,
At that same instant seven more are born.
Thus I cannot fully die or disappear,
For Owlglass will live on for ever.
It is a great artist who has made me.

The Back-passage
30   I have no idea how to write this prognostothingummy,
However, it would be a shame to lag behind.
Thus I will strive to apply myself to this,
And brew up a small prognosticatkin.
But before the foreturd you should know[3]

---

[1] The original text gives 'ezele', conflating *edele* (noble) with *ezel* (donkey).
[2] Proverbial: compare the German saying 'Unkraut vergeht nicht' ('a weed never dies'), or its modern Dutch equivalent 'onkruid vergaat niet'.
[3] The original gives 'protelloghe', combining *prologhe* (prologue) with *protelen* (to fart).

35 Dat ghi d'eerste beetken moet nuchteren eten,
's Morghens als ghy uut uwen bedde coemt ghesprongen.
Soo d'ouders pijpen sullen, so danssen die jonghen.
Ick wil u nu hier in 't smalle gaen verclaren
Wat ons toecomen sal van oude verre jaren
40 Ende wat ons eerghisteren staet te gheschieden,
Want dat gheleden is, is goet te bedieden.
Dus luystert naer my ende wilt den keest smaken.
Die minst gheslapen heeft sal aldermeest waken.
Al en come 't niet juyste alsoo 't hier staet ghescreven,
45 Denct 't sal noch comen, muechdy langhe leven.
Die 't niet en wil ghelooven, die gae sijn ganghen,
Hy en sal oock gheenen aflaet ontfanghen.
Ick pleghe te schrijven veel wonderlijcke grillen
Van ijseren, tinnen, houten en ghelasen brillen,
50 Hoe men 't volck nu daeraf siet vliën en wijcken,
Omdat si al leeren door die vingheren kijcken.
Swijcht nu Protelloghe, ick wil gaen beghinnen.
Tsjarent sullender veel meyskens liever naeyen dan spinnen.
Die meest in de kuecken is, crijcht die beste vinnen.

Van den eclipsis der manen
55 Eclipsis, mipsis, hipsis, pripsis, calipsis,
In 't hooghe schaelliënhuys, sittende op den tripsis,
Driëndertich halve mijlen van 't Drakenhoot,
Ontrent van sesthien scherpe puncten groot.
Ick en weet van naelden, messen oft spellen;
60 Gheraedt ghij er selve naer, ick en can niet tellen.
Den eclips sal dueren in 't keeren en in 't wenden al
Van dat hi beghint totdat hi voleynden sal,
Tsanderdaechs voor Bamisse, te vijfthien uren
Voor de noene, sal men dit al sien ghebueren.
65 Seer groot ende wonderlijck wort sijne operatie
In kisten, tesschen, borssen en lappen t'elcker spatie,
Sonderlinghe in de mijne, dies ben ick onverdult.
God betert, sey vrouw Backers, en het was huer schult.
Noch sal hy causeren veel siecten ende plaghen,
70 Door veel slampampens verquaedde maghen,
Leepe ooghen, roode nuesen en bevende handen.
D'oude wijfkens hebben ghemeenlick quade tanden.

35 That you must eat the first bite on an empty stomach
In the morning as you come rising out of your bed.
As the elders sing, so the youngsters will dance.
I will now explain for you in a shallow way
What things will come from many years ago
40 And what will happen the day before yesterday.
What has already happened is good to predict.
Thus listen to me and understand the true sense.
He that has least sleep will be woken up the most.
Although it might not happen just as it is written here,
45 Bear in mind that it will occur, should you live long enough.
Whoever will not believe it, he can go ahead,
But he will also not receive an indulgence.
I pledge to write about wonderful fancies,
About iron, tin, wood and glass spectacles,
50 Which show how people seem to flee and run,
Because they have learned to see with their fingers.
Shut up now, Back-passage, I will begin.
Next year many girls will rather sew than spin.
He that is most often in the kitchen catches the best morsels.

Of the eclipses of the moon
55 Eclipsis, mipsis, hipsis, pripsis, calipsis,
In the high-tiled house I am sitting on the tripod,[4]
Thirty-three half miles from the house of the Dragon,[5]
About sixteen sharp degrees in magnitude.
I know nothing about needles, knives or pins;
60 Calculate it for yourself, I cannot add.
The eclipse will last until it turns and goes all the way:
From the time it begins until it finishes,
The next day, Saint Bavo's,[6] at fifteen hours
Before noon, you will see that one must pay rent.
65 Most great and wonderful will be this operation,
Finding coins in chests, boxes, purses and clothes everywhere,
Especially in my place, where I go berserk.
God save us, said the landlady, and it was all her fault.
The eclipse will cause sicknesses and plagues,
70 Many bad stomach aches caused by drunkenness,
Dripping eyes, red noses and shaking hands.
Old wives frequently have rotten teeth.

---

[4] The word *tripsis* can describe both a piece of astrological equipment and a three-legged stool.

[5] *Huys* (house) can refer to divisions of the horoscope as well as buildings. To take this pun even further, town-houses were often known by symbols such as Dragon, Lion's Head, and so on in the early-modern period.

[6] Saint Bavo's Day falls on 1 October. Bavo himself has local significance, as patron of Ghent and Haarlem.

Van die regerende heeren des jaers
Venus en Mars sullen dit jaer meest regneren:
Mars in 't oorloghen en Venus in 't boeleren.
Ende in de winter comender noch drie in 't lant:
Monsieur Blaeubeck, Druypnuese en Clippertant.
Die niet en wil betalen, schabbeken is goet pant.

Van die vier tijden des jaers
Ende eerst van den lenten
Die lente beghint en springt uuter muyten
Als 't loof en die bloemkens beghinnen uut te spruyten.
Och, hoe vrolick sal wesen elck venuscamenierken,
Makende met die liefste een blijde chierken,
Als een dierken doorschoten met Venus' schichte!
't Is: 'Al goeden avont, cousijn', 'God groete u, nichte'.
Sy schicken 't seer lichte; 't is: 'Vaert wech verdriet'.
Maer corts daernaer gaet den buyck op dat men 't siet.
Dan is 't: 'Och lacen, och ermen, noyt meerder plaghen!'
't Ware al lecker dinck, moest men gheen kint draghen:
Men vonde nauwe een maecht op seven mijlen in 't ronde.
Sy ontsien het kintdraghen meer dan die sonde.
Dees leelijcke wijfs sullen 't oock seer quaet hebben,
Die de mans een luttelken fraey en delicaet hebben.
Want die leelicste vrouwen, het dient hier vertelt,
Sullen meest zijn met die jalousije ghequelt.
In dees tijt sullen sulcke mans niet om verroecken
't Wijf wel laten sitten en een schoonder soecken.
Dan sal 't wijf allesins loopen ende rinnen:
'Och, waer is dees man? Ick moet ontsinnen!'
Tsavonts als hy thuys coemt wordt er groot ghekijf:
D'een sal roepen en tieren, d'ander sal smijten op 't lijf.
Van sulck bedrijf soude men wonder verhalen:
'Ick behoef 't selve wel, ghi en dorft elders niet dralen',
Sal 't wijf segghen, 'Ick wou dattet ware d'laetste'.
Maer die de slaghen vangt die hevet 't quaetste.
Van sulcx vele te hooren ben ick wel ter cuere moe.
De pot loopt overe, nichte, sluyt die duere toe.

Van den somere
Als die lente uut is, 's morghens naer de noene,
Beghint de somere met den heeten saysoene.
Dan mueghen die meyskens wel, die seer verladen sijn,
Henlieden in Sint-Jorisvissop baden fijn.
Want door die groote hitte sal men dan seere sweeten.
Sonder vier sal men qualick ovens connen heeten.

Of the reigning Lords of the year
Venus and Mars will reign for most of this year:
Mars during wartime and Venus during love-season.
75 And in the winter three gentlemen will come to our land:
Messieurs Blueface, Dripnose and Chatterteeth.
For those unable to pay, a worn cloak pawns well.

Of the four seasons of the year
And first of spring
The spring begins and must spring out
When leaves and blossoms begin to grow.
80 Oh, how joyful every handmaid of Venus will be,
Making glad cheer with her lover,
Like a fawn changed by the arrow of Venus!
It is 'good evening, cousin', 'God greet you, niece'.
They treat all as very light; it is 'goodbye sadness'.
85 But soon thereafter they grow bloated, plain to see.
Then it is 'Oh woe, oh dear, never was I more wronged!'
It would be much too good if no-one had to bear a child,
You would not find a virgin for seven miles about.
They are more terrified by childbearing than sin.
90 Ugly wives will also have great suffering,
Those that have sweet, fair and charming husbands.
For the ugliest women, it should be told here,
Will be the most troubled by jealousy.
In this season such men are not stupid,
95 They leave their wife at home and seek a prettier one.
Then the wife will certainly race and run:
'Oh, where is my husband? I may go insane!'
At night, as he comes home, there will be great strife:
One will shout and scream, the other will lash out.
100 One might tell wonders of such a sight:
'I have the same to give, you should not go elsewhere',
The wife will say, 'I insist this time is the last!'
But he that catches the blows has the worst.
I am growing tired from hearing so many tales.
105 The pot runs over, niece, pull the door to.

Of the summer
When spring is out, the morning after the noon,
Summer begins with the hot season.
Then might the girls, those who want to,
Bathe finely in the suds of Saint George.[7]
110 Because of the great heat men will sweat a lot.
Without fire men will struggle to light their ovens.

---

[7] Compare the *Blue Barge*, line 130.

Dan comen die hontsdaghen en, soo 't volck wil callen,
Sullender alteveel misbrieven vallen.
Dan sal men oock thiende gheven van d'elfste schoven.
'␣t Is: 'Wacker knapen, wacker, laet seere hoven!'
Dan sullen wy wel gaen brassen en vullen ons maghe.
Kase en broot, is dat ghebrast? Meester, 't is de plaghe.

Van den herft
In den herft sal men de welgheleerde seere soecken
Om appelen te lesen in allen hoecken.
Dan sal men t'Antwerpen roepen om den cost:
'Hoort, mijnheeren, hoort! Ick hebbe goeden Rijnschen most!
Hael most, vrouwenlost die rueck en smaeck heeft!'
Diesulcke wel om een os te crijghen eenen baeck gheeft.
Dan sal 't sijn: druyfmisse, appelmisse en peermisse,
En dronckaerts sullen dan hebben kermisse,
Drinckende by maten, dat 's: met potten en pinten.
En door het overgheven sal de weerdinne wel quinten.
Dies sullender tsanderdaechs veel ligghen, ick wedde,
Seer stenende van die keldercortse te bedde.
Maer om haest te becomen van sulcken verseere,
So moeten si achtervolghen dese nuttelijcke leere:
Is 't dat van drincken u 's morgensvroech
Deert het hooft oft hant versleten beeft,
So sult ghi nutten voor u ghevoech
Van het hayr des honts die u ghebeten heeft.
Tsavonts droncken: ligt nere; 's morghens sieck: drinct were.
Dit is die leere van Alexander; d'een fenijn verdrijvet d'ander.
Jan Pockaert met sijn verrotte schinckelen
Mochte op dit pas wel beghinnen te hinckelen.
Och ghildekens, ghildekens, dat sal u temmen!
'␣t Is quaet water, sey de reygher, en hy en cost niet swemmen.

115

120

125

130

135

140

Then the dog days[8] come in, and people will backbite,
There will be a great many complaints to hear.
Then men will also give tithes from the eleventh sheave.
115 It is 'Wake up boys, wake up, let us have a feast!'
Then we will go to drink and fill our stomachs.
Cheese and bread, is that drinking? Sir, it is a scourge.[9]

Of the autumn
In the autumn men will search a lot for scholars
To leaf through apple trees in every place.
120 Then at Antwerp they will call at the market:
'Hear this, gentlemen, hear! I have good Rhenish cider!
You must buy it: women lust for its smell and taste!'
Whoever wants to gain an ox will give away bacon.[10]
Then it will be: grape-mass, apple-mass and pear-mass,
125 And drunkards will hold their fair-mass then,
Drinking in a measured way, that is, in half-pints and pints.
And through their charity the barmaid will be well rewarded.
Many of them will lie down the next day, I bet,
Sore afflicted by the cellar fever in their beds.
130 But to become free from such torment
They must follow this sober wisdom:
If you have morning sickness from drinking,
Should your head or hands start shaking
Then should you take for your health
135 A hair from the dog that has bitten you.[11]
Drunk in the evening: lie down; if sick in the morning: drink again.
That is the wisdom of Alexander; one venom counteracts the other.
John Poxy, with his rotten legs,
May very well start to hop on one of them.
140 Oh adulterers, adulterers, that will tame you!
This is bad water, said the heron, so he cannot swim.

---

[8] The *hontsdaghen* or *dies caniculares* are the hottest period of the year, and traditionally last from 19 July to 18 August. The name refers to the supposedly malign influence of the Dog Star Sirius, the alleged cause of heat and other misfortunes. Isidore of Seville states that Sirius 'doubles' the heat of the sun in this season, 'to the extent that bodies are liquefied and boiled', and is called 'dog star' because it 'inflicts sicknesses on to bodies' ('coniuncta cum sole duplicatur calor ipsius, et dissolvuntur corpora et vaporantur . . . Canis autem vocatur propter quod corpora morbo afficiat'): Isidori Hispalensis, *Etymologiarum sive Originum*, ed. W. M Lindsay (Oxford, 1911), 3: 71.14–15. The idea also occurs in Aristotle's *Physics* (199a2) and *Metaphysics* (1027a13).

[9] This appears to be another exchange between the narrator and his marot.

[10] The meaning of this line is obscure. It is probably intended to be read as a mock-proverb that, despite its gnomic tone, contains no real insight or wisdom.

[11] The idiom has the same meaning in both Dutch and English, where it is first documented in Heywood's *Dialogue of Prouerbes* (1546); Henry Bohn suggests that its ultimate origin is Italian. See Henry Bohn, *A Polyglot of Foreign Proverbs* (London, 1867), 91. The saying is attested in Dutch from the early sixteenth century: see J. Verdam, 'Het haar van den hond', *Tijdschrift voor Nederlandse taal- en letterkunde* 12 (1893), 141–9.

Van den winter

Men ghebiet ende laet weten van 's wintersweghen,
Dat ghi u moet van hout stofferen tedeghen,
Want 't sal cout sijn voorwaer in 't water als 't vriest.

145   God seghen u, compere, 't is wel gheniest.
Men sal niet veel coeyen in 't velt sien bijsen.
Jan Asschevijster sal het vier seer prijsen.
Daer wort sonder hout, steen, bert oft hamere
Ghemaect seer menighe gheschilderde camere.

150   Die winter is een vreemt ende onweert gast,
Maer Coppen Bontepelsse daer luttel op past.
't Sal reghenen als 't nat valt, ende sneeuwen mede,
Vriesen, haghelen en waeyen, soo 't laetstmael dede.
Och, hoe wel smaect by 't vier dan een lecker bete!

155   Vangt dat, sey de duyvel, en hi liet een schete.

Van pays ende oorloghe

't Wort oorloghe, 't wort pays; 't wort al dat men wille.
Raept op, knecht, sey de vrou, daer ontvalt mijn spille.
Door Martis' oppositie salder veel ghedrays wesen,
Maer door Venus' conjunctie sal 't wederom pays wesen.

160   Dit jaer en sal men niet veel kijven sonder spreken.
De vorsch sal dicwils teghen die crane willen steken.
De man sal op 't wijf dickwils vergrammen.
D'wijf sal 's mans hooft met eenen stoele kammen.
't Is tweëndertich jaer leden, luttel meer oft min,

165   Datter een oorloghe sal nemen haer beghin,
Daer sooveel ruyters sullen blijven ende knechten,
Datter seven vrouwen om een broeck sullen vechten.
Byloye, ick wil mijn broecken wel nauwe bewaren
Om daer eenen hoop vrouwen mede te vergaren!

170   Hoe ruyterlick sullen se malcanderen trommelen!
Dan sal ick in den hoop met al mijn broecken sommelen.
Ha ha, hoe sullen se onder die wijfs ghesletert sijn!
Een goey eerlijc vrouwe en mach niet verbetert sijn.

Van den goeden ende dieren tijt

Dit jaer sullen die vruchten eenen grooten loop hebben.

175   Al dat men ghegeven crijcht sal men goeden coop hebben.
Daer men leckerlick eet, sal men maken goey chiere.
't Sal al redelicken coop sijn, is 't niet te diere.
Het coren sal dit jaer vercocht worden by maten.

Of the winter
Of winter's ways one declares and expounds,
That you should gather up a great many sticks,
Since it will be cold in the water when it is frozen.
145 God bless you, my friend, if you sneeze.
One will not see many cows out rutting in the fields.
John Ashfarter will greatly praise the fire.
There will – without wood, stone, timber or hammer –
Be made a great many shit-coloured rooms.
150 The winter is an odd and unwelcome guest,
But Moneybags Finefurs gives it little thought.
It will rain when water falls, and snow appears,
Frost, hail and gales, much like the last time.
Oh, how nice a bite of meat tastes by the fire!
155 Catch that, said the devil, and he let out a fart.

Of peace and wartime
There will be war, there will be peace; there will be all that men will.
Pick it up, knave, said the woman, my bobbin fell there.
For Mars's opposition will cause great tumult,
But Venus's conjunction will bring peace.
160 This year men will not bicker without speech.
The frog will often want to stab the stork.
The husband will often be angry with the wife.
The wife will comb her husband's hair with a stool.
It is thirty-two years, a little more or less,
165 Since the war first took its beginning,[12]
There cavalrymen and infantry continue to die,
So that seven woman will fight for a pair of trousers.
By god, I will take care of my trousers now
So that I might have a whole heap of women!
170 How chivalrously they will beat each other up!
Then I will show off all my trousers in hope.
Ha ha, how the women will tear into them!
A good and honest wife needs no correction.

Of good and costly times
This year fruit will have a good load.
175 Anything you grab for nothing will be a good deal.
Where one eats plentifully, one makes joyful cheer.
All that is calculated cheaply, it is not dear.
The wheat will be sold in measures this year.

---

[12] A reference to the war with the duchy of Guelders (1502–43). During this conflict, the Gueldermen caused lasting and widespread damage to Antwerp and the surrounding area: see Michael Limberger, 'No Town in the World Provides More Advantages: Economies of Agglomeration and the Golden Age of Antwerp', in *Urban Achievement in Early Modern Europe: Golden Ages in Antwerp, Amsterdam and London*, ed. Patrick O'Brien, Derek Keene, Marjolein 't Hart and Herman van der Wee (Cambridge, 2001), 39–62.

Dies veel incomen heeft, het sal hem baten.
180 Men sal coren en haver ter merct brenghen in sacken.
T'Antwerpen sal men veel boeckweykoecken backen.
'Loopt, loopt, Lisken, loopt, die boter is goede coop!'
Men gheeft twee potten melcx voor eenen stoop.
Isser veel wijns ghewassen, men salder veel drincken.
185 Is 't anders, men sal se te poverlicker schincken.
't Sal goet sijn wijn te drincken met vollen horten,
Maer men sal gheen op 's vyleyns tafel storten.
Want datter ghebreck is, 't sy van anders oft van desen,
Van quade wijfs en salder ymmers gheen ghebreck wesen.
190 Want Lijse Vroechrijpe en Beele metten tuyten
Schrijven in 't vierde bladt die Hebreeusche cluyten:
'Hoort, goey mannen, hoort, wildy wat nyeus inbijten?
Een oude baghijne sal eenen nyeuwen foey schijten'.
Maer liever haddick die pensen van een vercken.
195 Rasch in 't jonckwijf, knecht, de vrouwe is ter kercken!

Van den loop ende cours der manen
Als die mane nyeu is, sal se seer cleen blincken.
Sulcke een groote koe hadde Gille Verclincken:
Als se vol is, sal se gheheel ront wesen,
Maer soudse altoos so blijven, het soude te bont wesen.
200 Als d'oude mane uut is, dan sal se weer vernyeuwen,
Die 't niet en wil ghelooven, die vraghe 't Hieuwen.
Al stondy op der kercken boven den weerhane,
Nochtans sal 't quaet pissen sijn teghen die mane.
Men vint veel mans t'Japick met quade broecken ane.

Van die veranderinghe des weers
205 Als 't schoon weer is en die quaey wijfs niet en kijven,
't En sal niet haest veranderen, willet alsoo blijven.
Maer als 't verandert en nat beghint te vallen,
Dan sal 't reghenen, haghelen oft seer sneeuballen.

Whoever has a high income, it will benefit him.
180   Men will bring wheat and oats to market in sacks.
In Antwerp men will bake many buckwheat biscuits.
'Come, come, miss, this butter is a bargain!'
Men will give two half pints of milk for one pint.
If much wine is harvested, we will drink a lot.
185   If the opposite is true, it will be scarcely poured out.
It will be good to drink wine with great gulps,
But you should not set it on a villain's table.
There will be a dearth, of one thing or another;
Of bad wives there will surely be no shortage.
190   For Louise Young-ripe and Belle Loose-hair[13]
Write on the fourth sheet of the Hebrew farces:
'Hear, good men, hear, do you want news to wolf down?
An old beguine will shit out a new bribe.'[14]
But I would rather speak about the belly of a pig.
195   Rush to the daughter, knave, the housewife is at church!

Of the cycle and path of the moon
When the moon is new, it will twinkle very brightly.
Giles Glass-clinking has such a great cow:
When she is full, she will be entirely round,
But should she stay like that, it will be too much.
200   When the old moon is done, then there will be a new one,
If you do not believe this, ask Mr Cut-off.
Although you stand on the church above the weathercock,
Nonetheless it will be difficult to piss against the moon.
Thus we find many a Japick man with foul trousers.[15]

Of the changing of the weather
205   When the weather is beautiful and evil women do not grumble,
It will not undergo change, as long as it stays the same.
But when it changes and water begins to fall,
Then it will rain, hail or blizzard severely.

---

[13] These figures also feature in the popular Flemish text *Les Evangiles des quenouilles* (*c.*1460), a mock-gospel supposedly dictated by a housewife while spinning, and interpolated with various interjections or 'commentaries' from other women. The work was published in 1520 in Dutch under the title *Die evangelien vanden spinrocke metter glosen bescreven ter eeren vanden vrouwen*, and printed in English as *The Gospelles of Dystaues* (*c.*1510). See Madeleine Jeay and Kathleen Garay, *The Distaff Gospels* (Peterborough, Ontario, 2006); G. J. Boekenooghen, *Die evangelien vanden spinrocke* (The Hague, 1910).

[14] Although the famous lay sisterhoods had declined since their thirteenth-century heyday, some beguinages did linger on into the sixteenth century. In fact, beguine communities were still in existence in the nineteenth century: see Walter Simons, *Cities of Ladies: Beguine Communities in the Medieval Low Countries 1200–1565* (Philadelphia, 2003).

[15] The whereabouts of Japick are unknown, but it seems to be a folkloric village of simpletons, akin to the English Gotham. See J. Cornelissen, *Nederlandsche volkshumor*, 6 vols. (Antwerp, 1929–38), I: 201–6.

Maer al siet de locht leelick, en vervaert u niet,

210 't En is niet al reghen dat altemet leelick siet.

. Want waer 't al reghen dat leelick siet op malcanderen,

Veel vrouwen souden dickwils in reghen veranderen,

Dies die mans hen drincken souden van droefheyt sat.

Vrouwe, wat lofdy u eyeren? De korf heeft een gat.

Van die principale steden

Van Antwerpen

215 T'Antwerpen sal 't in den winter op 't strate vuyl sijn.

Veel sullender spelen van cust nu mijnen cuyl fijn,

Laten hen lappen sien en 't gat aen de poorte vaghen.

Veel meyskens sullender nae d'oude behoorte waghen

Huer casteelkens te bestormen met cleen ghewelt.

220 Dan sal die vrouwe segghen: 'Meysken, daer is u ghelt'.

En als si sullen gheproeft hebben dat lecker morseel,

Dan sullen si gaen sitten in eenich bordeel

En crijghender dan die pocken door alsulck gheploch.

Gheraedt waer si varen? In 't gasthuys. Doen se? Jae, si toch.

225 Elck sal daer doen, maer 't wort in 't drinken goet bescheet.

'Beso los manos, seinnor de vuestra merceed'.

Die vroukens sullen gaen op si joffrouschs met doecken fijn.

'Car j'ay veu son robin, ma mere, je veulx Robijn'.

Van Bruessele

Die Bruesselaers en mueghen wi niet vergheten:

230 Al sijn se lecker, si mueghen noch wel kiecxkens eten.

Maer een quaet vuyl wijf dient wel ghesmeten.

Van Lueven

Vis disputare? Ita. Quid est ita? Ick en weet 's niet.

Soo sijdy dan victus; 't is een schotel bescheets, siet.

Soo sullen achter straten loopen dees jonghe clercxkens.

235 Maer die groote sullen maken seer luttel wercxkens

Van in huyskens van luxuriën 's nachs te loopen,

Al souden si boecken, cleeren en credit vercoopen.

Ende want se van den Keyenberch soo sijn besmit,

Daeromme so sijn se op dees dillekens temeer verhit,

But although the sky is ugly, do not be afraid,
210   It is not always rain that is ugly, but you.
For where it always rains people are ugly to each other,
Many women will often change into rain,
Thus their men should drink to drive out misery.
Woman, why praise your eggs? The basket has a hole.

Of the principal towns
Of Antwerp
215   In Antwerp the streets will be dirty in winter.
Many will play fine games of Kiss-my-arse,
Turning their backs and sweeping their back-gates.
Many girls will try to get, as an old custom,
Their castles stormed with a little violence.
220   Then will the women say: 'Girl, there is your living'.
And when they have sampled that sweet morsel,
Then they will go and sit in a brothel
And then catch the pox for all their ploughing.
Guess where they go? To the hospital. Do they? Yes, they do.[16]
225   Everyone will do that, but it is certain they will drink heartily.
'Beso los manos, senor de vuestra merceed.'[17]
Minor ladies will go about like real ladies, decked in finery.
'Car j'ai veu son robin, ma mere, je veulx Robijn.'[18]

Of Brussels
The men of Brussels we must not forget:
230   Although they are delicate, they do eat chickens.
But an evil, vile woman should be well beaten.

Of Leuven
Vis disputare? Ita. Quid est ita? I do not know.[19]
So you are the *victus*. It is a plate of shit, you see.
So young clerks shall wander through the back streets.
235   But the great will not bother the little scholars much
Who creep into houses of lust at night,
Although they must hawk their books, clothes and credit.
Because they are from Clownbergh they are so foolish,
They are fired up by these trollops,

---

[16]   Another exchange between Owlglass and the marot.
[17]   'I kiss your hands, my merciful lord' (Spanish).
[18]   'Because I saw his cock robin, I want to have his cock robin' (French).
[19]   A mock-student debate in pseudo-academic Latin. It reads: 'Do you wish to argue?' 'Yes'. 'What is the nature of "yes"?' Leuven was of course an important centre of scholarship during the early-modern period. Martin V founded the university there in 1425 as the first institution concentrating exclusively on the human sciences, 'a general school with all faculties, except for that of theology': *Charters of Foundation and Early Documents*, ed. Jos Hermans and Marc Nelissen (Leuven, 2005), 65. Erasmus, Vesalius, Mercator and Justus Lipsius were among the intellectuals active there.

240   Soodat kappe en kuevel dicwils blijft voor 't ghelach.
      Hou seg, hou! Is moeyer niet thuys? Alle goeden dach!

Van Ghendt
't Sal dit jaer te Ghendt dicwils al over noene gaen.
Want die clocke salder een telcken saysoene slaen.
Veel sullender maken den poyaert en den moyaert,
245   Maer de waghens sal men vinden ontrent den Hoyaert.
D'wijf die den tol ontfangt spreect beter dan een stomme;
Conde se niet spreken, ick gaver noch twee corten omme.
Waerdy te Ghendt by een meysken alleen in haer celle,
Wat soudy se doen? Omhelsen! Soudy? Jae ick.
        Dat 's een gheselle!
250   Preut, sey de duyvel, en hi werp eenen Wael in de helle.

Van Brugghe
't Is daer oock: 'Beso les manos', 'Jan, coemt, cust mi nou'.
't Isser al berockelt! Dies gheve ick hem eenen jou.
't Sal te Brugghe redelijck al goeden spoet hebben,
Maer die rijcke lieden sullen d'meeste goet hebben,
255   Dees meyskens wordender seer haestelijck vlugghe:
Gheeft men se eens de nope, si vallen op den rugghe.
Alle bate helpt, sey de zee, en si piste in de mugghe.

Van Mechelen
Hebt u nu cloeckelijck, ghi Mechelse hanssen,
Oft Sinte-Gurck sal tot uwent comen danssen.
260   Wacht dat ghi niet, hoe dat u wijf kijft oft bast,
Voren en woont daer men de torven tast.
En ghi wijfs, om vry te sijn van sulck achterdincken,
Wilt Sinte-Gurcken dapperlijck beschincken,
Oft hi sal comen danssen voor u duere onversaecht,
265   In teeken dat ghi voorslaept en de broeck oock draecht.
Voorwaer, die een quaet wijf heeft, is deerlick gheplaecht!

240 So that cap and coat are always for sale.
Hey, say hey! Is mother not at home? Good-day to all!

Of Ghent
This year it will often be noon all over Ghent,
Because the clock will toll once every hour.
Many will make themselves a drunk or a dandy,
245 But men will find wagons drawing through the Hoyaert.[20]
The woman who collects the toll speaks better than a mute;
If she does not speak I will give her two coins.
If you are in Ghent with a girl alone in her room,
What should you do? Embrace! Should you? Yes, I would!
    That's a good boy!
250 Fart, said the devil, and he chucked a Walloon into hell.

Of Bruges
It is there also: 'Beso les manos', 'John, come, kiss me now'.[21]
It is all crumpled! Thus I give him a jab.
It will be fairly good at Bruges despite adversity,
But the rich ones will have the most of the goods.
255 The girls will ripen very unexpectedly.
You give them a nudge, they fall on their backs.
Every little bit helps, said the sea, and he pissed on the gnat.[22]

Of Mechlin
Behave yourselves sensibly now, you Mechlinian idiots,
Or Saint Gurck will dance with all of you.[23]
260 No matter how your wife grumbles or shouts, watch that you do not
Go and live where you store your peat.
And you women, to free yourselves from such suspicion,
You must treat Saint Gurck to plenty of drinks,
Or he will come and dance for you at length and undaunted,
265 In the place where you sleep, and pull on your trousers as well.
Therefore, he that has an evil wife is sorely tormented.

---

[20] The old name for the hay-market at Ghent.

[21] This line seems to represent a scurrilous dialogue between a prostitute and a Spanish nobleman.

[22] A reference to a common Dutch proverb that describes any futile gesture or contribution: '"Every little helps", said the gnat, pissing in the sea.' For international variants, see Eric Partridge, *Dictionary of Catch-Phrases from the Sixteenth Century to the Present Day* (London, 1986), 123–4. The text comically inverts the roles of sea and gnat.

[23] Gurck is a fictional saint, whose name is perhaps taken from the town and chief diocese of Carinthia in modern-day Austria. This passage bears comparison with other medieval mock-hagiographies: see Martha Bayless, *Parody in the Middle Ages: The Latin Tradition* (Ann Arbor, MI, 1997), 57–92.

Van Iperen
'Die ruese coemt, den draeck die volcht ernaer',
Sullen de clocxkens spelen op den Tuyndach aldaer.
Al sijn die banckerotiers van de lotherie om den hoeck,
270 Nochtans schijt de lotherie in hueren broeck.
't Is wel 'lotherie, dieverie', soo men pleech te segghen,
Maer mocht ick 't hoochste lot crijghen, ick sou noch inlegghen.
Iperen sal nemmermeer in eenich beluyck quelen,
Want die borghers connen nu al crijchsghebruyck spelen.

Alle d'ander Brabandtsche ende Vlaemsche steden
275 Sullen alle dit jaer leven in grooter vreden,
Sooverre als 't volc malcanderen niet en ontbiedt voor recht,
Sooverre als nyemant en slaet, stoot, kijft oft vecht.
De reste sal men weten als 't al openbaer is.
Men sal gheen procureurs vinden die segghen dat niet waer is.

Conclusie
280 Adieu, tot weertastens toe, God wil u ghesparen wel.
Bidt voor my als ick achterstae, dat ick mach varen wel.
Finis.

Of Ypres
'The giant comes, the dragon follows after him':
The bells will play that song there on Thundaghe.[24]
Although bankrupts from the lottery are round the corner,
270   Nonetheless the lottery shits in their breeches.
It is true that 'lottery means robbery', as men swear and say.
But if I could snatch up the winning ticket, I would not pause.
Ypres will never suffer in any siege
For the citizens can already play all sorts of war-games.

All the other Brabantine and Flemish cities
275   All this year people will be living in greater peace,
As long as they send each other to court for justice,
As long as no-one slaps, punches, squabbles or fights.
The rest you will know when it is declared,
You will not find lawyers to swear this is not the truth.

Conclusion
280   Adieu, until we touch again, may God preserve you.
Pray for me when I turn away, that I may fare well.
Finis.

---

[24] The Thundaghe is a traditional festival held at Ypres on the first Sunday of August. The festival commemorates a military victory of 1383, in which the city repelled a combined force of Ghentish and English troops, supposedly with the assistance of Onse Lieve Vrouwe vanden Tuin (Our Lady of the Battlements). The occasion is marked by the ringing of church bells and processions of stilt-walkers, which are the 'giants' that Owlglass mentions. On the Thundaghe in the sixteenth century, see William Tydeman, *The Medieval European Stage, 500–1550* (Cambridge, 2001), 536–8.

PART II

Farces

.

The Farce of the Beggar

THE *Esbatement van den schuyfman* can be dated to the first decade of the sixteenth century. The best witness to its date is a note accompanying the single surviving copy of the text, which records that the play won first place in a *rederijkerfeest* held at Leuven in 1504. The same source also attributes the play to a chamber based at Tienen in the duchy of Brabant.[1] Although it does not specify which of the Tienen chambers was responsible for the piece, there are two possible candidates: *De Corenbloem* (The Cornflower), founded *c.*1480, and *De Fonteine* (The Fountain), which is first recorded as a competitor in the infamous Ghent *landjuweel* of 1539, but may have been active earlier.[2] Nonetheless, the issue is complicated by the final line of the play itself, which alludes to another chamber, the *Olyftack* (Olive branch). While there were no known chambers of this name in Tienen, as the work of Anne-Laure van Bruaene makes clear, the *olyftack* was a popular symbol among the *rederijkers*, presumably owing to its biblical resonances.[3] There are records of chambers with the name at Antwerp, Sint-Truiden, and a number of other cities.[4] This might suggest that the text was composed by the *factor* of another chamber on behalf of the Tienen *rederijkers*, who then performed the piece at the Leuven festival.

As is consistent with these muddled origins, the play owes its survival to a chamber that had no obvious part in either its composition or performance. The text is preserved in the *toneelcollectie* (theatre-library) of the chamber *De Pellicaen*, founded at Haarlem in *c.*1500.[5] The *Pellicaen* in fact dedicated itself to collecting plays from around the Low Countries. Its library originally consisted of fourteen volumes of manuscripts, each containing between twelve and twenty-six plays from a variety of sources, and including farces, table-plays and *spelen van sinnen*.[6] The *collectie* is

[1] W. M. H. Hummelen, *Repertorium van het rederijkersdrama 1500–ca.1620* (Assen, 1968), 92.

[2] J. Delmelle 'Géographie littéraire du Brabant. La Hesbaye thioise', *Le Folklore Brabançon*, 145–8 (1960), 569–70; A. van Elslander, 'Lijst van Nederlandse rederijkerskamers uit de XVe en XVIe eeuw', *Jaarboek de Fonteine*, 18 (1968), 29–60 (49).

[3] Anne-Laure van Bruaene, *Om beters wille: rederijkerskamers en de stedelijke cultuur in de Zuidelijke Nederlanden (1400–1650)* (Amsterdam, 2008), 262. For the scriptural connotations of the olive branch, see Genesis 8.11.

[4] Van Elslander, 'Lijst van Nederlandse rederijkerskamers', 24–5; Gary K. Waite, *Reformers on Stage: Popular Drama and Religious Propaganda in the Low Countries* (Toronto, 2000), 31; F. C. van Boheemen and T. C. J. van der Heijden, *Retoricaal memoriaal: bronnen voor de geschiedenis van de Hollandse rederijkerskamers van de middeleeuwen tot het begin van de achttiende eeuw* (Delft, 1999), 658–63.

[5] Van Boheemen and Van der Heijden, *Retoricaal memoriaal*, 351–2; Bart Ramakers, 'Voor stad en stadgenoten: Rederijkers, kamers en toneel in Haarlem in de tweede helft van de zestiende eeuw', in *Conformisten en rebellen: Rederijkerscultuur in de Nederlanden (1400–1650)*, ed. Bart Ramakers (Amsterdam, 2003), 109–24.

[6] The contents of the library were catalogued by C. G. N Vooys in three articles, 'Rederijkersspelen in het archief van "Trou moet blijcken", *Tijdschrift voor Nederlandse taal- en letterkunde* 45 (1926), 265–86; 'Rederijkersspelen uit het archief van "Trou moet Blijcken",

still held at the site of the original *kamer* in Haarlem, albeit with two volumes now missing.[7] The *Farce* is contained in the seventh of these volumes, along with several other comic texts, from cities as far afield as Antwerp and Diest.

In its production and preservation, *The Beggar* is therefore an illuminating piece. Its performance by a chamber not responsible for its composition suggests that *factors* might hire out their services beyond their own chambers. Likewise, its inclusion in the Haarlem *collectie* shows that successful plays could circulate freely between chambers, cities and regions. The text ultimately shows that the relationship between chambers could be more collaborative than competitive at times. However, it is important not to make too much of this, as it also seems that chambers might put their stamp on plays they took from elsewhere. There are some signs that *The Beggar* was at least partly rewritten by the Tienen *rederijkers*: as Erné and Van Dis observe, the play uses several terms that are particular to the eastern Brabantine dialect.[8] Similarly, the *Pellicaen* appears to have adapted *The Beggar* to meet its own needs. At least the motto that concludes the piece, 'Trou moet blijken' ('Truth will be shown'), is that of the Haarlem *kamer* rather than one of its counterparts in Brabant.

The Beggar itself belongs to the tradition of vagabond literature in medieval and Renaissance culture. While this probably owes something to Latin student poetry of the twelfth and thirteenth centuries, best represented by the Cambridge Songs and the verses attributed to Golias, by the end of the Middle Ages vagrancy was a recurrent theme in many popular and vernacular literatures.[9] The motif of the cunning wayfarer, deprived of all resources except for his guile, is central to much of the comedy of the period. Its informs the *picaro*-figures of early Spanish novels, such as *Lazarillo de Tormes* (1554) and Quevedo's *El Buscon* (c.1600), and is clearly present in English drama and 'coney-catching' pamphlets, ranging from John Awdeley's *Fraternity of Vagabonds* (c.1561) to the character of Autolycus in Shakespeare's *A Winter's Tale* (c.1611).[10] It also makes its way into the graphic art of the Low Countries in the sixteenth century, as beggars start to be depicted as 'cheats undeserving of any charity' in the work of Bosch, Van Leyden and Bartel Beham.[11] *The Beggar* provides an early example of this topos. Its two main protagonists are archetypal predatory beggars. This point is made clear from the outset, as both are given highly descriptive, almost allegorical names. 'Schuyfman' is derived from *schuiven*, 'to slide' or 'to push', and is close in meaning to 'drifter' or 'hustler', while the name of his companion 'Sloef' combines *sloeven* (drudge) with echoes of *slof* (idler). Ter Laan

---

Tijdschrift voor Nederlandse taal- en letterkunde 47 (1928), 161–205; 'Rederijkersspelen uit het archief van "Trou moet blijcken" (Slot)', *Tijdschrift voor Nederlandse taal- en letterkunde* 49 (1930), 1–25.

  [7] Hummelen, *Repertorium van het rederijkersdrama*, 58.

  [8] B. H. Erné en L. M. van Dis, *De Gentse spelen van 1539*, 2 vols. (The Hague, 1982), 1: 352.

  [9] Edwin Hermann Zeydel, *Vagabond Verse: Secular Latin Poems of the Middle Ages* (Detroit, 1966).

  [10] Two reviews of these literatures are Douglas C. Young, *Rogues and Genres: Generic Transformation in the Spanish Picaresque and Arabic Maqāma* (Newark, DE, 2004), and Linda Woodbridge, *Vagrancy, Homelessness, and English Renaissance Literature* (Urbana, IL, 2001).

  [11] Mark Koch, 'The Desanctification of the Beggar in Rogue Pamphlets of the English Renaissance', in *The Work of Dissimilitude*, ed. David G. Allen and Robert A. White (Newark, DE, 1992), 91–104 (91).

adds a further possibility, suggesting that 'Schuyfman' might be a pun of *schuyt-man* (shipman or mariner), since the characters occasionally discuss life at sea.[12] This would further stress the indigence of the pair, as even the work they have performed involves endless, wandering movement.

The fact that *The Beggar* makes use of these commonplaces, and at a comparatively early date, is interesting in the context of wider culture of the *rederijkerskamers*. As R. H. Tawney and others have argued, the shift from the medieval view of the poor man as 'friend of God' to the early-modern stereotype of the sly and 'wilful idler' coincides with the emergence of a capitalist economy in northern Europe.[13] It may even have been borne out of the new emphasis on enterprise such a change brought about, and its accompanying sense that individuals were responsible for their own financial success and failure. *The Beggar*'s use of this theme might therefore be seen as a further product of the chambers' *burgermoraal*. As beneficiaries of the mercantile, urban economy, it is perhaps inevitable that such attitudes would be current among the *rederijkers*.

Along with its dependence on the tradition of comic transients, the play also retains links with other comic forms. One especially strong influence is the French fabliau. The central trick of the text seems to be drawn from a version of the thirteenth-century *Le Sacristain*, in which the corpse of a monk is similarly tied to a donkey to create a bogus ghost, in an obvious parody of the legend of El Cid.[14] *The Beggar* is most likely derived from the same lost redaction of *Le Sacristain* that was reworked by the English chapbook *Dane Hew Munk of Leicestre* (*c.*1500): tellingly, both put the donkey in amorous pursuit of another animal, a detail which does not occur in any of the surviving French versions.[15] Again, the influence of French humour on Dutch dramatic texts remains insistent and immediate.

Over the last century or so, *The Beggar* has suffered from a markedly poor critical reception. Following the publication of Kalff's edition in 1889, a series of commentators have reacted with disgust to the brutality and amorality exhibited by the piece.[16] The scholar and historian Jan te Winkel dismissed it as 'al te ruwe' ('altogether too crude'), while Van Moerkerken defined it as 'onsmakelijk' ('distasteful').[17] Similarly, Jan ten Brink offered a lukewarm assessment of its merits, complaining that 'the entire play revolves around the efforts of a couple of wastrels to ensure that they will

---

[12] K. ter Laan, *Letterkundig woordenboek voor Noord en Zuid* (The Hague, 1952), 475.

[13] R. H. Tawney, *Religion and the Rise of Capitalism* (New York, 1926), 261–2. See also Paola Pugliatti, *Beggary and the Theatre in Early Modern England* (Aldershot, 2003), 19–20; William C. Carroll, *Fat King, Lean Beggar: Representations of Poverty in the Age of Shakespeare* (Ithaca, NY, 1996), 21–70.

[14] See Willem Noomen and Nico van den Boogaard, *Nouveau recueil complet des fabliaux*, 10 vols. (Assen, 1983–98), 7: 1–190.

[15] Melissa Furrow, *Ten Fifteenth-Century Comic Poems* (New York, 1985), 157–76.

[16] G. Kalff, *Trou moet blycken: tooneelstukken der zestiende eeuw, voor het eerst naar de handschriften uitgegeven* (Groningen, 1889), 55–80.

[17] Jan te Winkel, *De ontwikkelingsgang der Nederlandsche letterkunde II. Geschiedenis der Nederlandsche letterkunde van middeleeuwen en rederijkerstijd*, 2 vols. (Haarlem, 1922), 2: 377; P. H. van Moerkerken, *De satire in de Nederlandsche kunst der middeleeuwen* (Amsterdam, 1904), 105.

eat a good meal'.[18] Even Kalff himself, addressing the Society of Dutch Literature in 1921, felt it necessary to excuse *The Beggar* on the grounds that it reflects an outdated *smaak* (taste), although he added that 'it would be very naïve to believe that our descendants will value the literature of our time as highly as some of us do now'.[19]

There are some grounds for this squeamishness, since it is undeniable that the play contains a powerful current of cynicism and ruthlessness. Its central episode involves the two main characters breaking into the house of a grieving brother and sister, stealing their mother's corpse, and tying it to a donkey in order to convince them that their mother is haunting them. Furthermore, rather than punishing such sacrilegious behaviour, the piece rewards it as a singular piece of cunning, allowing the perpetrators to feed on the proceeds of their crime, and even receive extra payment for 'exorcising' the 'revenant' they have created. But in spite of its wilfully unpleasant contents, dismissing the play as clumsy or barbarous is unfair. If anything it is a thoughtful and sustained piece of black comedy, which manages to push the usually light-hearted structure of the farce in an innovative and uncomfortable direction. It is clear at the end of the piece that the victory won by the vagrants is at best a temporary one. While they may be well fed for the moment, they can only return to their life of 'drifting at the dyke-side', scrabbling at the margins of society (line 469). Indeed, when seen in the light of their extravagant protests of hunger at the beginning of the text, it becomes clear that the two are caught in a quasi-Sisyphean cycle of deprivation and desperation. As Herman Pleij has stressed, the elaborate jokes and fantasies about food that proliferated in the Middle Ages, such as Luilekkerland and the beggars' own wish for 'a horse stuffed in a sausage' (line 4), conceal genuine anxieties about the threat of starvation. As Pleij writes, 'one's daily bread . . . was a blessing in danger of being withdrawn at any moment' in this period.[20] With this in mind, the brutality of the text seems far less crude or gratuitously distasteful. Instead, it appears to complement the essentially ironic structure of the play, as its surface mischief and knockabout is poised precariously over the real hazards of malnutrition and death.[21] Just as the game played by the vagrants has a human corpse at its centre, so the text's own playfulness has mortality at its heart.

Another point in favour of the play is that it is one of the most visually spectacular comedies of the period. When its central trick is played out, for instance, it would have presented an amusing scene, as there is every likelihood that a live donkey would have been used in the performance. Other contemporary forms of play certainly incorporated live animals into their staging. The most famous of these is the annual pageant accompanying the *Fête de l'âne* (Feast of the Ass) in northern

---

[18] 'Schuyfman berust de geheele handeling op het streven van een paar landlopers, om aan een goed maal eten te komen': Jan ten Brink, *Geschiedenis der Nederlandsche letterkunde* (Amsterdam, 1897), 241.

[19] 'Om te gelooven dat ons nageslachtthe literary work of this time will set as high as one part of the audience it does. het letterkundig werk van dezen tijd even hoog zal stellen als een deel van het publiek het nu doet': G. Kalff, 'Bijlage I. Speech by the moderator. Toespraak van den voorzitter', *Handelingen en mededeelingen van de Maatschappij der Nederlandsche letterkunde* (1921), 7–18 (14).

[20] Herman Pleij, *Dreaming of Cockaigne*, trans. Diane Webb (New York, 2001), 117.

[21] On this point, see also Femke Kramer, *Mooi vies, knap lelijk: grotesk realisme in rederijkerskluchten* (Hilversum, 2009), 161–2.

France. E. K. Chambers summarises this peculiar custom as follows: 'A pretty girl, with a child in her arms, was set upon an ass, to represent the Flight into Egypt. There was a procession from the cathedral to the church of St Stephen . . . . A solemn mass was sung, in which *Introit*, *Kyrie*, *Gloria* and *Credo* ended with a bray.'[22] At the very least, the inclusion of an actual donkey in this ritual drama shows how easily such an animal could be used in the staging of *The Beggar*. The inclusion of a live animal, perhaps mounted with the straw figure of a dead woman, would be a simple way to add an arresting visual element to the performance of this farce. In other words, the play fully exploits the visual as well as auditory aspect of dramatic performance.

---

[22] E. K. Chambers, *The Medieval Stage*, 2 vols. (Oxford, 1903), 1: 286.

Hier Begint Een Esbatement Vande Schuyfman

De parsonages sijn dese
SCHUYFMAN, een fiel.
SLOEF, oock een fiel.
EEN DOVE VROUW.
DE SONE VANT LIJCKHUIJS.
EEN PASTOOR.

SCHUYFFMAN:	Och noijt meerder honger.
SLOEFF:	Och noijt meerder dorst.
SCHUYFFMAN:	Ghans lijff, ick slockte wel een olifants longere,
SLOEFF:	En ick adt wel van een paerde een worst.
SCHUYFFMAN:	Och die nu hadt een huijssbacken broot geschorst,
	Twaer recht om onsen mont mee te maecken.
SLOEFF:	Ghans lijff, mijn lippen beginnen te spaecken
	Van dorst; noijt duijpen so qualijck gestelt.
SCHUYFFMAN:	Wij hebben geen gelove.
SLOEFF:	Broot noch gelt.
	Tis al verscheurt, rock en caproen,
SCHUYFFMAN:	Wij en hebben gheen pluijsteringhe.
SLOEFF:	Coussen noch schoen.
	Gans oogen, tmach ons wel verdrieten.
SCHUYFFMAN:	Igo sulck heerschap als ter zee mach vlieten!
	Maer wij sijnder nu aff; ick ben lichter dan een vinck,
	Och, dat riemen, dat riemen!
SLOEFF:	Och ogen, dats al te vuijlen dinck!
	En dien stockvis te eeten, het docht mijn schande!
	Ick come niet meer te water!
SCHUYFFMAN:	Tjan, ick blijff oock liever te lande.
	Verbernen moet mast, schip, seijl en schuijt!
SLOEFF:	En alst dan qualijck gaet, veijn?
SCHUYFFMAN:	So machmen achter niet vuijt,
	Men moet tsolaes vanden crabben genieten.
SLOEFF:	Ja wadt gaen wij maecken?
SCHUYFFMAN:	Hertchiers worden; wij willen schieten,
	Want wij moeten onsen honger blusschen.
SLOEFF:	Wadt dingen? Rotganssen?
SCHUYFFMAN:	Neen, huijsmusschen.
	Wij sellent wel maecken, meuchdij swijgen.
SLOEFF:	Ke, wij sellen nergens niet een leur crijgen.
SCHUYFFMAN:	Tvolck sal seggen, ducht ick, bij gans doot . . .

Line numbers in margin: 5, 10, 15, 20, 25

---

* The Dutch text is taken from F. A. Stoett, *Drie kluchten uit de zestiende eeuw* (Zutphen, 1932), 1–27.

Here begins the Farce of the Beggar

The characters are these:[1]
BEGGAR, a rogue
TRAMP, also a rogue
A DEAF WOMAN
THE SON AT THE MORTUARY
A PRIEST

BEGGAR:	Oh, never was there greater hunger.
TRAMP:	Oh, never was there greater thirst.
BEGGAR:	God's body, I could gulp down an elephant's lungs.
TRAMP:	And I could eat a horse stuffed in a sausage.
BEGGAR:	Oh, that he now had a home-baked bread in his pocket, 5
	It would be perfectly suited for our mouths.
TRAMP:	God's body, my lips begin to split
	From thirst; never were wretches so evilly abused.
BEGGAR:	We have no hope –
TRAMP:	Bread nor money.
	It is all in shreds, like our shirts and caps. 10
BEGGAR:	We have no clothing –
TRAMP:	Socks nor shoes.
	God's eyes, it makes us most miserable.
BEGGAR:	God, that master the sea can get lost!
	But we are off now towards him; I am lighter than a finch,
	Oh, that rowing, that rowing!
TRAMP:	Oh God's eyes, it is too foul a thing! 15
	And eating that stockfish, it does me shame!
	Never again will I go to the water!
BEGGAR:	Saint John, I also prefer to live on land.
	Mast, ship, sail and barge should burn!
TRAMP:	And what if all goes badly, fellow?
BEGGAR:	We should not think in that way,
	We must find solace in scrabbling. 20
TRAMP:	Yes, what are we going to do?
BEGGAR:	We become archers; we will shoot,
	Since we must douse our hunger.
TRAMP:	For what sort of things? Wild geese?
BEGGAR:	No, house sparrows.[2]
	We will succeed, as long as you remain silent.
TRAMP:	Christ, we will not catch a crumb anywhere. 25
BEGGAR:	People will say, I guess, by God's death –

---

[1] A sixth character, the daughter of the dead woman, is not listed here, in spite of the prominent role she plays in the action.

[2] That is, the characters intend to commit a burglary, hunting their 'quarry' inside a house.

131

SLOEFF:	Wadt sellen sij seggen?
SCHUYFFMAN:	Wech stercke boven, verdient u broot!
.	Ons en sal nergens deucht geschien.
SLOEFF:	Wij, wij sellen bidden om twee arme schiplien,
	Wiens schip en scheer op de zee versoncken, 30
	En seggen, dat het altemael verdroncken.
	Dus swijcht! wij sullense wel verdoven.
SCHUYFFMAN:	Verdroncken? dat en soudense niet geloven,
	Het sou aen ons gemerckt seer schier sijn.
SLOEFF:	Ja wel, dan?
SCHUYFFMAN:	Maer tsou juijst quaet bier sijn. 35
	Tvolck ging ons alomme met steenen an.
	Wij moeten ijet anders vinden.
SLOEFF:	So sullen wij ontlenen dan
	En worden ergens petere, opdat wijt beseffen willen,
	Van een borse met gelde.
SCHUYFFMAN:	Hoe? soudijsse dan heffen willen?
	So werden wij oock verheven als van grooter waerden. 40
SLOEFF:	Hoe soo?
SCHUYFFMAN:	Tusschen hemel en aerden.
	Certeijn, wij blevender met die proije.
SLOEFF:	Hou veijn! ick vind en sie ginder een schaepskoije.
SCHUYFFMAN:	Een schaepskoije? daer maeckt ghij mij mede confuijs.
	Besietet wel, tis een dorphuijs. 45
	Daer mosten wij na den cost gaen sien.
	Wie sal ons in dese lange heij bespien?
	Mijn strotgadt verworgt van honger, dats claer.
	Ou! seg, ou
EEN DOVE VROU:	Godt weet, dats waer,
	De groesse was wel te tije afgesmeten. 50
SLOEFF:	Och rebben, her casenbroot, laet ons eten!
	Wij en connen van honger niet gespreecken!
	Teten? T'eten, hou seck!
VROU:	Dat wordt te sincxen elff weecken,
	Dat mijn man de papegaij aff schoot.
SCHUYFFMAN:	Wadt, dit wijff raest. Her een huijsbacken broot! 55
	T'eten! eten in onsen ijdelen sack!
VROU:	Hoe? wanneer? doemen die torven stack,
	Doemen die heij meijde, die noch op d'aerde leijt

TRAMP:	What will they say?
BEGGAR:	Away, rotten liars, earn your bread!
	Virtue will not shine on us.
TRAMP:	We, we will plead as two poor sailors,
	Whose ship and gear was sunk into the sea, 30
	And say that it is all drowned.
	So shut up! We will dupe them well.
BEGGAR:	Drowned? They would not believe that,
	It would have marked us very clearly.
TRAMP:	So, what then?
BEGGAR:	But it should be bad beer for us. 35
	People will go after us with stones,
	We must find something else.
TRAMP:	So we will go thieving, then.
	And become godfathers, before we know it,
	To a purse filled with money.
BEGGAR:	How should we raise that?
	We will also be raised, as though we are of greater worth. 40
TRAMP:	How so?
BEGGAR:	Between heaven and earth.[3]
	Surely if we continue we become prey.
TRAMP:	Hold your tongue! I think I see there a sheepfold.
BEGGAR:	A sheepfold? There you make me confused.
	Look sharp, it is a townhouse. 45
	We might go there to look for some grub.
	Who will see us in these tall bushes?
	My gizzard is choked with hunger, that is clear.
	Hey, I say, hey!
A DEAF WOMAN:	God knows, that is true.
	The pasture was closed long before time.[4] 50
BEGGAR:	Oh, God's ribs, give us bread and cheese, let us eat!
	We cannot speak for hunger!
	Let us eat? Let us eat, for pity's sake!
WOMAN:	It will be eleven weeks at Whitsun
	Since my husband shot the parrot.[5]
BEGGAR:	Why, this woman is mad. Give her home-baked bread! 55
	Let us eat! Put food in our idle sack!
WOMAN:	How? When? When they stacked the clods,
	After they mowed the hay, that still lay on the ground.

---

[3] That is, they will be 'raised' on the gallows.

[4] On the traditional character of the *weduwe*, see Ariadne Schmidt, 'Van de lusten geproefd. Wellust in het weduwebeeld in de vroegmoderne periode. Twee eeuwenoude weduwebeelden', *Jaarboek voor vrouwengeschiedenis* 20 (2000), 65–83.

[5] The shooting-guilds founded in various cities of the medieval Low Countries held annual contests to name a local 'king of the bowmen'. Traditionally, the target in such events would be a *papegaij* (popinjay), which could either be an actual bird, or a carved wooden figure.

SLOEFF:	Ick hoorde mijn dagen noijt sotter bescheijt.
	Houtse coutende, ick sal daer binnen verseijsen 60
	En, vind ick ijet, wij sullen tsamen preijsen.
SCHUYFFMAN:	Wij moeten eeten, dus sijt vast inde weere.
	En hebdij geen botermelck?
VROUWE:	Mijnen man trouden ick wel eere
	Int jaer voor d'oorloch van loreijne.
	Godt heb sijn lieve siel . . .
SCHUYFFMAN:	Ick wou, dat ghij inden vijver saet oft inde fonteijnne 65
	Oft aen een watermolen recht after dwiel.
SLOEFF :	Tuert, baes, tuert!
SCHUYFFMAN:	Parijst u, fiel!
	Al en hoort sij niet nobis haeren mots sou loncken.
SLOEFF:	En hebdij niet, goeij vrou, dat wij eens droncken?
	Onssen dorst en honker wort lancks so grover. 70
SCHUYFFMAN:	En hebdij geen speck?
VROU:	Wadt! ginder over
	Daer heb ick huijden een broot verworven,
	Want de vrouwe vanden huijsse is daer gestorven.
	Godt heb haer siele in allen doen!
	Men doet daer veel deuchden.
SLOEFF:	Ghans lijff! daer moeten wij henen spoen. 75
	Noijt beter tijdinge, siet, bij gants doot.
SCHUYFFMAN:	Wij crijgen elck wel noch een broot,
	Daer sellen wij ons honger mee slissen.
SLOEFF:	Loopt seer! wij en mogen daer niet missen,
	Int lijckhuijs daer geeftmen witten hoeff. 80
	Loopt darwaerts Schuijffman!
SCHUYFFMAN:	Ou, haest u, Sloeff!
	Want dees mare heeft niet, t'isser al ebbe,
	Maer int lijckhuijs ist al volle crebbe.
VROU:	Mij is leet, dat ick niet noch eenen tant en hebbe,
	Ick sou noch houwen, al moet ick nu swijgen. 85
	Ick sou noch eenen jongen knispaert crijgen,
	Al sout mijn corten mijnen pels terstont.
	Mij smelt noch wel boter in mijnen mont.
	Al schijn ick out, ick en heb maer negenwerff thien.
	Ick plach so gaeren den dans te sien 90
	En noch doe, al word ick verstooten,
	Om dat ick niet na en can getrooten.
	Maer nietemin ick mocht noch wel verfroijen.
	Adieu! ick wil mijnen pels gaen vloijen.
	Inne.

TRAMP:	I never heard more foolish prattle in all my days.
	Keep her talking, I will look inside there 60
	And, if I find anything, we will celebrate together.
BEGGAR:	We must eat: therefore, get yourself in there.
	Have you no buttermilk?
WOMAN:	I married my husband considerably earlier
	In the year before the war with Lorraine.[6]
	May God have his dear soul . . .
BEGGAR:	I wish you were set in a pond or in a fountain 65
	Or in a water mill right under the wheel.
TRAMP:	Say, boss, say!
BEGGAR:	Hush yourself, rogue!
	Although she does not hear, you need not shout so loud.
TRAMP:	And have you not, good woman, something we might drink?
	Our thirst and hunger mount up so greatly. 70
BEGGAR:	Have you no bacon?
WOMAN:	What? Over there,
	I have taken a loaf there today,
	For the woman of that house is dead.
	May God keep her soul in all circumstances!
	Men say she was very virtuous.
TRAMP:	God's body! We must go there quickly. 75
	We never had better tidings, by God's death.
BEGGAR:	We will each snatch up a loaf.
	There we will part with our hunger.
TRAMP:	Step lively! We will not fail there,
	In the mortuary they give you white bread for alms. 80
	Run over there, Beggar!
BEGGAR:	O, hurry yourself, Tramp!
	For this nightmare has nothing, it is all empty,
	But in the mortuary all is packed full.
WOMAN:	It grieves me that I do not have even one tooth,
	I wish I had one, even if I must fall silent now. 85
	I wish to catch hold of a young reveller
	Even if it immediately shortens my life.
	Butter still melts well in my mouth.
	Though I look old, I only have nine years times ten.
	I used to head out to see the dance, 90
	And do so still, although I am excluded,
	Because I can no longer keep the pace.
	But nonetheless I might well frolic now.
	Adieu! I will go and delouse my fur.
	She goes indoors

---

[6] Probably refers to the Burgundian war of 1474–7, fought between Charles the Bold and Louis XI of France, for possession of the territories of Alsace and Lorraine. Since the play dates from 1504 or slightly earlier, this is clearly a joke directed at the woman's age.

DE SONE VANT LIJCHUIJS: Och, och, de profundis!

DOCHTER: Och jae, voor alle doijen!   95
Godt wil haerder sielen ontfermen!
Eylaes! eylaes!

SONE: Wij en crijchgense niet weer, ten baet geen kermen.
Sij heeft betaelt, dat wij schuldich sijn.
Maer laet ons met haeste gaen sorchvuldich sijn,
Datse gekist waere en morgen begraven,   100
Ende noch doen backen, dat wij om goodswillen gaven
Voor haer siele ten eersten als vooren.
Godt salt al versien.

DOCHTER: Och, wij hebbense veel te vroech verlooren!
Och moertgen, moertgen, ay mij eijlaes!
Ghij waert ons so vrindelijck.

SONE: Wat baetet immers gebaert! tis al dwaes!   105
Sij most eens sterven, dus maeckt goeijen moet.
Hebben wij haer verlooren, so hebben wij tgoet.
En sij hadt veel gelts; elcks dies vroet is.
Dats nu al onse.

DOCHTER: Dats waer, hoet is,
Te bedt dat ick den rou verduere.   110
Maer het deert mij nochtans.

SONE: Waij, dats de natuere!
Dus en doet u selven niet meer gequels.
Eest niet beter een sack vol gelts
Dan een out wijff, hier sittende in d'asschen,
Diemen heffen en leggen moet, wasschen en plasschen,   115
Die niet doet dan crochgen, steenen en bulssen,
Knuetteren en schuddebollen, niessen en hulssen?
T'is quaet gequelt te sijn met ouwe vrouwen,

DOCHTER: Sij heeft lang nu gegaen.

SONE: Ick hoop, sij sal sijn behouwen.
Dus moeten wij gaen ons vrienden ontbieden   120
Ende oock wel vreemde lieden
Tijlijck, tegen morgen, voor alle saecken,
Om duytvaert te doen.

DOCHTER: Ja, en wij moeten oock lijck erreten maecken
En bereijen die koecken wel, want, t'is claer,
t' Moeter al blijven eetene.

SONE: Trouwen, dat is waer,   125
Al macht wadt costen, dats de manier.
T'en sal niet meer te doen sijn.

DOCHTER: Gaet en versiet ons van bier,
En doet een ham en tvleesch te vier.

THE SON AT THE MORTUARY: Oh, oh, de profundis![7]

DAUGHTER: Oh woe, for all the dead!   95
May God have mercy on their souls!
Alas! Alas!

SON: We do not get them back, it is better not to cry.
She has paid off what we owe,
But let us go with haste and arrange things
So that she is boxed up and buried in the morning,   100
Let us pay for a mass, that we give for God's sake,
In order to put her soul among the first and foremost.
God works all for good.

DAUGHTER: Oh, we have lost her much too early!
Oh mother, mother, ay me, alas!
You were so kind to us.

SON: What good is acting like this? It is all futile!   105
She had to die some time, so make yourself cheerful.
We have lost her, but we have also profited.
She had much money, like all that are wise,
That is all ours now.

DAUGHTER: That is true and how it is,
Mourning will not improve what I endure.   110
But it grieves me nevertheless.

SON: Well, that is nature!
Therefore do yourself no more torments.
Is not a sack full of money better
Than an old woman, sitting at the hearth,
That one must carry and set down, wash and help to piss,   115
Who does nothing but cough, moan and belch,
Complain and nod off, sneeze and retch?
It is an evil torment to live with old women.

DAUGHTER: She had lived for a long time.

SON: I hope her soul is saved.
Well, we must give our friends notice   120
And also many other people
Promptly, in the morning, before anything else,
To perform the obsequies.

DAUGHTER: Yes, and we must also make the funeral feast,
And bake bread, because, it is true,
Many may stay to eat.

SON: Indeed, that is true.   125
Although it may cost us, that is the custom.
We will not do anything more.

DAUGHTER: Go and buy us some beer,
And set a ham and meat on the fire.

---

[7] Penitential prayer used in the Office of the Dead. From Psalm 130.1: 'de profundis clamavi ad te Domine' ('Out of the depths I have cried to thee, O Lord').

	Des eens doot is dickwils des anders vrame.	
SONE:	Nu, men moetse gaen kisten.	
DOCHTER:	Och ja, oft sij weder quame.	130

So verlooren wij tgelt en haer kateijlen.
Men moet oock lijckbroot backen.

SONE: Dats waer, om deijlen.
Dlijck moet wech in d'aerde metten mollen zeijlen
Morgen vroech; wat sout hier maecken?

DOCHTER: Wij moeten te nacht immers waecken   135
Dlijck! ick come te nacht niet op pluijmen,
Dat seg ick u.

SONE: Tis de costuijmme.
Lieten wijt, schande soude in ons krielen.
Dus gaen wij bidden voor alien sielen.

Inne.

SLOEFF:	Loopt, Lepaert, loopt!	
SCHUIJFFMAN:	Hou, schuijm der fielen!	140

Mijn strotgadt verhangt van honger puere.

SLOEFF: Ick gaff u vlus een stuck broots.

SCHUIJFFMAN: Dats over lang duere.
Ick schocktte noch een paer baerssen wel ter kuere,
Al act ick een vercken, ten sou mij niet versaen.

SLOEFF: En oft ghij al mocht, wie sout u braen?   145
Ghij schocktet, peijs ick, wel een vlaemsche kase.

SCHUIJFFMAN: En ghij sijt gepurgeert als een ijdel blase.
Ghij schocktet wel op een halven osse
En een vierendel biers.

SLOEFF: Ick en sou, maer had ick den beecker met den rosse,
Ick souwen eens cussen sonder veel kouts.   150
T is tonsent al ebbe.

SCHUIJFFMAN: So soudij wel thien hoorenen mouts
Drincken teenen sitten sonder veel gesnaters,
Want ghij sijt schoontooch.

SLOEFF: Ghij seijlt ook qualijck met luttel waters,
Dat soud ick met u selven wel pijnen te tuijgen.

SCHUIJFFMAN: Die schiplien plegen gaern te suijgen.   155

SLOEFF: Alsse int diepste sijn, so ist al geluck en heijl.
Daert vuijt schaij gaet, ist al keij, veijl.

SCHUIJFFMAN: Dan begietmen tseijl.
Daer pleech ick gaern mijn ancker te sincken.

SLOEFF: Wa, ghij wint alomme den tap met drincken
Tot allen karmissen aen elcken cant,   160

	The death of one is often the other's gain.	
SON:	Now, one must box her up.	
DAUGHTER:	Oh yes, if she came back,	130
	Then we'd lose the money and her chattels.	
	We must also bake corpse-bread.[8]	
SON:	That is true, for handing out.	
	The corpse must go into the earth to sail with the moles	
	Early in the morning; what would it do here?	
DAUGHTER:	We must be sure to stay awake tonight.	135
	The corpse! Tonight I will not go to bed,	
	I tell you that.	
SON:	That is the tradition.	
	If we neglected this, shame should rise up in us.	
	Thus we go to pray for all souls.	

They go inside.

TRAMP:	Go, scoundrel, go![9]	
BEGGAR:	Hold off, scum of rascals!	140
	My throat is choked with pure hunger.	
TRAMP:	I just gave you a piece of bread.	
BEGGAR:	That happened long ago.	
	I should swallow a pair of perch as a good cure,	
	Even if I ate a porker, it would not content me.	
TRAMP:	And who would blame you, unless you had already eaten?	145
	You could swallow a Flemish cheese, I think.	
BEGGAR:	And you look as drained as an empty bladder,	
	You could swallow up half an ox	
	And a quarter of a beer-keg.	
TRAMP:	I should do so; if had I a beaker full of ale,	
	I would give it a kiss without much prattle.	150
	It is all gone, quick-smart.	
BEGGAR:	And you could drink ten horns of malt	
	In one sitting without much chattering,	
	For you are one clean sot.	
TRAMP:	You also sail poorly on shallow waters,	
	But this should make you and me truly brace the rigging.	
BEGGAR:	Sailors yearn to suck up waters.	155
TRAMP:	When the sea is deepest, then comes fortune and health,	
	Where it goes well, all is rejoicing, all is on hand.	
BEGGAR:	Then let us dampen the sail.	
	I yearn to sink my anchor there in that water.	
TRAMP:	Why, you always win first prize for drinking,	
	At every feast, in every way,	160

[8] *Lijckbroot* or *lijkbrood* (corpse-bread) was the Dutch and Flemish equivalent of Northern English arval bread, a form of spiced loaf distributed to the mourners at a funeral.
[9] We follow here Mak's suggestion for *lepaert*, 'deugniet, schurk, fielt' ('rascal, rogue, scoundrel'): J. J. Mak, *Rhetoricaal glossarium* (Assen, 1959), 238.

	Ghij sijt een biervliege.	
SCHUIJFFMAN:	Her, her, geeft mijn de hant,	
	Want ghij sijt gaeren bijden watere.	
SLOEFF:	En ghij opt lant.	
SCHUIJFFMAN:	Dats waer, daer de visschen stijgen.	
SLOEFF:	Nu fiel, al clappende sullen wij niet crijgen.	
	Wij mosten naer ons proije gaen spien.	165
	Waer is dlijckhuijs?	
SCHUIJFFMAN:	Ick hebt gesien.	
	Daer willen wij met haesten heen gaen trooten.	
SLOEFF:	Gans bloet, t'isser noch al gesloten.	
	Wie waert toch, die hier vreucht in schiepe?	
	En woonter niemant, peijnsick?	
SCHUIJFFMAN:	Sij hebben sorge, oft lijck ontliepe.	170
	Wij willen gaen bidden, als diet behoeven.	
	Waer op sullen wij bidden?	
SLOEFF:	Maer, op twee stercke boeven.	
	So seggen wij die waerheijt sonder jock.	
	Wij sullen wadt crijgen.	
SCHUIJFFMAN:	Dats waer, een grooten stock	
	Op ons ribben; maer dat willen wij vlien.	175
	Wij willen bidden op twee schamele schiplien	
	En seggen hen so, so sullen wijse best verdoven,	
	Dattet al verdroncken is.	
SLOEFF:	Ja, ja, dats best, dat sullense best geloven,	
	Want wij verdroncken eens de schoenen uijt onse hyelen.	
SCHUIJFFMAN:	Och, goeij vrienden, geeft wadt voor alle sielen:	180
	Twee arme schiplien, diet al gelaten hebben,	
	Schip en scherve, doen de zee ginck ebben,	
	Daer sij om haering souden vaeren,	
SLOEFF:	Ja den biertap . . .	
SCHUIJFFMAN:	Wa, swijcht! godt geeff u veel droever jaeren!	
	Off bidt selve, godt moet u schinden!	185
SLOEFF:	Och, geeff wadt, eedel hertelijcke vrinden!	
	(dat u nimmermeer en moet deucht geschien)	
	Wij hebbent toch al verloren.	
SCHUIJFFMAN:	So ghij moocht sien.	
SLOEFF:	En doet u charitate.	
SCHUIJFFMAN:	Och ja ghij, eerbaer lien.	
SLOEFF:	(Dat geluck en gesontheijt moet van u vlien!)	190
	Helpt toch ons arme capuijnen ter noot.	
DOCHTER:	Hout, waer sijde? daer is een broot!	
	Bidt voor de ziele van onse moedere.	
SCHUIJFFMAN:	Wadt, waa, niet dan broot?	
SLOEFF:	Wa vleijsch toe goedere!	
	Dat u allen u tanden moeten loteren!	195
SCHUIJFFMAN:	Gheeft ons een thienschen kaese.	

140

	You are a beer-fly.	
BEGGAR:	Hear, hear, give me a hand,	
	For you also yearn to be at the water.	
TRAMP:	And you on land.	
BEGGAR:	That is true: there the fish are dry.	
TRAMP:	Now rogue, with all this chatter we will not catch a thing.	
	We must go and spy near our prey.	165
	Where is the mortuary?	
BEGGAR:	I have seen it.	
	We will head over there, moving with haste.	
TRAMP:	God's blood, it is already shut now.	
	Who was it, who here has found joy?	
	Nobody lives inside, I think.	
BEGGAR:	They worry that the corpse will leap out.	170
	We will go and pray, like those it befits.	
	Who will we pray as?	
TRAMP:	Well, as two mighty crooks,	
	Then we tell the truth without a lie.	
	We will catch something.	
BEGGAR:	That is true, a great stick	
	On our ribs; but we want to avoid that.	175
	We will pray as two poor sailors	
	And tell them, we will make them believe,	
	That all we have is sunk.	
TRAMP:	Yes, yes, that is best, they will believe that	
	For we let the heels fall from our shoes once.	
BEGGAR:	Oh, dear friends, give something for all souls,	180
	Two penniless sailors, who have lost all,	
	Ship and cargo, when the sea turned ugly,	
	While they were cruising for herring.	
TRAMP:	Yes, at a beer-tap ...	
BEGGAR:	Why, silence! God give you many darker years!	
	Or pray for yourself, God will favour you!	185
TRAMP:	Oh, give something, noble goodhearted friends!	
	(So that virtue may never favour you again)	
	We have lost all.	
BEGGAR:	As you may see.	
TRAMP:	And perform your charity.	
BEGGAR:	Oh yes, do, honest people.	
TRAMP	(So that fortune and health may flee from you!)	190
	Help us poor wretches in need.	
DAUGHTER:	Hold on, where are you? There is a loaf.	
	Pray for the soul of our mother.	
BEGGAR:	What, what, nothing but bread?	
TRAMP:	Put it with meat!	
	May all your teeth come loose for this!	195
BEGGAR:	Give us a Tienen cheese.	

141

SLOEFF:	Ja, oft een cop botere,
	Ja, oft een stuck verckenvleijs, hoort ons bediet.
DOCHTER:	Godt help u, men geeft anders niet.
	Veel gevens staet tot grooten berespe.
	Dus bidt voor de ziele.
SLOEFF:	Wij sellen, geeft ons dan een hespe, 200
	Want hierme maecken wij lepen chiere.
SCHUIJFFMAN:	Och, geeft ons toch een cruijck met biere,
	Wij jagense met twee teugen, dats claer,
	Door onse strotgadt.
SONE:	Wie kijfter, suster, wadts daer, wadts daer?
	Compt in huijs, wil u versnellen! 205
	Wat isser gaens?
DOCHTER:	Tsijn twee gesellen,
	Die willen een hespe hebben hier veure
	Om godswillen.
SONE:	Godt help u, godt help u, sluijt toe de deure!
	Tsijn ruijters, sij steecken vol van liste.
	T is al gegeven.
SLOEFF:	Ick wilde gij beyd bijt lijck laecht inde kiste. 210
	Wij hebben ons hebbinge, gaen wij vrij fluijten.
SCHUIJFFMAN:	Ick wou wijsse enichsins mochten beguijten.
	Godt sal u oock so vuijt sijn hemelrijck sluijten,
	So ghij ons arme menschen doet, siet, bij gans roock!
SLOEFF:	Dat sal hij ons mee.
SCHUIJFFMAN:	Dat schadt ick oock. 215
	Comen wijder niet, so comen wijder nalijck.
SLOEFF:	Igo, alsmen derwaerts reijst, so gater qualijck.
	Tis veel te hooge; al best hier neer.
	Die daer gaet, fiel …
SCHUIJFFMAN:	Die en compt niet weer,
	Gelijckmen doet van Ceulen oft van Spiers. 220
SLOEFF:	Ick had liever te sijn voor een vadt biers,
	Daer noijt tap en was vuijt getrocken.
SCHUIJFFMAN:	Ghij segt waer, fiel.
SLOEFF:	Och dermen, ick sou so meesterlijck schocken:
	Ik ate een claverbladt metter lelijen
	Van labaijs broot.
SCHUIJFFMAN:	Wij zullen niet crijgen, bij gans martelijen, 225

TRAMP: Yes, or a cup of butter,
Yes, or a piece of swine-flesh, hear our plea.

DAUGHTER: God help you, we will give nothing further.
Giving too much leads to great shame
So pray for her soul.

TRAMP: We will, and then give us a ham,   200
Because we will help to make cheer.

BEGGAR: Oh, give us a pitcher of beer,
And we will chase it in two gulps, that is clear,
Down our gullets.

SON: Who speaks, sister, who is there, who is there?
Come into the house, will you be quick!   205
What is going on?

DAUGHTER: There are two companions,
They want to have a ham out here
For God's will.

SON: God help you, God help you, shut the door!
They are rogues, they are stuffed full of tricks.
All is lost.

TRAMP: I wish you were both by the corpse in the coffin.   210
Once we have our desire, we will head off wandering.

BEGGAR: I wish that we might trick them somewhat.
For this God will shut His kingdom to you,
Just as you did to us poor men, by God's sweat!

TRAMP: In this He will agree with us.

BEGGAR: I believe that too.   215
If we do not take everything, we will take almost everything.

TRAMP: God, if you travel that way, you are gone for ever.
It is much too high; all is for the best down here.
He that goes there, rogue . . .

BEGGAR: He will return no more,
It is not like going to Cologne or Spier.   220

TRAMP: I would rather be in front of a beer-keg,
Where the spigot was never turned off.

BEGGAR: You speak true, rogue.

TRAMP: Oh wretches, I would so expertly devour:
I would give a cloverleaf and lilies[10]
For good bread.

BEGGAR: We will catch nothing, by God's torments,   225

---

[10] The phrase 'claverbladt metter lelijen' suggests a coin stamped with lilies and clover. This seems to be a fanciful conflation of the florin, traditionally stamped with the *fleur de lis* of Florence, and the albus minted at Trier, which depicted a clover wreath around the circumference of the coin. A similar coin is also mentioned in the context of feasting in Daniël Heinsius's 'Lofsanck van Bacchus' (1616). Here it is described by a reveller 'des avonts voor de Vasten' ('in the evening before Lent') as 'het meeste dat ick wensch' ('the most that I wish for'): Daniël Heinsius, *Nederduytsche poemata*: *facsimile-uitgave van eerste druk 1616* (Bern, 1983), 20.

	Al meugen wij lange hier staen haecken.	
SLOEFF:	De deure is gesloten.	
SCHUIJFFMAN:	Wadt mogen sij maecken?	
	Gaet, betuertet heijmelijck neffens geen codt wadt.	
SLOEFF:	Hier is geen splete.	
SCHUIJFFMAN:	Ick sie deur tslotgadt.	
	Compt, kijckt, ghij saecht u dagen noijt sulck abuijs.	230
	Daer staet een baere te midden int huijs.	
SLOEFF:	Benedictije! dits immers een vuijl bedrijff!	
	Gans longeren, ick souwer mij aff vereenen.	
SCHUIJFFMAN:	En ick en sie daer niemant, noch man noch wijff.	
	Gans longeren! ick souwer mij oock aff verenen.	235
SLOEFF:	Sij sijn beij doot, sou ick menen,	
	So crijgen wij al ons hertsen gebruijcken.	
	T'is best, dat wij een luttel duijcken	
	En besien, hoet keeren sal eer een ure.	
SCHUIJFFMAN:	Waer mochten wij ons bergen?	
SLOEFF:	Achter dees schuere.	240
	Wij crijgen te botten noch sonder dralen.	
	Duijckt! twijff mocht ons te muijsemcel malen.	
DOCHTER:	Die doot is, men canse niet weer halen.	
	Dus wil ick de wijssheijt gaen besorgen	
	Aen onssen prochiaen tegen morgen,	245
	Dat duijtvaert eerlijcke werde volbracht.	
	Hij compt hier gaende, ick heb recht gewacht.	
	Ick wilt hen seggen, al mach ick mij schamen.	
	Heer, goeijen avont!	
PASTOOR:	Et in secula seculorum amen!	
	Belieft u ijet, ick ben voor cleijn en groot.	250
	Wadts u begeren?	
DOCHTER:	Och, mijn moertgen is doot!	
	Godt behoedse vanden helssche gecriele!	
PASTOOR:	Wachermen isse doot? godt heb haer ziele!	
	Sijt te vreden, wij moeten al eens sterven,	
	Soude wij d'euwige crone verwerven.	255
	Maer het deert mij met allen seere.	
	Wanneer sterff sij?	
DOCHTER:	Huijden morgen, heere,	
	Recht als de coster dwijwater droech.	

	If we stand babbling here for much longer.	
TRAMP:	The door is shut.	
BEGGAR:	What is it they are doing?	
	Go, furtively observe what occurs within the house.	
TRAMP:	There is no hole.	
BEGGAR:	I can see through the keyhole.	
	Come, look, you never saw such strangeness in all your days.	230
	There stands a bier in the middle of the house.	
TRAMP:	Benedicite![11] this is indeed a vile business!	
	God's lungs, I really fear for myself.	
BEGGAR:	And I see no-one there, neither man nor woman.	
	God's lungs! I really fear for myself as well.	235
TRAMP:	They are both dead, as I think.	
	So we collect all that our hearts desire.	
	It is best that we wait a little	
	And see how it will turn out for an hour.	
BEGGAR:	Where might we hide ourselves?	
TRAMP:	Behind this shack.	240
	We will be caught without delay.	
	Duck! The woman may grind us to mouse-flour.	
DAUGHTER:	You cannot summon back one that has died.	
	Therefore I will go to pass on the information	
	To our parson this morning,	245
	So that the funeral will be properly performed.	
	Here he comes now: I was right to wait.	
	I will tell him, although I may shame myself.	
	Sir, good evening!	
PRIEST:	Et in secula seculorum, amen![12]	
	If it pleases you, I am here for both small and great.	250
	What is it you seek?	
DAUGHTER:	Oh, my mother is dead!	
	God preserve her from hellish torments!	
PRIEST:	Alas, is she dead? May God have her soul!	
	Be in peace, we must all die eventually,	
	So that we can earn the eternal crown.	255
	But it pains me sorely nonetheless.	
	When did she die?	
DAUGHTER:	This morning, sir,	
	Just as the sexton drew the holy water.	

[11] 'Bless me', the opening petition of the Canticle of the Three Young Men, based on Daniel 3.57–88. This is the first of many allusions in the play to this particular canticle, which is traditionally recited at lauds on Sundays.

[12] 'And to the ages of ages, amen'. The concluding line of the *Gloria Patri* or *Doxologia Minor*, a prayer formula incorporated into the Magnificat and the Ordinary of the Mass, and often used to conclude medieval sermons. Many of the Priest's utterances consist of scraps parroted from liturgical sources.

PASTOOR:	Wanneer wildijse begraven?
DOCHTER:	Maer morgen vroech.
	Wij willense desen nacht gaen waecken. 260
PASTOOR:	Wel, ick sal gaen het graff doen maecken
	Van onsen coster; tsal al bereet wesen
	Tegen morgen.
DOCHTER:	Wel, hout daer heere, wilt misse requiem lesen.
	Daer sijn thien stuijvers een voor al,
	En voor de siele wilt bidden.
PASTOOR:	Requiescant in pace! wel, wel, ick sal. 265
	Ick wil al doen wat ick vermach.
	Gans longeren, quam dit alden dach!
	Maer neent, dus gae ick na d' oude zee
	Vigilie lesen, parce michi domine.

Inne.

SCHUIJFFMAN:	Gaet henen noch eens bekijcken!
SLOEFF:	So compt dan mee! 270
	Ick weet niet, watter ick vuijt mach vermoeijen.
SCHUIJFFMAN:	Ick en hoorder niemant spreecken noch loeijen.
	Ick moet immers kijcken, watse bedrijven.
SLOEFF:	Ick verseeker u, datse niet en kijven.
	Men salsse opt hooren niet betrapen, 275
	Sij dragent wel eens.
SCHUIJFFMAN:	Wa, sij leggen en slapen.
	Sij hebben te ruste geleijt hen hoot.
SLOEFF:	Liggense en slapen?
SCHUIJFFMAN:	Jase, bij gans doot,
	Nevent lijck; compt, haest u en besiet
	Door geen cleijn spleetgen.
SLOEFF:	Tis waer, en men wecktense niet, 280
	Al hieltmen hen handen en benen aff.
	Hoortse doch roncken!
SCHUIJFFMAN:	Gelijck de joden neven tgraff,

146

PRIEST:	When should she be buried?
DAUGHTER:	Early tomorrow morning.
	We want to hold a vigil for her this night. 260
PRIEST:	Well, I will go and have the grave made
	By our sexton; it will all be ready
	In the morning.
DAUGHTER:	Well, please dear sir, read a requiem mass.
	Here are ten *stuivers*[13] for everything,
	And for prayers for the soul.
PRIEST:	Requiescant in pace![14] Well well, so I will. 265
	I will do all that I am able.
	God's lungs, let this come every day!
	But it does not, thus I turn to the old ways
	To read vigilie, parce michi domine.[15]

They go in.[16]

BEGGAR:	Go hence and look again!
TRAMP:	Then come along! 270
	I do not know what to make of it.
BEGGAR:	I can hear no-one speaking or bellowing.
	I must indeed observe what they are doing.
TRAMP:	I assure you that they do not bicker.
	You will not catch them out by listening, 275
	They are very much as one.
BEGGAR:	What, do they lie and sleep?
	They are lying down to rest their heads.
TRAMP:	They lie and sleep?
BEGGAR:	Yes, by God's death,
	Next to the corpse, come, make haste and see
	Through this little crack.
TRAMP:	It is true, and you could not wake them 280
	If you hacked off their hands and legs.
	Hear their deep snoring!
BEGGAR:	Like the Jews near the grave,[17]

---

[13] The *stuiver* was a coin worth one twentieth of a guilder. It remained standard currency in the Netherlands until the early nineteenth century.

[14] Versicle from the Office of the Dead: 'may they rest in peace'.

[15] The First Lesson of the First Nocturne from the Office the Dead. It is taken from Job 7.16: 'parce mihi nihil enim sunt dies mei' ('spare me, for my days are nothing').

[16] Although the text simply states 'inne' at this point, subsequent events make it clear that the Priest returns to his own home, and only the Daughter re-enters the house.

[17] This allusion is unclear. It may refer to the custom of sitting on low stools during the post-burial period of Shivah, but otherwise it does not correspond to any standard Jewish mourning practice. Wolfgang Bunte believes that the passage may reflect a local custom, and sees it as evidence of 'the greater freedoms the Jews were allowed in the exercise of their religion' in the Low Countries, 'in contrast to the prevailing view of greater restriction' throughout the rest of 'Christendom' ('die grösseren Freiheiten, die den Juden – im Gegensatz zur herrschenden Auffassung von der grösseren

So leggensse gestreckt langs beijder baeren.

SLOEFF: Gans dagen, off wijder inne waeren,
Wij soudender thonen ons costuijmen.   285

SCHUIJFFMAN: Wij souden de schaeppraije immers ruijmen,
Want ick come van honger uijt mijnen sinne.
Isser nergens geen gadt?

SLOEFF: Siet geen veijnster! dat moeten wij inne.
Ick salder na climmen, geeff mijn den voet!
En dan sal ick de deure open doen.

SCHUIJFFMAN: Ghans lijff, soo doet!   290
Meugen wij botten, dat sal mij wel behagen.
Ick schranse te minsten voor drie dagen,
Was ickker in; ick weet wadt ick peijsse.

SLOEFF: De stadt is gewonnen, tis al behouwen reijsse.
Dlijck staet hier, compt inne, wilt vreucht hantieren.   295

SCHUIJFFMAN: Beijt fiel, wij moeten wadt vreemts versieren.
Ick hoope, ons compter aff vreucht en bate.
Wilt na mijn wachten hier op strate.
Ghij hoorden u dagen noijt setter bestel
Dan mij daer vooren compt.

SLOEFF: Ghans longeren, wel!   300
Her, her, geringe sonder enich dralen!
Ja, wadt ist nu?

SCHUIJFFMAN: Ginder staet een veulen, dat gae ick haelen.
Geen beter, rasch doet mij tdoot wijff vuijte!
Ontdoet de kiste!

SLOEFF: Gans doot, dit wordt een lepe cluijte.
Wel, wel, al sout ons noch rouwen tinden.   305
Wat sellen wij beginnen gaen?

SCHUIJFFMAN: Siet hier tveulen, helpttet mij ontbinden,
Gans lijff, noijt quader boeverije.
Her de coorde! houwet veulen ghije!
Tsal vlus een vremde personage wesen.

SLOEFF: Bijder doot, vrou ghijben die is verresen!   310
Tsou eenen in drome comen te vooren.
Nu bindtdet anden rinck vander dooren,
So salt staen huppelen, smijten en goijen,
En opten drempel sullen wij coren stroijen
En dan salt riecken, dus salt staen rammelen   315
Aende deure. Nu laeten wijt sammelen!
Sij sullen wonderlijck sien, als sij ontwecken.

SCHUIJFFMAN: Gans doot, dats waer, dus laet ons vertrecken
Ergens achter; noijt beter dinck om schoppen.
Noijt volck en machtmen badt bestoppen.   320

	They lie stretched out alongside the bier.	
TRAMP:	God's days, if we were inside,	
	We should perform in our true costumes then.	285
BEGGAR:	We would ransack the cupboards indeed,	
	For I go out of my senses with hunger.	
	Is there no hole anywhere?	

TRAMP: See this window! We must enter that.
I will climb up there, give me a leg-up!
And then I will open the door.

BEGGAR: God's corpse, then do it! 290
We might gorge, that will please me well.
I would guzzle for three days at least,
If I were inside; I know what I am thinking.

TRAMP: The city is taken, it is a successful voyage.
The corpse lies here, come inside, and you will have joy. 295

BEGGAR: Wait rogue, we must dress things to appear strange.
I hope we will come to joy and profit.
You wait for me here in the street.
You never heard in all your days a more foolish plan
Than came to me there.

TRAMP: God's lungs, well! 300
Well, well, quickly, without any delay!
Yes, what is it now?

BEGGAR: There stands a foal: I'll go and fetch that,
No deliberating, rush to get the dead woman out!
Undo the coffin!

TRAMP: God's death, this will be a crafty farce.
Well, well, although we could rue it eventually. 305
What are we starting to do?

BEGGAR: See, here is the foal, help me untie it,
God's body, there was never a more wicked swindle.
Here is the bridle! You hold the foal!
It will fast become a strange being.

TRAMP: By Death, dead lady you have risen! 310
It is like a thing that happens in someone's dream.
Now bind it underneath on the other side.
Now will it hop, strike and buck,
And on the doorstep we will strew some grain
And it will smell this, so it will make a din 315
Against the door. Now let us perform this plan!
They will see a wonderful thing, if they wake.

BEGGAR: God's death, that is true, so let us head off
Somewhere unseen; there was never a better thing for kicking!
There were never better people that one might rob! 320

enge gegenüber dem Christentum – in der Ausübung seiner Religion zugestanden sind'): Wolfgang Bunte, *Juden und Judentum in der mittelniederländischen Literatur (1100–1600)* (Bern, 1989), 249.

SONE:	Wie is daer veure? wat dient dat cloppen	
	Dus spaij bij nachte? ghij doet mij an vaer.	
	Wie is daer? ou! wie is doch nu daer?	
	Ghelooffdij, spreekt, oft het sal u verdrieten,	
	Ick sal u van boven met stenen begieten.	325
	Wadt manieren sijn dit! hoe tierdij aldus?	
DOCHTER:	Och, och, benedijste Dominus!	
	Och moeder gods, ick loop mijnder vaerde!	
SONE:	Wat isser noch?	
DOCHTER:	Ons moeder is te paerde!	
	Compt, sietet, ick en weet niet wattet meent!	330
	Ey! ey! ey!	
SONE:	Benedijste! wacharmen! noijt so vereent!	
	Mij sullen van grouwel de sinnen faelen.	
DOCHTER:	Och, och, ick duchte, sij sal ons te muijssemeel malen!	
	Eylacen, eylacen, wij moeten papen hebben!	
	Wadt mach dit bedien?	
SONE:	Och, ick ducht, dat is om dat wij geslapen hebben!	335
	Dit sal ons, ducht ick, ten leden vergaen.	
	Lopen wij geringe om den prochiaen.	
	Geringe! mij walcht van desen affgrijse.	
	Dus gaen wij, eer ick in meer grouwels rijse.	
SLOEFF:	Ja, ja, en wij gaen loopen om de spijse.	340
	Ick en hoorde mijn dagen van beteren ra.	
	Aent botten! aent botten!	
SCHUIJFFMAN:	Int schappra! int schappra!	
	Ick sal mij selven snoeren al versmoort!	
	Hier is de cant met den broije!	
SLOEFF:	Brengtet al voort!	
	Wij sellen nu hoven als quanten van lijven.	345
	Can ick, daer sal een sier niet blijven,	
	Ick en scheij niet, voor dattet al vuijtgemeten is.	
SCHUIJFFMAN:	Tuert, baes, wadt hier al te eeten is:	
	Gesoijen, gebraijen, goet vleesch gesmoockt	
	En een cruijck met biere.	
SLOEFF:	Dats goet, trouwen, tis voor ons gecoockt:	350
	Wij sijn hier vrienden, wij comense besoecken.	
SCHUIJFFMAN:	Dats waer, maar wisten sijt, sij souden ons vloecken.	
	Maer laet ons eeten, sij sellent betaelen.	
	Longeren, hoe schock ick!	
SLOEFF:	Laetse den pastoor gaen haelen!	
	Hij salse comen belesen, also ik houwe.	355
	Merckt doch, welcken personage!	
SCHUIJFFMAN:	Tdunckt mij sijn een vaerende vrouwe.	
	Ick en hoorde noijt spreecken van quader kecken,	
	Maer wistet de schout …	
SLOEFF:	Hij sou ons willen recken.	

SON:	Who is there before the house? What does that knocking mean
	This deep in the night? You make me afraid.
	Who is there? Hey! Who is there now?
	Believe me, speak, or you will regret it,
	I will rain on you from above with stones. 325
	What kind of behaviour is this? Why do you make such noise?
DAUGHTER:	Oh, oh, most blessed Dominus!
	Oh mother of God, I fear for my life!
SON:	What is the matter?
DAUGHTER:	Our mother is on horseback!
	Come, look at it, I do not know what this means! 330
	Ah! ah! ah!
SON:	Most blessed! Alas! I was never so terrified!
	My senses will fail out of horror.
DAUGHTER:	Oh, oh, I fear she will grind us to mouse-flour!
	Alas, alas, we must have a priest!
	What does this mean?
SON:	Oh, I fear this is because we have slept! 335
	I fear this will destroy our lives.
	Let us go quickly to the priest.
	Quickly! I sicken from this fright.
	Thus we go, before I rise into greater terrors.
TRAMP:	Yes, yes, and we rush to the feast. 340
	I never heard better advice in all my days.
	Such stuff to eat! Such stuff to eat!
BEGGAR:	In the cupboards! In the cupboards!
	I will smother myself, eating all this!
	Here is the side with the bread.
TRAMP:	Bring it all forth!
	We will dine now as fellows for our bodies' sake. 345
	I am able – there will not be a thing left,
	I will not leave until everything is swallowed.
BEGGAR:	Observe, friend, all that is here to eat:
	Roasted, baked, good smoked meat,
	And a keg full of beer.
TRAMP:	That is good, truly, it is cooked for us: 350
	We are friends here; we came to visit.
BEGGAR:	That is true, but if they knew it, they should curse us.
	But let us eat: they will pay.
	My lungs, how I guzzle.
TRAMP:	Let them go and fetch the pastor!
	He will come to pray, I guess. 355
	Mark that, what a figure!
BEGGAR:	It looks to me like a gypsy woman.
	I never heard tell of a crueller trick,
	But if the sheriff knew . . .
TRAMP:	He would want to rack us.

151

	Ick brengt u eens fiel, laet ons wel poijen!	
SCHUIJFFMAN:	Ghans dagen! wij sellen moeten verschoijen.	360
	Wij hebben ruwelijck bodt gebuijst.	
	Sij sullen vlus comen.	
SLOEFF:	Ick heb mijn dranck oock wel gehuijst.	
	Ick sou wel slaepen, sonder datmen mij sou wiegen.	
SCHUIJFFMAN:	Laet ons verseijssen!	
SLOEFF:	Wij willen vervliegen!	
	Dus laet ons hier ergens heijmelijck vlien	365
	En hooren watter sal aff geschien.	
DOCHTER:	Och, ick heb mijns heeren huijs gesien.	
	Laet ons cloppen! – noijt sulcken vaer –	
	Ou! seg, ou!	
PASTOOR:	Wadts daer? wadts daer?	
	Ghij clopt, al waerdij buijten kere!	370
	Wadt belieft u?	
SONE:	Och haest u, compt tonssent, lieve heere!	
	Geringe! want ons haer rijst recht op doort vermeten.	
PASTOOR:	Wat isser gaens? wat isser gaens?	
DOCHTER:	Ons moeder die is te paerde geseten,	
	Die gisteren sterff. Wie sach oijt dinck aldus?	
	Compt, beleestse, lieff heere!	
PASTOOR:	Te paerde! benedijste dominus!	375
	Wat segdij? ten sijn niet dan fantazijen.	
	Souwen de dooden te paerde gaen rijen?	
	En hoe compt ditte? wilt dit vuijtleggen.	
	T'is, peijnsick, miraeckle.	
DOCHTER:	Och heer, ick weet, ick salt u seggen:	
	Doen ick van u schiet, in waere saecken,	380
	Doen gingen wij dlijck sitten waecken,	
	Ende mits den vaecke, verstaet ons callen,	
	So sijn wij beijde in slaep gevallen.	
	En alst wij gelegen waeren ontrent een huere,	
	Ontsprongen wij, doen cloptense aen de duere.	385
	Certeijn, tis waer dat wij u hier verclaren.	
PASTOOR:	Swijcht toch, ick sou mij met allen vervaren.	
	So en hoorde ick noijt vremder, bij gans doot!	
	Och, daer schiet mij een geschot in mijn hoot:	
	Tdunckt mij ongelove tegens onse wedt.	390
	Wat, soudese te paerde rijden?	
DOCHTER:	Och tis certeijn waer, dus gaet toch met	
	En beleestse om meer quaets te weerne.	
PASTOOR:	Ick sal, maer ick en doets niet geerne.	
	Her mijn paert! want ick ben niet wel te voet,	
	En dus spaij te gaen en is oock niet goet.	395
	Nu paerdeken, gaet heenen in goods namen!	
	Godt hebbe alle zielen!	

152

	I will take you there one day, rogue, but now let us drink well!
BEGGAR:	God's days! We must depart. 360
	We have drunk a terrible amount.
	They will come soon.
TRAMP:	I have also gulped my drink.
	I could sleep well, without anyone rocking me.
BEGGAR:	Let us leave!
TRAMP:	We wish to flee,
	So let us find somewhere concealed here, 365
	And hear what will happen next.
DAUGHTER:	Oh, I have seen my lord's house.
	Let us knock! – there was never such fear –
	Ahoy, I say, ahoy!
PRIEST:	Who is there? Who is there?
	You knock as though you were lost, by Christ! 370
	What concerns you?
SON:	Oh hurry yourself, come to our home, dear sir!
	Quickly! For our hair rises right up from the sight.
PRIEST:	What is happening? What is happening?
DAUGHTER:	Our mother, who died yesterday,
	Is seated on a horse. Who ever saw a thing like this?
	Come, bless her, dear sir!
PRIEST:	On a horse? Most blessed dominus! 375
	What are you saying? It is nothing but fantasies.
	Should the dead ride on horses?
	And how has this happened? Can you explain it?
	I think it is a miracle.
DAUGHTER:	Oh lord, I know, I will tell you:
	When I went from you, these things are true, 380
	We quickly went to sit awake with the corpse,
	And sleep then came, understand our story.
	So it was that we both fell asleep.
	And as we were lying for about an hour,
	We rose up, when she knocked on the door. 385
	Certainly, it is true what we declare here.
PRIEST:	Silence, or I will grow frightened like the pair of you.
	I heard never a stranger thing, by God's death!
	Oh, in my head, a thought comes to me:
	It occurs to me that the damned are riding against us. 390
	Why should she ride a horse?
DAUGHTER:	Oh, it is certainly true, so come with us
	And bless her to ward off more evil.
PRIEST:	I will, but I do not fancy doing so.
	Bring my horse here, for I have difficulty walking,
	And it is also not good to delay going like this. 395
	Now, horsy, go forth in God's name!
	God have all souls!

SONE:	Eijlacijen, amen!
	Dus gaen wij; onssen ancxt waer quaet om sommen.
SCHUIJFFMAN:	Ghans honderden, siet onsen domine commen!
	Hij sidt beschaempt, al waert een wesele.
	Ou! guijlken, ou!
SLOEFF:	Het dunckt mij Balaam opten esele.
	Gans doot, hij salse comen besweren!
SCHUIJFFMAN:	Waer mochtemen beter boerde vercleren?
	Maer tsus, laet ons noch wadt vervliegen.
	Wij souden wel een kodt vol simmen bedriegen.
DOCHTER:	Och, och, ick hebse gesien!
SONE:	Siet heer, oft wij liegen.
	Och, lieff heer, beleestse off leijtse meet
	Wij crimpen van vaere.
PASTOOR:	Mee leijen? wadt benedijste!
	Waer ick thuijs, ick en quamer niet, mi weet ghijt al.
DOCHTER:	Och, och, lieff heer, beleestse!
PASTOOR:	Wel, wel, ick sal:
	Beatij quorum, voor alle geschreije . . .
	Och, benedijste! benedijste!
SONE:	En oftse dominus seije . . .
PASTOOR:	Et exultant quotidianum.
	Nunc dimittis; sijdij al stum?
	Ick besweer u: sijdij van goods wegen, spreeckt!
	De profudus en ast u ijet gebreeckt,
	Fec ut potentiam labia mea aperies.

Line numbers: 400, 405, 410, 415

SON:	Alas, amen!
	Thus we go; our fear truly cannot be calculated.
BEGGAR:	God's hundreds, see our lord come forth!
	He sits shamefully, all worried as a weasel. 400
	Hey, dobbin, hey!
TRAMP:	He looks to me like Balaam on the ass.[18]
	God's death, he will come to exorcise!
BEGGAR:	Where might you witness a better tale?[19]
	But hush, let us stage something further,
	We could easily fool a house full of monkeys. 405
DAUGHTER:	Oh, oh, I have seen them![20]
SON:	See sir, or do we lie?
	Oh, dear sir, bless her, or take her with you.
	We cringe from fear.
PRIEST:	Take her with me? What, benedicite!
	Were I at home now, I would not follow you: now you know all.
DAUGHTER:	Oh, oh, dear sir, bless them!
PRIEST:	Well, well, I will, 410
	Beati quorum,[21] for all shrieking …
	Oh, benedicite, benedicite!
SON:	And after they say Dominus …
PRIEST:	Et exultant quotidianum.[22]
	Nunc dimittis;[23] are you all tongue-tied?
	I cast you out: you, for God's sake, speak! 415
	De profudus and, since you have not finished it,
	Fec ut potentiam,[24] labia mea aperies.[25]

[18] This is an allusion to the famous episode of Numbers 22.22–8, in which a donkey ridden by the diviner Balaam is granted the power of speech, after its master beats it for stopping before an angel. The story, with its combination of miracle, revelation, inversion and folkloric anthropomorphism, acquired an important place in medieval festive culture across Europe: see Grace Frank, *The Medieval French Drama* (Oxford, 1954), 40–2; Hardin Craig, *English Religious Drama of the Middle Ages* (Oxford, 1960), 68.

[19] The text has 'boerde' here, the Middle Dutch equivalent of *fabliau*.

[20] That is, the horse and the cadaver.

[21] First verse of Psalm 31, the second of the Penitential Psalms, recited during litanies: 'Beati quorum remissae sunt iniquitates et quorum tecta sunt peccata' ('Blessed are they whose iniquities are forgiven, and whose sins are covered').

[22] This line appears to merge the second line of the Magnificat, 'et exultavit spiritus meus in Deo salutari meo' ('And my spirit hath rejoiced in God my Saviour'), with the petition from the Lord's Prayer, 'panem nostrum cotidianum da nobis hodie' ('Give us this day our daily bread').

[23] A canticle from the Divine Office, taken in turn from Luke 2.29: 'nunc dimittis servum tuum, Domine' ('now thou dost dismiss thy servant, O Lord').

[24] Probably a garbled version of a line from the Magnificat, from Luke 1.51: 'fecit potentiam in brachio suo' ('He hath shewed might in his arm').

[25] Opening versicle from the Divine Office. From Psalm 50.17: 'domine labia mea aperies et os meum adnuntiabit laudem tuam' ('O Lord, thou wilt open my lips: and my mouth shall declare thy praise').

	Segt op door dit groote les,	
	Oft ick besweer u, daermen den bitebau droech.	
DOCHTER:	Gaet wadt naerder, heer!	
PASTOOR:	Neen, ick ben na genoech.	420
	Die geesten sijn vrij van vremder aert.	
	Benedijcite! benedijcite!	
SONE:	Sij rijt ons na, noijt so vervaert!	
	Wadt sals geschien? Wij mogen wel kermen!	
	Eij! eij! eij!	
DOCHTER:	Wachermen! Wachermen!	
	Waer sal ick loopen? Dits een cranck bestel.	425
PASTOOR:	Och, och, de profundis! dat dacht ick wel.	
	Ick sal van anxte met luijder kelen crijten!	
	Aij! aij! aij!	
SLOEFF:	Ghans doot, ick sal van lachen slijten.	
	Mijn heere die blijfter inden brant.	
SCHUIJFFMAN:	Ick meen men noijt beter boerde vant.	430
	Ick gelooff dattet een aerdich cuerken is.	
	Ou, siet, tveulen loopt hem nae.	
SLOEFF:	Het meent dattet sijn muerken is.	
	T'is goet te sien dattet een naetuerlijck beestgen sijn,	
	En mijn heer meent dattet een geestgen sijn.	
	Laet ons na loopen en hooren sijn kermen.	435
PASTOOR:	Och, houwet veulen! eijlacij! wachermen!	
	Het wilt mij aen! wat mach hem porren?	
SONE:	Och lieve heer, wij souden niet dorren	
	Midts den geest, dier op present is:	
	Hij mocht ons te muijsemeel maecken en malen.	
PASTOOR:	Fijant aurez intendentis . . .	440
	Ick en weet niet, waer ick sta oft sitte.	
	Domine exaude! domine exaude!	
SCHUIJFFMAN:	Benedijste, heer, wadt dinck is ditte?	
	Ick en sach mijn dagen noijt vreemder bescheet.	
	Willet u quaet doen, heer?	

	Say it along with this great speech,	
	Or I'll cast you out, to where they sent the bogeyman.[26]	
DAUGHTER:	Get somewhat nearer, sir!	
PRIEST:	No, I am close enough.	420
	These spirits are wild and strange by nature.	
	Benedicite! Benedicite!	
SON:	She rides to us, never was I so afraid!	
	What will happen? We may well moan.	
	Ah! ah! ah!	
DAUGHTER:	Alas! Alas!	
	Where will I run? This is a deranged scene.	425
PRIEST:	Oh, oh, de profundis! It is as I knew!	
	I will cry from fear with a loud voice!	
	Ah! Ah! Ah!	
TRAMP:	God's death, I will die from laughing.	
	My lord carries a mark of shame for life.	
BEGGAR:	You might never want a better joke, I think,	430
	I believe that it is a pretty trick.	
	Oh, see, the foal runs to him now.	
TRAMP:	It thinks that is its mother.	
	It is good to see these beasts follow their nature,	
	But my lord thinks that they are ghosts.	
	Let us follow them and hear his moans.	435
PRIEST:	Oh, hold that foal! Alas! Alack!	
	It will get me! What is making it charge?	
SON:	Oh, believe me, sir, we would not dare	
	Because of the ghost, who is present there:	
	It will grind and mill us to mouse-flour.	
PRIEST:	Fiant aures intendentes …	440
	I do not know whether I stand or sit.	
	Domine exaudi! Domine exaudi![27]	
BEGGAR:	Most blessed sir, what is this thing?	
	I never saw a stranger event in my days.	
	Are you in danger, sir?	

---

[26] The *bitebau* mentioned by the text is an ogre from Germanic folklore. The Brothers Grimm place it alongside the werewolf, demon and *schim* (shade) as a type of 'wilder geist' ('malevolent spirit'), and note that gloves could apparently be made from its skin, 'aus dessen haut handschuhe geschnitten werden sollen': Jacob Grimm and Wilhelm Grimm, *Deutsches Wörterbuch*, 2 vols. (Leipzig, 1860), 2: 51. In Dutch the term came to describe any terrifying or unwanted force. A 1627 emblem by the Zeeland poet Jacob Cats refers to the 'blauwe scheen' ('blue look') that follows a rejected marriage proposal as 'een bitebau die yeder een ontsiet,/ Maer keert het spoock eens om, ten is so leelijck niet' ('a bitebau that everyone dreads, but when the ghost turns round, it is not so fearsome'): Hans Luijten and Marijke Blankman, *Minne- en zinnebeelden: een bloemlezing uit de Nederlandse emblematiek* (Amsterdam, 1996), 51.

[27] These three lines quote the second verse of Psalm 129: 'Domine exaudi vocem meam, fiant aures tuae intendentes in vocem deprecationis meae' ('Lord, hear my voice. Let thy ears be attentive to the voice of my supplication').

PASTOOR:	Och, lieve fijn mans, ick en weet.
	Ick lietet mij costen lant, zant en huijs, 445
	Dat ickx quijt waere.
SCHUIJFFMAN:	Wat, latet ons houwen, dit vreempt abuijs.
	Mij dunckt, het heeft u verde gedreven.
	Willen wijt houwen, heer?
PASTOOR:	Och jae, ick sal u veertich cronen geven!
	Ick was mijn dagen niet vervaert so seer.
	Och, houwet! houwet!
SLOEFF:	O! paerdeken o! ontfermpt u heer! 450
	Ghij most hier van mijn heer scheen.
	Houwet ghij van achter!
SONE:	Och, gesellen, woudijt opt kerckhoff leen
	En dattet lichaem worde in d'aerde gestelt,
	Wij sellen u geven goet gelt,
	Wadt ghijer aff eijscht, sonder lang sermoen. 455
	Wij biddent u, lieff quants!
SCHUIJFFMAN:	Waij, omdat ghijt sijt, so selent wij doen.
	Maer ten is geen spel vrij van jolijte.
PASTOOR:	Houdt daer, gesellen! maeckt mij den geest quijte!
	Ick wil gaen rijen en laetent u voort bestellen.
	Mijn herte beeft van vare.
DOCHTER:	Och voeret opt kerckhoff, lieff gesellen, 460
	Hout daer, siet! en willet bewaeren.
	Noijt geest en mocht ons meer beswaeren!
	Wij sullent u geheel en al bevelen,
	Doetter toch tbeste inne.
SLOEFF:	Wel, wel, wij selen.
	Wij sellender ons wel te degen in quijten. 465
SCHUIJFFMAN:	Wisten sij de waerheijt, tsou hen wel splijten.
	Godt heeft ons hier gesonden claer opter stee.
PASTOOR:	Adieu, lieve vrienden!
SLOEFF:	Adieu, heer domine!
	Wij willen gaen schoijen lanckx den dijcke.
SCHUIJFFMAN:	Wij waeren ons dagen noijt so rijcke, 470
	Want sij hebben, alst blijckt, ons tgelt gegeven seer vlijtelijck.
	Wij sullent oock wel verteeren derren jolijtelijck.
	God geeff datter morgen noch een moet sterven!
SLOEFF:	Wij sijn vande magen, wij sellen vant goet erfven,
	Want wij hebben, alst blijckt – dies vruecht in ons wast – 475
	Veel gelts gecregen.
SCHUIJFFMAN:	Ja, Ja, en wel gebrast
	Mits aerdige loossheijt, dier ick vol hucke.
SLOEFF:	So na leijt tgeluck den ongelucke.
	Dus gaen wij, als naeste vrinden, draven

PRIEST:	Oh, dear fine man, I do not know.
	I would let myself sell my land, garden and house, 445
	If I were freed from this.
BEGGAR:	What, let us hold it, this strange monster.
	It has driven you mad, so I think.
	Should we hold it, sir?
PRIEST:	Oh yes, I will give you forty crowns!
	I was never so badly frightened in all my days.
	Oh, hold it! hold it!
TRAMP:	Oh, horsy, oh! Do not pester the good sir. 450
	You must go from my lord here.
	You, hold the backside![28]
SON:	Oh, fellows, would you lead it to the churchyard?
	If you would drop the corpse into the earth,
	We will give you good money,
	Whatever you ask us, without a long sermon. 455
	We beg you, dear fellows!
BEGGAR:	Well, since it is you, we will do it.
	But this is a game freely played with jollity.
PRIEST:	Hold it there, fellows! Make sure I can escape the ghost!
	I want to get clear and let you do as you were asked.
	My heart shakes from fear.
DAUGHTER:	Oh take it to the churchyard, dear fellows, 460
	Hold it there, see! And it will stay there.
	No ghost may ever terrify us more!
	We will leave it to you in all matters.
	Do what is for the best.
TRAMP:	Well, well, we will.
	We will acquit ourselves well in doing this. 465
BEGGAR:	If they knew the truth, they would be torn in two.
	God has clearly sent us here for this purpose.
PRIEST:	Adieu, dear friends!
TRAMP:	Adieu, sir domine!
	We will go drifting along the dyke-side.
BEGGAR:	Never in our days were we so rich, 470
	For they have very quickly given us money, as shown here.
	We will also spend some of it in celebration.
	God grant that another may die in the morning!
TRAMP:	We are of his blood, we will inherit his goods,
	For we have, as you saw – this fruit grows in us – 475
	Received much money.
BEGGAR:	Yes, yes, and feasted well
	On this pretty trickery; I am sore burdened with it.
TRAMP:	So good fortune lies close to misfortune.
	And so we go, like the closest of friends, trotting

---

[28] The Sloeff is evidently addressing the Schuijffman in this line.

159

	Ten kerckehove waert.	
SCHUIJFFMAN:	Ja, en ons moeije begraven!	480
	En metten bucht sullen wij ons keeltgen laven,	
	Want mijn buijckgen staet nu al int ronde.	
SLOEFF:	Eerwaerdighe heeren, godt geeff u gesonde!	
	En neempt danckelijck, edele rethorisienen,	
	Dit vant olijfftackxken om druckx verclenen.	485

finis lang in dicht 605 regulen.
Par Trouw Moet Blijcken.

Item met dit voorgaende geschreven spel hebben die van Thienen den hoochsten prijss gewonnen tot Loven a° 1504.

Towards the churchyard.
BEGGAR: Yes, to bury our aunt!   480
And with the booty we will bathe our gullets,
For my belly stands all round now.
TRAMP: Worthy watchers, God send you health!
And take this thankfully, lords of rhetoric,
From the Olive Branch, to decrease sorrows.   485

Finis, this poem is 605 lines long.[29]
By Truth Will Be Shown.

Item: with this play written above have those from Thienen won the highest prize at Leuven, anno 1504.

---

[29]   The figures given by copyists tend to count unrhymed half-lines as full *regulen* in their own right. Compare the similar annotations for *Jack Sweet-tooth* and *The Barefoot Brothers*.

A Play of Three Lovers

*E*EN SPEEL *van drie minners* survives in a single unsigned copy, preserved in the same manuscript that contains the *Mock-Sermon on Saint Nobody*. Internal evidence suggests that the play was written shortly before the 1520s: its playful and light-hearted treatment of the clergy, for instance, places it in the first decades of the sixteenth century, as it stands in sharp contrast to the harshness of post-Reformation anti-clericalism.[1] Since the manuscript itself may have originated from Ghent, it seems likely that the play was composed for one of the chambers of that city, although there are no records to confirm this supposition.[2]

In its choice of material, *Three Lovers* demonstrates the curious mix of humanist and popular concerns that characterises *rederijker* drama more widely. Like several other *kluchten*, the text derives its basic plot from Giovanni Boccaccio's *Decameron* (*c.*1350).[3] The specific *novella* it draws from is the first story of the ninth day, itself a variant of the 'Entrapped Suitors' story-type, numbered 1730 in the Aarne–Thompson–Uther index.[4] In the Boccaccio story, one Madonna Francesca attracts the unwanted attentions of two Florentine exiles, Rinuccio and Alessandro. To deter her pursuers, she 'induces the one to enter a tomb and pose as a corpse, and the other to go in and fetch him out': both flee when they are challenged by the city's night watchmen.[5] However, while it follows this basic sequence to some extent, *Three Lovers* does not seem to have been based directly on Boccaccio. By the close of the Middle Ages the tale had been disseminated across northern Europe: the story was evidently known in German and French, as it appears in the work of Johannes Pauli, Hans Sachs and Nicolas de Troyes.[6] It also had some currency in the folklore of the Low Countries. Similar stories occur in the jest book *Een nyeuwe clucht boeck* (1564), a collection of popular anecdotes and tales, and in the legends associated with the 'Lange Wapper', a mythical shape-shifting trickster said to live in the River Scheldt at Antwerp.[7]

---

[1] See, for instance, Jan van der Noot, *Het theatre oft Toon-Neel*, in *Het bosken en het theatre*, ed. W. A. P. Smit (Utrecht, 1979), 184–387; Philips Marnix van Sint Aldegonde, *De bijenkorf der H. Roomsche kerke, met inleiding en varianten*, ed. A. Lacroix and A. Willems, in *De werken van Ph. van Marnix van Sint Aldegonde*, 2 vols. (Brussels, 1858), 1: 5–219.

[2] P. Leendertz, 'Eenige geneuchlijcke dichten', *Tijdschrift voor Nederlandse taal- en letterkunde* 20 (1901), 59–80 (59).

[3] René van Stipriaan, *Leugens en vermaak: Boccaccio's novellen in de kluchtcultuur van de Nederlandse Renaissance* (Amsterdam, 1996).

[4] Hans-Jorg Uther, *The Types of International Folktales*, Parts I-III (Helsinki, 2004).

[5] Giovanni Boccaccio, *The Decameron*, trans. G. H. McWilliam (Harmondsworth, 1972), 682–7.

[6] Hans Sachs, *Schwanken*, ed. Adelbert von Keller, 20 vols. (Stuttgart, 1860–90), 9: 424–9; Johannes Pauli, *Schimpf und Ernst*, ed. Johannes Bolte (Berlin, 1924); Nicolas de Troyes, *Grand parangon des nouvelles nouvelles*, ed. Krystyna Kasprzyk (Paris, 1970).

[7] Wim Hüsken, *Noyt meerder vreucht – compositie en structuur van het komisch toneel in de Nederlanden voor de Renaissance* (Deventer, 1987), 25; *Een nyeuwe clucht boeck: Een*

Of these retellings, the text which bears closest resemblance to *Three Lovers* is the Middle English *Lady Prioress* (*c.*1475), a poem of 250 lines once attributed to John Lydgate.[8] Like *Three Lovers*, *The Lady Prioress* increases the number of men pursuing its heroine to three, and compels the third to dress as a devil, eliminating the need for any outside agency such as Boccaccio's watchmen. It also makes the key addition of identifying each lover with a particular social class: hence the Lady Prioress is wooed by 'lordes and laymen and spryttualle', much like the Woman of the *Three Lovers*. Although it seems unlikely that *Three Lovers* was directly indebted to *The Lady Prioress*, which is only known in a single manuscript copy and therefore unlikely to have circulated widely, these similarities do imply a shared ancestor. Henry MacCracken has found evidence in *The Lady Prioress* to suggest it was derived from a lost fabliau, and this French text might also be the basis of *Three Lovers*.[9] In fact, *Three Lovers* does imply that it is modelled on a source already well known to its audience. The minimal use of exposition in the play, as the pursuers fall in with the Woman's scheme with little persuasion, indicates that its audience probably knew the story well enough to accept it without hesitation or rationalisation. Since an obscure English poem is unlikely to have attained such familiarity in the Netherlands, a common French source for *Three Lovers* and *The Lady Prioress* seems most plausible.

However, assuming that *The Lady Prioress* faithfully preserves the story on which *Three Lovers* is based, the Dutch piece does seem to depart from its plot in significant ways. The English text is noticeably systematic in the way it allocates a social class to each of the lovers. The three men pursuing the woman are each representative of a particular group: her suitors are respectively a 'young knyght', 'a parson of a paryche', and 'a burges of a borrow', a citizen or merchant of a local town. They therefore mirror the common medieval division of society into three estates, 'those who fight, those who pray, and those who work'.[10] The poem even uses this combination of classes as an opportunity to moralise on the correct social function of each group. The prioress obliquely reminds her suitors of their social obligations, even as she pretends to give in to their pleas: she hails the knight as 'ower patron, and ower precedent', and tells the libidinous parson 'we send for you, ouer worshype for to save'.[11]

zestiende-eeuwse anekdotenverzameling, ed. Herman. Pleij (Muiderburg, 1983); Johann Wilhelm Wolf, *Wodana* (Ghent, 1851), 11; Benjamin Thorpe, *Northern Mythology: North German and Netherlandish Popular Traditions and Superstitions* (London, 1852), 217–18. Further analogues are discussed in Ben Parsons and Bas Jongenelen, '*A Play Of Three Suitors*: A Neglected Version of the "Entrapped Suitors" Story (ATU 1730)', *Folklore* 119 (2008), 62–74.

[8] Melissa Furrow, *Ten Comic Poems* (New York, 1985), 3–30; Thomas D. Cooke, Peter Whiteford, and Nancy Mohr McKinley. 'XXIV: Tales', *Manual of the Writings in Middle English, 1050–1500*, ed. Albert Hartung. 11 vols. (New Haven, 1967–2005), 9: 3169; Seth Lerer, 'British Library MS Harley 78 and The Manuscripts of John Shirley.' *Notes and Queries* 235 (1990), 400–3.

[9] Henry Noble MacCracken and Merriam Sherwood, *Lydgate's Minor Poems*, Early English Text Society, os 192, 2 vols. (London, 1911–34), 1: 107.

[10] Christopher Dyer, *Making a Living in the Middle Ages: the people of Britain 850–1520* (London, 2003), 72. See also Ruth Mohl, *The Three Estates in Medieval and Renaissance Literature* (New York, 1962).

[11] Furrow, *Ten Fifteenth-Century Comic Poems*, 15–30.

Three Lovers, however, makes a curious substitution in its own cast of characters. It removes the 'burges' and replaces him with the less clearly definable figure of the *coster*. The office of *coster* is not as obviously emblematic of the laity as the English merchant, and has no automatic link to the urban middle class. The word itself is derived from the Latin *custos*, and is roughly equivalent to the English sexton or French *sacristan*, describing an officer charged with maintaining the buildings and grounds of a church. The position was usually occupied by laymen during the Middle Ages, as *costers* generally had professions alongside their ecclesiastic duties. For example, the burgher Laurens Janszoon Coster, who served as sexton of Haarlem's Sint-Bavokerk, was also a prominent businessman and city treasurer.[12] Nevertheless, while the *coster* is technically a layman, he has a noticeably greater attachment to the church than his counterpart in the earlier English text. Since he is only identified as *coster*, it is his service to the clergy that *Three Lovers* clearly wishes to emphasise. He functions here, in short, as a sort of honorary churchman. The effect of this alteration is therefore to shift the arrangement of classes in the story. The clerical estate is awarded a greater presence in the play, while the presence of the middle-class laity is minimised.

While there are some practical reasons for this alteration, as it does undeniably make sense for the *coster* to convey a coffin to the churchyard, it seems that a degree of self-interest underpins the revision. The *factor* responsible for the piece seems to be deflecting ridicule away from the social class of his chamber by removing the 'burges' character. The other classes are cruelly lampooned by the text: the Priest twitters in half-understood fragments of liturgy, while the Squire is given a series of tired chivalric and courtly-love clichés to quote, as he calls the Woman 'the measure of my heart', and evokes his word as a guarantee of truth (line 126). By exchanging the 'burges' for a quasi-clerical figure, the play removes any danger that a middle-class urban professional, a character like the *rederijkers* themselves, might be exposed to similar scorn. That this modification was deemed necessary is interesting, and it highlights a general point about the purpose of comedy for the *rederijkerkamers*. Rather like *The Blue Barge*, the text shows that *rederijker* humour could possess a strongly exclusionary function. Like the earlier monologue, it is careful to restrict the targets of its mockery to those groups beyond the door of the chamber; those within the fraternity are insulated against derision or humiliation. In other words, comedy here becomes a means by which the *kamer* can assert its own privileged, separate status. The sharp distinction between the mocker and the mocked is made to reinforce a social boundary, cordoning off the chamber from other groups, ridiculing outsiders while leaving the insiders in a position of safe detachment. Although *rederijker* comedy has often been seen as populist and even-handed in nature, designed to appeal 'to the people in the marketplace', in this case it seems more elitist than democratic: the rhetoricians' humour seems to be composed, in the words of E. de Jongh, 'for the amusement' and the benefit 'of the higher class'.[13]

---

[12] Lotte Hellinga and Clemens de Wolf, *Laurens Janszoon Coster was zijn naam* (Haarlem, 1988).

[13] 'De humor en de ernst van hun spleen . . . maakten hen gezien bij het volk . . . op het marktplein': P. J. Meertens, *Letterkundig leven in Zeeland in de zestiende en de eerste helft der zeventiende eeuw* (Amsterdam, 1943), 72; 'Voor de hogere klasse . . . een bron van groot vermaak':

A further remarkable feature of *Three Lovers* is its curious attitude towards the central figure of the Woman. As Barbara Hanawalt has noted, on the whole the 'Entrapped Suitors' story-type displays firm feminist sympathies.[14] The plot not only portrays women as intelligent, resourceful and inventive, but asserts their ability to preserve both their own integrity and that of the wider community. The Lady Prioress, for instance, is defending her own virginity and correcting a corrupt 'lord' through her trickery. In a similar vein, Boccaccio's Madonna Francesca is punishing 'the daring presumption of the lovers', putting down their harmful and excessive social aspiration.[15] The story, in effect, grants women the power and the judgement to correct any challenge to the existing order of things, even without male assistance.

Three Lovers, however, is markedly less laudatory in its portrayal of women. In fact, it could almost be described as an anti-feminist revision of the story. For instance, rather than finding herself pestered by her suitors, the Woman seems to have actively sought their attention. The play opens with her boasting of her beauty and cunning: she gloats that she is 'very heartily loved/ By callow boys' and has attracted three men that she intends to dupe, creating 'the greatest stupidity/ That ever was heard or seen' (lines 4–5, 16–17). The admissions of love she extracts from each suitor make it clear that she is punishing them only for desiring her. She does not even expose the suitors to public ridicule, or parade them before a figure of authority, like the women in most other versions. In *Three Lovers*, the suitors' degradation is staged for her amusement alone, not as a means of securing official or communal rebuke. Rather than defending the wider social order against interference, therefore, she exploits and encourages disruption for her own enjoyment. In short, *Three Lovers* redraws its source material to conform to the misogynous commonplace that women tempt men into 'ruin' and humiliation.[16] Overall, it presents a version of Boccaccio's story adapted for the emphatically male environment of the *kamers*.

Perhaps owing to these factors, the play does seem to have attained a degree of popularity among the *rederijkers*. Although its exact provenance is unknown, and despite the fact that it survives in only one manuscript, *Three Lovers* seems to have been widely known throughout the early-modern period and beyond. In the sixteenth and seventeenth centuries it was reworked by a number of playwrights, as the rhetoricians evidently thought it worth adapting to meet new political and aesthetic standards. The earliest and most important of its successors is the *Klucht van de bedrogen minnaars* ('Farce of the Mistaken Lovers'), written by Job Gommersz in 1565 for the *Blauwe Acoleyen* at Nieuwerkerk.[17] As J. J. Mak comments, Gommersz has 'clearly recast' *Three Lovers* 'with the Counter Reformation in mind'.[18] His play

---

E. de Jongh, *Tot lering en vermaak. Betekenissen van Hollandse genrevoorstellingen uit de zeventiende eeuw* (Amsterdam, 1976), 57.

[14] Barbara A. Hanawalt, *Of Good and Ill Repute: Gender and Social Control in Medieval England* (Oxford, 1998), 89.

[15] Boccaccio, *Decameron*, 688.

[16] R. Howard Bloch, *Medieval Misogyny and the Invention of Western Romantic Love* (Chicago, 1991), 14–15.

[17] Meertens, *Letterkundig leven in Zeeland*, 119–20; Arjan van Dixhoorn, *Lustige geesten: rederijkers in de noordelijke nederlanden (1480–1650)* (Amsterdam, 2009), 171–9.

[18] 'Job Gommersz' spel daarentegen is duidelijk in Contra-Reformatorische geest gecastigeerd': J. J. Mak, *Vier excellente cluchten*, Klassieke Galerij 46 (Antwerp, 1950), xi.

strips the narrative of even its most implicit anti-clericalism, moving the action away from a churchyard to a barn, and replacing the two clerical characters with 'een student' and 'een borghers sone' ('the son of a burgess'). In other respects, however, the *Klucht* remains faithful to the content and style of *Three Lovers*, even inserting the allegorical figure 'Subtyl Bedyeden' (Subtle Deceit) to spell out the anti-feminist moral of the earlier play.[19] In the centuries after Gommersz, the play was adapted four more times: as J. Franssoon's *Giertje Wouters* of 1623, Jan van Breen's *Bedrooge jalouzy* ('Mistaken Jealousy') of 1659, J. Pluimer's *De bedrooge vryers* ('The Deceived Friars') of 1679, and the anonymous *Fytje of, een Witte met een Zwarte* ('Fytje, or a White with a Black') of 1700.[20] In fact, the story retained its popularity in the Low Countries even later than these versions. Jurjen van der Kooi mentions two nineteenth-century songs which retell much the same story, an anonymous 'street-ballad' entitled 'De uitgezaagde minnaar' ('The Cut-Up Lover'), and Waling Dykstra's Frisian version 'De hingelmatte' ('The Hammock').[21] Although the origins of *Three Lovers* are uncertain, the material it introduced into the dramatic culture of the Low Countries retained a place there well into the modern period.

---

[19] W. M. H. Hummelen, *Repertorium van het rederijkersdrama 1500–ca.1620* (Assen, 1968), 49.

[20] J. A. Worp, *Geschiedenis van het drama en van het tooneel in Nederlan*, 2 vols. (Groningen, 1903–7), I: 454–5.

[21] Jurjen van der Kooi, 'De vrijers in de kast', in *Van Aladdin tot Zwaan Kleefaan: lexicon van sprookjes:ontstaan, ontwikkeling, variaties*, ed. A. J. Dekker, Theo Meder and Jurjen van der Kooi (Leuven, 1997), 387–90.

Een speel van drie minners, de coster, de pape ende de jonckere

Personen:
DWIJF
DE COSTER
DE PAPE
DE JONCKERE

DWIJF:
Ic mach wel seggen naer mijnen heesch
Smorgens: 'Staet up wel ghemaect vleesch'
Ieghens my zelven, alzoot wel schijnt,
Want ic ben zeker zeer hertelic ghemint
Van frisschen ghesellen, die naer mij staen.   5
Ic zal noch bont met hielen gaen,
Al en sauden gheen pijpers in peinse dien.
Daer isser drie, die mij vrihen;
Zij sullen saen commen, ic weet te vooren,
Maer ic zalse begecken, dats verlooren.   10
Virgilius of Aristoteles snel
En wierden noijnt beghect zo wel,
Als ic se beghecken zal saen!
Hola, ghinder comt eenen ghegaen;
Nu willic gaen loopen al in mijn huus.   15
Ghij sult hier zien dat meeste abuus,
Dat noijnt ghehoort was of ghesien.
Hij eijst certein, niet meer van dien,
Dus gae ic ligghen te mijnder veinster boven.[1]

COSTER:
Heere God, hoe mochtse mij verschoonen,   20
Niet min, die schoone eijst mij wel waert.
Van haer zo zaudic mij beloonen,

---

* The Dutch text is taken from Mak, *Vier excellente cluchten*, 1–15.

[1] The text may be missing a line at this point, since a couplet is incomplete here.

A Play of Three Lovers, the Sexton, the Priest and the Squire

Characters:
WOMAN
SEXTON
PRIEST
SQUIRE

WOMAN: I may say to my heart's content
To myself in the morning, 'Rise up,
Well-made flesh', for that is how it seems:
I am certainly very heartily loved
By callow boys, who gaze at me.
I will always go about in fur and heels,
Although pipers might not think much of me.[1]
There are three men who woo me;
They will soon come, I know this already,
But I will dupe them, that is for sure.
Virgil and Aristotle the quick
Were never gulled as well
As they will soon be fooled by me![2]
Hey, one comes from over there;
Now will I walk straight through my house.[3]
You will see here the greatest stupidity
That ever was heard or seen.
It is certainly him, no doubt about it,
Thus I go to my upper window.

SEXTON: Dear Lord, how you bless me,
No-one is as worthy to me as that beautiful one.
I should be well recompensed with her,

[1] A curious statement, perhaps intended to separate *rederijkers* themselves from being implicated in the play's foolery. Among the civic duties carried out by many chambers was the provision of music for festive occasions, and in fact several early *kamers* seem to have started life as musicians' guilds: see G. Kalff, *Geschiedenis der Nederlandsche letterkunde*, 7 vols. (Groningen, 1906–12), 7: 267; Natascha Veldhorst, *De perfecte verleiding: muzikale scènes op het Amsterdams toneel* (Amsterdam, 2004), 11–59. By claiming that musicians are not tempted by her beauty, the *wijf* possibly insulates the *rederijkers* from ridicule.

[2] A popular tradition, first documented in Henri d'Andeli's *Lai d'Arioste* (*c.*1250), describes how these wise men were each undone by women. According to these stories, Aristotle was once tricked into wearing a bridle and being ridden like a horse, while Virgil was suspended in a basket beneath his mistress's window, in full view of his neighbours. See Barbara Nolan, 'Promiscuous Fictions: Medieval Bawdy Tales and their Textual Liaisons', in *The Body and the Soul in Medieval Literature*, ed. Piero Boitani and Anna Torti (Cambridge, 1998), 79–106.

[3] The action here calls for a balcony, representing the upper storey of the Woman's house, the 'veinster boven' to which she refers. The rest of the action takes place on ground level, while the Woman observes from this vantage point.

	Ghefse mij troost, therte es verteert.	
	Hem, sec, hem, och wijde vermaert	
	Zijt ghij rusten, spreect doch een woort!	25
TWIJF:	Wie es daer?	
COSTER:	Ic bent, comt voort.	
	Ic ben hier te negen hueren,	
	Alzo ic u beloofde.	
TWIJF:	Fij, om ons ghebueren	
	Spreect heijmelic! Zijdij daer alleene?	
COSTER:	Hier en es niemant, groot noch cleene;	30
	Ic en dorste ooc niemant bringhen met mij,	
	Omdat tvolc zo clappachtich zij,	
	Zo komic alleene, als ghij ziet.	
	Och, zoet lief en troost ghij mij niet,	
	Zoe moet ict besterven in desen nacht.	35
TWIJF:	Ha, dat en meendij ooc niet!	
COSTER:	Ic doe bij sheerencracht!	
	Aylachen, waromme zo seghdij dat?	
	En haddic u zeker niet lief ghehadt,	
	Ic en hadde met desen couden winter	
	Hier niet ghecomen; ic meene men vinter	40
	Vele, zij en saudens niet hebben ghedaen.	
	Ic hebbe hier van desen jare ghestaen	
	Vervriesen, ic en conste nauwe vander stede	
	mijn voeten vertrecken. Up alle bede,	
	Laet mij toch inne en commes toe!	45
TWIJF:	Hebdij mij ooc lief?	
COSTER:	Oft ic doe,	
	Jae ic, ooc boven alle die leven!	
TWIJF:	Wel, wildij mij dan een sake belooven?	
COSTER:	Ja ic ende daer toe gheven	
	Wat dat es in mijnder macht.	
TWIJF:	Wildij bij mij slapen te nacht	50
	Zo moet ghij een stout werck beghinnen.	
	Ic hebbe een dootscrine staen hier binnen,	
	Die moet ghij gaen draghen te kerckhove waert;	
	Cruupter inne en weest niet vervaert	
	Met desen slaepelaken, verstaet mijn woort.	55
	Maer wat ghij siet, of wat ghij hoort,	
	Zo moet gij inde dootscrine bliven.	
COSTER:	Dat sal ic doen, rein bloeme van wijven;	
	Gheeft mij die scrine, ic cruper in.	
TWIJF:	Dat es den besten zin.	60
	Haut daer, gheluc en steect u duere!	
COSTER:	Ic sal wel ter kuere;	
	Ic sal daer binnen gaen ligghen swighen,	
	Mach ic aldus mijn lief ghecrijghen.	

	She may comfort me, for my heart is stifled.	
	Hey, I say, hey, oh widely renowned one,	
	Are you resting, do speak a word!	25
WOMAN:	Who is there?	
SEXTON:	It is I, come forth.	
	I am here at nine o' clock	
	As I promised you.	
WOMAN:	Fie, for our neighbours' sake,	
	Speak more softly! Are you alone there?	
SEXTON:	No man is here, great nor small,	30
	I dare not bring anyone with me,	
	Because people gossip so,	
	So I came alone, as you see.	
	O, sweet love, if you do not comfort me,	
	Then I must die during this night.	35
WOMAN:	Ha, you do not mean that!	
SEXTON:	I do, by God's strength!	
	Alas, why would you say that?	
	If I had no certain love for you,	
	I would not have come here	
	In this cold winter; I mean, you will find	40
	Many who would not have done so.	
	I have stood here throughout the year,	
	Frozen, I could barely move my feet	
	From this spot. I beg you,	
	Let me in to come to you!	45
WOMAN:	Have you love for me?	
SEXTON:	Surely,	
	Yes, I do, above life itself!	
WOMAN:	Well, will you swear something for me?	
SEXTON:	Yes, and I will give	
	Whatever is in my power.	
WOMAN:	If you want to sleep with me tonight	50
	You must begin with a bold task.	
	I have a coffin standing by here:	
	You must drag this to the churchyard,	
	Clamber in and do not be afraid,	
	With this bed sheet, understand my words.	55
	But whatever you see, or whatever you hear,	
	You must remain in the coffin.	
SEXTON:	I will do that, pure flower of womanhood!	
	Give me the box, I will clamber in!	
WOMAN:	That is the best attitude.	60
	Stand firm, good luck and get out of here!	
SEXTON:	I will follow this order well.	
	I will go there to lie inside in silence,	
	I may capture my love in this way.	

171

	Dats vetman, zo en darf ic niet claghen;	65
	Wanneer die clocke heeft twalef gheslaghen,	
	Zo zal ic gaen met mijnen lieveken onder.	
TWIJF:	Waer hoorde noijnt man van sulcken wonder?	
	Hoe heeft hem de dasaert laten beghecken!	
	Ic zie den pape, ic wil my decken;	70
	Hij heeft mij met allen huutvercooren.	
PAPE:	Hem, sec, hem!	
TWIJF:	Wie es daer?	
	Heer, zijt ghij datte?	
PAPE:	Ja ic, lieve minne.	
	Ic bidde u om Gods wille, laet mij inne,	
	Dat mij niemant en zie op strate!	
TWIJF:	Wat es de clocke?	
PAPE:	Thiene.	
TWIJF:	Wat, eijst zo late?	75
PAPE:	Jaet lief, laet mij tot hu daer boven.	
TWIJF:	Ja, wilt ghij mij dan een zake belooven	
	Ende die in desen nacht vulcommen?	
PAPE:	Ja ic, wat ooc es.	
TWIJF:	Zo zalt u vromen.	
PAPE:	Secht, wat wildij hebben ghedaen?	80
TWIJF:	Met desen slapelaken zo zult ghij gaen	
	Opt kerchof ende soucken een dootscrine;	
	Daer zuldy upsitten, al doet u pijne	
	Ende craken noten, die ic u zal gheven;	
	Maer al hoordij eenen gheest beven,	85
	Dien en beleest niet, maer craect heven stijf.	
PAPE:	Ja, dat zal ic gheerne doen, huutvercoren wijf;	
	Zal ic dan bij u slapen moghen?	
TWIJF:	Ja ghij, alst ghedaen es.	
PAPE:	Zo ben ic in hueghen.	
	Hoe langhe zal ic daer sitten moeten?	90
TWIJF:	Totter middernacht.	
PAPE:	Diet wilt besoeten,	
	Hij moet besueren; her, gheeft hier de noten.	
TWIJF:	Haud, daer zijn zij, siet!	
PAPE:	Dits wel ghescoten;	
	Ghij en ziet mij niet meer alleene.	
	God wil mij behouden van allen weene,	95
	Want dat ic bestae, het is dulheyt groot:	
	Vonden mij die gheesten, ic bleve doot,	
	Al waric stalen, - niet meer van dien.	
	Hola, ic hebbe de dootscrine ghesien.	

	That is excellent, so I do not need to complain;	65
	When the clock has struck twelve	
	Then I will go as my love commands.	
WOMAN:	Have you ever heard of such a marvel?	
	How has this dolt grown so foolish?	
	I see the priest, I will hide myself;	70
	He has chosen me above all others.	
PRIEST:	Hey, I say, hey!	
WOMAN:	Who is there?	
	My lord, is that you?	
PRIEST:	Yes, it is I, dear love.	
	I beseech you for God's will, let me in,	
	So that no-one should see me in the street!	
WOMAN:	What time is it?	
PRIEST:	Ten.	
WOMAN:	What, is it so late?	75
PRIEST:	Yes, it is, my love, let me come to you up there.	
WOMAN:	Yes, will you then promise me one thing,	
	And swear to perform it this night?	
PRIEST:	Yes, I will, whatever it is.	
WOMAN:	It will benefit you.	
PRIEST:	Speak: what would you have me do?	80
WOMAN:	With this bed sheet you will go	
	To the churchyard and search for a coffin;	
	There you will sit, even if it causes you pain,	
	And crack nuts, which I will give to you.	
	Even though you might hear a ghost shivering,	85
	Do not be afraid, but crack on boldly.	
PRIEST:	Yes, I will do that gladly, chosen woman;	
	Perhaps I will sleep with you then?	
WOMAN:	Yes, you will, when all is done.	
PRIEST:	So I am in joyfulness.	
	How long will I have to sit there?	90
WOMAN:	Until midnight.	
PRIEST:	Whoever will have the sweet	
	He must take the sour; hey, give me the nuts.	
WOMAN:	Hold on, there they are, see!	
PRIEST:	That is well thrown;	
	Soon you will never see me alone again.[4]	
	God will preserve me from all sorrow,	95
	For what I am doing is a great madness:	
	If the ghosts find me, I will be dead,	
	Even if I were steel – but no more of that.	
	Oh well, I have seen the coffin.	

---

[4] It is clear from the second half of this speech that the Priest is walking towards the graveyard as he recites these lines.

	Daer up willic gaen sitten craken vaste	100
	Met desen slapelaken. Uut allen laste	
	Wilt mij God helpen, huut allen saken!	
	Ay, hoe hert es de die!	
COSTER:	Wat horic daer craken?	
	Het zijn dode beenderen, ic ghemesse mijn zinnen,	
	Eylachen, wachaermen!	
PAPE:	Wat es hier inne?	105
	De doot gaet spreken, ay mij, ay mij,	
	Veni creator domine,	
	Groot Magnificat, ende tvers met allen!	
COSTER:	Eylacen, of ic huut ware!	
PAPE:	Wat zals ghevallen?	
	De doot wilt huut, ic ben verlooren.	110
	Ic sal stijf up de kiste duwen.	
COSTER:	Ghij sult mij versmooren!	
	Hoordijt gheest, sit vander scrinen!	
DE PAPE:	Ic en quam mijn daghe in meerder pijnen;	
	Water ende bloet sweet ic van vare!	
TWIJF:	Beter collacie, verre noch nare,	115
	En was ghesien, dan hier up zal vallen.	
	Ic hebber twee beghect met allen:	
	Den pape, den coster, God moet vromen.	
	Ic weet wel, die derde zal ooc schiere comen.	
	Dat es een joncker, hoort mijn ontdecken,	120
	Maer ic zallen ooc zo wel beghecken.	
	Hij comt, ic ziet, wel hij eijst certein!	
JONCKER:	O liefelic beelde, o liefelic grein,	
	Die ic met herten hebbe huutvercooren,	
	Ghij staet in mijnder herten plain	125
	Boven alle, die zijn gheboren!	
	Hem, sec, hem!	
TWIJF:	Wie es daer vooren?	
JONCKER:	Ic lief, ghij weet wie ic sij!	

	I will sit there and crack right away	100
	With this bed sheet. Away from all burdens,	
	God will help me, away from all sorrows!	
	Ay, how hard this one is!	
SEXTON:	What do I hear cracking there?	
	It is dead bones, I am losing my senses,	
	Alas, alack!	
PRIEST:	What is in here?	105
	The corpse begins to speak, ay me, ay me,	
	Veni creator domine,⁵	
	Great Magnificat, and all the other verses!⁶	
SEXTON:	Alas, I would be out of here!	
PRIEST:	What will happen?	
	The dead will out, I am lost.	110
	I will firmly push down on the chest.	
SEXTON:	You will smother me!	
	Hear me, ghost, get off this coffin!	
PRIEST:	I never had more suffering in all my days;	
	I sweat water and blood from fear!⁷	
WOMAN:	A better show, far nor near,	115
	Was never seen, than the one happening here.	
	I have fooled two, amongst others:	
	The priest and the sexton, God bless them.	
	I know well, the third will come here too.	
	He is a squire, hear my words,	120
	But I will also dupe him well.	
	He comes, I see, it is certainly him!	
SQUIRE:	Oh cherished picture, oh cherished jewel,	
	That I with my heart have chosen,	
	You stand as the measure of my heart	125
	Above all the others that have been born!	
	Hey, I say, hey!	
WOMAN:	Who is there before me?	
SQUIRE:	I, dear, you know who I am!	

---

⁵ 'Come creator Lord': part of the liturgy recited at Pentecost, and used in the ordination of clergy. The speech of priest characters in *kluchten* typically incorporates scraps of liturgy and prayer, generally as oaths: compare the *Farce of the Beggar*, line 249 *et passim*.

⁶ The Magnificat is part of the Liturgy of the Hours, based on the canticle sung by Mary to Elizabeth in Luke 1.46–55. It derives its name from its opening line, 'Magnificat anima mea Dominum' ('My soul doth magnify the Lord').

⁷ A blasphemous allusion to the Passion: 'But one of the soldiers with a spear opened his side, and immediately there came out blood and water' (John 19.34). The phrase 'water ende bloed', usually prefixed with 'sweete' or 'zweette', is a common tag in Dutch penitential lyrics, sermons and other devotional texts: see for instance D. F. Scheurleer, *Een devoot ende profitelyck boecxken* (The Hague, 1889), 19; François van Veerdeghem, *Leven van Sinte Lutgart (tweede en derde boek)* (Leiden, 1899), 78; Johannes Brugman, *Verspreide sermoenen*, ed. A. van Dijk (Antwerp, 1948), 129; G. Kalff, *Middelnederlandsche epische fragmenten* (Arnhem, 1968), 258.

TWIJF:	Wat heeft de clocke?
JONCKER:	XI of daerbij;
	Laet mij inne up gheloove als nu!
TWIJF:	Ic en ghelove niemande!
JONCKER:	Ende ic begheert an u
	Up trauwe, up vrientschap, sonder aerch.
TWIJF:	Dat en mach niet wesen.
JONCKER:	Om eenen guldenen berch
	En mesdadic u niet in dorperheden!
TWIJF:	Hebdij mij ooc lief?
JONCKER:	Jaic, zijt tevreden
	Ende laet mij inne, het zal u vromen.
TWIJF:	Wildij mij dan een sake vulcommen,
	Die ic u bidden zal nu ter tijt?
	Zo zuldij bij mij slapen.
JONCKER:	Jaic, sonder respijt.
	Al dadij mij inde helle gaen,
	Ic saudt doen,
TWIJF:	Zo eijst ghedaen.
	Houdt, ziet daer es eens sduvelshabijt!
JONCKER:	Dits emmer een vremt fautsoen!
TWIJF:	Up een cort, dat moetty an gaen doen
	Ende slepen dese ketene lancx ter strate
	Te kerchovewaert.
JONCKER:	Ic en zals niet laten.
	Maer wat dijnge zal ic daer bedrijven?
TWIJF:	Dat zal ic u segghen. Ghij sulter bliven
	Ende soucken een dootscrine, die daer staet;
	Die suldij bringhen sonder verlaet
	Hier voor mijn huus in deser nacht.
JONCKER:	Ic en zalt niet laten.
TWIJF:	Zo haest u al u macht
	Ende brinctse hier ende datter in zij.
JONCKER:	O liefelic lief, ic bringhse u vrij,
	Maer seght mij, hoe staet mij dit habijt?
TWIJF:	Met allen frisschelic.
JONCKER:	Nu siet, dat ghij in waken zijt;
	Ic bring u de dootscrine voor u huus.
	Mij dijnct, ic en gaver niet om een gruus,
	Al quaem mij Sathanas selve jeghen.
	Niet meer van dien, tes best ghesweghen.
	Ic ben ant kerchof. - Wat zie ic ghinder
	Met eenen slapelaken? Van grooter hitten
	Zo gaet mijn haer recht up staen.
PAPE:	Bijder doot van mij selven, wat gaet ghinder?

130

135

140

145

150

155

160

WOMAN:	What says the clock?
SQUIRE:	Eleven or thereabouts;
	Let me in, believe me as I say it now! 130
WOMAN:	I believe no man!
SQUIRE:	And I desire you
	In loyalty, in friendship, without error.
WOMAN:	That might not happen.
SQUIRE:	For a mountain of gold
	I will not corrupt you with coarseness!
WOMAN:	Do you have love for me?
SQUIRE:	Yes, I do, are you satisfied? 135
	Now let me in, it will benefit you.
WOMAN:	Will you perform a thing for me,
	That I beg of you now at this hour?
	Then you will sleep with me.
SQUIRE:	Yes, I will, without delay.
	Although you should send me into hell, 140
	I will do it.
WOMAN:	So it is done.
	Hold on, see, there is a devil's costume.
SQUIRE:	This surely is a peculiar shape!
WOMAN:	In short, you must put that on
	And trail this chain through the streets 145
	To the churchyard.
SQUIRE:	I will not fail you.
	But what would you have me do there?
WOMAN:	That I will tell you. You should stay there
	And search for a coffin, standing there.
	You should bring this without delay 150
	Here before my house this very night.
SQUIRE:	I will not back down.
WOMAN:	So hurry with all your might
	And bring it here along with its contents.
SQUIRE:	Oh dear love, I bring it to you freely.
	But tell me, how do I look in this habit? 155
WOMAN:	Dreadful in every way.
SQUIRE:	Now see that you are awake;
	I will bring the coffin to you before your house.
	I occurs to me that I care not a speck
	Even though I might run into Satan himself.
	No more for now, it is best to be silent.[8] 160
	I am at the graveyard – What do I see there
	With a bed sheet? From great fear
	My hair starts to stand up straight.
PRIEST:	By the death of myself, what approaches there?

---

[8] As before, the Squire is moving towards the graveyard during this speech.

	Het es een duvel, noijnt meerder vaer,	165
	Eylachen, wachaermen!	
COSTER:	Es de duvel daer,	
	Zo sal hij mij draghen inde helle!	
PAPE:	Wat sal ic doen nu, arem gheselle?	
	De doot spreect ende de duvel comt;	
	Nu ben ic eewelicken verdomt;	170
	Ic en hadde mijn daghe noijnt meerder verdriet!	
JONCKER:	Tes een gheest, hij ruert hem, ziet!	
	Ons Heer behoude mij mijnen zin!	
PAPE:	De duvel spreect.	
COSTER:	Wilt hij hier in,	
	Zo com ic met allen huut mijner memorien!	175
JONCKER:	Was ic tot deser crancker victorien	
	Te nacht up tkerchof nu ghesonden!?	
PAPE:	De duvel zalt hier al verstoren;	
	Ic en quam mijn daghe in meerder vreesen!	
COSTER:	Ic wilde, ic verkeeren mochte in een meese;	180
	Ic en darf mij verrueren noch verporren.	
JONCKER:	Of ic mijn keten rammelde, zoudic durren?	
	Om te ziene, of ic hem saude cuenen vervaren	
	Ende vreeselic burrelen ende baren,	
	Of ic Lucifer waer met allen?	185
	Tru, hou, ha, hai!	
PAPE:	Wat zals ghevallen?	
	Ic loope, of ic vare huut mijnen sinnen!	
JONCKER:	Ic dancke der hemelscher Coninghinnen,	
	Dat ic den doden hebbe verjaecht.	
	Nu willic gaen loopen onversaecht	190
	En laden de dootscrine up mijn lijf.	
	Helpe, zielgaten, zou weecht zo stijf,	
	Ic en salse nauwe connen verdraghen.	
COSTER:	Nu varic ter hellen, ic mach wel claghen:	
	De duvel heeft de scrijne gheladen!	195
JONCKER:	Ic valle in onmacht, staet mij in staden	
	Godalmachtich, de doot gaet spreken!	
COSTER:	De duvel wilt mij den hals breken.	
	Hij laet mij vallen, och waric huut!	
	Ic en hoorde mijn daghen noijnt zulc een gheluijt,	200
	Eylachen, de duvel leit hier vooren!	
	Nu willic gaen loopen, noijnt zulcken tooren,	
	Tot mijnen lieve met grooten node.	
	Eylachen ghinder staet noch een dode	
	Onder thuus van mijnen lieve;	205

	It is a devil, I never felt more fear,	165
	Alas, alack!	
SEXTON:	It is the devil there,	
	He will drag me into hell!	
PRIEST:	What will I do now, poor lad?	
	The dead speak and the devil comes;	
	Now I am for ever doomed;	170
	I never had more trouble in all my days!	
SQUIRE:	It is a ghost, he is raising himself, see!	
	Our Lord preserve me and my senses!	
PRIEST:	The devil speaks.	
SEXTON:	He wants to come in here	
	So I will escape with all my wits intact!	175
SQUIRE:	Was I for this feeble victory	
	Sent to the churchyard in the night?	
PRIEST:	The devil will overturn all here;	
	I never had more terror in all my days!	
SEXTON:	I wish I might change into a mouse;	180
	I do not dare to move or stir myself.	
SQUIRE:	Will I clatter my chains, will I dare?	
	To see if I should scare him away	
	With terrible booing and baaing,	
	As though I were Lucifer with all the demons?	185
	Troo, hoo, ha, hai!	
PRIEST:	What is happening?	
	I run, or I go out of my senses![9]	
SQUIRE:	I thank the Queen of Heaven,	
	That I have driven away the dead man.	
	Now I will go walking untroubled	190
	And load the coffin on to my back.	
	Help, dear body, it weighs so much,	
	I will barely be able to drag it.	
SEXTON:	Now I go to hell, I may well moan:	
	The devil has picked up the coffin.	195
SQUIRE:	I fall into a faint, keep me in wholeness	
	God almighty, the dead man is speaking!	
SEXTON:	The devil wants to break my neck.	
	He lets me fall, oh, were I out of here!	
	I never heard in all my days such a noise.	200
	Alas, the devil leads here from the front![10]	
	Now I wish to run – I never had such misery –	
	To my love with great need.	
	Alas there stands another dead man	
	Under the house of my love;	205

---

[9] The Priest exits here, or at least steps outside of the playing area.
[10] The Sexton apparently jumps out of the coffin at this point.

	Ic zal mesvallen van desen meskieve,	
	Niet min de schoone eijst mij wel waert.	
JONCKER:	En was mijn daghen noijnt zo vervaert,	
	Doen ic den doode hoorde spreken.	
	Ic zie wel, hij heeft hem dueghesteken;	210
	Nu willic gaen laden de scrine ghereet.	
PAPE:	De duvel comt weder, noijnt aergher besceet;	
	Nu zal ic met allen mijnen zin verliesen.	
COSTER:	Wat zal ic doen?	
PAPE:	Ic zal tlopen kiesen,	
	Want ic zie wel, ic ben verlooren.	215
JONCKER:	Die dode zijn beede hier, noijnt zulcken toren.	
	Willic de scrine laten vallen	
	Ende steken mij duere?	
TWIJF:	Staet stille met allen,	
	Alle drie, also ghij sijt!	
PAPE:	Waer sullen wij vlien als nu ter tijt?	220
	De duvel comt, laet mij nu inne!	
JONCKER:	Ic en ben gheen duvel!	
COSTER:	Zo doet ons bekennen,	
	Wie ghij zijt.	
JONCKER:	Ic wone hier in de ste	
	Ende ben een mensche.	
PAPE:	So doe ic me,	
	Ic en ben gheen gheest, al dinckes u.	225
COSTER:	Voorwaer, noch icke!	
JONCKER:	So seght ons, wie ghij zijt!	
COSTER:	Ic ben de costere.	
PAPE:	Ende ic de pape.	
JONCKER:	Ende ic de joncker, die woont hier bij.	
COSTER:	Bijder doot van mij zelven, zo hoor ic vrij,	
	Wat hebdij mij vaers ghedaen te nacht!	230
PAPE:	Ic was bijna doot.	
JONCKER:	Ende ic was in onmacht;	
	Tes wonder, dat ic bleven ben in mijnen zin	
COSTER:	Hoe quaemdij daer?	
JONCKER:	Dat icker verleet toe ben,	
	Minne van vrauwen dedet mij doen,	
	Dier mij tot dwanc.	
COSTER:	Dats mijn fautsoen,	235
	De minne van vrauwen dedet voorwaer.	
PAPE:	Ende ic, certein!	
JONCKER:	Ic hoore wel int openbaer,	

	I will collapse from this mishap,
	No-one is as worthy to me as that beautiful one.
SQUIRE:	I was never so afraid in all my days,
	As when I heard the dead speak.
	I see well, he has fled away;
	Now will I take up the coffin, right away.
PRIEST:	The devil comes again, I never had worse terror;
	Now I will lose all my senses.
SEXTON:	What will I do?
PRIEST:	I will choose to run,
	Because I see well that I am lost.
SQUIRE:	Both dead men are here, I never knew such troubles.
	Should I let the coffin fall
	And make my escape?
WOMAN:	Stand still all of you!
	All three, you as well!
PRIEST:	Where will we flee to at this hour?
	The devil comes, let me in now!
SQUIRE:	I am not a devil!
SEXTON:	So do tell us
	Who you are.
SQUIRE:	I live here in the town
	And am a man.
PRIEST:	Just like me:
	I am not a ghost, whatever you think.
SEXTON:	Truly, nor am I!
SQUIRE:	So tell us who you are!
SEXTON:	I am the sexton.
PRIEST:	And I the priest.
SQUIRE:	And I the squire who lives near here.[11]
SEXTON:	By the death of myself, did I hear clearly?
	What shocks you have caused me this night!
PRIEST:	I was almost dead.
SQUIRE:	And I was in a faint,
	It is a wonder that I kept hold of my senses.
SEXTON:	How did you come to do this?
SQUIRE:	I was led to it,
	The love of a woman drove me to it,
	This compelled me to do it.
SEXTON:	That is my reason,
	The love of a woman did it, in truth.
PRIEST:	And I, certainly!
SQUIRE:	It is clear now I hear it spoken,[12]

The line numbers appearing in the right margin: 210 (at "I see well, he has fled away"), 215 (at "Because I see well that I am lost"), 220 (at "Where will we flee to at this hour?"), 225 (at "I am not a ghost, whatever you think"), 230 (at "What shocks you have caused me this night!"), 235 (at "That is my reason").

---

[11] Gommersz's adaptation of the play inserts a protracted fight between the characters after these revelations; this and comparable additions extend the piece by nearly six hundred lines.

[12] Literally, 'I hear it well in the telling'.

Wij zijn alle drie verdult
Van eender vrauwen.

COSTER: Tes al der minnen scult
Van vrauwen, die ons bedrooghen heeft,   240
Daer groote subtijlheijt an cleeft,
Want alle de wijse hier te vooren,
Die van vrauwen waren ghebooren,
Waren alle van vrauwen bedroghen tsamen;
Hier bij en durvens wij ons niet scamen,   245
Dat met ons es dus ghevallen.
Orloef, Gods gracie beware ons allen!

Explicit.

We are all three duped
By a woman.

SEXTON: It is all the fault of love
For women which has deceived us,   240
Great cunning clings there,
For all the wise men here before us,
They were born from women;
They were all deceived by women in the same way;
Because of this we need not be ashamed of ourselves,   245
For that which has befallen us here.
Farewell, God's grace preserve us all!

Explicit.

Cornelis Everaert, *The Farce of the Fisherman*

T HE HIGH LEVEL of sophistication which *rederijker* comedy could attain is best encapsulated by the *Esbatement vanden visscher*.[1] The play is the work of Cornelis Everaert, described by J. J. Mak as 'a little-known genius of his time . . . no rhetorician and few poets before or after him reached the same heights in the comic genre'.[2] Everaert was certainly one of the most energetic and productive playwrights of the first three decades of the sixteenth century. During his time as *factor* for the Bruges chambers *Drie Santinnen* (The Three Female Saints) and *De Heilige Geest* (The Holy Spirit), Everaert produced some thirty-five known plays, and is the probable author of numerous others.[3] According to one scholar's calculations, this figure amounts to about two thirds of the total number of plays produced during his lifetime.[4] Alongside composing his own work, he also collected and transcribed the plays of earlier playwrights, such as those of Anthonis de Rovere, whose *Quiconque vult salvus esse* ('Whoever wishes to be saved') owes its preservation to Everaert.[5]

Everaert himself was born in *c*.1480 into the wealthy burgher class of Bruges.[6] Despite his prolific output he can only be considered an amateur poet, belonging to the generation before the emergence of professional writers such as Matthijs de Castelein. Like his father before him, also apparently named Cornelis, his principal business was as a dyer and fuller. This was one of the most prestigious and lucrative trades in the cloth-making economy of Flanders and, as a wealthy and prominent citizen, Everaert was intimately involved in many aspects of public life at Bruges.[7] Alongside his duties with the two chambers of rhetoric, he also served as *clerc van den Aerdchiers*, the official secretary to the shooting-guild of Saint Sebastien. His earliest known play is the *Spel van Maria Hoedeken* (1509), a piece dealing with the

---

[1] The most recent edition of the play is *De spelen van Cornelis Everaert*, ed. W. N. M. Hüsken, 2 vols. (Hilversum, 2005), 2: 628–44.

[2] 'Everaert moet gezien worden als een in zijn tijd miskend genie, aangezien geen enkele rederijker en maar weinig toneeldichters voor of na hem in het komische genre een hoogte hebben bereikt als hij': J. J. Mak, 'Everaert', in *De Nederlandse en Vlaamse auteurs van middeleeuwen tot heden met inbegrip van de Friese auteurs*, ed. G. J. van Bork and P. J. Verkruijsse (Weesp, 1985), 197.

[3] J. F. Willems, 'Cornelis Everaert, tooneeldichter of Bruges. Cornelis Everaert, tooneeldichter van Brugge', *Belgisch museum voor de Nederduitsche tael- en letterkunde en de geschiedenis des vaderlands* 6 (1842), 41–51.

[4] Gary K. Waite, 'Reformers on Stage: Rhetorician Drama and Reformation Propaganda in the Netherlands of Charles V, 1519–1556', *Archiv für Reformationsgeschichte* 83 (1992), 211.

[5] W. M. H. Hummelen, *Repertorium van het rederijkersdrama 1500–ca. 1620* (Assen, 1968), 16.

[6] The best account of Everaert's life and activities available in English is Wim N. M. Hüsken, 'Cornelis Everaert and the Community of Late Medieval Bruges', in *Drama and Community. People and Plays in Medieval Europe*, ed. Alan Hindley (Turnhout, 1999), 110–25.

[7] On Everaert's political and social affiliations, and the presence of these in his work, see Samuel Mareel, 'Entre ciel et terre: le théâtre sociopolitique de Cornelis Eveaert', *European Medieval Drama* 12 (2008), 93–108.

traditional story of the foundation of the rosary, which is partly set in Bruges.[8] From this date until his apparent retirement in 1538, he produced at least twelve further *zinnespelen* and seven farces, along with several miscellaneous and occasional pieces. He was also probably involved in the contest hosted by the *Heilige Geest* in 1517, a lavish event lasting ten days, and marked by processions of relics and official entries by the competing *kamers*.[9] Most of his plays are preserved in a manuscript compiled by Everaert himself, now held at the Royal Library of Brussels. This includes several valuable annotations on the texts, as Everaert often records the circumstances of a play's composition or performance. The manuscript also preserves its author's personal motto, 'So reine verclaert', both an anagram of Everaert's name and a brief artistic manifesto, translating as 'so purely declared'. Everaert died on 14 November 1556.

Much of the critical work on Evaraert has been concerned with his relation to the religious controversies of the 1520s and 1530s. As his service in numerous official positions might suggest, Everaert probably remained a staunch Catholic throughout his life, even during a period in which Lutheran ideas were beginning to filter into the Low Countries, and often into the chambers themselves.[10] As Kalff writes, in its overall spiritual framework, his work is 'orthodox in doctrine' and may in fact have been intended to 'help keep the old faith alive'.[11] On the few occasions that he does respond directly to new ideas on religious observance, as in his *Spel vanden nyeuwen priestere* ('Play of the New Priest'), he is invariably dismissive of the Protestants' conclusions. Nevertheless, despite his fundamental conservatism and his position within the ruling group of Bruges, Everaert still engaged vigorously with several contemporary issues, including corruption within the priesthood. In so doing he often drifted close to the unorthodox positions he explicitly repudiated. A number of his plays are concerned with ecclesiastic abuses and are invariably outspoken, often dangerously so. As Herman Pleij states in a recent assessment: 'the

---

[8] See Lynette R. Muir, *Love and Conflict in Medieval Drama: The Plays and their Legacy* (Cambridge, 2007), 33–4; Wim Hüsken, '"Van incommen en begheert men scat noch goet": Cornelis Everaert and the Rosary', in *European Theatre 1470–1600. Traditions and Transformations*, ed. Martin Gosman and Rina Walthaus (Groningen, 1996), 119–29.

[9] A. van Elslander, 'Lijst van Nederlandse rederijkerskamers uit de XVe en XVIe eeuw', *Jaarboek de Fonteine* 18 (1968), 29–60 (29); Anne-Laure van Bruaene, *Om beters wille: rederijkerskamers en de stedelijke cultuur in de Zuidelijke Nederlanden (1400–1650)* (Amsterdam, 2008), 209.

[10] See for instance J. Duveger, 'Lutherse predicatie te Brussel en het process tegen een aantal kunstenaars (april–juni 1527)', *Weltenschappelijke tijdingen* 36 (1971), 221–8; Alistair Duke, *Reformation and Revolt in the Low Countries* (New York, 2003), 101–24. There is some question, however, whether Everaert is responsible for the *Heilige Geest*'s pro-Lutheran entry for the Ghent *landjuwel* of 1539, which is not credited to him and does not appear in the *bundel* of texts he compiled. On this issue, see Nelleke Moser, *De strijd voor rhetorica: poëtica en positie van rederijkers in Vlaanderen, Brabant, Zeeland en Holland tussen 1450 en 1620* (Amsterdam, 2001), 131–2; W. van Eeghem, 'Cornelis Everaert op het Landjuweel te Gent (1539)', *Toneelgids* 25 (1938), 1–7.

[11] 'Een tiental zijn geestelijke spelen, die zuiver in de leer zijn en ertoe kunnen hebben bijgedragen het oude geloof in stand te houden': G. Kalff, *Geschiedenis der Nederlandsche letterkunde*, 7 vols., Section 3 (Groningen, 1906–12), 3: 61.

greater part of the *rederijkers* ask questions in their work about the ins-and-outs of the Catholic church, and many of them go even further by putting characters on stage who openly voice their doubts about traditional religious truths. This is certainly true of Cornelis Everaert, even in well-behaved Bruges.'[12]

The frequent proximity of Everaert's work to the ideas of the Reformers was apparently noted by his contemporaries, as his work was at times treated as heretical or seditious. According to Everaert himself, his plays occasionally ran foul of the civic authorities, and he was 'verboden te spelene' ('forbidden to play') two of them in particular. In 1530 his *Spel van donghelycke munte* ('Play on the Debased Coinage') attracted official censure for reasons that he does not disclose, while a further piece entitled *Spel van den crych* ('Play of the War') was apparently suppressed for its attacks on clerical greed and political corruption: as Everaert complains, 'was my verboden te spelene om dat ic te veil de waerheyt in noopte' ('I was forbidden to play it, and owing to that was forced to conceal the truth').[13] Moreover, as Buitendijk contends, the speed with which his work was forgotten after his withdrawal from public life shows that it was equally objectionable to conservative Catholics and to radical Protestants alike.[14] His indiscriminate movement between the two camps ultimately led to his rejection by both.

Everaert's work then presents an intriguing set of contradictions, not unlike the writing of Erasmus, to which it is often compared.[15] Although rigorously Catholic in their stated principles, his plays contain a thread of dissatisfaction, one which overlaps with many Protestant concerns. As Gary Waite aptly observes, 'in most of his religious plays he defended the essentials of Catholic orthodoxy while at the same time criticising materialistic piety and clerical abuses'.[16] In other words, the work of Everaert seems to present a stage in which the dividing lines between orthodox and unorthodox are not quite fully drawn. Pre-dating the Counter-reformation and the disturbances of the 1560s, when it became imperative to choose a particular side, Everaert could allow both the established religion and the newer ideas to intersect in his writing. He could launch stinging critiques against the church without necessarily crossing over into the opposing side. At this stage, it might be said, Protestant concerns were simply part of the bloodstream of the intellectual culture of the Low Countries, and had yet to crystallise fully into a cohesive heretical position.

This quiet affinity with some of the Reformers' views is evident in *The Farce of the Fisherman*, the piece translated here. This dates from c.1531, during the latter half of

---

[12] 'De meesten onder hen stellen in hun werk vragen over het reilen en zeilen van de moederkerk, en velen gaan vervolgens nog verder door personages in hun spelen op te voeren die openlijke twijfels uitspreken over de traditionele geloofswaarheden. Dat geldt zeker voor Cornelis Everaert in het brave Brugge': Herman Pleij, *Het gevleugelde woord: geschiedenis van de Nederlandse literatuur, 1400–1560* (Amsterdam, 2007), 637.

[13] Hummelen, *Repertorium*, 20; Wim Hüsken, 'Wie wás Cornelis Everaert nu eigenlijk?', *Jaarboek van de Maatschappij der Nederlandse letterkunde* (2006), 138.

[14] W. J. C. Buitendijk, *Het calvinisme in de spiegel van de Zuidnederlandse literatuur der Contra-Reformatie* (Groningen, 1942), 108.

[15] See for instance Reinder P. Meijer, *Literature of the Low Countries: A Short History of Dutch Literature in the Netherlands and Belgium* (The Hague, 1978), 79.

[16] Gary K. Waite, *Reformers on Stage: Popular Drama and Religious Propaganda in the Low Countries* (Toronto, 2000), 203–4.

Everaert's career. On the face of it, the farce would seem to offer little room for doctrinal or devotional concerns. It is at root a light domestic comedy, with its cast of characters restricted to the Fisherman, his Wife, and their three sons. Nonetheless, as Herman Pleij has stressed, it is often in such 'homely and trivial settings' that the *rederijkers* addressed their most serious concerns, and delivered their most pointed 'illustrations of the truth'.[17] Accordingly religious issues do cross into Everaert's narrative at a number of points, and the play has resonances with several contemporary debates. A central theme in the play is the sacrament of confession. The farce as a whole revolves around an act of confessing, as this generates the doubts over the Wife's fidelity that govern its second half. While the couple are at sea, caught in a storm and believing that death is imminent, the Fisherman urges his Wife to confess to him, telling her that 'everyone is a confessor in direst need' (line 89). She agrees, thereby seeking absolution for her sins from another member of the laity, rather than from an ordained priest.

At first glance, there is little that is problematic here. As Robert Guiette remarks, the confession in the play does not contravene practices that 'have long been supported by the western church': confession to laymen is in fact expressly recommended by a number of authorities, should a priest be unavailable, and if death is close at hand.[18] However, the play manages to extend this point in interesting ways. In the final segment of the text, the Wife claims that her husband has always been her confessor, since she regularly confides in him as part of their married life. As she explicitly states, he is entitled to be called 'mijn capelaen' ('my pastor') at all times, as hearing her confess is one of his normal functions: 'Since the time that I first slept with you/ There are things I never confessed to parsons nor priests,/ But only to my parish pastor and you' (line 254–6). He is therefore the equivalent of a priest for her, allocated the same status, the same title, and carrying out much the same role.

In raising the issue of lay confession, and then confirming its normality and ubiquity, Everaert draws perilously close to the Reformers' challenge to accepted practice. The play is in fact not far away from demonstrating Luther's blunt formulation that 'every Christian is a confessor'.[19] This again shows how readily Everaert's interest in ecclesiastic issues could lead him to express opinions that were not entirely orthodox. Of course, his farce is not intended as a wholesale or even conscious attack on the traditional teachings of the church. As Mak stresses in his edition of the play, the militant implications of these statements are not fully embraced by Everaert, as he 'keeps the holiest issues subordinate to comical settings or plot', and 'can blithely keep writing pious medieval plays and – *o sancta simplicitas* – stay within the same medieval dramatic tradition'. Nonetheless, the fact remains that the issue is still raised here, and that *The Fisherman* does border on heresy in its treatment: as Mak goes on to say, 'it is true that the "lay confession", in terms of its content, is

---

[17] 'Die huiselijke en grappige tafereeltjes gebruikt ter illustratie van een Waarheid': Herman Pleij, 'De sociale funktie van humor en trivialiteit op het rederijkerstoneel', *Spektator* 5 (1975–6), 108–27 (127).

[18] 'C'est qu'en effet, la confession aux laiques a été pratiquée assez longtemps dans l'Église d'Occident': Robert Guiette, *Forme et senefiance: études médiévales* (Geneva, 1978), 82.

[19] Martin Brecht, *Martin Luther: Shaping and Defining the Reformation, 1521–1532* (Minneapolis, MA, 1990), 20.

not something encouraged by the church'.[20] The play thus shows that Everaert, while remaining impeccable in his stated allegiances, does share many of the same ideas that will later become cornerstones of Protestant doctrine. His work is the product of an intellectual atmosphere in which heterodox ideas are freely circulating, as he absorbs them without committing himself to the Lutheran cause, seemingly unaware of how close he comes to dissent.

However, what makes *The Fisherman* exceptional as a comedy is its subtle manipulation of audience expectation, and particularly the way in which this is focused on the figure of the Wife. While most comedies of the period are content to invoke stock characters and allow them to perform their functions with little deviation or innovation, the Wife occupies a much more complex position. If anything she becomes a means of overturning stereotypical characterisation and accepted truisms. For the first half of the play, her actions and words connect her with various traditional conceptions of femininity, as she moves systematically through guises drawn from anti-feminist literature. From the outset she adopts the posture of a typical shrewish wife, nagging her husband, resisting his authority, and obstinately challenging his instructions. She also recounts with obvious relish some of the spiteful tricks she has played on him: 'When you came home well soused,/ I obstructed your way with a bench' (lines 104–5). Given the play's maritime setting, her stubbornness and aggression recalls the folkloric wife of Noah, who similarly disputes her husband's knowledge of God's word.[21] She also encompasses many of the characteristics of an Eve-like temptress. Her acquisitive fantasies, as she imagines how much money good fish might raise at market, are responsible for luring her husband into mortal danger, and nearly destroying him. The asides she speaks to the audience build on these connotations, as she gloats about how she will dupe her husband and 'dizzy him with illusions' (line 181).

Finally and most critically, she reveals herself to be an adulteress. When her husband instructs her to confess her sins, in the belief that both he and she are about to die, she responds by telling him that her children are not his. This segment of the play has numerous analogues, such as the thirteenth-century fabliau *Du chevalier qui fist sa fame confesse*.[22] These are invariably anti-feminist in tone, explicitly asserting the general venality and untrustworthiness of women. The confession also recalls the folkloric device of the 'rash boon', as the husband is unable to beat his wife once he has sworn not to hurt her, again casting the wife as a wayward element requiring male discipline.[23] The wife therefore embodies many of the charges traditional misogyny levels against women, recalling Proverbs 19.13 in her 'wrangling . . . like a

---

[20] 'Hij kan daartegenover rustig zijn middeleeuws-vrome spelletjes blijven schrijven en – *o sancta simplicitas* – naar dezelfde middeleeuwse traditie . . . en de heiligste zaken dienstbaar blijven maken aan de kluchtige situatie of verwikkeling . . . al is het waar, dat de "lekenbiecht", waar het hier om gaat, toen van kerkelijke zijde niet meer werd aangemoedigd': J. J. Mak, *Vier excellente cluchten*, Klassieke Galerij 46 (Antwerp, 1950), xvii.

[21] On this tradition, see Lucy de Bruyn, *Woman and the Devil in Sixteenth-Century Literature* (Tisbury, 1979), 132–6.

[22] Willem Noomen and Nico van den Boogaard, *Nouveau recueil complet des fabliaux*, 10 vols. (Assen, 1983–98), 4: 227–44.

[23] See T. P. Cross and W. A. Nitze, *Lancelot and Guenevere: A Study of the Origins of Courtly Love* (New York, 1970), 32–62.

roof continually dropping through', and St Jerome in her 'finding lovers' to 'minister to the indulgence of her lust'.[24]

Yet the conclusion of the play breaks utterly with this logic. In a final twist, which Kalff finds particularly praiseworthy, Everaert allows the Wife to transcend the misogynistic categories he has evoked through her.[25] By the end of the piece, the Wife has proved that her husband's suspicions are baseless. Although she has told him that two of their children are the sons of a priest and a servant, she reveals that these are merely aspects of the husband's own identity: in other words, the children are indeed his. She has also taught him a lesson in forgiveness and the importance of compromise, since it is his angry response to her minor admissions that caused her to make ostensibly graver disclosures. Furthermore she embodies these qualities herself, graciously pardoning her husband for his suspicions in the final lines of the farce.

What is important here is that the Wife has not just managed to prove her dedication to her husband, but has gained a position of moral authority in the text. Hence she both delivers the concluding address of the play and earns her husband's deference, not only by manoeuvring him into asking for forgiveness, but also by reminding him of his servitude to her. The text does not merely contradict the earlier stereotypes it invokes, but implicitly argues that women may impart moral wisdom, rather than being innately unruly or corruptive. In sum, Everaert uses conventional notions of womanhood in a highly self-conscious manner, voicing these ideas in order to collapse them, and to expose them as groundless fictions. The farce amounts to a defence of femininity in general: its narrative enacts the final message it delivers, providing evidence that women 'suffer from spiteful mouths', and drawing proof of this from the audience's own preconceptions (line 277). As befits a piece written for the chamber of *Drie Santinnen*, the three female saints, Everaert's piece has an emphatically pro-feminist thrust. It therefore merits attention, both as an artistic achievement and as a counterpoint to the casual misogyny of such texts as *Three Lovers* and *The Blue Barge*.

[24] Jerome, 'Against Jovinianus', in *The Principal Works of St. Jerome*, trans. W. H. Fremantle, ed. Philip Schaff, Select Library of Nicene and Post-Nicene Fathers Second Series VI (New York, 1893), 383. See also the texts assembled in Alcuin Blamires, Karen Platt and C. William Marx, *Woman Defamed and Woman Defended: An Anthology of Medieval Texts* (Oxford, 1992).

[25] Kalff, *Geschiedenis der Nederlandsche letterkunde*, 3: 68.

Esbatement vanden visscher

Personen:
DE MAN
TWIJF
DEN EERSTEN ZUENE
DEN TWEESTEN ZUENE
DEN DERDEN ZUENE

DE MAN:	Suer broot, salich broot!
TWYF:	Ten mach anders wesen niet.
MAN:	Diet pacientich beaerbeyt tsynder noot.
WYF:	Suer broot, salich broot!
MAN:	Sy moetent beslaeven cleen ende groot,
	Die visschen willen in desen vliet.
WYF:	Suer broot, salich broot!
MAN:	Ten mach anders wesen niet.
	Met Godt zynse gheresen ziet, ic wilt bethooghen.
WYF:	Wye? De visschers?
MAN:	Jae et blyct voor ooghen.
	Want sinte Pieter, thooft der kercken,
	Wast niet een visscher, om claer bemercken,
	Met sint Andries, zynen broeder,
	Sint Jacop de meerder, ende Marien behoeder,
	Den heleghen sint Jan ewangeliste?
WYF:	Daer of serteyn ic niet en wiste.
	Waerent ooc visschers in huerlieder tijt?
MAN:	Trauwen, warent niet? Alsse Christus ghebenendyt
	Riep, warense noch met den nette besich.
WYF:	Esmen dat in onsen wette lesich,
	So willict ten rechten wel ghelooven.
MAN:	Waenge dat ic hu wil met lueghenen verdooven?
	Tes waerachtich waer, my wel versindt.
WYF:	So zyn de visschers met Godt wel bemindt.
MAN:	Scriftuere doet blycken.
WYF:	Man, zonder beswycken,
	Tes best, dat wy ons om visschen voughen
	Mueghelic wy sullen Godt te bet ghenoughen,
	Naer dat hy de visschers zo uut vercoren heift.
MAN:	Hy es quaet om helpen, die den moet verloren gheift.
	Wel hem, die hem up Godt betraut.
WYF:	Man, zoomen ziet ende anscaut,
	Tweder es lustich, claer ende zoet.
	Et zoude my dyncken wesen goet,

Line numbers: 5, 10, 15, 20, 25, 30

* The Dutch text is taken from Mak, *Vier excellente cluchten*, 17–33.

The Farce of the Fisherman

Characters:

MAN
WIFE
FIRST SON
SECOND SON
THIRD SON

MAN:	Hard-earned bread, holy bread![1]	
WIFE:	Everything else does not matter –	
MAN:	When you work patiently to meet your needs.	
WIFE:	Hard-earned bread, holy bread!	
MAN:	They must slave away, the small and great,	5
	Whoever would fish in these waters.	
WIFE:	Hard-earned bread, holy bread!	
MAN:	Everything else does not matter.	
	Only one may rise through God alone, I will swear.	
WIFE:	Who? The fisherman?	
MAN:	Yes, and it is plain to see.	10
	Take Saint Peter, the head of the church,	
	Was he not a fisherman, mark it clearly,	
	With Saint Andrew, his brother,	
	Saint James the Greater, and the preserver of Mary,	
	The holy Saint John the Evangelist?	15
WIFE:	I certainly did not know any of this.	
	Were they fishermen in their lifetime?	
MAN:	In truth, were they not? When blessed Christ	
	Called, they were all busy with their nets.	
WIFE:	If this is what our faith teaches	20
	Then I will believe it is the truth.	
MAN:	Do you think I stop your ears you with lies?	
	It is wholly true, understand me well.	
WIFE:	So the fishermen are loved by God.	
MAN:	Scripture does prove it.	
WIFE:	Man, without doubt	25
	It is best that we set out to fish.	
	I hope we will please God well,	
	Since he has picked out the fishermen in this way.	
MAN:	He that loses heart is deprived of help.	
	But he that trusts in God is well.	30
WIFE:	Man, as you can see and tell,	
	The weather is cheerful, bright and sweet.	
	I think it will turn out well,	

[1] Literally 'sour bread' ('suer broot'), although we follow Mak in reading this figuratively.

191

	Dat wy budtkins vynghen, et waere proffyt.	
MAN:	Kir lieve wyf, doch daer of vermyt!	35
WYF:	Dat wy budtkins vynghen, twaere proffyt.	
MAN:	Ic bems te vreden, als nu ter tyt,	
	Maer cleen winnynghe zal ons dies ghenaecken.	
WYF:	Dat wy budtkins vynghen, twaere proffyt.	
	Mueghelic winnynghe zal up ons daken.	40
	Cont ghy moorghen in tyts ter maerdt gheraken,	
	Verwytsme, enge van elc budt niet een grootken hebt.	
MAN:	Nu met corten woorden int boodtkin stept.	
	Uwes raedts te doene wordic een ghenietere.	
	Godt hebs deel ende myn heere sinte Pietere.	45
	Dits van lande ghesteken in Gods bevelen.	

Hier moet zyn de manniere ghemaeckt van een cleen sceipken.

WYF:	Benedicite, zietme tvisch ligghen spelen!	
	Wy sullen nu budtkens vanghen by hooppen.	
	Siet waer ghunder een gheernaert comt ghelooppen	
	Achter een cabeljaeu, diese voor huer jaecht!	50
MAN:	Wat comt ghunder?	
WYF:	Tes een crabbe, die draecht	
	Een rochghe up den hals, wat vreimder gheveerte!	
	Siet hoe vast houdtseze byden steerte,	
	De rochghe en can huer keeren noch wenden,	
MAN:	Ghunder ligghen mussels by groote benden;	55
	Twaere best, dat icse om vanghen voere.	
WYF:	De zee dynctme over al in stranghen roere;	
	Tvisch houdt bruloft ofte keermesse serteyn.	
MAN:	Tesser al met vreuchden, groot ende cleyn;	
	Tscynt datse ter baeren looppen om prys.	60
WYF:	Siet, ziet ghunder een budt ende een pladys,	
	Die ghejaecht zyn van eenen hondt!	
MAN:	Siet dan ghunder! Een woester goet rondt	
	Wil eenen scelvisch dooghen uut steken.	
WYF:	Tscynt dat de tonghe ten besten wil spreken	65
	Om tsaemen met accoorde te verlyckene.	
	Ic en can my niet versaden van kyckene;	

	We will catch flounder, and gain profit.	
MAN:	God damn,[2] beloved wife, be quiet about this![3]	35
WIFE:	Were we to catch flounder, it would profit us well.	
MAN:	I am content as things now stand,	
	But some small income would help us out.	
WIFE:	Were we to catch flounder, it would profit us well.	
	I hope some income will come our way.	40
	If you can get to market on time in the morning,	
	I swear, you will have a *grootken*[4] for each flounder.	
MAN:	Now cut short your words, step into the boat.	
	It will benefit me to follow your counsel.	
	God and my lord Saint Peter have my thanks.	45
	From the land we slip into God's hands.	

Here must a small ship be produced in some way.

WIFE:	Bless me, see me acting like a fish!	
	We will now catch flounders by the pile.	
	See over there a shrimp comes rushing	
	After a cod, which drives him onwards.	50
MAN:	What is coming from over there?	
WIFE:	It is a crab, which draws	
	A skate around his neck, what an odd spectacle!	
	See how he has seized it fast by the tail;	
	The skate can neither twist nor turn.	
MAN:	Over there lie mussels in great clusters;	55
	It would be best if I went there and grabbed them.	
WIFE:	It strikes me that the sea is steering us crookedly;	
	The fish are having a wedding feast or festival for sure.	
MAN:	They are all full of joy, great and small;	
	It seems they are running a race for prizes.	60
WIFE:	See, see over there a flounder and a plaice;	
	They are being chased by a dog!	
MAN:	Look over there! A good round oyster	
	Wants to poke out the eyes of a haddock.	
WIFE:	It seems that the tongue desires to speak	65
	So that they may come to an agreement.	
	I cannot tire myself from looking,	

---

[2] The Dutch has 'kir' here, a deliberate bastardisation of the liturgical formula *Kyrie eleison* ('Lord, have mercy').

[3] The text seems to be missing a line here, despite the fact that it stems from Everaert's own autograph copy. At least, the following lines contain a *rondeel* that is not fully concluded.

[4] A *grootken* is defined by the humanist grammarian Petrus Curius as half a *stuiver*: Petrus Curtius, *Pappa Rerum Maxime Vulgarium Congesta per Locos in Puerorum Gratiam* (Antwerp, 1570), f.E1. The coin circulated in Brabant and Utrecht throughout the sixteenth and seventeenth centuries; a Hague ordinance of 1617 fixed its value at sixteen *minutae*, 'in moneyer's weight, the twentieth part of a grain': Albert R. Frey, *A Dictionary of Numismatic Names* (New York, 1917), 97, 151.

	Ic sate hier al de nacht zonder te verlanghene.	
MAN:	Wy moesten peynsen om budtkins te vanghene,	
	Souden wy moorghen gheraken ter vente.	70
WYF:	Ic consenteirt met blyden atente.	
	Veel budtkens te vooren ic ghunder sach.	

Hier moet ghemaect zyn een rommelynghe als een dunderslach.

MAN:	Wat hooric daer?	
WYF:	Een dunderslach,	
	Alzoo my dochte, met fellen oreeste.	
MAN:	Godt wil ons besceermen van tempeeste;	75
	Den Heleghen Gheeste wil draeghen ons vaene.	
WYF:	De zeede beghunt zo rude te ghaene.	
	O godt van omme te slaene ons sceipkin behoet!	
MAN:	Staet ons by, weerdich helich bloet;	
	Ic zalhu eeuwich dienen met herten vlugghe.	80
WYF:	O sinte Michiel buten Brugghe,	
	Wilt doch beede ons sielen bewaeren!	
	Ic zye ghunder commen twee felle baeren,	
	Tscynt ofse ons inde zee erven willen.	
MAN:	Wy moeten ons bereeden, zoo wy sterven willen.	85
	De doot duchtich comt ons bestoken.	
WYF:	Haddic doch eerst myn biechte ghesproken,	
	Ic waerts te gheruster in myn doot	
MAN:	Elc es een biechtvaer in duterste noot.	
	Dit moetge ghelooven zonder bedriechte.	90
	In noode mach elc hooren biechte,	

	I could sit here all night without losing interest.	
MAN:	We must think about catching flounder	
	If we want to go and sell them in the morning.	70
WIFE:	I agree with glad awareness.	
	Earlier on I saw many flounder over there.	

Here must be made a rumbling like a thunderclap.[5]

MAN:	What do I hear there?	
WIFE:	A thunderclap,	
	I thought, with a great deal of uproar.	
MAN:	God will protect us from this tempest;	75
	The Holy Spirit[6] will bear up our banner.	
WIFE:	The sea begins to grow so rough.	
	Oh God, keep our ship from overturning!	
MAN:	Stay by us, dear holy blood;[7]	
	I will praise you always with my whole heart.	80
WIFE:	Oh Saint Michael, outside Bruges,[8]	
	Pray for us so that our souls are preserved!	
	I see two vicious waves coming there,	
	It looks as though they will pitch us into the sea.	
MAN:	We must ready ourselves, for we will die.	85
	Doughty death comes to assail us.	
WIFE:	If I had first uttered my confession today	
	I would be assured in my death.	
MAN:	Everyone is a confessor in direst need.	
	You must believe this, no word of a lie.	90
	Anyone may hear confession in time of need,	

[5] As Worp comments, this is a simple enough effect to create on stage, and requires little in the way of special equipment: J. A. Worp, *Geschiedenis van het drama en van het tooneel in Nederland*, 2 vols. (Groningen, 1903–7), 1: 179.

[6] Everaert's allusion to the 'Heleghen Gheeste' refers to the *patroon* of the Three Female Saints, and not to the chamber of this name also active in Bruges. The two chambers had in fact been entangled in a lengthy legal dispute over use of these insignia, which was heard before the court of Flanders. The controversy was finally settled in 1494: see A. Schouteet, 'Inventaris van het archief van de Brugse rederijkersgilden van de H. Geest, van de Drie Santinnen en van het H. Kruis op het Stadsarchief van Brugge', *Handelingen van het Genootschap voor geschiedenis Société d'émulation te Brugge* 114 (1977), 380–2; Hüsken, 'Cornelis Everaert', 111.

[7] The 'helich bloet' refers to a cloth held in the Basilica of the Holy Blood in Bruges, which purports to contain blood wiped from the body of Christ by Joseph of Arimathea. This, like the chambers themselves, was an important part of civic celebration at Bruges. From 1311 onwards, the relic has been used in the annual *Bloedprocessie* (literally, Blood-procession) around the city on Ascension Day. In the early-modern period this occasion often overlapped with the activities of the *rederijkers*: in 1517, for instance, the *processie* incorporated a *wedstrijd* (contest) among a number of Flemish and Brabantine chambers, hosted by the *Heilige Geest* of Ghent. As *factor* of the chamber, Everaert was probably involved in this event. See Van Elslander, 'Lijst van Nederlandse rederijkerskamers', 48; August de Winne, *Door arm Vlaanderen* (Ghent, 1904), 215–25.

[8] This line refers to Sint-Michiels, a town close to Bruges, now a suburb of the city.

	Om te beteren der sonden ghebreken.	
WYF:	So laet ons dan ons biechte spreken	
°	Tjeghens elc anderen up een cort,	
	Want ons noot nu daer toe port,	95
	Up dat wy cryghen der hellen inducie.	
MAN:	Knyelt neder, dat hu Godt gheve absolucie.	
	Als ghy hu biechte sult hebben ghedaen,	
	So sallic ooc te biechten ghaen	
	Ende tjeghens hu myn quaet vermonden.	100
	Dus seght eerst tgrosse van uwe sonden,	
	Dat hu Godt zyn gracie wil gheven.	
WYF:	Ic gheve my besculdich man: eens hebbic bedreven,	
	Doen ghy thuus quaemt wel by drancke,	
	Ondersteldic hu den wech met eenen bancke,	105
	Daer ghy over vielt twee quaede scenen,	
	Om dat ic zoude hu dronkescip ontwenen.	
	Wat ic daer in mesdede, dats my leedt.	
MAN:	Ende voort?	
WYF:	Anhooret tbesceet:	
	Up de selve tyt, up de selve vaert,	110
	Doen ghy dus droncke te bedde waert,	
	Binnen dat ghy laecht in slaeps verduusteren,	
	Te wylen ghynghic hu buerse pluusteren,	
	Daer ic een dobbel stuver uut nam.	
	Tsanderdaechs maect ic van hy een ghuut gram,	115
	My ghelatende zonder ontbeerren.	
	Doen ghynct ghy van erheyt vloucken, zweerren,	
	Maer ic en ruste niet voor ic hu wech jouch.	
MAN:	Ghy moet hu wachten sulc onghevouch	
	Huwen man meer te beradene;	120
	Et mochte pooghen ons beeden te scadene,	
	Want by sulcke felheyt, vaet myn ontcnooppen,	
	Soudic up een huere al tmyne verlooppen,	
	Dies ons naecken mochte groot verdriet.	
WYF:	Ey, ic sals my wachten.	
MAN:	Ende voort, verstaet tbediet,	125
	Onthoudet woort van mynen bevelene:	
	Ghy moet hu wachten van meer te stelene	
	Tghelt uut myn buerse, vaet myn ghebriefte,	
	Want tes gherekent simpel diefte	
	Voor Gods ooghen, ghesproken plat.	130
	Eist daer mede al?	
WYF:	Daer es noch wat,	
	Twelc my alder meest doet verswaeren.	
MAN:	Ghy moet hu sonden al openbaeren,	
	Of anders en doocht hu biechte niet.	
WYF:	Ey, ey, ey!	

	To make restitution for your sins.	
WIFE:	So then let us speak our confessions	
	Telling each other and keeping it short,	
	For our need now forces us to do so,	95
	So we might obtain freedom from hell.	
MAN:	Kneel down, so that God may give absolution.	
	When you have done with your confession,	
	Then I will make my confession as well	
	And disclose to you how I am sinful.	100
	Thus you should reveal the grossest of your sins first,	
	So that God may give you His grace.	
WIFE:	I accuse myself before you, husband: once I connived,	
	When you came home well soused,	
	I obstructed your way with a bench,	105
	You fell over this, receiving two painful shins,	
	In this way I showed you to avoid drunkenness.	
	Because I offended you with this, it is my regret.	
MAN:	And more?	
WIFE:	Listen to this account:	
	At the same time, in the same place,	110
	When you were thus lying drunk in bed,	
	You lay within your darkened sleep;	
	I went to plunder your purse,	
	I took a double *stuiver* out of it.	
	The day after I made you an angry man,	115
	I nagged without ceasing.	
	Then from anger you started to curse, to swear,	
	But I did not rest until I drove you away.	
MAN:	You should hold off doing such wickedness	
	To damage your husband in this way.	120
	It would be detrimental to us both,	
	For out of such malice, hear my words,	
	There may come a time when I do run away,	
	This might bring us great sorrow.	
WIFE:	Oh, I will hold off.	
MAN:	And more, listen carefully,	125
	Hold on to every word of my commands:	
	You must refrain from stealing more	
	Money out of my purse, understand me well,	
	For it is simply reckoned as theft	
	In God's eyes, to speak plainly.	130
	Is that all?	
WIFE:	There is something else,	
	Which does trouble me above all.	
MAN:	You must lay bare all of your sins,	
	Otherwise your confession is not complete.	
WIFE:	Oh, oh, oh!	

197

MAN:	Wilt ghy scuwen svyants bedriechte, ziet: 135
	De biechte en mach niet zyn ghespleten.
WYF:	Sulge die sonde moeten weten?
	Noijnt en ghesciede my meerder blaemen.
MAN:	Seghse vry zonder scaemen.
	Ic belove hu in svyants spyt, 140
	Nummermeer en doe icx hu verwyt.
	Want seghgese niet, ghy blyft verloren
	Ende versteken uut Gods rycke vercoren.
	Dus en wilt hu biechte niet wesen spennelic.
WYF:	Lieve man, hu es wel kennelic, 145
	Dat wy thuus hebben drye zuenen,
	Waer of den houdtsten es de ghuenen,
	Die hu ende my alleene behoort.
MAN:	Ende dander?
WYF:	Verstaet myn woort:
	Dander daer naer, in biechten gheseyt, 150
	Es myn scnaepens kynt inder waerheyt.
	Ic biddu willet int beste verstaen.
MAN:	Ende den derden?
WYF:	Behoort mynen capelaen.
	Nu weitge van myn biechte et rechte slodt.
MAN:	Huwen capelaen?
WYF:	Jaet, zoo helpt my Godt, 155
	De rechte waerheyt hebbic hu ontloken.
MAN:	Hadget niet in biechten ghesproken,
	Hier gheseyt met goeden motyfve,
	Ic hadge gherooft vanden lyfve.
	Maer nu laetict om der biechten wille. 160
WYF:	Tes seker waer, wel lieve gille.
	Sout ghy hu tmywaerts met sulker nyt spoen?
	Ghy beloofdet my, ghy en zouds my gheen verwyt doen.
	Godt zoudtge plaghen, engeme hyet mesdeit.
MAN:	Trauwen ic kent, ic bem ghevreit. 165
	Ic houdeme ghepayt als ten tyden.
WYF:	Nu wilt hu sonden ooc belyden
	Ende seghtme hu quaet, naect ende bloot styf!
MAN:	Tempeest es over. Ten es gheen noot wyf,
	Dat ic tjeghens hu ontlaste my. 170
	Wy zyn ooc den lande vaste by.
	So wel zoudic my noch eens verclaeren.
	Voor mynen pasteur.
WYF:	Hebbic zoo ghevaeren
	Nu ghy zyt wetende de secreten myn,
	Dat ic niet en mach weten de secreten dyn? 175
	Dit mach my wel spytten int overlegghen.
	Maer non forche, men mach gheen biechte versegghen

198

MAN:	You must speak up to chase off the devil, see:	135
	Confession may not have two faces.	
WIFE:	Are you sure you must know these sins?	
	I have never been blamed more in the past.	
MAN:	Speak freely without shame.	
	In spite of the devil, I promise you	140
	I will not give you any more reproof.	
	For if you do not tell them, you will be lost	
	And thrust out of God's chosen kingdom:	
	Therefore you should not let your confession fail.	
WIFE:	Beloved husband, you know very well	145
	That at home we have three sons,	
	Of these, the oldest is the one	
	That belongs to you and me alone.	
MAN:	And the next oldest?	
WIFE:	Hear my words:	
	The next oldest, I say in my confession,	150
	Is my servant's child in all truth.	
	I beg you to understand it as best you can.	
MAN:	And the third?	
WIFE:	Belongs to my pastor.	
	Now you know the truth at last from my confession.	
MAN:	Your pastor?	
WIFE:	Yes, so help me God.	155
	The straight truth I have revealed.	
MAN:	Had you not uttered this in confession,	
	Spoken it here for an honest cause,	
	I would have robbed you of your life,	
	But now I will not because it is your confession.	160
WIFE:	It is surely true, well-beloved husband.	
	Would you act so forcefully against me?	
	You swore to me you would do me no harm.	
	God should torment you if you do wrong.	
MAN:	I accept the truth, as I am duty-bound.	165
	I hold my peace for the time being.	
WIFE:	Now will you also lay bare your sins	
	And tell me your wrongs, naked and entirely bare!	
MAN:	The storm is over. There is no need, wife,	
	For me to unburden myself to you.	170
	We are also very near land.	
	I intend to declare myself soon	
	To my pastor.	
WIFE:	I am in such danger	
	Now that you have knowledge of my secrets,	
	And I may not know your secrets in turn?	175
	All of this pains me when I think of it.	
	But never mind, one may not share a confession,	

199

	Up spaeus verwatenesse ofte ban.	
	Ic weddic up myn hoede worde, zo ic best can.	
	En hy my onghenouchte wil doen den baers,	180
	Ic salhem vry wel doen waenen waers.	
	Al weet hy myn biechte, ic en achs een gruus.	
MAN:	Godt danck, wy zyn ommers by huus,	
	Daer wy te wuennenne zyn ghewuene.	

Hier moeten commen drie cnechtkens al hynckel den vaer wellecomme heeten.

EERSTEN ZEUNE:	Wellecomme vaer!	
MAN:	Godt loontge zuene;	185
	Hu anzien my therte in roere brynt,	
	Puer van blyscepe.	
TWEESTEN ZEUNE:	Goeden dach vaere!	
MAN:	Wech, ghy hoerekynt!	
	By hu zoudic druck raepen licht.	
DERDEN ZEUNE:	Dach vaer!	
MAN:	Hefge, ghy paepenwicht!	
	Van hu zo steictme puer de walghe.	190
WYF:	Kir, et doet dat men hu byden balghe	
	An een ghalghe moet inden wynt cnoopen.	
	Waeromme smytget?	
MAN:	Laetet hoerekynt loopen,	
	Sendet binnen spapen bewelven!	
WYF:	Wel en eist al niet vanden selven?	195
	Elc kynt comt hu uut vrienscepe thouven	
	Ende ghy sceltse en smytse. Godt moetge bedrouven!	
	Wat hebben hu de kynders mesdaen?	
MAN:	Sent uwen cnaepe ende capelaen	
	Elc et zyne, dat hem behoort.	200
WYF:	Besiet, waer mede dat ghy comt voort.	
	Tsyn alhu kynders, wel lieve ketyf.	
MAN:	Myn kinders?	
WYF:	Jae.	
MAN:	Wel lieve wyf,	
	Payt een ander met sulc een clucht.	
WYF:	Ic segghe waer!	
MAN:	En hebt gheen ducht,	205
	Dat ic hu gheloove een hynckel luus.	
WYF:	Tsyn al hu kynders.	
MAN:	Dits ommers abuus!	
	En beleidt ghy niet, by goeden besceede,	
	Doen wy waeren up de zeede	

	Under the pain of the pope's curse or ban.	
	I feel I must be on my guard, as best I can,	
	Since this fellow wants to do me harm.	180
	I will pretty well dizzy him with illusions.	
	Although he knows my confession, I care not a speck.	
MAN:	Thank God, we are nearly at the house	
	Where we are accustomed to live.	

Here three boys must come one after the other to welcome their father.

FIRST SON:	Welcome father!	
MAN:	God reward you, son.	185
	The sight of you brings my heart to joy,	
	To pure bliss.	
SECOND SON:	Good day father!	
MAN:	Away, you whoreson!	
	I should quickly grow sick from you.	
THIRD SON:	Dear father!	
MAN:	Begone, you priest's brat!	
	I am filled with pure loathing for you.	190
WIFE:	Lord, it is fitting that men should hang your body	
	On a gibbet where it will twist in the wind.	
	Why are you angry?	
MAN:	Let the whoreson march away,	
	Send it to dwell with the priest!	
WIFE:	Well, is it not true that they are all yours?	195
	Each child comes to greet you out of friendship	
	And you scold and lash out. May God curse you!	
	What have these children done to you?	
MAN:	Send to the servant and to the pastor	
	What belongs to them, each his own.	200
WIFE:	See here, you do not know what you say.[9]	
	They are all your children, well-beloved caitiff.	
MAN:	My children?	
WIFE:	Yes.	
MAN:	Well, beloved wife,	
	Delight another with such a farce.	
WIFE:	I speak the truth!	
MAN:	Then have no doubt	205
	That I do not believe you by one single louse.	
WIFE:	They are all your children.	
MAN:	This is entirely wrong!	
	Did you not admit it, by good humility,	
	When we were on the sea,	

---

[9] We accept here Mak's suggested rendering for this line: 'Je weet niet, wat je zegt'. Everaert's Dutch translates literally to 'see here, be wary of what you bring forth'. Presumably this means that the Wife is warning the husband against reacting too hastily, as she is about to reveal her deception.

	In biechten? Hoe cunger tjeghen stuenen?	210
	Seytge niet: man ic hebbe drye zuenen,	
	Daer doutste of behoort hu ende my,	
	Dander behoort myn cnaepe. Voort zeyt ghy:	
	Den derden behoort mynen capelaen.	
	Deidt ghy my dit niet in biechten verstaen?	215
	Dit en cunge loochghenen varre noch naer.	
WYF:	So ghy seght man, tes seker waer.	
	Ic kenne, dat ict hu zoo verleet.	
	Nochtans zo zynt hu kynders ghereedt,	
	Verstonge mynder meenynghe advys.	220
MAN:	Synt myn kinders?	
WYF:	Jaet.	
MAN:	So maectme dat wys,	
	Dat ict te rechten ghelooven mach.	
WYF:	Dat sallic doen zonder verdrach,	
	In dien ghy my ghevet audiencie.	
	Ic weet wel, ghy gheven zult sentencie,	225
	Dat waerachtich wort myn bediet.	
MAN:	Myn daghen en hoordic vreimder liet.	
	Seght up, laet hooren hu motyf!	
WYF:	Ghy zyt myn man ende ic hu wyf.	
	Ic hebbe hu ende ghy my ghetraut.	230
	Dus es ons houdtste zuene, alst naut,	
	Huwe ende myn duer shuwelicx bant.	
MAN:	Daer of hebbic goet verstant;	
	Wy en zyn van dien in gheenen twiste.	
	Tes van dander twee hoerekynders, dat ic gheerne wiste,	235
	Hoe ghy wilt, datse my bestaen.	
	Want ghyse by uwen cnaepe ende capelaen	
	Hebt ghehadt, naer hu selfs belyden.	
WYF:	Ic salt hu segghen zonder vermyden;	
	Wilter naer hooren, wel lieve vrient:	240
	Noijnt en wassic van te vooren ghedient,	
	Dan sichtent dat ic hu te manne nam.	
	Ende noijnt ic met hyemande ter zee en quam,	
	Dan met hu te gheender hueren,	
	Daer ghy ghedaen hebt al tlabueren	245
	Van roeyen, van stieren ende dier ghelycke.	
	Ende waer ic met hu ghae in eeneghen wycke,	
	Altoos ghaet ghy vooren ende ic comme achtere.	
	By desen dienst, zonder scande of lachtere,	
	Syt ghy myn cnaepe, mids welcken dan	250

	In confession? How can you deny this?	210
	Did you not say: husband, I have three sons:	
	Of these the oldest belongs to you and me,	
	The other belongs to my knave. Then you said:	
	The third one belongs to my pastor.	
	Did you not tell me this in your confession?	215
	You cannot deny this, far nor near.	
WIFE:	As you say, husband, it is certainly true.	
	I know that I confessed this to you.	
	Nonetheless they really are your children,	
	You misunderstood the meaning of my speech.	220
MAN:	They are my children?	
WIFE:	Yes.	
MAN:	So let me know	
	What I should rightfully believe.	
WIFE:	I will do that without delay,	
	If you will give me an audience.	
	I know you will give the correct verdict,	225
	After my true explanation.	
MAN:	I have heard nothing stranger in all my days.	
	Speak on, let me hear your reasons!	
WIFE:	You are my husband and I your wife.	
	I have taken you as you took me:	230
	Thus our oldest son, it follows,	
	Is yours and mine bound by marriage.	
MAN:	I have good understanding of all this,	
	On this point we have no disagreement.	
	It is for the other two bastards I would argue,	235
	How will you explain that they are mine?	
	For it is from your servant and your vicar	
	That you had them, as you yourself stated.	
WIFE:	I will tell you without hesitation;	
	You should hear this, well-beloved friend,	240
	Never before was I serviced frontally,[10]	
	Until I took you as a husband,	
	And I never went to sea with any man,	
	Except you, never in any hour,	
	For you have done all the labour:	245
	The rowing, the steering, and the like.	
	And wherever I go with you, by any route,	
	Always you go before and I come after.	
	From these services, without shame or indignity,	
	You are my servant, which entails that	250

[10] A common euphemism for intercourse: it also occurs, for instance, in Karel van Mander's 1604 life of the notoriously libidinous painter Filippo Lippi, with much the same meaning. See Karel van Mander, *Het schilder-boeck: facsimile van de eerste uitgave* (Utrecht, 1969), 206.

	Hu dit kynt behoort, wel lieve man.	
	Verstaet te vullen mynder meenynghe woort doch!	
MAN:	Wat au?	
WYF:	Ontbeyt, hoort noch!	
	Sichtent dat ic by hu hebbe gheslaepen	
	En wassic te biechte voor costers noch paepen,	255
	Dan tjeghens myn prochghyepape ende hu.	
	Dus hebt ghy gheweist, ter tyt van nu,	
	Myn capelaen. Aldus by desen	
	So moet dit ooc hu kyndt wesen.	
	Nu weit ghy mynder meenynghe concluus.	260
MAN:	So doende zoudic commen thuus;	
	By dien zoudic worden ghevreidt.	
WYF:	Tonrechte ghy de kinders mesdeidt,	
	Die hu uut blyscepe quaemen tjeghen.	
MAN:	Ic waende, dat ghy hu hadt mesdreghen;	265
	By dien wierdic tot gramscepe gheport.	
	Waer in dat ic hu hebbe ghedaen te cort,	
	Dat willic betren naer myn begheerren.	
WYF:	Alsicker om peynse, tmach my wel deerren,	
	Dat ghy my betrauwen zout sulc een cleynicheyt.	270
	Soudic doen sulc een onreynicheyt?	
	My zoude ghescien der scanden anclevenesse.	
MAN:	Wyfveken zyt te vreden, ic bidge verghevenesse,	
	Ghy en sult my niet meer in sulc gheclach vynden.	
WYF:	Daer by moetense een ommeslach vynden,	275
	Vrauwen die becommert zyn met sulc ghebrec,	
	Of zy zouden up der quaeder bec	
	Haestelic ryden zonder veel delays.	
	Een lueghen gheloghen om thebbene pays	
	Es beter dan metter waerheyt te houdene ghekyf.	280
MAN:	Wye dat ghy zyt, man ofte wyf,	
	Esser tusschen hulieden hyet secreits ghebuert,	
	Syt te vreden ende niet en puert	
	In elc anders mesdaet groot noch cleene.	
	Leift met payse tsaemen ghemeene	285
	Ende dect elc anders eere, daer ghy muecht.	
WYF:	So salhu ghescieden voorspoet ende duecht	
	Ende de eeuweghe vruecht naer dit leven,	
	De welcke vruecht hulieden wil gheven	
	Den Heleghen Gheest, in wiens vruecht playsantelic	290
	De Drye Santinnen tryonpheren tryonphantelic.	

Amen.

	This child belongs to you, well-beloved husband.	
	Do understand the meaning of the words I say!	
MAN:	What next?	
WIFE:	Be still, and listen!	
	Since the time that I first slept with you	
	There are things I never confessed to parsons or priests,	255
	But only to my parish pastor and you.	
	Thus you have been, from that time to this,	
	My pastor. Therefore, because of all this,	
	This child must also be yours.	
	Now you know my meaning at last.	260
MAN:	And I become calm in doing so,	
	With this I will be satisfied.	
WIFE:	You were wrong to mistreat the children,	
	Who came out to you with joy.	
MAN:	I assumed that you had misbehaved;	265
	I was driven to anger by this,	
	In whatever way that I have done you wrong,	
	I will eagerly seek to redress it.	
WIFE:	As I think of it, it hurts me greatly,	
	That you thought so little of me.	270
	Would I do such dishonour?	
	Such a shameful past would cling to me.	
MAN:	Darling wife, content yourself, I beg forgiveness,	
	You will never again find such thoughts in me.	
WIFE:	Women who are wronged in this way	275
	Must find a resolution for it,	
	Or must quickly flee without delay	
	And suffer from spiteful mouths.	
	To tell a lie in order to have peace	
	Is better than having strife for the sake of truth.	280
MAN:	Whatever you may be, man or woman,	
	If there is some secret between the two of you,	
	You ought to be content and not peer	
	Into each misdeed, great or small.	
	Live with peace in accord together	285
	And guard each other's honour, whenever you can.	
WIFE:	You will then have prosperity and virtue,	
	And eternal joy after this life,	
	Which joy will be given to you	
	By the Holy Spirit, in whose joy pleasantly	290
	The Three Female Saints rejoice in triumph.[11]	

Amen

---

[11] The three *santinnen* in question are Mary Magdalene, Barbara and Catherine. On the chamber's iconography see N. Geirnaert, 'De miniatuur met de Drie Santinnen. Een nieuwe datering van het cartularium van de Brugse rederijkerskamer van de Drie Santinnen', *Brugs Ommeland* 23 (1983), 243–8.

Jan van den Berghe, *Jack Sweet-tooth*

MUCH LIKE *The Farce of the Beggar*, *Hanneken Leckertant* owes its survival to the chamber of the *Pellicaen* in Haarlem. The text is also part of the *Pellicaen's* play-library, where it is preserved in the same manuscript as a number of other farces, including *The Beggar*.[1] Like many other dramas included in this collection, *Jack Sweet-tooth* is accompanied by a brief note giving some information about its original performance. This states that the play was entered by the Antwerp chamber *De Violieren* (The Gillyflower) into a *feest* held by *De Lelie* (The Lily) at Diest in 1541. It also apparently won first prize at the contest.[2] If the note is accurate, then *Jack Sweet-tooth* represents continued success for *De Violieren*, one of the most celebrated and prestigious of the Brabantine chambers. The group received its name after gaining overall victory at a *landjuweel* in Leuven in 1478, and in 1510 was officially recognised as the oldest chamber in Antwerp, despite a rival claim to this position by *De Goudbloem* (The Marigold). In 1490 it gained an annual bursary from the ruling council of Antwerp as a mark of its value to the city, and this continued to be paid until 1587. At the Ghent *landjuweel* of 1539 it won the 'highest prize', consisting of four silver canteens and 'a silver cup weighing four ounces'.[3] In total, the chamber took part in no fewer than fifteen festivals of rhetoric throughout the sixteenth and seventeenth centuries, either as organiser or competitor.

Unlike the note accompanying *The Beggar*, the annotation attached to *Jack Sweet-tooth* also records the name of its author. The manuscript states that 'fecit Jan van den Berghe' ('Jan van den Berghe made it [the farce]'). Van den Berghe is a comparatively shadowy figure among sixteenth-century *factors*, as little is known about his life outside the chambers. Even his place of birth is uncertain. One contemporary source calls him 'M. Jan van den Berghe, alias van Diest', implying some connection with the Diest area of Brabant; this, however, cannot be corroborated, as the two names do not appear together in any other record.[4] Nevertheless, despite his obscurity, his activities as a playwright and poet are fairly well documented.[5] The first mention of Van den Berghe occurs in 1537, when he succeeded one J. Casus as appointed *factor* of the *Violieren*. He was therefore probably responsible for the plays which attained first prize at the Ghent festival two years later.[6] Some time after *Jack Sweet-tooth* won first place at

---

[1] Bart Ramakers, 'Voor stad en stadgenoten: Rederijkers, kamers en toneel in Haarlem in de tweede helft van de zestiende eeuw', *Conformisten en rebellen: rederijkerscultuur in de Nederlanden (1400–1650)*, ed. Bart Ramakers (Amsterdam, 2003), 109–24 (115).

[2] W. M. H. Hummelen, *Repertorium van het rederijkersdrama 1500–ca. 1620* (Assen, 1968), 93.

[3] 'Ende wy speelden daer een seer goet spel, daer wy af hadden den hooghen en meesten prys, vier selveren cannen, te samen ix merc. Ende den factuer, voor synnen persoen, j silveren cop van iiij onsen': C. Kruyskamp, *Dichten en spelen van Jan van den Berghe* (The Hague, 1950), xi.

[4] Philippe-Felix Rombauts and Theodoor van Lerius, *De liggeren en andere historische archieven der Antwerpsche Sint Lucasgilde, onder zinspreuk: Wt ionsten versaemt*, 2 vols. (Antwerp, 1961), 1: 178.

[5] The details and records quoted here are taken from W. van Eeghem, 'Rhetores Bruxellenses', *Revue belge de philologie et d'histoire* 15 (1936), 47–78, 57.

[6] Hummelen attributes one of the plays to him, the *Spel van de graci Gods*: see Hummelen,

Diest, Van den Berghe seems to have transferred his services to *Den Boeck* at Brussels. *Den Boeck* was one of the oldest chambers in the Low Countries, and ranks among the most illustrious: apparently founded in 1401 to supply music for the ducal court, in 1417 it boasted Duke John IV of Brabant as a member, and from the 1480s even had its own *speelhuys* (playhouse) for performances.[7] Van den Berghe is first named as *factor* of the Brussels chamber in 1543, and the remaining records of his career refer to plays he composed for *Den Boeck*. The last of these dates from 1556, and Van den Berghe appears to have died shortly afterwards, in *c*.1559.

Alongside *Jack Sweet-tooth* and a number of *refreins*, two other major works by Van den Berghe are still extant. The earliest of these, *De wellustige mensch* ('The Voluptuous Man'), dates from 1551, and is notable for its strong Protestant convictions: Waite describes it as 'a long and complex play which splices a Lutheran theology onto the traditional "spiritual pilgrimage" format'.[8] Slightly later is the scathing legal satire *Het leenhof der ghilden* ('The Court-Record of the Guilds'), a 'rijme cluchtische wijse' ('farcical poem') that made its way into print in 1564. A third play, *Ghanseman* ('The Gooseherd'), is listed but has not survived. Judging from its title, this no doubt continues the mockery of rural manners and habits which forms an important strand in *Jack Sweet-tooth*.

While *Jack Sweet-tooth* is in many respects as 'merkwaardig' ('remarkable') as Mak and Coigneau judge it, it also revisits many of the central preoccupations of *rederijker* comedy.[9] One widespread feature that is particularly prominent in the farce is the theme of food. Its plot contains the same thread of dietary humour found in *The Beggar*, *Prognostication* and *Saint Nobody*: in fact, it takes this to a higher and more elaborate pitch than is found elsewhere, referring to a wide range of specific foodstuffs, from the humble *booterham* (bread-and-butter) and *zoetemelk pape* (sweet-milk porridge) to relatively luxurious types of pastry, such as the *roffioel* and *vlaey*. The play concerns the efforts of the spoiled child Jack and his neighbour Philip Loser to inveigle expensive food from Philip's mother. She for her part forces her son to subsist on a diet of beans, and compels him to spend his days spinning thread, but hurries to purchase fine food when he feigns illness. Therefore, much like *The Beggar* and *The Barefoot Brothers*, the play is built around a central ruse which is intended to extort food from a vulnerable target. Branching off from this main strand are several episodes which play further with the themes of eating and digestion, creating linguistic and visual jokes around this core. At one point Jack teases Philip by alternately offering and withdrawing a spoonful of pudding, and there is an extended sequence in which Philip, ignorant of all but the most rudimentary meals, inadvertently makes a series of puns on rich foodstuffs. As in other farces, food is presented as deeply desirable, and its attractiveness

---

Repertorium van het rederijkersdrama, 130.

[7] Dirk Coigneau, '"Den Boeck" van Brussel: een geval apart?', *Jaarboek de Fonteine* 49–50 (1999–2000), 31–44.

[8] Gary K. Waite, *Reformers on Stage: Popular Drama and Religious Propaganda in the Low Countries* (Toronto, 2000), 72. See Jan van den Berghe, 'The Voluptuous Man', trans. Peter King, *Dutch Crossing* 28 (1986), 53–107.

[9] J. J. Mak and Dirk Coigneau, 'Jan van den Berghe', *De Nederlandse en Vlaamse auteurs van middeleeuwen tot heden met inbegrip van de Friese auteurs*, ed. G. J. van Bork and P. J' Verkruijsse (Weesp, 1985), 69.

serves as a spur for the rest of the action.

However, despite the key role played by food in *rederijker* comedy generally, the play's treatment of the theme is not without idiosyncracies. In certain respects it differs sharply from other, similar plays. As its games and puns with food might suggest, *Jack Sweet-tooth* does not share the underlying sense of anxiety that is clearly present in comparable texts. Its attitude is more ludic, as here food can be treated frivolously and casually, as an occasion for sport rather than fear. It is more of a toy than a desperate necessity, something to be played with and treated with amusement. This nonchalance is further underscored by the ease with which Philip's mother assembles a banquet of rich fare: despite her obvious poverty she is able to acquire 'sweet milk, and warm rice,/ A roasted pullet or a partridge . . . tartlets, flans and pastries' within a few lines (lines 382–4). In essence, the play draws on a more recognisably festive standpoint than some other plays, treating the feast as a source of pure enjoyment, rather than a cause for fear or anxiety.

This basis in festive culture, especially the practices and themes associated with carnival, is visible throughout the play. It can be clearly witnessed in the central binarism of the text. The action of *Jack Sweet-tooth* revolves around an opposition between the two houses of Philip and Jack, one dedicated to work and disciplined austerity, the other to feasting and the relaxation of rules. This is the binarism of *Vastenavond* itself, a night of celebration before Lent's long period of abstinence, which even commemorates the coming 'fast' in the first syllable of its name. The same idea occurs in pictorial work, such as a pair of prints Pieter van der Heyden produced in 1563, entitled *De magere keuken* and *De vette keuken* ('The Meagre Kitchen' and 'The Fat Kitchen').[10] Although *Jack Sweet-tooth* was certainly not performed at Shrovetide, since the *landjuweel* for which it was written fell in July and August, the logic of carnival is still embedded in the text.[11] Its two main characters draw on the same conflict that carnival also ritualises, pitting the feast against work and moderation.

Given this grounding in festive custom, it is unsurprising that a number of the characters in the play seem to be part of a common stock of types and forms. The Philip Loser character, for instance, appears to be a traditional or even folkloric invention. He also features in *Vuyl sause* ('Dirty Sauce'), an engraving issued by the Antwerp printer Hieronymus Cock some time after 1550 (Fig. 5). Here he is part of 'a boorish company', including a 'slattern seated on the floor . . . her hair streaming from beneath her untidy cap', and a 'bearded gentleman . . . about to season his pan of eggs with the discharge from his nose'. Philip himself is presented as a 'loutish youth' who will, according to the accompanying verses, 'van blyschap over dat ey eens danssen' ('dance with joy over that egg').[12] This last detail recalls the insatiable hunger, or reckless greed, he demonstrates throughout *Jack Sweet-tooth*.

---

[10] The theme is discussed in Dennis P. Weller, Cynthia von Bogendorf Rupprath and Mariët Westermann, *Jan Miense Molenaer: Painter of the Dutch Golden Age* (Raleigh, NC, 2002), 139–41.

[11] W. N. M. Hüsken, '1 augustus 1541: de klucht *Tielebuys* van Willem Vrancx wordt als welkomstspel gespeeld op het landjuweel van Diest. De kluchtentraditie in de Nederlanden', *Een theatergeschiedenis der Nederlanden. Tien eeuwen drama en theater in Nederland en Vlaanderen*, ed. R. L. Erenstein (Amsterdam, 1996), 106–11.

[12] Walter S. Gibson, 'Some Flemish Popular Prints from Hieronymus Cock and his Contemporaries', *The Art Bulletin* 60 (1978), 673–81.

Figure 5. Philip Loser (Lippen Loer) 'dancing for an egg'. Jan Verbeeck (attrib.), *Vuyl sause* ('Foul Sauce'), *c.*1560. © Trustees of the British Museum.

Other figures in the play have a similar status, also being variants of traditional types. For instance, the pompous scholar Doctor John Pedlar-quack has a clear resemblance to the figure of Maestro Grillo from the Italian *commedia dell'arte*.[13] Pedlar-quack and Grillo are both self-satisfied *medici fisici* who gradually prove themselves dishonest and 'unqualified' as the performance progresses, and finally receive their come-uppance at its conclusion.[14] But most importantly, the play's central character of Jack Sweet-tooth also occurs elsewhere. The figure of the over-indulged child or *moederskindje* (mother's boy) is a common one in *rederijker* drama. One close analogue is the irresponsible title-character of Wilhelm Elias's *Tielebuys*, a play also staged as part of the 1541 feast.[15] Other examples of the same topos are provided by *The Blue Barge* (lines 87–123) and the table-play *Van den ouden, ende lang-*

---

[13] On the *commedia* in the Low Countries, see R. L. Erenstein, 'De invloed van de commedia dell'arte in Nederland tot 1800', *Scenarium* 5 (1981), 91–106.

[14] M. A. Katritzky, *The Art of Commedia: A Study in the Commedia dell'Arte, 1560–1620* (Amsterdam, 2006), 32.

[15] W. N. M. Hüsken, B. A. M. Ramakers and F. A. M. Schaars, *Trou moet blijcken. Bronnenuitgave van de boeken der Haarlemse rederijkerskamer 'de Pellicanisten'*, 8 vols. (Assen: Uitgeverij Quarto, 1992–8), 7: 389–422.

hen Aernout ('Of the old master and tall Aernout').[16] The spoiled and unruly Jack is therefore one of a number of troublesome youths in the literature of the chambers.

In introducing this figure as its protagonist, the play reflects an important issue for the chambers. Many of the productions of the *rederijkers* either directly appeal to the young or focus on aspects of their growth or training. Even when not satirising the excesses of youthful disobedience, the *spelen* often show particular concern for the spiritual development of adolescents. This is illustrated by the 1539 Ghent *landjuweel*, where a number of the plays were *Everyman*-style moralities, focusing specifically on characters identified as 'een jongeman' ('a young man').[17] On the one hand, this apprehension about the young can be attributed to the urban context which the chambers inhabited. The cities of the Netherlands contained a large population of apprentices and servants, most of whom would have been teenagers or young adults.[18] This concentration of youngsters led to inevitable concerns over public order, and occasionally resulted in large-scale disturbances. Throughout the sixteenth century there were attempts in Mechelen, Brussels, Ghent and other cities to suppress seasonal games involving the young for fear of unrest.[19] Adolescents were also held responsible for much of the sectarian rioting of the 1560s: as Peter Arnade writes, 'the Antwerp pensionary Jacob van Wesenbeke blamed the violence in Antwerp on a classic quartet of '*enfans, jeusnen, garçons, et canaille* . . . . Van Vaernewijck's account of iconoclasm in Ghent in several instances mentions the participation of children and youths'.[20]

The *rederijkers*' insistent focus on the conduct of the young, and on the need to coach them correctly, therefore stems from an unavoidable aspect of life in the early-modern city. But alongside this, it also extends from one of the appointed social functions of the chambers. The chambers did see themselves as centrally concerned with educating and informing the communities in which they operated: as Wim Hüsken writes, the chambers held themselves duty-bound to 'instruct citizens . . . in their commonly shared belief'.[21] Many chambers in fact focused their efforts directly on youths, incorporating vernacular schools and training their younger members in literacy, deportment and citizenship, as well as providing some basic knowledge of religion and classical literature.[22] Thus the founding statues of *De*

---

[16] See T. J. I. Arnold, *Veelderhande geneuchlijcke dichten, tafelspelen ende refereynen* (Utrecht, 1977), 72–88.

[17] B. H. Erné and L. M. van Dis, *De Gentse spelen van 1539*, 2 vols. (The Hague, 1982), 1: 340–68, 434–68.

[18] Fernand Braudel, *Civilization and Capitalism, 15th–18th Century: The Perspective of the World* (Berkeley, NC, 1992), 179–86.

[19] M. Vandecasteele, 'Letterkundig leven te Gent van 1500 tot 1539', *Jaarboek de Fonteyne* 16 (1966), 3–57; Herman Pleij, 'Eind juli 1551', in *Een theatergeschiedenis der Nederlanden: tien eeuwen drama en theater in Nederland en Vlaanderen*, ed. R. L. Erenstein (Amsterdam, 1996), 112–19.

[20] Peter J. Arnade, *Beggars, Iconoclasts, and Civic Patriots: The Political Culture of the Dutch Revolt* (Ithaca, NY, 2008), 111.

[21] Wim Hüsken, 'Civic Patronage in Early Fifteenth-Century Religious Drama in the Low Countries', in *Civic Ritual and Drama*, ed. Alexandra F. Johnston and Wim N. M. Hüsken (Amsterdam, 1997), 120.

[22] See Herman Pleij, *Nederlandse literatuur in de late middeleeuwen* (Utrecht, 1990), 158–91.

Barbaristen (Saint Barbara) at Aalst pledge that the chamber will provide its junior *guldebroeders* with 'instruction so they themselves will be skilled and proficient in reading, writing and oration, and from this gain and learn the way to salvation and a sense of reasoned understanding'.[23] The frequent reference to the young in the work of the *rederijkers* therefore stems from this instructive purpose, their function 'as schools for the education of the rising patriachate'.[24]

By charting the punishment and correction of a poorly raised youngster, *Jack Sweet-tooth* touches on this wider preoccupation. In fact, a number of critics have noted its 'leerzame bedoeling' ('educational intent') or 'paedagogische strekking' ('pedagogic purpose'), despite its Prologue's claims to the contrary.[25] What is perhaps surprising is the actual solution that is offered. Although the play is never in any doubt that Jack should be physically castigated to remedy his behaviour, endorsing the 'birch cake' which Master John inflicts on him, it is just as keen to punish his punisher. Although the play ends with John's diagnosis that Jack should receive 'birch cakes...on his ribs...if he would have delicious things' (line 531–2), a parallel moral is provided by Jack's mother after she has beaten John himself: 'learn not to flog other people's children' (line 529). In other words, despite its implicit belief that children need to be kept in line for the good of society as a whole, the play is really a defence of the family as a private, self-contained unit. Society may suffer when a coddled child runs amok, but it has no apparent right to displace the authority of a parent. In effect, what the play reveals is that the chambers placed limits on their own instructive role. Although it asserts that outside forces should intervene to raise a child correctly, it also takes care not to challenge traditional patterns of authority, seeing parental control as the only proper check on the excesses of adolescence.[26]

[23] 'Instructie wesende int lesen, scriven ende prononchieren putter ende bequamer te wordene den zij gheweest en zijn, ende daeruut ontfangen ende leeren den wech der salichden ende den sin des redelicx verstants': F. de Potter and J. Broeckaert, *Geschiedenis der stad Aalst*, 2 vols. (Ghent, 1875), 1: 142.

[24] Herman Pleij, 'Novel Knowledge: Innovation in Dutch Literature in the Fifteenth and Sixteenth Century', in *Making Knowledge in Early Modern Europe: Practices, Objects, and Texts, 1400–1800*, ed. Pamela H. Smith and Benjamin Schmidt (Chicago, 2007), 115.

[25] P. H. van Moerkerken, *De satire in de Nederlandsche kunst der middeleeuwen* (Amsterdam, 1904), 101; G. Kalff, *Geschiedenis der Nederlandsche letterkunde*, 7 vols., Section 3 (Groningen, 1906–12), 3: 150.

[26] On the limits of the education provided by the *kamers*, see also Oscar Westers, *Welsprekende burgers* (Nijmegen, 2003), 38, which concludes that 'de serieuze, leerzame kant van de rederijkerij lijkt al met al geen groot succes te worden' ('the serious, instructive aspect of the chamber seems all in all not to have been a great success').

Hanneken Leckertant

Item Hier volcht Een prologe vant naervolgent Esbatement van Hanneken Lecker tant

Prologe

DEERSTE:	Vreucht is ons begeeren.	
TWEEDE:	Vreucht sijn ons motijven.	
DEERSTE:	Vreucht is ons hanteeren.	
TWEEDE:	Vreucht is ons begeeren.	
DEERSTE:	Vreucht wij nu vermeeren –	5
TWEEDE:	Voor mannen en wijven.	
DEERSTE:	Vreucht is ons begeren.	
TWEEDE:	Vreucht sijn ons motijven.	
DEERSTE:	Daerom, goede borgers, om vreucht te verstijven	
	Sullen wij hier spelen een aerdighe cluyt –	10
TWEEDE:	Die belachelijck is, om vreucht te bedrijven	
	Tot elckx gerijven, verstaet het besluijt –	
DEERSTE:	Van Hanneken Leckertant, een aerdighe guijt,	
	En van Lippen Loer met sijn moer die altijt most spinnen.	
TWEEDE:	Dan creech hij een schottel bonen voor sijn snuijt,	15
	Maer Leckertant haelden de soetemelckx pap binnen.	
DEERSTE:	Lippen docht mee altijt met hert en sinnen	
	Om aende soetemelckx pap te geraecken –	
TWEEDE:	En hij en wist niet hoe hij dat sou beginnen;	
	Maer Hanneken gaff hem raet, verstaet die saecken –	20
DEERSTE:	En seyden: hij most hem seer sieck gaen maecken.	
	Hij deet oock also nae Hannekens vermeten –	
TWEEDE:	Waer door hij oock quam om allerley lekkernij te smaecken;	
	Maer ten laetsten moste hij noch berckenstruijven eaten –	
DEERSTE:	Van Mr. Jan Luerquack, ten dient niet vergeten,	25
	Diese oock coocktten voor Hanneken, so ghij sult hooren.	

* The Dutch text has been reproduced from Kruyskamp, *Dichten en spelen*, 61–88. Used with permission.

Jack Sweet-tooth

Item: Here follows a prologue from the ensuing farce, of Jack Sweet-tooth

Prologue

FIRST:	Joy is our desire.
SECOND:	Joy is our purpose.
FIRST:	Joy is our pursuit.
SECOND:	Joy is our desire.
FIRST:	Joy we now increase –
SECOND:	For men and women.
FIRST:	Joy is our desire.
SECOND:	Joy is our purpose.
FIRST:	For this end, good citizens, for strengthening joy,
	We will play here an amusing farce –
SECOND:	One that is comical, to create joy,
	Free to all, understand what happened –
FIRST:	To Jack Sweet-tooth, an amusing chap,
	And to Philip Loser, with his mother, who spun most of the time –
SECOND:	He always found a dish of beans before his nose,
	As Sweet-tooth took the sweet-milk porridge within him.[1]
FIRST:	Philip also plotted, constantly, with heart and mind
	Scheming how to reach the sweet-milk porridge –
SECOND:	Yet he did not know how he should begin,
	But Jack gave him counsel, understand these things –
FIRST:	And said: he must go and make himself very sick.
	He then did as Jack's plan demanded –
SECOND:	By this he also came to taste the sumptuous treat;
	But at the end he had to eat the birch-cakes –
FIRST:	Of Doctor John Pedlar-quack, but do not forget,
	These also were cooked for Jack, as you will hear.

Line numbers in right margin: 5 (line 5), 10 (line 10), 15 (line 15), 20 (line 20), 25 (line 25)

[1] The *zoete pap* at the centre of the play is a type of rudimentary pudding, a sweetened porridge made of wheat or barley and flavoured with spices, along the same lines as the English frumenty. According to an eighteenth-century recipe, this 'goede podding' could be made with raisins, ground nutmeg, pieces of white bread, lemon and orange peel, succade, almonds or melted butter: Noel Chomel, *Algemeen huishoudelijk-, natuur-, zedekundig-, en konst- woordenboek*, 7 vols. (Leiden, 1778), 5: 2777–8. In spite of its relative simplicity, in medieval folklore and popular literature the *pap* often features as an archetypal desirable foodstuff. The Brothers Grimm, for instance, preserve the story 'Der süße Brei', in which an enchanted cooking-pot produces the porridge inexhaustibly; likewise, in the English *fabliau* 'The Vnluckie Firmentie' (*c.*1572), attributed to one 'G. Kyttes', a bridegroom's fixation with the dish ruins his wedding night. Pleij also quotes a popular *kerstliedje* (Christmas carol) in which Mary demands of her husband 'Jozef, maak voor ons een zoete pap, en snel een beetje, gauw' ('Joseph, make for us a sweet porridge, and a little quicker, go'): Herman Pleij, *Sprekend over de middeleeuwen* (Utrecht, 1991), 72. The pudding still serves much the same function in modern Dutch nursery rhymes, such as 'Kleine katrijne' ('Little Catherine'): Nellie van Kol, *Kinderversjes* (Alkmaar, 1923), 53.

TWEEDE:	Daerom most hij wesen met vuysten gesmeten
	Van Hannekens moeder, die haer daerom ging verstoren.
DEERSTE:	Dit sullen wij spelen, om vreucht te orboren,
	U ter eeren, goede borgers, om vrolijck te wesen. 30
TWEEDE:	En oft wij ijet faelgierden, ons faulten wilt smoren,
	So sult ghij doen als die waerdich sijt gepresen.
DEERSTE:	Maar eer wij beginnen, hoort wadt wij u voorlesen:
	Bewaert wel u buijdels voor der pickaerts practijcken –
TWEEDE:	So hebt ghij niet voor eenich ongheluck te vresen 35
	Oft dat een ander met u gelt sal gaen strijcken.
DEERSTE:	Wij bidden u altsaemen, armen en rijcken,
	Wilt noch niet wech wijcken naer ons vermonden plaen –
TWEEDE:	Maer staet een weijnich stil, wij beginnen van stonden aen.

Fijnis vanden prologe. Lang 39 regulen.

Volcht spel onder aen.
Item Hier volcht het Esbatement van Hanneken Leckertant

De personages sijn dese:
GOEY VROU VEUGHE, een vrou
HANNEKEN LECKERTANT, duijpenachtig
VRECKE WEBBE
LIPPEN LOER, Vrecke Webbens soon, spinnende
MEESTER JAN LEUREQUACK

SECOND:	He was struck with fists for this
	By Jack's mother, who quickly grew riled from it.
FIRST:	This we will play, to spread joy,
	To honour you, good citizens, to make you joyful – 30
SECOND:	And if we fail in this, you should overlook our flaws,[2]
	You should do as those who are worthy of praise –
FIRST:	But before we begin, hear what we teach you:
	Guard your purses well from the schemes of pickpockets –
SECOND:	So you do not have to fear any misfortune, 35
	Or fear that another should go off and spend your money.[3]
FIRST:	We pray for you all the same, poor men and rich men,
	You should not wander away from our planned adventures –
SECOND:	But stand still a while, we begin as of this time.

The end of the prologue. 39 line long.

The play follows below.
Item: Here follows the farce of Jack Sweet-tooth

> *The characters are these:*
> GOOD WIFE CODDLE, a woman[4]
> JACK SWEET-TOOTH, babyish[5]
> MISERLY WEAVER[6]
> PHILIP LOSER, Miserly Weaver's son, spinning
> DOCTOR JOHN PEDLAR-QUACK

---

[2] The text has *smoren*, literally 'smother', 'stifle'. We follow Krusykamp's suggestion of *bedekken*, 'cover over'.

[3] An interesting but not unprecedented reminder of the perils of attending plays in open public spaces. Similar warnings to the audience occur in no fewer than four of Everaert's works, including his earliest play, *Maria Hoedeken* (1509): see J. W. Muller and L. Scharpé, *Spelen van Cornelise Everaert*, 3 vols. (Leiden, 1898–1920), 3: 559. Other plays also refer to the dangers of *zakkenrollers*, including *Een spel van sinne van Charon* (1551) and Anthonis de Roovere's *Quiconque vult salvus esse* (c.1470): see G. Jo Steenbergen, *Het landjuweel van de rederijkers* (Leuven, 1951), 113.

[4] Her name is derived from the verb *veuge*, or *voegen* in Modern Dutch, meaning 'accommodate' or 'oblige'.

[5] *Hanneken* is a diminutive of Jan or Johannes, in much the same way that Jack or Johnny is a diminutive of the English John.

[6] The character's forename is a play on *vrek* (miser) and *vrouwke* (miss, or madam). As her surname states, she is a weaver by trade. As elsewhere in pre-industrial Europe, weaving and spinning flax were predominantly female domestic occupations in the Low Countries, especially outside the cities. See for instance the fourteenth-century song 'Wi willen van den kerels zinghen' ('We wish to sing of the peasants'), which ridicules various aspects of rural life, and contains the lines, 'Dan comt tot hem sijn wijf, de vule,/ Spinnende met enen rocke,/ Een sleter omtrent haer mule' ('Then his wife comes to him, spinning with a distaff, and with rags hanging out of her mouth'): C. C. van de Graft, *Middelnederlandsche historieliederen* (Ypres, 1904), 61.

VEUGE:	Alle goeden dach! ick ben ommers op graeckt;	40
	Hadde ick nu wadt goets, dat leckerlijck smaeckt,	
	Dat Hanneken mijns soons mage mocht verteren!	
	Leet hij oock gebreck, och! tsou mijn deren,	
	Want noijt man en sach kint so subtijl van liste.	
	Waert dat de Prince van Oraingien wiste	45
	Hoe edel dat hij is in al sijn voorstel,	
	Hij sout mij affnemen / ja hij, dat weet ick wel.	
	Geen fraijheijt en is aan hem vergeten;	
	En al wadt lecker is / can hij wel eeten,	
	So natuerlijck groeijt hem d'edelheijt int lijff.	50
	Grove spijse, seit hij / die maeckt de leden stijff,	
	Dies moet ick hem alle lieffelijckheijt bien.	
	Van hem sal mij noch deucht en eere geschien,	
	So eens tot mij een wijse vrouwe sprack.	
	Oock heeft mij geseijt Meester Jan Leurquack,	55
	Dat hij is geboren, so hij in boecken las,	
	Inde beste planeet die in den hemel was.	
	Dus twaer tegens natuere, dede ick hem leet.	
HANNEKEN:	Moeijer! Ou!	
VEUGE:	Wadt ist?	
HANNEKEN:	Is dwidtmoes noch niet gereet	
VEUGE:	Neent sone.	
HANNEKEN:	Dats mij een alte grooten verdriet.	60
	Trouwens, ghij seijt mij gisteren, en dedij niet?	
	Dat ghij mij nu sout wadt lecker coocken.	
VEUGE:	Ick salt doen, kint, ick moet tvier eerst stoocken,	
	Maar 't is uuijte, mij dunckt ick geen en hebbe.	
	Slaept noch / ick gaen om vier tot die Vrecke Webbe,	65
	Suldij Hanneken? en sijt wadt gerust.	
HANNEKEN:	Ja ick, moeijer, maer ghij en hebt mij niet gecust,	
	Dat sal ick clagen tot Lijse mijn nichtgen.	
VEUGE:	Nu cust mij / En ist niet een vrindelijck wichtgen?	
	Wie en sou hem sijn willeken niet gehingen?	70

Vrecke Webbe spreeckt tot haar soon Lippen

| | Spint! wildij. | |
| LIPPEN (*spinnende*): | Suldij mij dan t' eeten bringen? |

CODDLE:	To all good day![7] I have been up for a while; 40
	If I only had something good now, that tastes delicious,
	That might fill the belly of my son Jack!
	Should he also go without, oh! it should hurt me,
	For a man never saw a child so subtle of guile.
	If it were that the Prince of Orange knew[8] 45
	How noble he is in all his business,
	He would deprive me of him, yes he would, I know it well.
	No grace is wanting in him;
	And he very much likes to eat all that is delicious,
	Nobility of body occurs so naturally in him. 50
	Coarse food, he says, makes his limbs stiffen,
	Therefore I must give him every lovely thing.
	Joy and honour will bless me through him,
	So a wise woman once said to me.
	Also Doctor John Pedlar-quack has told me 55
	That he was born, so he read in books,
	Under the best planet that is in the sky.
	Thus it would be against nature if I did him grief.
JACK:	Mother! hey!
CODDLE:	What is it?
JACK:	Is the white mash ready yet?[9]
CODDLE:	No, son.
JACK:	This is altogether a great sadness for me. 60
	In truth, you told me yesterday, did you not,
	That you would cook something delicious for me now.
CODDLE:	I will do so, child, I must stoke the fire first,
	For it is out; it seems to me I have no flame.
	I will go to Miserly Weaver for fire; sleep now, 65
	Will you, Jack? And be calm.
JACK:	Yes, I will, mother, but you have not kissed me;
	I will report this to my cousin Lise.
CODDLE:	Now kiss me: is he not a darling child?
	Who would not do everything he wishes? 70

Miserly Weaver speaks to her son Philip

WEAVER:	Spin, will you!
PHILIP (*spinning*):	Will you then bring me something to eat?

---

[7] This might suggest that *Jack Sweet-tooth* was initially played during the afternoon, i.e. during daylight hours. As Kalff points out, plays would often refer to their time of performance, especially if they departed from the usual practice of being staged in the evening: Kalff, *Geschiedenis der Nederlandsche letterkunde*, 3: 519.

[8] As Krusykamp observes, this should be read as a later interpolation, since Willem of Orange only became an important figure in the Netherlands after 1559, when he was made *stadhouder* of the emergent republic.

[9] *Dwidtmoes* is evidently an alternative name for the sweet-milk porridge mentioned in the Prologue.

WEBBE:	Peijnsdij alre om eeten, seght, onaerdich gast?	
LIPPEN:	En soudick niet? ick hebbe doch alden nacht gevast;	
	Ten is geen wonder al quelt mij de honger straff.	
WEBBE:	Spint mij alder eerst dien rocking aff,	75
	Eer ghij van eeten spreect, vuijl slappe leure!	
VEUGE:	Mij dunckt, vrecke Webbe sidt voor haer deure;	
	Noijt en sach ick wijf int werck so vierich!	
	Goeden dach, Webbe, sijdij al eeven gierich?	
	Sal u herte nimmermeer sijn vervult?	80
	Wie sal tgoet verteeren dat ghij winnen sult?	
	Ghy slaeft als eene die in dachuere spidt?	
WEBBE:	Wiet verteeren sal?	
VEUGE:	Ja.	
WEBBE:	Dien loeris, die daer sidt,	
	Daer sorghe noch eere in en schuijlt.	
	Hij sidt daer alre om eeten en muijlt;	85
	Nochtans en heeft hij nau drie draijen gesponnen.	
VEUGE:	Webbe, al en is den cost noch niet gewonnen,	
	Kinderen moeten eeten, wadt baetet geseijt?	
	Hanneken mijn soone heeft wel een uere geschreijt	
	En geroepen om die witmoes pappe.	90
LIPPEN:	Sweepen, mijn herte quackelt vandien clappe!	
	Mocht ick daer aff eens vol steecken mijnen crop	
	Daer gaff ick omme mijnen besten top;	
	Van sulcken cost sou mijn herte verblijen.	
WEBBE:	Ghij sult u wel met een schootel bonen lijen!	95
	Hebdij honger, verslaet daer mede uwen lost.	
LIPPEN:	Ja, dats oock dagelijckx mijnen besten cost;	
	Maer quam u vrijer, die sou wadt leckers crijgen.	
WEBBE:	Wadt segdij daer?	
LIPPEN:	Niet moeijer, ick ga swijgen.	
	Daer wasse bijcans geterden op haeren teen!	100
	Maer om die witmoes pappe peijnsick alleneen,	
	Mocht ick daer op mijn tanden eens wetten,	
	Ick sou mijnen buijck so viercant setten	
	Als een biertonneken, vrij sonder sparen.	
VEUGE:	Webbe, wij souden van ons voorleden jaren	105
	Wat couten, gaefft pas en sweech Lippen stille.	
LIPPEN:	Teerlinck! daer ontvalt mijn mijnne spille!	

WEAVER:	Are you already thinking about eating, tell me, ungrateful sponger?
PHILIP:	Why should I not? I have fasted the whole night;
	It is no wonder then that hunger inflicts torment on me.
WEAVER:	First spin for me all that is loaded on the distaff, 75
	Before you speak of food, you vile slothful scrap!
CODDLE:	It seems to me that Miserly Weaver sits before her door;
	I never saw a woman so fiery in her work!
	Good day, Weaver, are you still just as grasping?
	Will your heart never be satisfied? 80
	Who will enjoy the goods you have gained?
	You slave like a digger in the fields.
WEAVER:	Who will enjoy it?
CODDLE:	Yes.
WEAVER:	This scrap, who sits there,
	Who does not think about the honour in duty.
	He sits there, and everything from his mouth is about eating; 85
	Even though he has barely spun three threads.
CODDLE:	Weaver, although it is costly and gains nothing,
	Children need to eat, what more needs to be said?
	Jack my son has been shrieking for an hour
	And shouting for his white mash porridge. 90
PHILIP:	God's tears, my heart quakes from the blow!
	I must stuff my belly full of that,
	I would give my best spinning-top for it;
	My heart would rejoice from such a meal.
WEAVER:	You will content yourself with a dish of beans! 95
	If you are hungry, that will soothe your appetite.
PHILIP:	Yes, that is my main meal every day,
	But if your lover came, he would get something delicious.
WEAVER:	What did you say there?
PHILIP:	Nothing mother, I fall silent.
	She nearly stepped on her toe then![10] 100
	But I always think on that white mash pudding,
	If I might sharpen my teeth on it just once,
	I would stretch my belly so far outwards
	I'd be like a beer barrel, without hiding the truth.
CODDLE:	Weaver, we should speak a little 105
	Of our early years, if Philip falls silent and gives us a break.
PHILIP:	Dice![11] There falls my working spindle!

---

[10] That is, turning around with alarm after Philip's allegation.

[11] The use of *teerling* as an expletive perhaps stems from the episode recorded in Matt. 27.35, in which the Roman soldiers, after mocking and beating Christ, 'divide his garments, casting lots' for them. Other texts of the period also connect dicing with immorality more broadly. In the mock-prophecy *Pronstelcatie van meester Malfus Knollebol* (1561), for instance, handling dice is equated with masturbation, and is further made to recall the mocking of Christ. The text declares, 'Hant van den teerlinck, oft hi sal u hoonen' ('hands off those dice, or it will shame you'):

Eeten! / eeten! / off dwerck en sal niet willen sijn.

WEBBE: Wadt doedij mij al verdriets, ghij vuijle cockijn!
Ghij waert weert dat ick tot uwen hooffde ginck. 110

VEUGE: Sijt te vreden, Webbe, 't is al kinder dinck!
Gheefft hem teetene / en daer mee gedaen.
Och heere! ick blijve hier oock te lange gestaen;
Hanneken sal hem hebben / al waer hij sodt.
Hebdij geen vier?

WEBBE: Ja ick, in mijnen lolle podt. 115
Een coolken oft twee; suldijt wel ontsteecken.

VEUGE: Ja ick / daer toe weet ick al aerdighe treecken,
Ick en machs niet hebben na mijnen geneuchge.
Adieu, vrecke Webbe!

WEBBE: Adieu, goeij vrou Veughe,
Compt hier bij ons spinnen, indient u belieft. 120

VEUGE: Ick sal comen, had ick mijn Hanneken gerieft;
Ick weet wel, hij schreijt van grooten hongere.

LIPPEN: Ick sou wel eeten, bij gans longere!
Mijnen buijck valt in tot aan mijn rebben.

WEBBE: En ick sal heden geen vree mogen hebben! 125
Van eeten en rust niet uwen clepele;
Nu hout die schotele en dien lepele,
Daer is oock broot / wilt nu wel brocken!
Ick sal u gaen ander vlas op rocken;
Die wil eeten, die moet oock werkens beginnen. 130
Ick mach u bonen gaen halen hier binnen,
Mij dunckt, ghij hebt veel te lange geseten.

LIPPEN: Ramp hebbe dleet! moet ick al weer boonen eten?
Sal ick mijn leven met sulcken cost verslijten?
Och waerse doot / quets alle die ses mijten 135

I must eat, I must eat, or no work will happen.

WEAVER: You do me such torments, you foul rogue!

You deserve to have me swiping at your head. 110

CODDLE: Do not be displeased, Weaver, it is all a childish thing!

Give him something to eat and then it is done.

Oh Lord, I have also stayed here for too long;

Jack will be acting as though he were a madman.

Do you have a fire?

WEAVER: Yes, I have, in my brazier.[12] 115

One coal or two: they should burn well.

CODDLE: Yes, I think so, I know how to handle them nicely,

But I have not taken all that I wanted.[13]

Adieu, miserly Weaver!

WEAVER: Goodbye, good wife Coddle,

Come here to spin with us, if you wish. 120

CODDLE: I will come, once I have I satisfied my Jack;

I know well that he is shrieking with great hunger.

PHILIP: I should eat well, by God's lungs!

My belly falls in on my ribs.

WEAVER: And I might not have any peace today! 125

Your tongue does not rest from talking about eating;

Now take your dish and your spoon,

Here is also some bread, it will break well![14]

I will give you more flax for the distaff;

He that would eat, he must start by working. 130

I may fetch some beans for you from inside,

It seems to me you have sat much too long.

PHILIP: Calamity have my grief! Must I always eat beans?

Shall I waste my life with such food?

Oh if she were dead, I would take the six pennies[15] 135

Hinke van Kampen, Herman Pleij, Bob Stumpel, Annebel Venmans and Paul Vriesema, *Het zal koud zijn in 't water als 't vriest: zestiende-eeuwse parodieen op gedrukte jaarvoorspellingen tekstuitg. met inleiding en commentaar* (The Hague, 1980), 89.

[12] The text has *lollepot*, a small earthenware pot filled with embers or hot ash, and used as a personal heater. Since this receptacle was often secreted beneath the skirts of women, it has obscene connotations here. These implications are often exploited in folk literature, and probably explain why *lollepot* or *pot* is contemporary Dutch slang for a lesbian: see Willy Louis Braekman, *Hier heb ik weer wat nieuws in d'hand: marktliederen, rolzangers en volkse poëzie van weleer* (Brussels, 1990), 101–9. Since a *lollepot* will only heat its possessor, the fact that Weaver owns one further underscores her meanness and selfishness.

[13] Kruyskamps holds that this probably refers to the *buurpraatje* (gossip) that Coddle sought in lines 66–7, and which Weaver has not relinquished. In light of the references to *lollepotten*, however, the statement clearly has sexual connotations: since she is probably a widow, the text suggests that she does not 'have all that I wanted' at home. See Kruyskamp, *Dichten en spelen*, 68.

[14] That is, because there is in fact no bread in the dish.

[15] The text has *mijt*. Since the *mijt* was one forty-eighth of a *stuiver* in Flanders, and of even less value in Brabant, this is hardly the 'groote somme' Phiip claims. On the *mijt*, see *Blue Barge*, n.48.

	Die sij gepodt heeft, een groote somme,	
	Daer soudick dan al waeffelen coopen omme,	
	Soetemelckxken / coecken / appelen / en peeren.	
	Ick sal vrij dat goeijken wel anders verteeren,	
	Dwelck sij mij nu dus vroeijlijck verspaert.	140
WEBBE:	Hebdij schier gebrockt, seght, luijen draijlaert?	
LIPPEN:	Ja ick, moeijer.	
WEBBE:	Hout! steeckt dat onder u snuijte	
	En eet mij geringe die schotel uuijte,	
	So dat ghij u dan weder aent spinnen rast.	
LIPPEN:	Aijmij, ick was schier van honger geheel verlast!	145
	Mijn herte dat clopt, hoort, al waert een steen.	
HANNEKEN:	Wel become mij datte / ende dan noch een;	
	Hier op en sal ick immers geen tanden breecken.	
LIPPEN:	Nu wel, ick gae Hanneken Leckertant spreecken;	
	Hij heeft, weet ick wel, die witmoes pappe gereet.	150
	Hij compt hier gaende / siet, bij gans sweet,	
	Met een groote teijl pappen inde hant!	
HANNEKEN:	Dach Lippen Loer!	
LIPPEN:	Dach Hanneken Leckertant!	
	Wadt eet ghij daer?	
HANNEKEN:	Ick eete al watte.	
LIPPEN:	Aij, 't is witmoes pappe, wat goeijer cost is datte!	155
	Laet mij toch mee eten / uijt uwer teijlen,	
	Ick sal u van mijn goeij bonen deijlen,	
	Ghij en aet u dagen noijt beteren cost.	
	Wildij, goey Hanneken?	
HANNEKEN:	Ick en hebs geen lost,	
	Lippen, u bonen sijn mijn veel te hert.	160
	Siet, sij hebben vellen so dicke als een bert!	
	Dunckt u dat goeijen cost? hoort toch desen goeijen bloet!	
LIPPEN:	Jaet / want moeijer seijt / sij sijn voort stoppen goet.	
	En aet ick geen boonen met groten hoopen,	
	Mijn dermen, seijt sij, souden wech loopen;	165
	En dan most [ick] sterven / met een groote pijne.	
HANNEKEN:	Mij en lust nochtans niet gestopt te sijne;	
	Ik hou mij al open / so ick best can.	
LIPPEN:	Hanneken, laet ons mangelen, sijdij een man;	
	Ick sal u dat versch steertgen toe geven, siet!	170
HANNEKEN:	Neen manneken, ghij en hebt mij noch daer niet!	
	Meijndij mij te verdullen? ick en ben geen boer!	
	Hoe gaerne waerdij aan mijn pappen, Lippen Loer!	
	Ghij en haelter niet, ghij hebt te cort geschooten.	

	That she has hoarded, a great sum:	
	With them I then should go to buy waffles,	
	And sweet-milk, cakes, apples and pears.	
	I will freely devour those treats and more,	
	All that she stingily keeps from me now.	140
WEAVER:	Are you almost broken apart, tell me, you lazy sluggard?	
PHILIP:	Yes, I am, mother.	
WEAVER:	Quiet! Stick that under your snout	
	And quickly empty the dish for me,	
	So that then you can return again to spinning.	
PHILIP:	Ay me, I was almost wholly freed from hunger!	145
	My heart does clap, hear it, as would a stone.	
JACK:	This pleases me well, and so does this one;	
	I will indeed break no teeth here.	
PHILIP:	Well now, I go to speak with Jack Sweet-tooth;	
	He has, I know well, the white mash porridge at hand.	150
	He is approaching now, I see it, by God's sweat,	
	With a great bowl of porridge in his hand!	
JACK:	Good day Philip Loser!	
PHILIP:	Good day Jack Sweet-tooth!	
	What are you eating there?	
JACK:	I am eating something.	
PHILIP:	Ay me, it is white mash porridge, what good food that is!	155
	Let me also eat, out of your bowl;	
	I will treat you to some of my good beans,	
	In all your days you never ate better food,	
	Will you, good Jack?	
JACK:	I have no wish to do so,	
	Philip, your beans seem to me much too hard.	160
	See, they have skins as thick as a plank!	
	You think that is good food? Hear this simple fool!	
PHILIP:	Yes, it is, as my mother says, they are good for blockages.[16]	
	If I did not eat beans in great heaps	
	My guts, she says, should race away;	165
	And then I must die, in great pain.	
JACK:	Nonetheless I have no desire to be blocked up;	
	I keep myself all open, as best I can.	
PHILIP:	Jack, let us swap, if you are a man;	
	I will give you this fresh rump steak, see![17]	170
JACK:	No, little man, you have not caught me there!	
	You intend to fool me? I am no peasant!	
	How much you yearn for my porridge, Philip Loser!	
	You will not have it, you have shot too short.	

---

[16] That is, they promote constipation.
[17] The original plays with the similarity between *steert* (tail, backside) and *stiertje* (bull, beef).

LIPPEN:	Deijlt mij nu, ick sal u geven al mijn kooten	175
	Die ick thuijs hebbe en hier in mijnen sack,	
	En dien top oock, daer eens een pinne in stack;	
	Ick salt u al geven / noot mij te gaste!	
HANNEKEN:	Lippen, eet bonen, so blijven u darmen vaste!	
	Dees pappe sou u veel te qualijck smaecken.	180
LIPPEN:	Ick hou, cost icker nochtans an geraecken,	
	Ick sou met haer spelen alte schoonen spel.	
HANNEKEN:	Lippen Loer, dat gelooff ick herde wel,	
	Niet veel en sout ghij met haer slapen!	
	Maer offt ick u deijlden, soudij wel gapen	185
	Wijt genoech / om in te steecken nae mijn gevoech?	
LIPPEN:	Ghapen, segdij? ja ick, siet is dat wijdt genoech?	
	Suldijt wel in steecken / sonder genaecken?	
HANNEKEN:	Ick staeck wel die heel teijle in u caecken!	
	Tjan, Lippen / u aensicht is wel gecloven,	190
	Ghij sout wel gaepen / tegen eenen hoven;	
	Daer sou wel een catte metter jongen in woonen.	
LIPPEN:	Nu deijlt mij pappe!	
HANNEKEN:	Neen Lippen, eet boonen!	
	Dees pappe en waer u niet gesont.	
LIPPEN:	En ghij soutse mij steecken inden mont?	195
	Ick en seyts niet, als ick niet doen en woude.	
HANNEKEN:	Nu gaept dan / en doet beij u oogen touwe.	
	Ick salse u in steecken sonder respijt.	
LIPPEN:	Willick dan gaepen?	
HANNEKEN:	Jae ghij, Lippen, gaept wijt!	
LIPPEN:	Noch wijder gapen? dat sal ick doen.	200
HANNEKEN:	Wadt dunckter u off, is dit niet een goet fatsoen?	
	Alle de ghene die hier nu sijn vergaert,	
	Die noijt en sagen eenen grooten gapaert,	
	Die mach hier comen / en sien hem nu.	
LIPPEN:	Waer blijft ghij Hanneken? steeck in, haest u!	205
	Ick wachter, siet, naer, en doet mij geen loos.	
HANNEKEN:	Neen ick, trouwens, Lippen / maer gaept ghij altoos?	
	Doet u oogen vast toe / en dat ghij niet en kickt!	
	Hout / ghij hadt mijn hant bijcans oock opgeslickt	
	Metten lepele / ick spranck uijtten weghe.	210

PHILIP:	Hand it to me now, I will give you all of my jacks[18] 175
	That I have in the house and here in my pocket,
	And that spinning-top as well, in which a nail was once stuck;
	I will give you all: invite me to dine!
JACK:	Philip, eat your beans, so your guts hold fast!
	This porridge would suit your tastes poorly. 180
PHILIP:	I know that if I could get my hands on it
	I would play a very splendid game with it.
JACK:	Philip Loser, I believe that very well,
	You would not fall asleep if you had it!
	But if I give it to you, could you open up 185
	Wide enough, so that I might stick it in easily?
PHILIP:	Open up, you say? Yes, I can, see, is that wide enough?
	Can you ram it in well, without touching the sides?
JACK:	I could well cram the whole bowl into your craw!
	By Saint John, Philip, your face is truly split, 190
	If you would gape like that beside a farm,
	A cat might well leap in there with her kittens.
PHILIP:	Now dole out the porridge!
JACK:	No, Philip, eat the beans!
	This porridge is not wholesome for you.
PHILIP:	But you said you would shove it into my mouth. 195
	I don't say things that I will not or cannot do.
JACK:	Now then open up, and close your two eyes.
	I will push it into you without delay.
PHILIP:	Should I open up then?
JACK:	Yes, you should, Philip, open wide!
PHILIP:	Even wider open? I will do that. 200
JACK:	What do you think of this? Is this not a good spectacle?
	Any of you that are now gathered here
	That never saw a great yawner,
	They may come forward and see one now.
PHILIP:	Why hold yourself back, Jack? Put it in, hurry yourself! 205
	I wait for it, see, do not leave me empty.
JACK:	No, in truth I will not, Philip, but do you always gape so?
	Shut your eyes fast, and do not stir!
	Hold on, you almost swallowed my hand too,
	Along with the spoon, but I sprang out of the way. 210

---

[18] In Dutch *kootjes* (anklebones), since the playing-pieces were originally made from sheep's knuckles. The game is also called *bikkelspel* (knuckle-play). Interestingly, one of the playing-pieces seems to have been dubbed the *boer* (the farmer) in some versions of the game, as Daan prints a song meant to accompany the game, which begins 'Zeg boer waar is je vrouw? Zeg boer waar is je arme vrouwe?' ('Say, farmer, where is your wife? Say farmer where is your poor wife?'): Jo Daan, *Wieringer land en leven in de taal* (Wieringen, 1981), 69–70. The offer of jacks may therefore be a response to Jack's earlier statement, in which he denies being a *boer*.

LIPPEN:	Ja, ja, ghij en doeget niet te degen.
	Was dat pap?
HANNEKEN:	En ist niet?
LIPPEN:	Tsijn boonen, ick houwe.
HANNEKEN:	Hoe meijndij, dat ick u bedriegen souwe?
LIPPEN:	Ja ghij, twaeren bonen / ghij hebt mij verdult.
HANNEKEN:	Nu, ick sal insteecken, dat ghijt sien sult.
	Gaept wijt, ick en sal niet meer met u gecken.
LIPPEN:	Ja, dats beter.
HANNEKEN:	Siet Lippen eens lecken!
	Wat segdij daer aff, quant / smaeckt u dat niet badt?
LIPPEN:	Ghij hadt mij vlus bedrogen / ick seijde wel dat,
	Quansuijs offt ick niet beters en wiste.
HANNEKEN:	Ghij sijt een geselleken van schalcken liste,
	Dat ghij wel bonen kent voor witmoes pappe
LIPPEN:	Ick heb verstant, al en draech ik geen cappe!
	Och, hoe wel smaeckt datte / Noch eens, och! och!
HANNEKEN:	Nu, gaept dan!
LIPPEN:	Hanneken Leckertant / noch! noch!
HANNEKEN:	Hoe gaet dat keelgat open, al waert een sluijsse.
LIPPEN:	Noch! noch!
HANNEKEN:	So seijt de soch oock vanden gasthuijse.
	'Noch! noch!' ja, ghij singt al eenen sanck.
	Neen, Lippen, uwen derm is mij veel te lanck.
	Ick hebbe u gegeven / dat ick u jonne;
	Ghij ater wel vol een haering tonne
	Eer dat uwen buyck sou sijn versaeijt.
LIPPEN:	Ke, noch een lepeltgen!
HANNEKEN:	Lippen, hout u gepayt!
	Ick wil dit selve steecken in mijnen mage.
LIPPEN:	Dat ick sulcken cost moch eeten alle dagen,
	Ick sou oock worden een aerdich pronckere.
HANNEKEN:	Men sou u eer lang noch heeten mijn jonckere,
	Gelijckemen mij doet / ick sal vlus ridder zijn.
	Om dat ick leckerlijck eete ben ick dus fijn;
	Dan en sidt ick oock nemmermeer inden roock,
	Dies ben ick so schone.
LIPPEN:	Besiet mij eens oock!
	Ben ick niet goetaerdich en jent van leden?

215

220

225

230

235

240

PHILIP:	Yes, yes, but you did not satisfy me.
	Was that porridge?
JACK:	Was it not?
PHILIP:	It is beans, I know.
JACK:	What are you thinking, that I would have betrayed you?
PHILIP:	Yes, you have: it was beans, you have fooled me.
JACK:	Now, I will stick in something you can see.	215
	Open wide, I will not toy with you further.
PHILIP:	Yes, that is better.
JACK:	See Philip drooling!
	What do you say about that, pal? Does it taste good to you?
PHILIP:	You have betrayed me even so, as I said.
	As though I did not know better.	220
JACK:	You are a companion of the clever rogues,
	Since you can distinguish beans from white mash porridge very well.
PHILIP:	I have insight, although I wear no cap![19]
	Oh, how good that tasted, more, oh, oh!
JACK:	Now, open up then!
PHILIP:	Jack Sweet-tooth, more, more![20]	225
JACK:	How that gullet swings open, as though it were a sluice-gate.
PHILIP:	More! More!
JACK:	So says the sow as well at the clinic.
	'Snort! snort!' Yes, you both sing the same song.
	No, Philip, your gut is much too long for me.
	I have given you all that I wished;	230
	You could eat a barrelful of herring
	Before your belly would be sated.
PHILIP:	Hey, one spoonful more!
JACK:	Philip, close your mouth!
	I will stick this into my own tummy myself.
PHILIP:	That I might eat such food all day long!	235
	I should also strut like a fashionable gentleman.
JACK:	Men would call you monsieur before long,
	Much as they do to me. I will soon be a knight,
	Because I eat delicious things, and so am fine;
	Also I never sit in the smoke,	240
	So I am so clean.
PHILIP:	Behold me as well!
	Am I not goodly and graceful of body?

---

[19] Philip's *cappe* is the biretta worn by medieval masters or doctors after their conferment ceremony. This was worn not only formally but as an everyday marker of status and profession: see Laura F. Hodges, *Chaucer and Clothing: Clerical and Academic Clothing in the General Prologue* (Cambridge, 2005), 204–8.

[20] In Middle Dutch *noch* (again) is also onomatopoeia for the sound of a pig, somewhat like the English 'oink'.

HANNEKEN:	Ja ghij, al waerdij uuijt eenen stronckeijck gesneden,
	Viercant gedraijt / als een mulders stock.
LIPPEN:	Ick, heb ick niet goet fatsoen in desen rock? 245
HANNEKEN:	Ja ghij / ghinck deur de mouwe een strepe.
LIPPEN:	En heb ick oock niet een aerdige nepe?
	Die mij wel besiet / ick ben een fraij geselleken.
HANNEKEN:	Ghij hebt een nepe als een akerwelleken,
	Daermen de cluijten opt lant me breeckt ontwee. 250
LIPPEN:	Aij, van dees bonen doet mijnen buijck so wee!
	Tis jammer, ick ben anders net en propere.
HANNEKEN:	Uwen cost is te groff / en ghij sijt sopere;
	Ghij most al leijen een ander leven.
LIPPEN:	Ghij segt wel, Hanneken / maer wie sout mij geven? 255
	Mijn moeijer is veel te vreck en quaet.
HANNEKEN:	Tjans hoij, Lippen / ick weet u goeijen raet,
	Dat ghij u moeijer wel sult verschalcken.
LIPPEN:	Ick spronge van blijsscap op tot aen de balcken,
	Cost ghij dat gedoen en mijnen commer stelpen. 260
HANNEKEN:	Sijt te vreden, ick sal u wel helpen,
	Dat ghij wel sult verlacken den blieck.
LIPPEN:	Maer hoe soo?
HANNEKEN:	Ghij sult u gaen maecken zeer sieck,
	Crochen, steenen / en clagen van veel gebreecken
	En seggen uwen buijck is al vol steecken, 265
	En dat ghij moet eeten, om u verfraijen,
	Pasteijkens / taerkens, / roffioelen en vlaijen.
	Ghij sullet so crijgen / ick derffis mij beroemen.

228

JACK:	Yes, you are, as though you were cut out of an oak stump,	
	Square-carved, like a miller's block.[21]	
PHILIP:	Do I not have a good figure in these clothes?	245
JACK:	Yes, you have, as you are always in sleeves and stripes.[22]	
PHILIP:	But do I not have a neat waist?	
	I am a fair companion to whoever sees me.	
JACK:	You have a waist like a field roller,	
	With which men break up clods in the meadow.	250
PHILIP:	Ay, my belly does gripe from these beans!	
	It is a shame, I am otherwise neat and proper.[23]	
JACK:	Your food is too coarse, and you are so particular;	
	You must lead another life at once.	
PHILIP:	You speak truly, Jack, but who would give it to me?	255
	My mother is much too miserly and spiteful.	
JACK:	Saint John's head, Philip, I have some good advice for you	
	That you might use to outwit your mother.	
PHILIP:	I would jump for joy up to the rafters	
	If you could do that to stop my sorrow.	260
JACK:	You ought to be happy, I will help you,	
	So that you may well catch a sprat.	
PHILIP:	But how so?	
JACK:	You should make yourself seem very sick,	
	Coughing, grumbling and complaining about much suffering,	
	And saying your belly is all full of gripes,	265
	And that in order to recover you must eat	
	Pasties, tartlets, turnovers[24] and flans.[25]	
	You will have them, I give you my honour.	

---

[21] Probably the axle on which the mill-wheel was set.

[22] This suggests that Philip is wearing fool's motley. He appears in this costume in Verbeeck's *Vuyl sause*.

[23] Philip appears to be farting during these lines. Beans have of course been linked to flatulence since antiquity. For instance, Cicero records that 'the Pythagoreans are forbidden to eat beans, which cause considerable flatulence and are thus inimical to those who seek peace of mind': Jonathan Barnes, *Early Greek Philosophy* (Harmondsworth, 2001), 165–6.

[24] The recipe for *roffioelen* is preserved in Gheeraert Vorselman's *Een notabel boecxke van cokerije* (*c*.1501). It consisted of crescents of pastry, filled with pulped apple, chopped nuts and cinnamon, and fried in a shallow pan. See *Eenen nyeuwen coock boeck: kookboek samengesteld door Gheeraert Vorselman en gedrukt te Antwerpen in 1560*, ed. Elly Cockx-Indestege (Wiesbaden, 1971), 204–5. The cake also appears in the earliest Dutch account of the Land of Cockaigne, as Cockaigne's 'banken ende stoelen' ('benches and stools') are apparently fashioned from it: Herman Pleij, *Dreaming of Cockaigne*, trans. Diane Webb (New York, 2001), 432.

[25] The text refers to *vlaey*, a sort of sweet tart made with egg yolks and milk, and filled with a mixture of grated fruit soaked into white bread. It could apparently hold various fillings: a cookbook of 1667, for instance, contains a recipe for *vlayken van citroenen* (*vlaey* of lemon). See Marleen Willebrands, *De verstandige kok. De rijke keuken van de gouden eeuw* (Bussum, 2006), 20.

LIPPEN:	Alsulcken cost en hoordick noijt noemen:
	Platteijrkens / quaertgens / en pompornoelen, quant? 270
HANNEKEN:	Hoe segdij dat? dats immers quaet verstant!
	Tsijn pasteijkens, taerkens en roffioelen.
LIPPEN:	So sou ick alleenskens tverstant gevoelen.
	Maer off ick so dede / sout hem wel schicken?
HANNEKEN:	Jaet / want u moeijer salder haer aff verschricken, 275
	Om dat sij uwer sieckten is ongewone;
	En want ghij dan sijt een eenich sone,
	Sij soude u herde noij laten sterven.
LIPPEN:	Ick salt doen / al soud ick de peeper bederven.
HANNEKEN:	Maer wadt ghij doet, maeckt altijt een wemoedig getier. 280
VEUGE:	Waer sijdij Hanneken?
HANNEKEN:	Moeijer, ick ben hier
	Bij Lippen Loer; dus moeijer en sijt niet gram.
VEUGE:	Neen ick, kint.
HANNEKEN:	Moeijer, eenen witten bootterham
	Haddick seer geerne.
LIPPEN:	Longeren en rebben!
VEUGE:	Compt in huijs, mijn kint, ghij sullet hebben; 285
	Twaer schae, leet gebreck sulcke schoone spruijte.
WEBBE:	Waer blijffdij Lippen, en hebdij noch niet uijte?
	Mij dunckt, van uwen wercke crijch ick cleijn gebruijck.
LIPPEN:	Och neen ic, moeijer, mijnen buijck! mijnen buijck!
	Ach mijnen buijck die doet mij al te zeere. 290
WEBBE:	Sijdij dan sieckt soone?
LIPPEN:	Dat weet godt den heere!
	Och noijt en was ick so vol sieckten gelaijen!
	Moeijer, siedij niet mijn hoot staen draijen?
	Mij duckt daer in wonen pijpers en bommers.
WEBBE:	Kint, u hooft staet stille.
LIPPEN:	Moeijer, het draijt jommers? 295
	Och noijt so en leet ick meerder smerte.
	Aij mij, die milte smijt daer op mijn herte!
WEBBE:	Smijt u de milte?
LIPPEN:	Och ja, sij niet doet dan smijten.
	Aij noijt so seere / als mij die mieren bijten.
	Mijn dermen tegen een vechten en sammelen. 300
WEBBE:	Vechten u dermen?

PHILIP:	I never heard the names of all these foodstuffs:
	Flat eggs, farthings and undergrowths, my friend?[26] 270
JACK:	How can you say that? That really is poor comprehension!
	Those should be pastries, tartlets and turnovers.
PHILIP:	I feel that I understand all these things.
	But if I did this, should it turn out well?
JACK:	Yes, it would, as your mother will be terrified 275
	By the fact that your sickness is strange;
	And since you are her only son,
	She would never let you die, in truth.
PHILIP:	I will do it, though it should cause her grief.
JACK:	But whatever you do, always make a mournful din. 280
CODDLE:	Where are you Jack?
JACK:	Mother, I am here
	With Philip Loser, so do not be grumpy, mother.
CODDLE:	I will not, child.
JACK:	Mother, some white buttered bread:[27]
	I have a great yearning for that.
PHILIP:	Lungs and ribs!
CODDLE:	Come into the house, my boy, you will have it; 285
	If I let such a sweet one go without it would be a shame.
WEAVER:	Where are you lounging, Philip, have you finished?
	It seems to me that I get little profit from your work.
PHILIP:	Oh no, poor me, my stomach! my stomach!
	Ay, it is my belly that makes me all sore. 290
WEAVER:	Are you sick then, son?
PHILIP:	The Lord God knows that!
	Oh, I was never so loaded full of sickness!
	Mother, can you see that my head is spinning?
	I fear pipers and drummers reside in there.
WEAVER:	Child, your head stands still.
PHILIP:	Mother, does it not spin? 295
	Oh, I was never grieved with more pain.
	Ay me, my spleen pounds up against my heart!
WEAVER:	Your spleen pounds?
PHILIP:	Oh yes, it does nothing but pound.
	Ay it was never so severe, as though ants bite me.
	My guts fight and bicker with one another. 300
WEAVER:	Your guts bicker?

[26] According to Van der Heijden, Philip here mishears *pasteitje* for *platte eitje* (flat egg, often referring to insect eggs or nits), *taartje* for *kwartje* (a coin worth a quarter of a guilder), and *roffioel* for *paddenstoel* (toadstool). Given the context, the confused terms are no doubt sexual innuendos. See M. C. A van der Heijden, *Hoort wat men u spelen zal: Toneelstukken uit de Middeleeuwen* (Utrecht, 1968), 404.

[27] Jack refers to the *boterham* here, a primitive sandwich made with a single slice of buttered bread, still eaten in the Low Countries.

LIPPEN:	Hoordijse niet rammelen?
	Ick sorge, die doot sal mij genaecken.
	Moeijer, hoordij daer niet mijn lever craecken?
	Och noijt en leet ick meerder pijn!
	Ick sal sterven.
WEBBE:	Lieff kint, wadt mach u sijn?
	Meuchdij ijet quaets hebben ingenomen?
LIPPEN:	Neen ick, moeijer, 't is mijn vande bonen gecomen.
WEBBE:	Van de bonen segdij?
LIPPEN:	Ja, die niet en deugen.
WEBBE:	En sout ghij gheenen goeijen brij meugen?
	Ick souts u coocken eenen vollen ketele.
LIPPEN:	Neen ick, moeijer, set mij in vaeijerkens setele,
	Mij wort so cranckelijck, ick moet wat rusten.
WEBBE:	Lieff kint en sou u nergens naer lusten?
	Segt u gebreck en laetet mij weten.
LIPPEN:	Moeijer, ick sou gaerne vlaykens eeten
	En plateijerkens, wilt mij die copen, siet.
WEBBE:	Plateijerkens, kint? die en ken ick niet;
	De eyeren sijn rondt die de hennen leggen.
LIPPEN:	Goey Vrou Veuge die salt u wel seggen;
	Gaet, haeltse nu rasschelijck sonder draelen.
WEBBE:	Suldij wel sitten?
LIPPEN:	Ja ick.
WEBBE:	Ick gaese haelen.
	Och, noijt en was mijn herte so swaer!
	Hou seck, hou! isser niemant thuijs?
VEUGE:	Jaet, wie is daer
WEBBE:	Ick bent, goey vrou Veuge, comt tonsent geringe!
VEUGE:	Wadt isser te doene?
WEBBE:	Mijn handen ick wringe,
	Lippen Loer wilt sterven, noijt meerder noot!
VEUGE:	Waer houwet hem?
WEBBE:	Sijnen buijck is bijcans doot!
	Noijt kint ter werrelt en leet meer ongemack.
VEUGE:	Twaer best dat ghij ginck tot meester Jan Leurequack;
	Dat is een meester die veel consten thoont.
WEBBE:	Ick en weet niet waer die groote meester woont;
	Want hulpe soeck ick vroech en laete.
VEUGE:	Hij woont hier, siet, inde rechte strate;
	Daer en is nijemant die hem helpen mach badt.
HANNEKEN:	Wil ick hem halen?
WEBBE:	Hanneken doet doch dat.
	Gaen wij, ick salt u lonen, lieve gebueren.

Line numbers: 305, 310, 315, 320, 325, 330, 335

PHILIP: Do you not hear the clamour?
            I worry that death will overcome me.
            Mother, do you not hear my liver crack?
            Oh I never suffered greater pain!
            I will die.
WEAVER: Dear child, what is affecting you?   305
            Have you perhaps swallowed something bad?
PHILIP: No, I have not, mother – it comes from my beans.
WEAVER: From the beans you say?
PHILIP: Yes, nothing but badness.
WEAVER: Then you would prefer to have some good gruel?
            I could cook a kettle full for you.   310
PHILIP: No, I would not, mother. Sit me in father's chair,
            I grow so sickly; I must rest a while.
WEAVER: Dear child, would you like to go somewhere?
            Tell me your needs and let me know.
PHILIP: Mother, I would like to eat some flan   315
            And flat eggs. Will you buy those for me, see?
WEAVER: Flat eggs, child? I do not understand that.
            The eggs that hens lay are round.
PHILIP: Good Wife Coddle will tell you;
            Go, get them now, quickly without pause.   320
WEAVER: You will stay here?
PHILIP: Yes, I will.
WEAVER: I'll go to fetch them.
            Oh, my heart was never so heavy!
            Hey, I say, hey! Is there no-one at home?
CODDLE: Yes? Who is there?
WEAVER: It is I, good wife Coddle. Come quickly to our home!
CODDLE: What is the matter?
WEAVER: I wring my hands.   325
            Philip Loser will die: there was never greater need!
CODDLE: What ails him?
WEAVER: His stomach is almost dead!
            A child has never suffered greater decline in the world.
CODDLE: It would be best if you went to Doctor John Pedlar-quack,
            Who is a master of very many sciences.   330
WEAVER: But I do not know where this great master lives;
            I will be searching for help for a long while.[28]
CODDLE: He lives here, see, in the next street:
            There is nobody that he will not help if asked.
JACK: Shall I fetch him?
WEAVER: Jack, do just that.   335
            Let us go; I will reward you, dear neighbours.

---

[28] Literally 'early and late'.

LIPPEN:	Ick hope nu oock mijn querne te rueren;
	Hanneken geraijde dat wel beschelijck.
VEUGE:	Hoe vaerdij, Lippen?
LIPPEN:	Och, noyt so weelijck!
	Mij overquam vlus een alte quaijen vlage. 340
VEUGE:	Waer lettet u, Lippen?
LIPPEN:	Al in mijn mage
	Ende in mijnen buijck princepalijck;
	En hout mijn hoot / mij wort so qualijck.
	Ick gevoele daer wadt na mijn blase cruijpen.
VEUGE:	Webbe, oft ghij hem maeckte een goet suijpen 345
	Oft een papken, ten waer hem niet ongesont.
LIPPEN:	Och, dat sou mij wel helpen inden mont.
WEBBE:	Goey Vrou Veuge / ick en cans niet, comt, wijset mij!
MEESTER:	Waer ist Hanneken?
HANNEKEN:	Meester, 't is hier bij;
	Maer eerst voor al so moet ick u ontsluijten: 350
	Al gelaet hem Lippen Loer seer cranck van buijten,
	Hij en is vrij niet sieck, al spreeckt hij flouwe.
MEESTER:	Wadt ledt hem dan?
HANNEKEN:	Tjan, dat hij geernne souwe
	Eens leckerlijck eeten / dwelck ick hem riedt,
	Dat hij hem sou sieck maecken, verstadij tbediet? 355
	So heeft hijt gedaen, daer na moettijt passen.
MEESTER:	Eest soo?
HANNEKEN:	Jaet, meester.
MEESTER:	So sal ick mee brassen.
	Nu genoch van dien, ik hebbe tverstant.
	Sijn wij schier bijt huijs, Hanneken Leckertant?
HANNEKEN:	Siet, hier ist, gaen wij naerder ons tweester. 360
MEESTER:	Goeden dach, ghij vrouwens!
WEBBE:	Wellecomme meester.
	Mijn kint wilt sterven / het wert u geclaecht.
VEUGE:	Meester Jan, oft ghij sijn water besaecht?
	Sout ghij u dies wel dorren onderwinden?
MEESTER:	Wat segdij? waer sout ghij mijns gelijcke vinden? 365
	Sulcken meester als ick ben / en was noch noijt gebooren.
	Ick besie dwater wel in eenen koehooren,
	Mij en roeckx, crijg ick tgelt rechs in mijn tessche;
	Oock besie ickt wel in een leeren flessche.

PHILIP:	I also hope to use my mortar and pestle now;[29]
	Jack's advice was well thought-out.
CODDLE:	How are you, Philip?
PHILIP:	Oh, I was never so unwell!
	Just then I experienced a very severe attack. 340
CODDLE:	Where does it hurt you, Philip?
PHILIP:	All in my tummy
	And in my belly principally;
	And hold my head, I have fallen so ill.
	I felt something there inflate my bladder.
CODDLE:	Weaver, make a good tonic for him,[30] 345
	Or a pudding, that will not disagree with him.
PHILIP:	Oh, that in my mouth would help me out.
WEAVER:	Good Wife Coddle, I do not know how, come, tell me!
DOCTOR:	Where is it, Jack?
JACK:	Master, it is close by here.
	But I must let you know this first of all: 350
	Although Philip Loser shows himself to be very ill outwardly,
	He is well and not sick, much as he speaks of illness.
DOCTOR:	What afflicts him then?
JACK:	By Saint John, he desires
	A delicious meal, and so I advised him 354
	That he should make himself sick; do you understand my meaning?
	So he has done it: you too must go along with this.
DOCTOR:	Is that so?
JACK:	Yes, it is, master.
DOCTOR:	So I will also play along.
	Now enough about that, I have understood you.
	Are we nearly at the house, Jack Sweet-tooth?
JACK:	See, here it is, the two of us can go in. 360
DOCTOR:	Good day, you women!
WEAVER:	Welcome, master.
	If my child should die, it will go badly for you.
CODDLE:	Doctor John, have you inspected his water?
	Do you wish to undertake this yourself?
DOCTOR:	What do you say? Where else would you find my equal? 365
	A master like me has never been born before.
	I can read water in a cow's horn,
	I think nothing of it, as long as I catch money in my purse;
	I could also read it in a leather flask.

---

[29] That is, to grind food with his teeth.

[30] Gheeraert Vorselman's recipe for a *suijpen* reads as follows: 'Om te maken een suypen voor eenen crancken oft siecken mensche. Neempt twee doren van eyeren oft drie ende lutterken bloemen. Dan temperet beyde te samen seer wel onder een. Dan ghiet daer wijn ofte bier inne' ('To make a tonic for an ill or sick man. Take the yolks of two eggs or three and a little flour. Then beat both together very well into one. Next pour wine or beer into this'): *Eenen nyeuwen coock boeck*, 115.

	Meendij dat ick geen water besien en can?	370
VEUGE:	Ja ghij, en belght u doch niet, goeij meester Jan!	
	Wij bidden / cost ghij hem gehelpen lichte.	
MEESTER:	Ick sal tgebreck wel sien uuijt sijnen gesichte,	
	Ghij en dorft mij daerom geen water togen.	
	Heij, laet ons sien dlock in sijn oogen:	375
	Dees knecht en mach niet eeten erten / bonen / noch loock	
	Het hout hem al inde mage.	
WEBBE:	Meester, dat seijt hij oock.	
MEESTER:	Dees knecht is zeere inden buijck gequelt;	
	Sijn dermen sijn binnen al vrempt gestelt,	
	Sij leggen gewrongen gelijck eenen palinck leijt.	380
WEBBE:	Meester Jan / 'tis oock seecker also hij seijt.	
MEESTER:	Rassch! haelt hem soetemelckxken / en werm rijsken,	
	Een gebraijen hoenken oft een patrijssken,	
	Haelt hem taertgens / vlaijkens en pasteijkens,	
	Haelt hem wittebroot / en gedoopte eijkens,	385
	Haelt hem gebotert bierken voor een medecijnken,	
	Braet hem kiecxkens / laet hem rijnswijnken	
	Drincken / so mach sijn pijne wadt worden gestilt.	
HANNEKEN:	Ja, ja / daer stoot ghij hem rechs daer hij vallen wilt.	
	Lippen Loer sal nu eens vaeren inde feeste.	390
WEBBE:	Siet, hier ist meester.	
MEESTER:	Nu, met lichten geeste!	
	Set hier van als, wilt u selven toeven!	
LIPPEN:	Dees witmoes pappe wil ick eerst gaan proeven,	
	Op dat ick daarmede mijnen noot ontlaste.	
VEUGE:	Webbe, segt den meester dat hij oock toetaste,	395
	Oft hij spraeckx u schant inde tavernne.	
WEBBE:	Meester, eedt oock!	
MEESTER:	Wel vrouwe, herde gernne!	
	Dat kiecxken tast ick ane / dat leijt mij naest.	
LIPPEN:	Meester, dat ghij u niet te seere en haest,	
	Ick moet van dien oock een beetgen behouwen.	400
HANNEKEN:	Dats goet ondersproocken.	
MEESTER:	Wel zoone, in trouwen,	
	Ick en sal u den cost niet al ontvremen.	
	Wadt ou / desen siecken sal wel wadt innemen;	
	Hij werckt op sijn stucken, hij haest hem te degen.	

236

	Do you mean to say that I cannot read water?	370
CODDLE:	Yes, you are right, but I meant no offence, good doctor John!	
	We beg you, you must help him quickly.	
DOCTOR:	I will diagnose from looking at his appearance;	
	You do not have to bring me water from him.	
	Hey, let us see the pupils in those eyes:	375
	This lad may not eat peas, beans nor garlic,	
	It all damages him in the stomach.	
WEAVER:	Master, he said that as well.	
DOCTOR:	This lad is severely wounded in the belly;	
	His guts within are all strangely laid out,	
	They lie ravelled up the way an eel lies.	380
WEAVER:	Master John, this is also just as he said.	
DOCTOR:	Hurry! Get him sweet milk, and warm rice,	
	A roasted pullet or a partridge,	
	Get him tartlets, flans and pastries,	
	Get him white bread, and poached eggs,	385
	Get him butter beer as a remedy,[31]	
	Roast him chickens, give him Rhenish wine	
	To drink, so that his pain may be silenced.[32]	
JACK:	Yes, yes, you have shoved him right where he wants to fall.	
	Philip Loser will now go to a feast for once.	390
WEAVER:	See, here it is, doctor.	
DOCTOR:	Now, in good humour,	
	Set it all down here. You will cheer yourself with this!	
PHILIP:	I wish to sample first this white mash porridge,	
	So that I may satisfy my desire with it.	
CODDLE:	Weaver, tell the doctor that he may eat as well,	395
	Or he will shame you with speech in the tavern.	
WEAVER:	Master, eat as well!	
DOCTOR:	Well woman, I wanted to hear that!	
	I will taste that chicken that lies next to me.	
PHILIP:	Doctor, you should not stuff yourself in haste:	
	I must also have a little from that.	400
JACK:	That is well said.	
DOCTOR:	Well, son, in truth,	
	I will not steal this meal from you.	
	What-ho, this patient should surely take something;	
	He that works at a fixed rate hurries himself greatly.	

[31] Probably a version of the tonic or *sluipen* mentioned in line 306.
[32] As Worp notes, the language of this speech, with its use of enjambment and its concluding 'effect', recalls the folk remedies found throughout the period: J. A. Worp, *Geschiedenis van het drama en van het tooneel in Nederland*, 2 vols. (Groningen, 1903–7), 1: 149. Parodies of these texts were common: for a discussion and an example, see W. L. Braekman, 'Een "Konstboecxken" met een spotrecept door een "ongeleerden sottoer" (ca. 1595)', *Volkskunde: tijdschrift voor de studie van de volkscultuur* 105 (2004), 327–45.

LIPPEN:	Die schootel is uuijte; setse uuijtte wegen!	405
HANNEKEN:	En can Lippen niet schoon schuetten schieten?	
LIPPEN:	Dit gebotert bierken wil ick binnen gieten.	
	Aij mij / dat doet mijn mage verwarmen;	
	En met dat soetemelckxken spoel ick mijn dermen.	
MEESTER:	En ick aen dit pasteijken / so ick schatte.	410
LIPPEN:	Eet properlijck, meester, ontbeijt watte!	
	Ick moet van die spijse oock eeten mede.	
MEESTER:	Ick sal beijen also ons koeijen dede.	
HANNEKEN:	Lippen vreest te verliesen sijn paertgen.	
LIPPEN:	Nu aen dees vlaijen en aen dit taertgen!	415
	Mijn bloet verblijt hem / tot in mijn teenkens.	
MEESTER:	Hout daer, Lippen! cnaecht aan die beenkens!	
LIPPEN:	Neen meester, tvleijssken sal mij ock wel smaecken.	
HANNEKEN:	Siet, hoe vol steeckt Lippen beij sijn caecken!	
	Vrij, knecht, crijget oppe / waerom soudijt sparen?	420
WEBBE:	Och! nu sal alle mijn potgelt qualijck varen,	
	Dat ick lange so wijsselijck so gespaert hebbe.	
VEUGE:	Ick hebt u wel lange geseijt, Vrecke Webbe,	
	Dat ghij daer mede so sout varen in inde.	
	Ghij gaeft veel te groven cost uwen kinde;	425
	Nu en valt u int leste niet dan tegenspoet.	
LIPPEN:	Aij mij! dees pasteijbrocxkens sijn oock seer goet	
	Ende dit rijnswijnken mijn herte verblijt.	
WEBBE:	Betert het niet, mijn soone?	
LIPPEN:	Jaet, moeijer, metter tijt.	
HANNEKEN:	Hij swemt in vreuchden als een endde kuijckentgen.	430
LIPPEN:	Moeijer, hou!	
WEBBE:	Wadt ist kint?	
LIPPEN:	O suijckertgen, suijkertgen	
	Geeff mij voor die bitterheijt in mijn kele!	
WEBBE:	Lieff Lippen, zone, ghij eet so vele,	
	Ick en siet niet / waer ickt al halen sal.	
LIPPEN:	Lieff moeijer, die sieckte verteret al.	435
MEESTER:	Ja, so doende soudij noch veel behoeven!	
	Wadt segdij doch van dese jonge boeven,	
	Weeten sijt haer ouders niet aff te strijen?	
	Gans doot / ick en saechs niet langer te lijen.	
	Hou, Lippen Loer, ick wil u noch badt verheugen.	440
	En soudij geen bercke struijven meugen?	
	Ghij souter fraij aff worden en heel gesont.	
LIPPEN:	Moeijer, ick moet bercke struijven eeten terstont,	
	Meester Jan Leurequack heeftet gesproocken.	
WEBBE:	Wat cost is datte?	

PHILIP:	This dish is empty; put it out of the way!	405
JACK:	Can Philip not shoot the shuttle beautifully?[33]	
PHILIP:	I will pour that butter beer within me,	
	Ay me, that does warm my stomach;	
	And with that sweet milk I rinse my guts.[34]	
DOCTOR:	And I with this pastry, as I enjoy myself.	410
PHILIP:	Eat with restraint, master; hold back a little!	
	I must also eat some of this food.	
DOCTOR:	I will wait the way our cow does.	
JACK:	Philip is afraid to lose his share.	
PHILIP:	Now on to this flan and on to this tartlet!	415
	My blood rejoices, down to my toes.	
DOCTOR:	Hold on there, Philip! Gnaw on the small bones!	
PHILIP:	No, master, I will taste the meat instead.	
JACK:	See how Philip stuffs his cheeks full.	
	Eat up freely, lad, why should you leave any?	420
WEAVER:	Oh, now all my savings will be sorely depleted,	
	All that I have so wisely hoarded for so long.	
CODDLE:	I told you before, miserly Weaver,	
	That this would happen to you in the end.	
	You gave too much coarse food to your son;	425
	Now in the end it has brought you nothing but misery.	
PHILIP:	Ay me! These pastry scraps are also very good	
	And this Rhenish wine cheers my heart.	
WEAVER:	Is that not better, my son?	
PHILIP:	Yes, it will be, mother, in time.	
JACK:	He swims in joy like a young duckling.	430
PHILIP:	Mother, ouch!	
WEAVER:	What is it, child?	
PHILIP:	Oh, sweetmeats, sweetmeats,	
	Give them to me for the bitterness in my throat!	
WEAVER:	Dear Philip, son, you eat so much,	
	I do not know whether I can afford it all.	
PHILIP:	Dear mother, the sickness consumes it all.	435
DOCTOR:	Yes, and if you continue, you will need much more!	
	What can you say about these young crooks,	
	Do they not know how to gull their parents?	
	God's death, I cannot lie like this any longer.	
	Well, Philip Loser, I will play with you some more.	440
	But could you not also eat birch cakes?	
	You would find that suitable and entirely healthy.	
PHILIP:	Mother, I must eat birch cake immediately.	
	Doctor John Pedlar-quack has commanded it.	
WEAVER:	What food is that?	

[33] That is, work hard, with reference to the weaving his mother forces him to perform.
[34] Since *spoel* (rinse, wash) can also mean 'spindle' or 'bobbin', this is a further pun on weaving.

MEESTER:	Ick salt wel coocken.	445
	Geefft mij eenen bessem / dat ick mach stoocken tvier.	
	Sedt ditte wech en gaet altsaemen van hier,	
	Ick en wil mijn conste niemant leeren.	
	Nu Lippen, ghij sult u gaen ommekeeren;	
	Doet uwen rock uuijte / ghij leves te sachtere.	450
LIPPEN:	Hoe, sal ick bercken struijff eeten van achtere?	
MEESTER:	Men sal u wadt strijcken tegent vercoelen.	
LIPPEN:	Ist oock goeijen cost?	
MEESTER:	Dat suldij wel gevoelen.	
	Her! her! Lippen, eet nu leckernije!	
LIPPEN:	Aij mij! lijeff meester! wat maeckt ghije?	455
MEESTER:	Tsijn die bercken struijven / die ick u bieck.	
LIPPEN:	Aij mij! meester Jan, ick en ben niet sieck!	
	Wech, wech met uwen bercken struijven!	
MEESTER:	So salmen dees jonge boeven huijven	
	Die haer Ouders aldus willen bedriegen!	460
LIPPEN:	Ick en sals niet meer doen.	
MEESTER:	Suldij noch liegen?	
LIPPEN:	Neen ick lieff meester, laet mij nu gaen.	
MEESTER:	'Neen ick, lieff meester' segdij, siet dat ghij u	
	Niet en maeckt meer sieck.	
LIPPEN:	Neen, meester, dats gedaen.	
MEESTER:	Adieu, Lippen, peijnst om die morgen soppe!	465
LIPPEN:	Wadt ou! die leckere beetgens comen mij suerlijck oppe!	
	Ja, bercken struijven! ick en salt niet vergeten.	
	Ontbeijt / Hanneken Leckertant moetse oock eeten,	
	Dat sal mijn pijne wadt doen versoeten.	
	Hij compt hier gaende op sijn voeten,	470
	Ick weet wel, hij heefter naer grooten lost.	
HANNEKEN:	Wel, Lippen, hoe sijdij gevaren?	
LIPPEN:	Noijt beteren cost!	
	Sij soude u goet sijn, want ghij sijt teere.	
HANNEKEN:	So sal ickse oock eeten, wilt ghodt den heere.	
	Ick salder mijn moeijer om gaen senden.	475
LIPPEN:	Ja, maer ghij sult een roeij vinden op u lenden;	
	Ick en begeer niet meer alsulcken hindere.	
HANNEKEN:	Wadt segdij, Lippen?	
LIPPEN:	Mijn moeijer compt gindere.	
	Haer verlangt zeere hoet met mij mach wesen.	
WEBBE:	Wel Lippen, hoe ist?	

DOCTOR:	I will cook it up.	445
	Give me a broom, so that I may stoke a fire.	
	Set this aside, and all of you go from here,	
	I do not wish to divulge my art to anyone.	
	Now Philip, you must turn yourself around,	
	Get out of your tunic, to improve your life.	450
PHILIP:	Why, will I have to eat birch cake from behind?	
DOCTOR:	It will protect you against cooling.[35]	
PHILIP:	Is it also good food?	
DOCTOR:	You will know that soon enough.	
	Here! Here! Philip, now eat this delicacy!	
PHILIP:	Ay me! Dear master! What are you doing?	455
MASTER:	These are the birch cakes that I baked for you.	
PHILIP:	Ay me! Master John, I am no longer sick!	
	Away, away with your birch cakes!	
DOCTOR:	In this way one puts the hood on those young crooks[36]	
	Who try to deceive their parents in this manner!	460
PHILIP:	I will not do it any more.	
DOCTOR:	You will not lie again?	
PHILIP:	No, I will not, dear master. Let me go now.	
DOCTOR:	'No, dear master', you say: see that you	
	Do not make yourself seem sick again.	
PHILIP:	No, master, that is over.	
DOCTOR:	Adieu, Philip. Think about your morning sops![37]	465
PHILIP:	Eugh! The delicious pieces come back up sourly!	
	Yes, birch cakes! I will not forget them.	
	Wait, Jack Sweet-tooth must also eat them,	
	That will sweeten my pain somewhat.	
	He is coming here on his feet,	470
	I know well that he has great desire for this.	
JACK:	Well, Philip, how did you get on?	
PHILIP:	I never had better food!	
	You should try some yourself, since you are so delicate.	
JACK:	Then I will also eat them, as the Lord God wills it.	
	I will send my mother to get them.	475
PHILIP:	Yes, but you would find a rod on your bottom:	
	I can no longer bear such a nuisance as him.	
JACK:	What do you say, Philip?	
PHILIP:	My mother approaches from over there.	
	She very much wants to know how things are with me.	
WEAVER:	Well, Philip, how is it?	

---

[35] A pun foreshadowing Philip's beating: *strijken* means both 'to protect' and 'to strike'.

[36] That is, as in falconry.

[37] A *morgensoppe* consists of pieces of bread soaked in milk, traditionally eaten for breakfast. According to Kruyskamp, the line refers to the 'opfrissing' ('refreshment') Philip has just received from the Meester, figuratively waking him from his fantasies: Kruyskamp, *Dichten en spelen*, 84.

LIPPEN:	Moeijer, al genesen!	480
	Die bercken struijven maecken mij gesont en vet.	
WEBBE:	Ick salsse u oock noch coocken altemet,	
	Als u eenich pijne sou meugen deeren.	
LIPPEN:	Tjans hoij, ick en souse niet meer begeeren;	
	Ick sal liever boonen eeten/en seer spinnen.	485
WEBBE:	Nu laet ons in huijs gaen / en dwerck beginnen.	
	Wel, gaet voort / hadde ich nu goeij avontuere.	
VEUGE:	Om bercken struijffen loop ick nu rasch duere;	
	Tis verloren, mijn kint moet hebben sijn gemack.	
	Ick heb geen geluck / hier compt meester Jan Leurquack!	490
	Meester Jan, compt / gaet met mij sonder toeven en beijen;	
	Ghij moet Hanneken bercken struijven bereijen,	
	So ghij voor Lippen Loer deet, verstadijt wel?	
MEESTER:	Ick wil hem geernne verwermen sijn vel;	
	Maer ghij en mostes niet sien, dus gaet wat wech dan.	495
VEUGE:	Gheernne, in trouwen.	
HANNEKEN:	Wellecome, meester Jan.	
MEESTER:	Gherass! haelt my eenen bessem, doet mijn beheet!	
	En doet uwen rock uuijt/en u ondercleet.	
	Wij sullen gaen speelen een vremde cluijte.	
HANNEKEN:	Daer is den bessem/mijn cleeren doe ick uijte;	500
	Coockt nu bercken struijven/thoont u practijken!	
MEESTER:	Nu sal ick u rugge gaen bestrijcken,	
	So dat ghij sult lachen als een huerpaert.	
HANNEKEN:	Aij mij! meester, wadt doedij?	
MEESTER:	Sijt niet vervaert;	
	Ick sal u noch al beter hebben vrij.	505
HANNEKEN:	Aij mij! aij mij! meester, waerom sladij mij?	
	Sijn dat de bercken struijven? tsijn een goet jaer!	
VEUGE:	Ontbeijt! wel wat schreijen hoor ick daer?	
	Ist dat niet Hanneken Leckertant die daer weent?	
	Hoe? sijn dat de bercken struijven/die ghij meent?	510
	Ja, meester Jan, dat sal u veel meer costen oock:	
	Hout datte en datte! Hoe smaeckt u dat vuijstloock?	
HANNEKEN:	Moeijer, hij heeft mij al met rocijen gchouwen.	
VEUGE:	Daer voor sal hij stockvisch sonder botter cnouwen.	
	Hout dat en datte!	
MEESTER:	Och, 'tis genoch, hout stille.	515
HANNEKEN:	Moeijer, smijt stijff!	
MEESTER:	Och, ick deet om beters wille!	

PHILIP:	Mother, all better!	480
	Those birch cakes made me healthy and well.	
WEAVER:	I will cook more of them right away	
	In case you experience any more pain.	
PHILIP:	Saint John's head, I can bear no more;	
	I would rather eat beans and carry on spinning.	485
WEAVER:	Now let us go home, and begin work.	
	Well, go on, I have had enough adventure now.	
CODDLE:	I race now after birch cakes, ever in a rush,	
	All is lost: my child must have them made for him.	
	I have no fortune. Here comes Master John Pedlar-quack!	490
	Doctor John, come with me without delay or pause.	
	You must prepare birch cakes for Jack,	
	Just as you did for Philip Loser. Do you understand me?	
DOCTOR:	I will enjoy heating his skin for him;	
	But you must not look, so go away now.	495
CODDLE:	I will, in truth.	
JACK:	Welcome, Doctor John.	
DOCTOR:	Hurry! Get me a broom, do as I command!	
	And take off your tunic and your underclothes.	
	We are going to play a strange farce.	
JACK:	There is the broom, I am out of my clothes;	500
	Cook the birch cakes now, show me your arts!	
DOCTOR:	Now I will sweep your behind,	
	So that you will laugh like a workhorse.	
JACK:	Ay me! Master, what are you doing?	
DOCTOR:	Do not be afraid,	
	I will make you all better soon.	505
JACK:	Ay me! Ay me! Master, why do you spank me?	
	Is that the birch cakes? It is a good year for them!	
CODDLE:	Wait! Well, what is that shrieking I hear there?	
	Is that not Jack Sweet-tooth who cries out in there?	
	How? Is that the birch cakes that you meant?	510
	Yes, Doctor John, you will also pay for that:	
	Take that and that! How do you find that fist of garlic?	
JACK:	Mother, he has cut me with rods all over.	
CODDLE:	He will gnaw on stickfish without butter for that![38]	
	Take that and that!	
DOCTOR:	Ouch, it is enough, hold still!	515
JACK:	Mother, strike firmly!	
DOCTOR:	Oh, I did it out of good intent!	

---

[38] The text refers here to the dried fish known in English as 'stockfish', a term itself derived from the Middle Dutch *stokvis*. Since this literally translates to 'stick fish', possibly owing to the infamous hardness of its meat, a similar pun is created in the original. See the discussion in Dirk Boutkan, 'Pregermanic Fish in Old Saxon Glosses', in *Speculum Saxonum: Studien zu den kleineren altsächsischen Sprachdenkmälern*, ed. Arend Quak (Amsterdam, 1999), 11–26 (24).

	Hout oppe, hout oppe! / wildij mij vermoorden?	
WEBBE:	Wel vrou Veuge! vichten, met veel woorden?	
	Mij dunckt, jaesij / ick en weet wadt bedien mach.	
LIPPEN:	Siet, meester Jan Leurequack sidt oock inden slach;	520
	Al is hij loos en schalck, hij wordt ook verdult.	
HANNEKEN:	Ja, Lippen Loer, dat is al u schult.	
LIPPEN:	Hebben u die bercken struijven qualijck getoeft?	
HANNEKEN:	Dat weet ghij wel.	
LIPPEN:	Ick hebs oock geproeft,	
	Dus gae wij even swaer geladen naer tstede.	525
WEBBE:	Hout, goey vrou Veuge, geeft vrede, geeft vrede!	
	Laet u gespreecken/hoe hebdijt aldus gemaeckt?	
MEESTER:	Aij mij! ick ben ommers uuijten druppe geraeckt!	
VEUGE:	Leert noch der lieden kinderen castijen!	
MEESTER:	Voorwaar, Leckertant sou hem dickwijls wel lijen	530
	Met bonen/gaeffdij hem op sijn rebben	
	Berckenstruijven, als hij wadt leckers wil hebben;	
	Ick wedde, 't sou een kint werden ten inde.	
VEUGE:	Wyse, discrete / notabele, geminde –	
LIPPEN:	Hier mede uwen oorloff –	
WEBBE:	Soot best betaempt –	535
LIPPEN:	Nemen wij, Violierkens, uuijt jonsten versaempt.	

FINIS. Lang in dicht 561 regulen.

Is gespeelt bij die Violieren van Antwerpen indie feeste der Lelijen in Diest ao 1541 en hebben den oppersten prijs gehadt.

Fecit Jan vanden Berge.

	Hold up, hold up! Do you want to murder me?	
WEAVER:	Well, wife Coddle! Is she fighting, with many words?	
	It seems to me that yes, she is: I will look to see why.	
PHILIP:	See, Doctor John Pedlar-quack is also trapped in there;	520
	Although he is clever and sharp, he has also been fooled.	
JACK:	Yes, Philip Loser, this is all your fault.	
PHILIP:	Have you sampled the birch cakes in a hard way?	
JACK:	You know that full well.	
PHILIP:	I have also tried them,	
	Thus we brought home an equal share.	525
WEAVER:	Hold, good wife Coddle, make peace, make peace!	
	Let me speak with you, what have you done?	
DOCTOR:	Ay me! I am at least out of danger.	
CODDLE:	Learn not to flog other people's children!	
DOCTOR:	In truth, Sweet-tooth should satisfy himself	530
	With beans; give him birch cakes	
	On his ribs, if he would have delicious things;	
	I bet that would turn him into a good child.	
CODDLE:	Wise, discreet, notable, beloved –[39]	
PHILIP:	Your end is also here –	
WEAVER:	As this was our best attempt –	535
PHILIP:	Take leave of us, the Gillyflower, gathered with joy.	

FINIS. The length of this poem is 561 lines.

Played by the Violets of Antwerp at the festival of the Lilies in Diest anno 1541, where it took first prize.

Written by Jan vanden Berghe.

---

[39] This and the subsequent lines are addressed to the audience.

A Farce of the Barefoot Brothers

THE RELATIONSHIP between the chambers and early Protestantism is one of the most complex issues of the period, and one that has generated a great deal of critical debate. Towards the end of the sixteenth century, contemporaries of the *rederijkers* were often quick to view them as irredeemably steeped in heresy. For instance, in G. A. Bredero's *Spaanschen Brabander* (1617), there is an extended joke at the expense of what were by now outdated organisations clinging to hackneyed aesthetic principles. In an ironic tribute to the chambers, Bredero primarily ridicules the groups for their stylistic excesses, but also mentions their links to suspect religious ideologies:

> Dat waaren liens vol perfeccy, en van devine eloquency,
> Yghelijck woordeken datse aggeerde, of nomineerde, dat
>   was een sentency.
> Het minste datse sproocken dat was een reffiereyn, en dat so
>   exstruvagant
> Van uytspraack, trots een Oostersche Phar-heer, of Luyter-
>   sche Predikant.[1]

> (Their lines were full of perfection and divine eloquence,
> Each word they wrote or uttered was a full sentence.
> The meanest thing they spoke was a refrein, and that so
>   extravagant
> In diction, that it would suit a German pastor, or Lutheran
>   preacher.)

Much the same conclusion was also reached by an English visitor to the Netherlands. In 1561, Richard Clough, an agent of Sir Thomas Gresham in Antwerp, reported that the 'companies of Reteryck' first spread 'the worde of God ... in thys contrey', and compared their work to 'the bokes of Martyn Luter'.[2] Again, the chambers are seen as 'nests of heresy', deeply enmeshed in the propagation of Protestant ideas.[3]

While these claims are certainly overstated, as is shown by the long careers of committed Catholics such as Cornelis Everaert at Bruges and Anna Bijns at Antwerp, they mirror the suspicions civic authorities often showed towards *rederijker* drama. With its volatile mix of riotous comedy and vernacular religious instruction, their *spelen* were often considered a potential threat, or held responsible for actual outbreaks of violence. Although city councils were usually sympathetic to the *rederijkers*' concerns, since both were members of the same social class, they were at

---

[1] Gerbrand Adriaensz Bredero, *Spaanschen Brabander*, ed. C. F. P. Stutterheim (Culemborg, 1974), 167–8.

[2] John William Burgon, *The Life and Times of Sir Thomas Gresham*, 2 vols. (London, 1839), 1: 379–80.

[3] Alistair Duke, *Reformation and Revolt in the Low Countries* (Cambridge, 2003), 106.

times forced to put aside their tolerance and impose punitive measures, especially when prompted by higher authorities such as the imperial court or the church. The most notorious case of this involves the revolt at Ghent in 1539, which followed a *landjuweel* in the city some weeks earlier. In 1540 Charles V issued an edict blaming the disturbances squarely on the 'comedien' of the 'Camern der Rhetoricker', seeing the plays as vehicles for seditious Protestant doctrines.[4] Owing to this ordinance, a number of authorities had no option but to ban the printed edition of the Ghent *spelen*, forbidding its further publication and circulation.

The Ghent episode was, however, merely part of a long line of investigations and prosecutions. At Amsterdam the city effectively withdrew its support for the chambers between 1525 and 1559 after a series of plays attacking monastic orders, the sacraments and other aspects of devotion were performed, including one which depicted monks as demons fishing for gold.[5] Graver still, the Amsterdam chambers were implicated in the Anabaptist riots of 1535: when the city's *stadhuis* was seized by dissenters, many were carrying musical instruments and other pieces of equipment that belonged to the city's chambers.[6] At Antwerp there was also a growing sense of unease, and the city authorities brought progressively sharper penalties against rhetoricians thought to be disseminating inflammatory ideas. In 1546 Jacob van Middeldonck, *deken* of *De Damastbloem* (The Damask Flower), was ordered to complete a pilgrimage for producing a suspect play, *Den boom der scriftueren* ('The Tree of Scripture').[7] Van Middeldonck was certainly more fortunate than two later poets, Peter Schuddematte of *De Violieren* and the printer and rhetorician Frans Fraet: Schuddematte was beheaded in 1547 for composing an anti-clerical *ballade* and *spel van zinne*, while Fraet followed him to the scaffold in 1558.[8] Other cities in the Netherlands treated the chambers with similar hostility, especially after the iconoclastic riots of 1566 cemented official opinion against them. In 1568 Heynszoon Adriaanszen of the Haarlem chamber *De Pellicaen* was hanged, allegedly for writing lyrics in which 'papen' ('priests') were derided as 'apen' ('monkeys').[9]

While the penalties were certainly brutal, especially in the latter half of the century, the prosecutions themselves were not entirely without foundation. It is clear that some heterodox activity did emanate from the chambers. The plays staged at

[4] Leonard Verduin, 'The Chambers of Rhetoric and Anabaptist Origins in the Low Countries', *Mennonite Quarterly Review* 34 (1960), 192–6 (194).

[5] Gary Waite, 'On the Stage and in the Streets: Rhetorician Drama, Social Conflict and Religious Upheaval in Amsterdam, 1520–1550', in *Rederijkers: conformisten en rebellen. Literatuur, cultuur en stedelijke netwerken (1400–1650)*, ed. Bart Ramakers (Amsterdam, 2003), 162–73.

[6] J. A. Worp, *Geschiedenis van den Amsterdamschen schouwburg 1496–1772* (Amsterdam, 1920), 8–9; Andrew Pettegree, *Reformation and the Culture of Persuasion* (Cambridge, 2005), 94.

[7] S. J. van Mierlo, '"Den boem der Schriftueren" en het geval Jacob van Middeldonck', *Verslagen en mededelingen van de Koninklijke Vlaamse academie voor taal- en letterkunde* (1939), 889–905.

[8] R. Ryckaert, 'Een Antwerpse brief aan Symmachus. Analyse van het "Totten goetwillighen leser" in de Antwerpse spelen van Sinne (1562)', *Spiegel der letteren* 46 (2004), 1–32 (22); Paul Valkema Blouw, 'The Van Oldenborch and Vanden Merberghe pseudonyms, or, Why Frans Fraet had to die', *Quaerendo* 22 (1992), 165–96, 245–72; E. Hofman, 'Liederen en refreinen van Frans Fraet?', *Spiegel der letteren* 42 (2000), 227–58.

[9] Conrad Busken Huet, *Het land van Rembrand* (Haarlem, 1946), 269.

Amsterdam, for instance, were not merely outspoken or scurrilous in their satire, but seem to have been inspired by the apocalyptic teachings of Melchior Hoffman.[10] Likewise, as Leonard Verduin observes, it is unlikely to be a coincidence that early Reformed churches, such as La Vigne at Antwerp or La Rose at Lille, imitated the chambers by adopting similar names.[11] Nevertheless it is equally obvious that the dangers were at times more perceived than actual, extending more from nervousness amongst the magistrates and councils than from any real threat. Even tried and tested work could attract suspicion in the right circumstances. One example of this is *Hecastus*, a humanist reworking of *Everyman* produced by Georgius Macropedius in 1538. In his prologue to the printed edition of the play, Macropedius complains that it suffered 'a zoilorum dentibus' ('at the teeth of detractors') and provoked some level of 'contentionem' ('controversy') after its first staging.[12] This is in spite of the fact that its material was already several decades old, that the play itself was written in Latin, and that it was performed in the relatively restricted environment of De Hieronymusschool, the grammar school at Utrecht.

Perhaps an even stranger instance of this controversy is provided by the farce translated here, *De bervoete bruers*.[13] The episode in which this play was involved has been thoroughly outlined by Willem van Eeghem and Anne-Laure van Bruaene.[14] The play was first staged on 9 April 1559 at Brussels. It was performed as part of a day-long celebration of the Peace of Cateau-Cambrésis, signed by Elizabeth I, Henry II and Philip II earlier that month.[15] The farce was performed by the chamber of *De Corenbloem* (The Corn Flower), a fraternity founded in 1477, which had close associations with the city's tapestry industry and with the shooting-guild of Saint Sebastian.[16] The celebrations evidently took the form of a small-scale competition, as the *Corenbloem* was awarded first prize for its entry. However, in the weeks following this festival there were a number of complaints from the Franciscan community of Brussels. One friar even preached a public sermon against the play, and against the weavers and dyers for performing it, denouncing its staging as 'een schande' ('a disgrace'). The surviving text of the play also mentions that the players had been publicly 'blamed' and even 'taunted' for their involvement (lines 15, 27). A particular bone of contention was the fact that an actual Franciscan habit had been used as a costume in the performance.

In spite of these criticisms, the *Corenbloem* decided to stage the play a second time on 21 September. This time its venue was the highly public setting of the central square of Brussels, the Grote Markt. While this decision was hardly likely to calm the situation, the play was preceded by a new prologue of forty lines which makes

[10] Waite, 'On the Stage and in the Streets', 164.

[11] Verduin, 'Chambers of Rhetoric and Anabaptist Origins', 195.

[12] Raphael Dammer and Benedikt Jessing, *Der Jedermann im 16. Jahrhundert: die Hecastus-Dramen von Georgius Macropedius und Hans Sachs* (Berlin, 2007), 36.

[13] Willem van Eeghem, *Drie schandaleuse spelen (Brussel 1559)* (Antwerp, 1937), 3–26.

[14] Anne-Laure van Bruaene, *Om beters wille: rederijkerskamers en de stedelijke cultuur in de Zuidelijke Nederlanden (1400–1650)* (Amsterdam, 2008), 115–17, 123.

[15] On the significance of the treaty for the southern Netherlands, see Louis Sicking, *Neptune and the Netherlands: State, Economy, and War at Sea in the Renaissance* (Leiden, 2004), 443–50.

[16] H. de Keyser, 'De Brusselse rederijkers in de opstand', *Tijdschrift voor Brusselse geschiedenis* 1 (1984), 121–33.

some effort to defend the piece and its performers. Taking the form of a dialogue between a weaver and 'Prologue', this denies any malicious intent, and claims that the tapestry workers had no participation in staging or writing the piece. To hedge its bets even further, it pays lavish praise to Emperor Charles V, who was born in Flanders in 1500, and his daughter Margaret of Parma, appointed governor of the Netherlands by Charles's successor, Philip II, in 1559 (lines 4–5). Interestingly, it also deflects attention away from the anti-fraternal content, claiming that the 'barefoot brothers' of the title are 'poor children' rather than Franciscans, even though the play deliberately evokes both senses of the phrase (line 30). Apart from these cosmetic revisions, the play seems to have remained unchanged.

The response to this second performance was swift. An investigation was immediately ordered by Antoine Perrenot de Granvelle, prime minister to Margaret of Parma, Philip II's regent in the Netherlands. He appointed Henri de Booms, procurator-general of Brabant, to look into the situation. No doubt De Granvelle feared that the play was not merely anti-clerical but actively Protestant in its sympathies, as De Booms had already proved himself a dogged pursuer of heresy. In 1553 he led an investigation into the workshop of the famous Utrecht painter Anthonis Mor, whose clients included Philip II, Maximilien II, Mary I, and De Granvelle himself.[17] De Booms was certainly vigorous and thorough in his examination of the *Corenbloem*, seizing the manuscript of the controversial play, and collecting testimonies from a wide range of parties. He questioned witnesses to the original performance, a number of the city's Franciscans, and members of the *Corenbloem* itself. Among the *rederijkers* he interrogated were the actors of the farce, some senior members of the chamber and Franchoys van Ballaer, *factor* of the chamber and probably father to one of the actors.[18]

The rhetoricians were clearly shaken, as they took great care not to implicate themselves. They claimed that the play was not their responsibility but the work of an unknown author, and that it had been performed in Antwerp 'tanderen tyde' ('some time ago').[19] They also alleged that they had found the piece in a book owned by Nicolaas Rombouts. Rombouts was a figure of some repute, and the chamber evidently named him to capitalise on his respectability. At seventy years old he was a *rederijker* of fifty years' standing, and the uncle of a former *factor*. He may also have been related to the glass-painter Rombouts, who produced the spectacular windows of Antwerp cathedral, and died at Brussels in *c*.1530.[20] Nonetheless, as Van Bruaene comments, naming this particular man was a risky strategy. In 1527 'Nicolaas Rombouts had been one of the leading men of the Lutheran group', who had ' hidden Lutheran books and tapestry designs with anti-papal themes in his house'.[21] In their

[17] Henri Hyams, *Antonio Moro, son œuvre et son temps* (Brussels, 1910), 35.

[18] Van Eeghem, *Drie schandaleuse spelen*, 5. On Van Ballaer, see P. Pikhaus, *Het tafelspel bij de rederijkers*, 2 vols. (Ghent, 1988–1989), 1: 95.

[19] Van Eeghem, *Drie schandaleuse spelen*, 81.

[20] Jean Helbig, *De glasschilderkunst in België, repertorium en documenten*, 2 vols. (Antwerp, 1951), 2: 91.

[21] Anne-Laure Van Bruaene, '"Of the king's edict I do you no command": Vernacular Literary Networks and the Reformation in the Low Countries', *Archive for Reformation History* 99 (2008), 229–55 (241).

other statements the *rederijkers* were more circumspect. For his part Van Ballaer would not claim authorship of the text as a whole, although he freely admitted that the prologue was his work. In fact he seems to have recited this section of the play personally during the performance on 21 September.

While the inquiry continued, tensions were heightened still further by the performance of a second play on 29 September. This was a piece with the title *Een tafelspel van twee sotten* ('A Table-Play of Two Fools').[22] The play was staged by *Het Mariacransken* (The Crown of Mary), and contained a series of jokes apparently directed at the sacrament of the altar. It is unclear whether the play was an act of deliberate provocation, or merely an innocent entertainment whose staging happened to be poorly timed. While either possibility is likely, the fact that Van Ballaer was also factor of the *Mariacransken* at least raises some questions.[23] At any rate, a further investigation was launched after complaints about the play were submitted by two priests. The *rederijkers* again faced official questioning, and this time were even more guarded in their testimony. The *Mariacransken* claimed it had obtained the *tafelspel* from a young man of Lier or Mechelen, whose name no-one knew, in exchange for a selection of *refreins*. Van Ballaer added that the text had been in the archive of the chamber for at least sixty years. This was confirmed by an elderly member of the group, Pauwels Thielmans, who swore that he had played a role in the piece some forty years ago, even going so far as to recite his part before the procurator-general.[24] It was also argued that any jokes concerning the sacraments were not intended seriously, and the play had twice been played before the priest of Sint-Goedele without raising any objections. This particular clergyman was, however, conveniently dead, and was therefore unavailable for questioning by De Booms.[25]

The investigation spread even further afield. By October it had extended to the chamber of *Den Boeck* (The Book), the oldest and most active of the Brussels *kamers*. On 24 October 1559 the members of *Den Boek* played *Een tafelspel van drie sotten* ('A table-play of three fools') at the wedding of Jan de Fuytere, a prominent citizen and land agent of Bosvoorde.[26] Much like the *Play of Two Fools*, at least one audience member thought the play a mockery of the Eucharist, and duly reported it to the authorities. His outrage was hardly universal: during the brief investigation that ensued, the brother of De Fuytere lodged his own complaint, disappointed that *Den Boek* had not staged the livelier farce he originally requested.[27] The *rederijkers* for their part argued that that they had no intent to offend their viewers. This explanation satisfied Henri de Booms, who ordered that the *rederijkers* should make an official apology to the church, but imposed no further penalties. Perhaps emboldened by this perceived leniency, or believing that the authorities were now favourably disposed towards them, *De Corenbloem* wrote to De Booms asking for the manuscript of *The Barefoot Brothers* to be returned. As it transpired, this

---

[22] Van Eeghem, *Drie schandaleuse spelen*, 27–40.
[23] K. ter Laan, *Letterkundig woordenboek voor Noord en Zuid* (The Hague, 1952), 351.
[24] Van Eeghem, *Drie schandaleuse spelen*, 83.
[25] Van Bruaene, *Om beters wille*, 116.
[26] Van Eeghem, *Drie schandaleuse spelen*, 41–56.
[27] Van Bruaene, *Om beters wille*, 116.

move was very poorly judged. On 26 January 1560 the central government of the Hapsburg Netherlands answered their impudence by issuing a *plakkaat*, a form of emergency edict normally reserved for periods of civic disorder. This stated that all plays, songs and *refreins* would henceforth be submitted for inspection, and could only be performed once approval had been obtained from both religious and secular authorities. The *Corenbloem* had clearly pushed its luck too far.

It is difficult to know what to make of this affair, and especially of the play which triggered it. On the face of it, *The Barefoot Brothers* seems fairly mild in terms of its anti-clerical satire. Not only is it more concerned with the usual *esbattement* themes of food, theft and knock-about, but the charges it makes against the friars are largely conventional in character. Most stem from the tradition of anti-fraternal satire, which was already several centuries old by this point. For instance, the claims that friars live in idleness, extort fine foodstuffs and ignore the poor dates back to William of Saint-Amour's *De Periculis Novissimorum Temporum* (1256), a text which was, as Penn R. Szittya and Arnold Williams have shown, 'the wellspring of a long tradition of attacks on the friars'.[28] The ability of the main Franciscan to wander into Hans's home might also recall this tradition, since *De Periculis* charges the friars with being 'penetrantes domos' ('creepers into homes').[29] The farce is therefore evoking a series of familiar caricatures, rather than raising new or specific complaints. There is also some overlap with anti-monastic traditions. The fact that the chief antagonist is a *framineur*, the head of his community's infirmary, recalls a satiric motif first found in Bernard of Clairvaux's *Apologia ad Guillelmum Abbatem* (1125). In this widely read satire on Cluny, Bernard also targets the monastic infirmary as a seat of sloth and greed, describing it as a place where 'healthy and strong young men are opting out of the common life' and taking to bed all day instead: 'you bandage yourselves before receiving a wound, bewail the sound limb, ward off the undealt blow'.[30]

The use of this material considerably blunts the edge of the farce. The conventional nature of its accusations, and the fact that many are at root more appropriate to monks than friars, mean that the play can hardly be judged a vitriolic outcry against the order. This is further reinforced by the speech of Mild-of-Heart praising the conduct of the friary. Even if this is intended ironically, it does at least commend the founding ideals of the Franciscans, rather than denying their validity altogether. The satire of the farce is further dulled by the openly venal nature of the poor man and his wife, who are the opponents of the friars in the play. These roguish, acquisitive figures fall conspicuously short of their surname Goetbloed (Good-blood): in the *rondeel* that opens the play, for instance, Hans pleads that 'I would go to work if I had some soup', evidently believing that he should be rewarded before he has done anything that might warrant it (line 52). Likewise the fact that the Infirmarian is permitted to exercise his office as confessor, absolving Hans at the play's conclusion, suggests a basic acceptance of the authority of his order.

---

[28] Penn R. Szittya, 'The Antifraternal Tradition in Middle English', *Speculum* 52 (1977), 287–313 (287); Arnold Williams, 'Chaucer and the Friars', *Speculum* 28 (1953), 499–513.

[29] William of Saint-Amour, *De Periculis Novissimorum Temporum*, ed. G. Geltner, Dallas Medieval Texts and Translations 8 (Leuven, 2007), 57.

[30] Bernard of Clairvaux, 'An Apologia for Abbot William', in *The Cistercian World: Monastic Writings of the Twelfth Century*, trans. and ed. Pauline Matarasso (Harmondsworth, 1993), 53.

But what makes the play all the more difficult to gauge is its occasional movement towards a more militant position. This is most noticeable when the infirmarjan is branded a 'lollaert' by Hans (line 130). Such a term is highly loaded. On the one hand, it could simply be taken in its literal sense, as 'mumbler', playing further on the friar's claim that his brothers 'have spent three hours praying this night' (line 113). However, it is also possible that the term is designed to evoke ideas of heresy. *Lollaert* also refers to a member of the so-called Brethren of the Free Spirit, a lay 'movement' formally pronounced heretical in 1312, despite the fact that it was in reality 'no organised sect at all' but a range of 'individual mystics in communication with like-minded friends and followers on an informal basis'.[31] It is possible that the text is alluding to this specific heresy, since friars were at times confused with alleged practitioners of the Free Spirit.[32] It may also be evoking heterodoxy more generally: by the time the play was produced there had been no prosecutions for the heresy for over a century, and *lollaert* had developed into a more generalised term for any religious eccentric.[33] The fact remains, however, that labelling a friar *lollaert* carries serious connotations. In particular, it evokes a well-established line of attack against the friars. It echoes the frequent claim that the mendicants are themselves a heretical group, that their rules are based in heterodoxy rather than sound doctrine: as Szittya writes, 'other ecclesiastic groups and individual churchman of all orders had often been attacked for falling into immorality . . . but the mendicant orders were attacked primarily as an institution, whose claim to the *vita apostolica* was false and whose legitimacy as religious orders was suspect'.[34] Given this background, deploying such a term against a friar seems calculated to strike a nerve, no matter how obliquely.

Similarly, the episode in which the infirmarian strips off his habit in order to beat Hans and his wife also contains problematic symbolism. Again, on the surface it seems a fairly innocent gesture, one which might be intended to preserve the sanctity of the vestment. It might also serve to dilute the satire still further, since the disrobing breaks the dramatic illusion of the play. The friar's claim that he is now a 'worldly' layman is a statement of fact, since he was apparently played by the ropemaker Jan de Knibbere: this in turn highlights how the play is merely a pretence, not a depiction of actual friars' conduct (line 314).[35] However, as before, this detail can

---

[31] Malcolm D. Lambert, *Medieval Heresy: Popular Movements from the Gregorian Reform to the Reformation* (Oxford, 2002), 205. See also Gordon Leff, *Heresy in the Later Middle Ages: The Relation of Heterodoxy to Dissent, c.1250–c.1450* (Manchester, 1999), 308–400; Walter Wakefield and Austin Evans, *Heresies of the High Middle Ages* (New York, 1991).

[32] Robert Lerner, *The Heresy of the Free Spirit in the Later Middle Ages* (Berkeley, CA, 1972), 43–5.

[33] See for instance the lyric 'Van dat niemen en can ghedoen hi en es begrepen' ('Of that which no-one can do or else he is blamed'), in which the narrator complains that 'Men seghet dat ic ijdelheit soeke/ Latic ende ic's niet en roeke,/ Men seghet dat ic een lollaert si' ('Men tell me that I seek idleness, I let them and do not care, men say that I am a lollard'): P. Blomaert, 'Van dat niemen en can ghedoen hi en es begrepen', *De Dietsche warande* 1 (1855), 134–6. The last documented trial for the heresy was that of Hans Becker in 1458 at Mainz: see Lerner, *Heresy of the Free Spirit*, 177–81.

[34] Penn R. Szittya, *The Antifraternal Tradition in Medieval Literature* (Princeton, 1986), 7.

[35] Van Eeghem, *Drie schandaleuse spelen*, 81.

be construed in more radical terms. It is difficult to overlook the fact that when the friar casts off his habit he cancels his membership of the church, openly emphasising his basic similarity to the lay characters. This equalisation becomes clearer still when Hans and the infirmarian exchange blows, and discuss their punches in the same culinary, carnivalesque terms, announcing 'have a sample of our food' and 'take here a knucklebone of great value' (lines 323–4). The physical contact they make with one another, and the uniformity of the language they use, serves to emphasise their essential sameness.

But what is especially problematic is the sheer nonchalance with which the friar shrugs off his vestments. In reality, stripping off the cope was a much graver issue for a friar: as one late-medieval source has it, 'the levynge of oure clothis ... bitokeneth/ forsakyng of oure reule'.[36] The play, however, makes this badge of separateness a mere cosmetic difference, one that can be put on or off quite casually. Again, the difference between cleric and layman is tacitly dissolved, or at least made to appear negligible. This line of reasoning is taken even further at the end of the play, when its central trick is revealed. Here Hans and Gertrude claim that their household is in fact entitled to be called a religious foundation, no less than the actual friary next door. They even argue that they are more deserving of donations than the Franciscans, and are supported in this judgement by the authoritative character of the Bailiff.

All of this veers uncomfortably close to arguments made by the Reformers. Most severely, it echoes the fundamental Lutheran doctrine of universal priesthood. Luther formalised this idea in his *Babylonian Captivity* (1520), declaring that 'we are all equally priests, as many of us as are baptized'.[37] The play's consignment of laity and priest to the same basic position moves close to this viewpoint, as it also erodes the distance between them, highlighting their essential equality. The fact that a real Franciscan habit was used only reinforces this confusion of the two estates, and may well be why the friars responded with particular vehemence to this feature of the performance. There is a further hint of Lutheranism in the final lines of the play, when Hans, Gertrude and their children are permitted to retain the food they have stolen. This has clear echoes of Luther's insistence on the importance of charity, which led him to reinterpret the Mass as a form of fellowship with the poor, and to denounce uncharitable priests as unworthy of their office.[38] The play is putting these ideas into dramatic form, diverting a charitable presentation from an undeserving friar into the hands of the urban poor. All things considered, the play does present several inflammatory ideas, even if these are couched in traditional comedy and apolitical slapstick. Heterodoxy is never more than implied, but it remains present nonetheless.

---

[36] *The Reply of Friar Daw Topias*, in *Political Poems and Songs Eelating to English History, Composed during the Period from the Accession of Edw. III to that of Ric. III*, ed. Thomas Wright, 2 vols. (London, 1859–61), 2: 68.

[37] Martin Luther, 'On the Babylonian Captivity of the Church', *Martin Luther: Selections from his Writings*, ed. John Dillenberger (New York, 1961), 65. See Norman Nagel, 'Luther and the Priesthood of All Believers', *Concordia Theological Quarterly* 61 (1997), 283–4.

[38] Ursula Stock, *Die Bedeutung der Sakramente in Luthers Sermonen von 1519* (Leiden, 1982), 248.

To compound the problem still further, few answers are provided by the records of De Booms's investigation. Even though full transcripts of the interviews have been preserved along with the texts of the *schandaleuse spelen*, these documents are far from illuminating. They shed little light on the extent of the disquiet caused by the plays, and say even less about the intentions of the *rederijkers*, and whether or not they were deliberately courting controversy. Aside from the issue of the Franciscan habit, which was only criticised for its appearance on the stage, and not for the specific use to which it was put, there are few other explicit allegations made against the performers. The testimonies of witnesses are almost uniformly evasive and imprecise, as time and again members of the audience claim not to have seen or heard the play fully or to have missed crucial parts of the performance. As Van Bruaene summarises, according to the records, most audience members 'had not seen the play all the way through, or could not recall it very well, or had only heard rumours about it; they did not know who the actors were or had not seen them properly, since they had their backs to the players'.[39] There may well be some truth to these statements, as rhetorician drama may not have demanded the complete attention of those present, especially since many *spelen* were staged during feasts and other celebrations. The abiding impression, however, is of a reluctance to give information: the witnesses did not want to incriminate themselves by highlighting their presence at a scandalous production. The testimonies of the *rederijkers* are even cagier. There is a suspicious consistency to their depositions, as the same core details are echoed throughout them, with little elaboration between individual statements. It seems, as Van Bruaene concludes, that these actors did what they did best when confronted: they play-acted, performing in accordance with a pre-arranged script.[40]

All in all, despite these questions, it seems safest to conclude that the episode does not represent an outbreak of defiantly Protestant-inspired outspokenness, like the Ghent *landjuweel* or the Amsterdam plays two decades earlier. Although the *rederijkers* closed ranks when accused, the farce was probably intended to be the genial, traditional farce it appears to the modern reader. Perhaps the most revealing detail is the fact that the *Corenbloem* requested the text of the play to be returned before De Booms's investigation had concluded. This suggests that the chamber genuinely did believe that the play contained nothing out of the ordinary, or at least nothing that could be considered exceptionally offensive by the court. They were confident that the satire was within accepted limits, and so they could afford to request their manuscript back. At the very least they were convinced that they could rely on the support of secular authorities such as the procurer-general, having done nothing that might disturb this traditional relationship: this perhaps underlies their decision to perform the farce a second time, despite the vocal resentment of the friars.

This point in turn reveals something interesting. Even though the *Barefoot Brothers* does not represent a departure from the norm, it does show that a fair degree of anti-clerical sentiment and implicit radicalism was part of that norm. The fact is that the text does contain traces of more incendiary ideas, overlapping

---

[39] 'Ze hadden het spel niet volledig gezien of herinnerden het zich niet zo goed, hadden hun informatie maar van horen zeggen, wisten niet wie de acteurs waren of hadden ze niet goed gezien doordat ze met hun rug naar de spelers toegekeerd zaten': Van Bruaene, *Om beters wille*, 117.

[40] Ibid., 117–18.

with the Reformers' concerns at a number of points; yet nonetheless the *rederijkers* seemed confident that De Booms would deem the text harmless and conventional. The rest of the evidence also supports this point. When the other two suspected plays are considered, for instance, the same conclusion suggests itself. It is certainly strange that the plays were staged at all: the other Brussels chambers must have known of the scandal, especially since many *rederijkers* were members of more than one chamber, such as Van Ballaer himself. Again, the fact that the actors did not modify their material shows that this form of humour was not judged to be abnormal. Jokes about the Mass did not strike them as being sufficiently exceptional to attract suspicion, even in a climate of heightened tension and unease. Likewise, the repeated attempts by witnesses to distance themselves from the drama might be seen in the same light. On the one hand, the refusal of those questioned to co-operate fully with the inquiry highlights a lack of concern for the allegations, a sense that nothing too outrageous occurred in the Grote Markt or at De Fuytere's wedding. If the witnesses' sensibilities were offended by what they saw, they would certainly have echoed the friars and priests in denouncing the plays.

However, on the other hand, the fear of being implicated shows that those interrogated tacitly agreed with the charges, in principle at least. Their anxiety suggests that they did believe the chambers might well be guilty of attacking the church, and that they too ran the risk of being drawn into the prosecutions. In sum, the testimonies show a clear expectation that *rederijker* drama could potentially be offensive, but that this was nothing extraordinary or warranting special concern. Overall the episode at Brussels, like the work of Cornelis Everaert at Bruges, shows that the accepted limits of *rederijker* comedy were quite far from those of strict orthodoxy. At least before the enactment of the 1560 *plakkaat*, anti-clericalism was accepted as a natural part of comedy, even to the extent of verging on heresy.

Een esbatament van De Beruoete Bruers

Een esbatament van De Beruoete Bruers, van ses personagijen, met een Prologhe, gespeelt door De Corenbloem te Brussel op 9 April 1559 en op St. Matheusdag 1559

De Prologhe

PROLOGUE: Frans van ballaer
LEGWERCKERE: een legwercker

PROLOGUE: Goids mildelycke goetheyt / diet al veruult
den hemel hier bouen / en deerde beneden
moet becrachtighen / in trouwen ghehult
onsen Coninck van spanien van hier geleden
de hertoghinne van perma vol goeder seden   5
ons regente wil god wel bewaren
op dat wy moghen rusten in peys en in vreden

LEGWERCKERE: wel ghy Corenbloemkens wat suldy verclaren
salt van den beruoetenbruerkens weder wesen
daer wy legwerckers soo seer om syn begresen   10
en van sommighe rabouwen gheheeten
ic rade v allen by den sweeten
dat ghy hier voor allen dit volc vertelt
datter niet eenen legwercker me en heeft ghespelt
twort ons noch verweten op den dach van heden   15
dat wyt ghedaen hebben

PROLOGUE: wa vrint syt te vreden
Coomt vry hier bouen en wilt ons wel verstaen
heb dyer eenighe lachterdeel aff ontfaen
tes ons leet alsulcx ghewagen

LEGWERCKERE: neen siet / een voor al moet ick v vraghen   20
ofter ghy vanden seluen weder sult spelen
soo wilic dat ghy bekent na mijn beulen
datter noyt legwerckere me en heeft te doene ghehadt
noch noch en heeft

PROLOGUE: kenlyck es dat
niemant en heefter noyt me gespeelt van uwen knechte   25
en als ment wel verstaet te rechte
ten es op niemant schimp gedaen
en wildy sit neer / het selue vermaen
suldy noch eens hooren de vremde cuerkens
want schamel wichtkens zyn beruoete bruerkens   30
daer Cousen noch schoenen en syn om aen te doene
dus salment noch eens spelen in den seluen fautsoene

LEGWERCKERE: tes mij alleleens wat dat ghy speelt
als wy legwerckers niet en worden ghequelt

* The Dutch text is reproduced from Van Eeghem, *Drie schandaleuse spelen*, 3–26.

A Farce of the Barefoot Brothers

A farce called *The Barefoot Brothers*, with six characters and a prologue, played by The Cornflower in Brussels on 9 April 1559, and on Saint Matthew's Day 1559.[1]

The prologue

          PROLOGUE: Frans van Ballaer
          WEAVER: a tapestry worker

PROLOGUE:	God's gentle goodness, that entirely fills	
	Heaven above and the earth beneath	
	Ought to support, bound by honesty,	
	Our Spanish king, who was born here,	
	And the duchess of Parma, full of the finest virtues.	5
	God will guard our regent well,	
	So that we may remain in peace and calm.	
WEAVER:	Well, you Cornflowers, what will you perform?	
	It will concern the barefoot brothers once again,	
	For which we tapestry weavers are so famous,	10
	And which causes some to call us rebels.	
	I advise you all, by God's sweat,	
	That you should declare to all the people	
	That not one tapestry weaver has written	
	A word of this, though we have been blamed up to now	15
	As though we had done so.	
PROLOGUE:	Well, friend, be satisfied,	
	Come up here and be sure to tell us,	
	Did you take any laughter from this?	
	It will upset us if you did not.	
WEAVER:	No, you see, for all this I must ask you	20
	Whether you will play the same piece,	
	I wish that you would swear as I demand	
	That no tapestry weaver had a hand in it,	
	Nor has any now.	
PROLOGUE:	That much is certain.	
	No-one from your workforce played along with it,	25
	And if you heed this advice well,	
	Then nobody will be taunted.	
	If you will sit here, the same thing	
	You will hear again, the strange adventures,	
	As poor children are the barefoot brothers	30
	Without stockings or shoes to put on their feet.	
	Thus we will play it again in the same manner.	
WEAVER:	It does not concern me what you play	
	As long as tapestry weavers are not dealt hard words,	

---

[1] The Feast of Saint Matthew falls on 21 September.

	want tsy arm oft ryck ia watter left	35
	tes quaet lyden daermen gheen schult toe en heeft	
	dus wilic om hooren rusten mijn sinnen	
PROLOGUE:	gheeft dan audientie men sal terstont beghinnen	
	ghy goede heeren / van dat hier wort ghedaen	
	hoort en swycht / en wiltet in tbeste slain	40

Het Esbatament

HANS GOETBLOET:	Peeter de packere
TRUIJCKEN DWIJFF:	Jan eenen tymmerman
EEN FRUMINUER:	Jan de knibbere
MILT VAN HERTEN:	Laureys visschere
EENEN BALLU:	Hans ballaer
DIE (7 OF 8) KINDERS	

Juecht Sticht Vruecht

Jan de knubber die heuet ghescreuen
dbehoort hem toe / vindet willet hem geuen
coerebloemken

HANS:	bij mijnder trouwen jck ben wel een arm katijf	
	jc ha eens de wille om tsijne een franmunuer	
	maer jc moeste als een ander trouwen een wijff	
	docht mij al keijl deijl / thuwelijcx bedrijff	
	maer den sanck jn thuwelijck es drou tonnuer	45
	sonder blijschap soe leuick int ghetruer	
	midts dlast der kinderen en daermoede swaer	
	de fortuijne valt mij altijt euen stuer	
	maer tes verloren gheclaecht jc segt openbaer	
	tsal beteren hopick noch hier near	50
	waer sijdij truijken	
TRUIJCKEN:	hier hans goet bloet
HANS:	jc ginghe te wercke haddic een soppe
TRUIJCKEN:	den hongher mact mij benaest verwoet
HANS:	waer sijdij truijken
TRUIJCKEN:	hier hans goet bloet
HANS:	aermoede hout ons jn tegenspoet	55
TRUIJCKEN:	en van hongher draijt mijn hoot gelijck eenen doppe
HANS:	waer sijdij truijken
TRUIJCKEN:	hier hans goet bloet
HANS:	jc ginghe te wercke haddic een soppe
	want den dach die es hooge oppe
TRUIJCKEN:	wat sullen wij maken
HANS:	ic en weet voerwaer	60

	Whether you are poor or rich in life	35
	It is bad to hear things said about you that are untrue.	
	Thus I hope you will let us be as you play.	
PROLOGUE:	Give us permission and we will begin,	
	With what we intend here, you good gentlemen.	
	Listen in silence, and hold this for the best.	40

The farce[2]

HANS GOODBLOOD: Peter de Packere
GERTRUDE, HIS WIFE: Jan, a carpenter
AN INFIRMARIAN: Jan de Knibbere
MILD-OF-HEART: Laureys Visschere
A BAILIFF: Hans Ballaer
THE (7 OR 8) CHILDREN

Youth causes joy

Jan de Knubber has transcribed this.
It belongs to him: if you should find it, give it to him.
Cornflower

HANS:	Upon my word I surely am a poor caitiff.	
	I once had the desire to be an infirmarian	
	But I was forced, like many others, to take a wife.	
	The state of wedlock is entirely difficult for me	
	As the songs of marriage are sombre in tone.	45
	Without bliss I live in tribulation	
	With the heavy burden of children and poverty.	
	Fortune has always imposed on me.	
	But complaining is no help, I always say.	
	Things will improve, I hope, some time from now.	50
	Where are you, Gertrude?	
GERTRUDE:	Here, Hans Goodblood.	
HANS:	I would go to work if I had some soup.	
GERTRUDE:	Hunger almost drives me mad.	
HANS:	Where are you, Gertrude?	
GERTRUDE:	Here, Hans Goodblood.	
HANS:	Poverty has us in decline.	55
GERTRUDE:	And hunger spins my head like a spigot.	
HANS:	Where are you, Gertrude?	
GERTRUDE:	Here, Hans Goodblood.	
HANS:	I would go to work if I had some soup.	
	For now the day is nearly over.	
GERTRUDE:	What will we do?	
HANS:	I do not know for sure.	60

---

[2] The manuscript preserves the names of the original actors, recorded during the procurator-general's investigation; we reproduce these here. Note the inclusion of 'Hans Ballaer' as the Bailiff, who could well be a relative, possibly a son, of the *factor* Franchoys van Ballaer.

TRUIJCKEN:	wij en hebben ghelt noch broot	
HANS:	dat blijct hier claer	
TRUIJCKEN:	jc werde jnt ouerdincken plats moedeloos	
HANS:	pacientie es ons goet altoos	
TRUIJCKEN:	waer suldij werck vinden hans goet bloet	
HANS:	godt sal ons hulpen / mact eenen moet	65
	tgheluck comt somtijts aen gewaijt	
TRUIJCKEN:	gister auont aten wij gelijck den haen craijt	
	gheen armer jnt stadt nu jc wedde	
HANS:	ons kinderkens ghinghen al singhen te bedde	
	voer haerlien eten / en te mijnen bevroene	70
	jc en claechde niet vondick iet te doene	
	en sal den tijt noch niet verkeeren	
	och heere der heeren	
TRUIJCKEN:	schut droefheijts verseeren	
	al eest dat wij bloot sijn van vrinden en maghen	
	jc sal gaen spinnen nempt gij uwen cruijwagen	75
	en trect jnde stadt jn alle hoecken	
	die wat winnen wilt moet alomme soecken	
	al eest dat wij lijden swaer abstinencie	
	god saelt beteren	
HANS:	en de paciencie	
	die prijstmen voer een groote duecht	80
	dies ben ic wat van herten verhuecht	
	maer het valt ons te lastich	
TRUIJCKEN:	dicwils qualijck eten	
HANS:	altoos jn roere	
TRUIJCKEN:	en de kinderen bescheten	
	elck mach wel weten van onse vijten	
HANS:	wij slapen jnt stroo	
TRUIJCKEN:	en soper jn de habijten	85
	daermoede compt ons geheel betrapen	
HANS:	ons kinderen gaen dicwils sonder eten slapen	
	dwelck mij dert bouen maten al	
	nu jc trecke gheluck soecken vare alst zal	
	en neme ter mertwaert mijn vertreck	90
	somtijts heeftmen daer cruijwageners gebreck	
	och mocht mij eenen stuijuer winninge toe loopen	
TRUIJCKEN:	Daer ghingic terstont broot om coopen	
	och kinderkens daer mach v naer verlanghen	
	want het es den joncxkens een swaer verstrangen	95
	hongher te lijden oft sulcx torment	
	hier esser seuen oft acht omtrent	
	dijer grootelijck naer ligghen en gapen	
HANS:	peijs truijken laet de kinderkens slapen	
	eer sij ontwaken gij sult wat verhoeren	100

hier nempt hij sijnen cruijwagen

GERTRUDE:	We have no gold or bread.	
HANS:	That much is clear.	
GERTRUDE:	I cannot think what to do but despair.	
HANS:	Patience is always a good dish.	
GERTRUDE:	Where will you find work, Hans Goodblood?	
HANS:	God will help us, you must take heart.	65
	Sometimes luck comes in a flurry.	
GERTRUDE:	Yesterday all we had to eat was what the cock crowed:	
	There is no-one poorer in this town, I bet you.	
HANS:	Our children were all singing in bed	
	Before we ate dinner. And I will tell you this,	70
	I would not complain if I had something to do,	
	And I would not fritter away time then,	
	O king of kings.	
GERTRUDE:	Shake off your sadness,	
	Even though we are unaided by friends and family.	
	I will go spinning. Take up your wheelbarrow	75
	And trundle into town into every corner;	
	He that would prosper must search everywhere,	
	Even though we suffer such privation,	
	God will make it better.	
HANS:	And patience	
	Is prized as a great virtue:	80
	That brings joy to me, in my heart.	
	But it is hard for us.	
GERTRUDE:	Usually with nothing to eat.	
HANS:	Always in strife.	
GERTRUDE:	And the children covered in shit.	
	Everyone can see our hardship plainly.	
HANS:	We sleep on straw –	
GERTRUDE:	And have holes in our clothes.	85
	Poverty completely imprisons us.	
HANS:	Our children often go to sleep without eating,	
	Which causes me pain above all else.	
	Now I will go and search for luck as well as I'm able,	
	I head for the market place in my travels,	90
	Sometimes the vendors need barrowmen there,	
	Oh, if a *stuiver* of profit would run my way –	
GERTRUDE:	Then I would go straightaway and buy bread with it.	
	Oh children, you may yearn for this,	
	Since it is a severe sentence for youngsters	95
	To live with hunger or similar torment.	
	Here we have seven or eight or so,	
	Who are all greatly hankering and craving.	
HANS:	Peace, Gertrude, let the children sleep:	
	Before they wake up you will hear from me.	100

Here he takes up his wheelbarrow.

rammel sammele ruijmpt van voren
nu hef jc een lieken op sender envie
die altoos truert en es nemmermeer blije

hier singt hij

    tgheluck es mijn partije
    daerom en mach jc niet trueren   105
    voerspoet dat blijft op dsije
    altoos tachter en niet te vueren

FRUMINUER: hoe suldij v tieren hoe suldij v gelaten
hoe comdij al sammelen achter straten
mijn bruerkens en cunnen niet gerusten   110
al en mach v niet te slapen lusten
laet haerlien doch ligghen met vreden
want sij hebben te nacht drij uren gebeden
voer de salicheijt des weerelts dies seker sijt

HANS: en jc gaen jaghen iewers om proffijt   115
wettij niet broerken hier iewers iet omtrent

FRUMINUER: hulp godt neenick / tes hier een arm conuent
gaet elders oft gij crijcht wat op v snotgat

HANS: jc ha lieuer x stuijuers voer sulcken lot plat
ke laet v gramschap sincken dat biddic v toch   120
en gaet jn v celle

FRUMINUER: dats waer droncken soch
wilt ghij mij heeten jn mij celle gaen
En jc ben die pater de gerdiaen
heft v van hier saen / oft v nact verdriet
van mijnen clauwen

HANS: tians hoij dat en begere jc niet   125
adieu gerdiaen en sijt niet verstoort

FRUMINUER: gaet laetsien en hebt v alst behoort
oft ghij crijcht van mijnen handen eenen tuck

HANS: bij vidts musschen ic ha lieuer beter geluck
wa siet mij desen lollaert wat hij versiert   130
maer hij es noch nuchter en qualijc gebiert
her her dits naer een ander geweste
jc treck ter mert / het dunct mij dbeste
daer commet profijt met hoopen groot
winne winne winne broot winne broot   135
jc worde puer gram voer jc noch eens alsoo
tsus jc wil gaen sitten wachten / jc sal noch werden vroo

MILT VAN HERTEN: therte verblijt mij jn douerdincken der duecht
der beruoeten broes / dat jc ben bewuecht
haerlien te doen aelmoesen ten dach ter eeren   140

Rattle, rumble, get out of the way
Now I have a song without hope
For those who are always sad and never joyful.

Here he sings.

   Luck is my accomplice,
   Therefore I may not complain,   105
   Success keeps its place
   Always behind me and not before.

INFIRMARIAN: Why are you doing this? Why do you behave so?
   Why do you come so loudly through the streets?
   My brothers are not able to rest.   110
   Even though you might not want to sleep,
   Let them all lie in peace,
   For they have spent three hours praying this night,
   For the salvation of the world, you can be sure.

HANS: I am going about hunting for some profit: 115
   Have you a little something for me, brother?

INFIRMARIAN: By God's help, no. This here is a poor community.
   Get lost or you will receive something up your snot-hole.

HANS: I would rather have ten *stuivers* instead of that.
   Boy, let your anger die down, that much I ask you,   120
   And get back in your cell.

INFIRMARIAN: What was that, you drunk?
   Did you order me to get back in my cell?
   But I am the leader of this friary,
   Get out of here quickly, or you will regret it,
   At my hands.

HANS: John's head, I have no desire for that.   125
   Adieu, guardian, and do not be upset.

INFIRMARIAN: Get away and behave as you ought,
   Or you will receive a smack from my hands.

HANS: By Vitus's sparrows,[3] I would prefer to have better luck
   Than this mumbler wishes me to have,   130
   For he is abstemious and has a troubled mind.
   Well, I will head to another area.
   I will go to the market, I think that is best.
   Profit comes in great heaps there:
   Profit, profit, profit, bread, profit, bread.   135
   I will turn into a madman if I go on like this.
   So I will sit and wait. I may grow merry from this.

MILD-OF-HEART: My heart cheers me in thinking about the virtues
   Of the barefoot brothers. I am moved
   To see them give alms to honour the day.   140

---

[3] Hans's oath alludes to the common superstition that eating sparrows would cause Sydenham's chorea, or Saint Vitus Dance: see 'Popular Medicine in Germany', *Chamber's Journal* (1878), 783–4.

sij singhen sij lesen / sij doen gods loff vermeeren
alsmen daghelijcx jn clooster mach aenschouwen
sij hebbent soberlijck midts tijts benouwen
dus willicse recreeren met planteijt van spijsen
en oock met wijne diet therte doet verjolijsen   145
want eens welde en es niet armoede altijt
haddick iemant diet droeghe jc werde verblijt
holla jc sien ghinder eenen cruijwagener staen
hans goet bloet dien wil jc gaen spreken aen
oft hij van desen wercke wilde sijn de boo   150
hans goeden dach

HANS: wa dat en hoor ic niet noo
goeden morghen / bon joer naer v gelieuen

MILT VAN HERTEN: hans soudij mij niet willen gerieuen
om spijse te voeren / om wel betalen

HANS: waer soudict voeren

MILT VAN HERTEN: ic saelt v verhalen   155

HANS: nu laet hooren sonder veel rammoers

MILT VAN HERTEN: ghij sultse gaen voeren ten beruoeten broes
en segt den gerdijaen dat jc hem laet weten
dat jc te noenen met hem wil commen eten
daer es rintvleesch en schapen vleesch en wijn   160
en daer es broot segt hem wij moeten vrolijc sijn
want van spijsen sendic hem volle plantteijt
nemt daer es een stuck gelts voer uwen aerbeijt
dus rijt duere sonder veel gheschals

HANS: been monsuer been

MILT VAN HERTEN: hoe ghij sprect wals   165
die tale en can jc mij niet bevroen

HANS: verstadijs niet

MILT VAN HERTEN: neennick

HANS: jc segghe jc saelt gherren doen
jc steke mij derwaert te desen keere

MILT VAN HERTEN: hoordij wel hans

HANS: wat belieft v

MILT VAN HERTEN: groeten mij seere
hier met orloff god sij uwen troostere   170

HANS: godt wil v geleyen / maer jc weet een ander cloostere
daert bat van doene es jc segt v vrij
nu hij aen laetsien jc lijde voer bij
met oorloue heer pater gerdijaen
dat jc voer v clooster jn dmijn mach gaen   175
je lijde voer bij sonder veel rammoers
blijft ghij jn uwen met uwen broers
nu ben jc leden ken achs niet een gruijs
noijt soo vrolijck jc ben nu bij huijs
jc wedde de gerdijaen wert nu getrompeert   180

	They sing, they read, they increase God's praises	
	As you may see daily in their cloister.	
	They live frugally, with even less at times:	
	And so I will please them with a bowl of food	
	And also with wine that will delight the heart.	145
	For it is good to have comfort and not constant poverty	
	I would be happy if I had someone to transport it.	
	Hey, I see a barrowman standing over there.	
	It is Hans Goodblood. I will go and ask him	
	If he would be interested in this work.	150
	Hans, good day.	
HANS:	Well, I do not hear that often.	
	Good morning, or bonjour if you prefer.	
MILD-OF-HEART:	Hans, would you be willing to help me	
	To deliver this food? I will pay you.	
HANS:	Where should I take it?	
MILD-OF-HEART:	I will tell you.	155
HANS:	Now let me hear it, without further delay.	
MILD-OF-HEART:	You should go and take it to the barefoot brothers,	
	And tell the guardian that I notify him	
	That I will come and eat with him at noon.	
	Here is beef, and mutton, and wine,	160
	And there is bread. Tell him we must be merry	
	Since I send him a full platter, laden with food.	
	Here is a sum of money for your labour,	
	So take it there without a great noise.	
HANS:	Bien, monsieur, bien.	
MILD-OF-HEART:	Oh, you speak French,	165
	I cannot manage to speak that tongue.	
HANS:	You do not understand it?	
MILD-OF-HEART:	Not me.	
HANS:	I said I would be glad to do it,	
	I will take myself to where you have sent me.	
MILD-OF-HEART:	Listen well, Hans.	
HANS:	As you please.	
MILD-OF-HEART:	I salute you sincerely.	
	Here, goodbye. May God protect you.	170
HANS:	May God lead you. But I know another cloister	
	Where there is great need, I say it freely.	
	Now he cannot see me I go further along.	
	With my apologies, father guardian,	
	I pass by your cloister to my own.	175
	I go further along without a great noise.	
	I pray you stay inside with your brothers.	
	Now I am past and I care not a jot,	
	I have never come back home so happy.	
	I wager the Guardian is cheated now.	180

tjanshoij mij kueken es nu gestoffeert
woef hijda wat blijder knecht
laet jnne truijken jc bringhe goeij vrecht
van vruechden quackelt mij leuer en longere

TRUIJCKEN: och ons kinderen hebben zoe grooten honghere 185
brengdij gheen auentueren met allen

HANS: truijken den terlinck es nu al wel geuallen
siet wat jc bringhe / est niet wel gemact

TRUIJCKEN: ja hans hoe sijdij hier aen geract
jc bidde v dat ghij mij de fortuijne verclaert 190

HANS: dit ben jc verhueuert jn een ure herwaert
dat rint vleesch / dats schaps vlesch wilt jn vruechden vleten
dats boter kese / hij es seck bedreten
en daer es een goede flessche met wijne

TRUIJCKEN: nu hebbic redene om blijde te sijne 195
ons huijs wert nu vol vruechden

HANS: ter eeren des daechs willen wij verhuechden
dus hout v gherust van dies jc doe

TRUIJCKEN: wa eens welde en es altoos gheen armoe
maer wilt der fortuijnen mij verclaren 200

HANS: doeghet tvleesch te vuere sonder plaren
jc sal v trelaes gheheel vertellen

TRUIJCKEN: nu laet ons gaen ter kuekenen sonder quellen
om de spijse te beredene ts meer dan tijt
ons kinderen nact vruecht en jolijt 205

MILT VAN HERTEN: Die clocke es elue of daer omtrint
jc wil mij gaen ter tafelen voeghen
ten beruoten broers jn dat conuint
jn vruechdelijcke collacie sullen wij ploghen
tfij hem diet qualijck genoeghen 210
holla jc voer tcouents porte
ic trecke best de belle naer de behorte

FRUMINUER: wie es daer

MILT VAN HERTEN: jc ben milt van herten
goeden dach vaer gerdiaen en v lijdelijcke smerte
com jc v boeten / en met v eten 215
vuijt goeder vrintschap jn mij vervleten
heb jc gesonden spijse / esse ooc bereet

FRUMINUER: wat spijse

MILT VAN HERTEN: hoe wettijs niet

FRUMINUER: neenick godt weet
en hier es qualijck teten te deser stonden

MILT VAN HERTEN: en jc hebbe heden hier spijse gesonden 220

	By John's head, my kitchen is stuffed.	
	Fantastic, yes. What a happy knave I am.	
	Let me in, Gertrude; I bring a good cargo.	
	My liver and lungs are quacking with joy.	
GERTRUDE:	Oh, our children have so great a hunger,	185
	You had better not bring trouble for us all.	
HANS:	Gertrude, the die has fallen favourably now,	
	See what I bring. Is it not well made?	
GERTRUDE:	Yes, Hans. How did you come by this?	
	I bid you tell me how this turn comes about.	190
HANS:	I was given this within the last hour.	
	This is beef, this is mutton, which you may bathe in,	
	This is butter, cheese, which is very soft,	
	And there is a good flask of wine.	
GERTRUDE:	Now I have reason to be joyous,	195
	Our house will now be filled with delights.	
HANS:	We will be joyful, to honour this day,	
	Therefore you must please do as I do.	
GERTRUDE:	For once we have comfort and not constant poverty,	
	But you should further explain this good fortune to me.	200
HANS:	I acquired this meat without any flimflam.	
	I will tell you the whole story.	
GERTRUDE:	Let us go to the kitchen now without delay,	
	To prepare the food, for now is the time.	
	Our children hanker for joy and jollity.	205
MILD-OF-HEART:	The clock is at eleven or thereabouts.	
	I will convey myself to the dining table	
	Of the barefoot brothers, in that convent.	
	In joyful company we will celebrate.	
	Fie on him that thinks badly of this.[4]	210
	Holla, I am before the convent door,	
	I had better pull the bell, as custom dictates.	
INFIRMARIAN:	Who is there?	
MILD-OF-HEART:	I am Mild-of-Heart,	
	Good day, father guardian; I come to relieve you	
	Of your doleful sorrow, and to eat with you.	215
	Out of good fellowship I was obliged	
	To send you food, some of it ready to eat.	
INFIRMARIAN:	What food?	
MILD-OF-HEART:	Do you not know?	
INFIRMARIAN:	I do not, God knows	
	At this time there is merely paltry food in here.	
MILD-OF-HEART:	But I have sent some food here today,	220

[4] This line appears to be a Dutch rendering of the Old French 'honi soit qui mal y pense', the motto of the Order the Garter. This in turn suggests that Mild-of-Heart wishes to be seen as a member of the nobility; his professed inability to speak French, however, places him outside this group.

en jc omboot dat jc selue jn persoone
soude commen eten

FRUMINUER: wa een boone
hier en es spijse commen noch gheenen dranck

MILT VAN HERTEN: en jc sanse heden morgen / vrij en vranck
om dat wij vroelijcheijt souden hantieren   225

FRUMINUER: en wie was de bode die v wilde bestieren

MILT VAN HERTEN: wie hij was

FRUMINUER: ja

MILT VAN HERTEN: het was hans goet bloet

FRUMINUER: wa dats eenen luerefaes jc mact v vroet
om elcken te tromperene tsij groot oft cleene

MILT VAN HERTEN: hij beloefdet mij met worden reene   230
dat hijse bringhen souwe sonder eenich ghetruer

FRUMINUER: die woent hier bij tes onslien gebuer
die ons meer leets doet dan jc sou connen verhalen

MILT VAN HERTEN: jc saelt weder gaen eijsschen sonder fallen

FRUMINUER: neen laet staen jc sallen gaen casstijen   235
hij saels hem op een ander tijt vermijen
dus jc danck v der jonsten menichfout
hij zal van mij haest crijghen assout

HANS: truijken es de spijse al ghereet
het es bijder noenen soe jc meene   240
en datse verberde dat waer mij leedt
dus dect de tafele pijnet dammelaken te spreene

TRUIJCKEN: ghij beghint ons soperheijt meer te breene
hier en es lijwaet / ammelaken noch ammelakens kint
want sulcken haue en hebben wij twint   245

HANS: nu sedt de tafele brengt de juweelen

TRUIJCKEN: en hier en sijn gheene

HANS: bringt dan die erden teelen
roept ons kinderen bringt vleesch broot en wijn

TRUIJCKEN: siet daer eest al

HANS: willecom moetij alle sijn

DIE KINDERS: gheloent vaerken

HANS: jc sal mij mes gaen stellen te wercke   250
den honger heeft v lien beuanghen soe jc mercke
jn den naem godts sitten wij hier nere
wildij alle eten

DIE KINDERS: ouwie mon pere

HANS: kinderkens sprect ws muerkens tale
al ben jc van verre jc en ben geen wale   255
nu elck grijpe syn deel dan suldij eens drincken

TRUIJCKEN: jc wachs hans

HANS: tsa wilt mij schincken
ter eeren van den coninck dit es den cloot

	And I stated that I myself in person	
	Would come to eat.	
INFIRMARIAN:	This is strange.	
	No food has come here, nor any drink.	
MILD-OF-HEART:	But I sent it this morning, freely and honestly,	
	So that we should celebrate joyfulness.	225
INFIRMARIAN:	And who was the messenger that you sent?	
MILD-OF-HEART:	Who was he?	
INFIRMARIAN:	Yes.	
MILD-OF-HEART:	It was Hans Goodblood.	
INFIRMARIAN:	Well, that is one bad apple, I have you know,	
	He deceives everyone, for goods both big and small.	
MILD-OF-HEART:	He promised me with honest words	230
	That he would bring it all without a pause.	
INFIRMARIAN:	He lives close by here as our neighbour,	
	He does more mischief to us than I can say.	
MILD-OF-HEART:	I will go to demand it back without fail.	
INFIRMARIAN:	No, stay put, I will go to challenge him.	235
	He will have pleasure at a future time.	
	Thus I thank you a great deal for this.	
	He will receive a beating from me at once.	
HANS:	Gertrude, is the food all ready?	
	It is noon by now, I think,	240
	And if the food is burned that would pain me.	
	So lay the table, try to spread the tablecloth.	
GERTRUDE:	You are becoming soft-headed from starvation.	
	Here is a cloth: we have no tablecloth, or clothing for the children.	
	We lack such things and do not possess them.	245
HANS:	Now set the table and bring forth the jewels.	
GERTRUDE:	But there are none here.	
HANS:	Then bring the earthenware plates.	
	Summon our children, bring meat, bread and wine.	
GERTRUDE:	See, there is everything.	
HANS:	All must be welcome.	
THE CHILDREN:	Greetings father.	
HANS:	I will put my knife to work.	250
	Hunger has overcome you so, I see.	
	In the name of God we sit down here.	
	Now all should eat.	
THE CHILDREN:	Oui, mon père.	
HANS:	Children, speak your mother tongue,	
	Although I am from far away, I am not French.	255
	Now each grab his share; you then should also drink.	
GERTRUDE:	I am waiting, Hans.	
HANS:	Ah, I will serve up.	
	For the honour of the king, that is the sentiment,	

	roept alle gelijck monsuer leroij boor	
DIE KINDERS:	monsuer leroij boor / al vuijt al vuijt	260
TRUIJCKEN:	nu hans gij sijt gerdijaen	
HANS:	en daer vruecht bij spruijt	
	soe sijdij ghij die mater van desen conuente	
TRUIJCKEN:	van onser auentueren salmen noch hooren vermaen	
HANS:	jc bringt v matere	
TRUIJCKEN:	jc wachs gerdijaen	
HANS:	hebbic mijn boetschap qualijck gedaen	265
TRUIJCKEN:	ghij schint om te siene een weeldich patere	
HANS:	en gij sijt van de rochghen de matere	
	die nu verheuen sidt nae den rechten roes	
TRUIJCKEN:	tswaer / en mijn kinderen sijn de beruoeten broes	
	ten es gheen spel sij doent jn nerste	270
	den hongher bracht ons dicwils jn queste	
	waer duer wij quamen jnt groot gequel	
	maer wat dunck v nu	
TRUIJCKEN:	het gaet hier wel	
	dies jc van vreuchden dat bacxken sal vuijt poijen	
HANS:	nu kinderkens den wijn doet ons verfroijen	275
	dus laet roncken de kele en laet een lieken singen	
TRUIJCKEN:	singt voren hans	
HANS:	dat sijn de dinghen	
	hem seek hem	

hier singense altemale

	wij sijn der gilden al verre vermaert	
	maer al jn ons borse soe en schuijlter niet	
	den meesten tijt vintmen ons vergaert	280
	hij schont sijn weluaert die van ons vliet	
	jc sal ons singhen trecht bediet	
	daer aff den aert	
	jnt sulck volck varen sal	
	hoort ouer al	285
	men vinter een groot getal	
HANS:	jc sitte met blijschap jn mijnen masesteijt	
	spijse en dranck hebben wij planteijt	
	godt sij gheloeft diet ons heeft verlent	
	nu kinderkens gaet slapen	290
TRUIJCKEN:	nu kinderkens gaet slapen jnt stroo	
DIE KINDERS:	vaerken en muerken goijen nacht	
FRUMINUER:	by gans dermen het mach mij wel spijten	
	dat jc verloren hebbe aldus de spijse	

	Cry all at once: monsieur le roi, boire![5]	
THE CHILDREN:	Monsieur le roi, boire! All empty, it's all empty.	260
GERTRUDE:	Now, Hans, you are the guardian.	
HANS:	And joy springs from that.	
	In that case, you are the mother of this convent.	
GERTRUDE:	We will not hear any rebuke for our adventures.	
HANS:	I bring you more, mother.	
GERTRUDE:	I wait, Guardian.	
HANS:	Have I done my duties badly?	265
GERTRUDE:	You appear to resemble a wealthy father.	
HANS:	And you are the mother superior of this convent,	
	Who sits rejoicing now after a well-earned feast.	
GERTRUDE:	For sure, and my children are the barefoot brothers.	
	This is not a game, they are brothers in earnest.	270
HANS:	Hunger often forced us to roam around,	
	Which caused us to come into great trouble,	
	But what do you think now?	
GERTRUDE:	It goes well here,	
	With joy I will pour that pan out.	
HANS:	Now children, the wine does cheer us,	275
	Thus let our throats ring and let us sing a song.	
GERTRUDE:	Sing forth, Hans.	
HANS:	These are the important things,	
	When all is said.	

Here they sing together.

	We are the most famous of all the guilds,	
	But nothing lurks in any of our purses.	
	Most of the time you will find us gathered,	280
	He that flees from us does harm to his wealth.	
	I will sing a true tale for us	
	About the character	
	That dwells within these people.	
	Listen all of you:	285
	One finds a great many of them.	
HANS:	I sit here with bliss in my majesty,	
	We have food and drink plentifully.	
	Glory be to God, who has arranged this for us.	
	Now children, go to sleep.	290
GERTRUDE:	Now children, go to sleep in the straw.	
THE CHILDREN:	Father and mother, good night.	
INFIRMARIAN:	By God's guts, it makes me very sorry	
	That I have lost the food in this way.	

---

[5] The text's French is curious here as it gives 'drink' in its infinitive form, *boire*, rather than the imperative *buvez*. It is not clear whether this is deliberate, since Hans's use of French is otherwise competent.

	sij sitten van vruechden en tieren en crijten	295
	dies jc van gramschap ter quaetheijt rijse	
	ja hans goet bloet / hebdij de spijse	
	gij suit noch stock visch eeten jn corten tijden	
	nu hans goet bloet wilt mij belijden	
	hoe sijdij aen dese spijse gheract	300
	die mij gesonden was / es hier gestact	
	gij sullent becoopen het es al mijne	
HANS:	compt drinct een tuechsken van desen wijne	
	proeft hoe hij smaect hij es seer costelijck	
FRUMINUER:	swijcht en mact mij niet verbostelijck	305
	raubaut / boeue en mijns ontdraegere	
HANS:	hout v backuijs oft jc sal sijn hans de veriagere	
	van voer mijn clooster tot jn v celle	
FRUMINUER:	ghij en sijt zoe coene niet	
HANS:	jck ben / maer holla van dijen gequelle	
	waerdij werlijck jc sou v slaen	310
	maer aen tghestelijck volck daer en com jc niet aen	
	dus kiesic tschoonste ten naesten trappe	

Fruminuer trect de crapproen vuijte

FRUMINUER:	siet daer de crapproen van mijnder cappe	
	paep aff als weerlijck dus sijn de dinghen	
HANS:	hoe suldij vuijt uwen garen springhen	315
	hebbic anders ghedaen dant behoort	
	moijt mij te rechte verstaet dat woort	
	laet sien wie ghelijck sal hebben op dit pas	
FRUMINUER:	ou ghij spetael guijt gij en hebt maer den bas	
	sijdij soe coene compt hier jnde bane	320
HANS:	her her gerdiaen gij moetter ane	
	hout daer een pocie van onser spijsen	
FRUMINUER:	nemt daer cnoockel poer van grooten prijse	
HANS:	wat meijndij ghij luijsack	
FRUMINUER:	wat segt gij lecplateel	
HANS:	nempt dat en datte	
FRUMINUER:	nempt daer oock wel v deel	325
HANS:	moort moort moort	
TRUIJCKEN:	holla wat mach daer schuijlen	
	ombeijt ere jc sal jnt bescheet daer moeten huijlen	
	hier es water om tvier te coelen	
	gerde leen	
FRUMINUER:	soch / ghij suit oock wat geuoelen	

	They sit with joy and chant and cry:	295
	And so rage and anger rise within me.	
	Yes, Hans Goodblood, you have the food,	
	You will also eat stickfish before long.[6]	
	Now, Hans Goodblood, you will tell me	
	How you could have gained all this food,	300
	Which was sent to me, but is stacked up here.	
	You will pay; it is all mine.	
HANS:	Come drink a touch more of this wine	
	Judge how it tastes; it is very costly.	
INFIRMARIAN:	Shut it, and do not make me wrathful,	305
	Thief, brigand, and pilferer from me.	
HANS:	Hold your tongue or I will become Hans the Hunter,	
	From my cloister to the inside of your cell.	
INFIRMARIAN:	You are not that brave.	
HANS:	I am, but stop your yelling.	
	I would slap you if you were worldly,	310
	But I do not come near clergymen.	
	I choose the best of what is available.[7]	

The Infirmarian takes his habit off.

INFIRMARIAN:	See there the cope of my order;	
	I cast priesthood off: I am worldly, this is how things stand.	
HANS:	However much you spring out of your gear	315
	I have done as I ought to in every way.	
	I have right on my side; understand these words:	
	Let us see which one of us equals will claim the right.	
INFIRMARIAN:	Oh, you foolish rogue, you have nothing but a voice,	
	If you are so brave come here within my reach.	320
HANS:	Well, well, Guardian, you can have this,	
	Have a sample of our meal there!	
INFIRMARIAN:	Take here a knucklebone of great value!	
HANS:	What do you think, you sluggard?	
INFIRMARIAN:	What do you say, lickplatter?	
HANS:	Take that and that!	
INFIRMARIAN:	Take there also your fair share!	325
HANS:	Murder, murder, murder!	
GERTRUDE:	Hola, what causes this racket here?	
	Pipe down, or I must cry out because of this.	
	Here is water to cool the fire!	
	Accept this on loan!	
INFIRMARIAN:	Ouch! You will also feel some!	

---

[6] Compare the similar joke in *Jack Sweet-tooth*, line 474. As in the earlier play, 'stickfish' is a pun on *stok vis*, a notoriously tough salted cod, which came to be known as 'harde-harde' in parts of Guelders: see Dirk van Delft, *Heike Kamerlingh Onnes. Een biografie. De man van het absolute nulpunt* (Amsterdam, 2005), 147.

[7] Literally 'I choose the best of the nearby staircases'.

	leelijcke dante gij oude mare	330
EENEN BALLU:	vre vre stilt v van desen ghebare	
FRUMINUER:	jck begheer recht	
HANS:	et moij ousij	
FRUMINUER:	heere tes dese popelare	
HANS:	swijcht / laet mij spreken	
FRUMINUER:	jc heijssche correxcie	
TRUIJCKEN:	heere balu jc stelle mij in v protectie	
	vanden grooten ouerlast mijnen man gedaen	335
BALLU:	segt mij dbescheet	
FRUMINUER:	hoort mijn vermaen	
HANS:	heer ballu hij comt hier ghegaen	
	en mact veel beroers	
FRUMINUER:	ghij hebt gestolen de spijse van mijn broers	
HANS:	contrarie es waer	
BALLU:	wat wildij al segghen	340
FRUMINUER:	hoort de warheijt / ic salse vuijt legghen	
	spijse ontfinck hij om te bringen jn ons conuent	
	en hij en heeftse niet brocht	
HANS:	jc leter ontrent	
	en jc hebse gheuoert	
BALLU:	waer segt sonder veel rammoers	
HANS:	en daert mij belast wat tot de beruote broers	345
FRUMINUER:	sulck was dbeuel	
HANS:	trouwen dat kinick	
	en heb icse ontvoert een dief soe ben ick	
	ten beruoten broers	
FRUMINUER:	ghij hadt gelijck wart gedaen	
HANS:	matere roept de broers	
TRUIJCKEN:	wel gerdijaen	
	compt hier mijn kinderkens voer dees famillie	350
	op ulieden sal hier werden een consillie	
HANS:	siet hier mijn heere saelt qualijck blijcken	
	sullen dese de beruoete broers qualijck ghelijcken	
	van cleederen nact merct dit faetsoen	
	want sij en hebben noch cousen noch schoen	355
	dus den noot dede mij de spijse hier bringhen	
BALLU:	heer gerdijaen wat sijn de dinghen	
	heeft hij qualijck gelijck gheeft mij tverstant	
	dits wel een conuent der beruoeten broers want	
	arm en bijstier es gheheel tconuent	360
FRUMINUER:	hij heeft gelijck voer waer jc kent	
	dies jc hem jonne de spijse en den dranck	
	die hij heeft gehadt heden den ontfanck	
	want al eest dat wij soperlijck moeten leuen	
	wij moeten pacientich sijn want godt verheuen	365
	heeft veel beruoeten broers jn dit saijsoen	

	Ugly aunt, you old mare!	330
A BAILIFF:	Peace! Peace! You must desist from this.	
INFIRMARIAN:	I demand justice.	
HANS:	Et moi aussi.	
INFIRMARIAN:	Sir, it is this deceiver.	
HANS:	Shut it, let me speak.	
INFIRMARIAN:	I request restitution.	
GERTRUDE:	Lord bailiff, I put myself in your protection,	
	Because of the great trouble done to my husband.	335
BAILIFF:	Tell me what happened.	
INFIRMARIAN:	Hear my complaint.	
HANS:	Lord bailiff, he comes over here	
	And makes a real ruckus.	
INFIRMARIAN:	You have stolen the food from my brothers.	
HANS:	The contrary is the case.	
BAILIFF:	How will you all plead?	340
INFIRMARIAN:	Hear the truth, I will explain it.	
	He took some food to bring to our convent,	
	And he did not deliver the same.	
HANS:	I accepted it,	
	And I have transported it.	
BAILIFF:	Tell the truth without further delay.	
HANS:	I was told to take it to the barefoot brothers.	345
INFIRMARIAN:	Such was the instruction.	
HANS:	Trust I understand this,	
	And I have taken it, thief as I am,	
	To the barefoot brothers.	
INFIRMARIAN:	That is what you should have done.	
HANS:	Mother, call the brothers.	
GERTRUDE:	Well, Guardian,	
	Come here, my children, for this family,	350
	We will hear a verdict spoken about you all.	
HANS:	See here, my lord, it will surely be proven,	
	That these are surely like the barefoot brothers.	
	Quite without clothing, mark their condition,	
	For they have neither socks nor shoes,	355
	And so their need made me bring the food here.	
BAILIFF:	Sir Guardian, what do you say about this,	
	Has he spoken correctly? Give me a solution.	
	This is truly a community of the barefoot brothers because	
	This whole convent is poor and wretched.	360
INFIRMARIAN:	He is right, therefore I concede.	
	And so I grant him the food and the drink	
	That he was given to have for his own	
	For everything demands that we must live soberly,	
	We must be patient because God is gladdened,	365
	Having a lot of barefoot brothers this season.	

	dus jc vergheeft hem gherne van sijn pinioen	
	en schelt hem quijte al dat hij mij heeft mesdaen	
BALLU:	hans danct den pater wij willen gaen	
	want hij es cause van uwen weluaren	370
HANS:	vader al dat jc ghedaen hebbe / jc salt verclaren	
	aermoede waert dijer mij toe brocht	
	al mij goet al waert verchocht	
	en es niet ses stuijuers wert op dees tijt	
	en willet mij vergheuen sonder resspijt	375
	bidde ic v minnelijck duer godts bitter doot	
FRUMINUER:	jc vergheeft v gherne.	
BALLU:	jn ws lijdens weder stoot	
	sijt pacientich wij willen scheijden	
HANS:	tkindeken van maria wil v allen geleijden	
	en elck diet ghehoort heeft oft ghesien	380
	tot compassijen voecht uwer herten engien	
	op de beruoeten broers / vaet ons ontbinden	
	want gij sullent hier namaels vinden	
	eest dat ghij hier doet duechdelijcke wercken	
TRUIJCKEN:	op de ermmen wilt ontdoen v vlercken	385
	duer compassien soe vercrijchdij godts gracie	
	en der jngelen vruecht naer sleuens spacie	
	daer ons wil bringhen met duechden volleest	
	De vader de soene den heijlijghen gheest	

Amen. Finis est.

lanck drij hondert en sesenvijftich regulen
ghespelt te brussel vande coerebloemme anno 1559

	And so I release him in earnest from his obligation	
	And absolve him of all he has done to me.	
BAILIFF:	Hans, thank the father so we can go,	
	For he is the cause of your prosperity.	370
HANS:	Father, I will declare all that I have done:	
	It was poverty that brought me there.	
	If all of my goods were sold	
	They would not be worth six *stuivers* at this time.	
	Will you forgive me without delay,	375
	I beseech you with love and for God's bitter death.	
INFIRMARIAN:	I forgive you earnestly.	
BAILIFF:	You will rise out of your suffering,	
	Be patient: we will part.	
HANS:	May the child of Mary always lead you,	
	And let everyone who has heard or seen this	380
	Move their heart to true compassion	
	For the barefoot brothers. Let us part,	
	For you will find heaven here	
	When you do virtuous works.	
GERTRUDE:	You will gain your wings from the poor men,	385
	So through compassion you will receive God's grace,	
	And angels' joy in your allotted span.	
	We will be brought there with the highest virtues:	
	The Father, the Son, the Holy Spirit.	

Amen. Finis est.[8]

Length: three hundred, seven and fifty lines
Played in Brussels by the Cornflower, anno 1559

---

[8] 'It is finished'.

BIBLIOGRAPHY

Ackermann, Elfriede Marie, *Das Schlaraffenland in German Literature and Folksong: Social Aspects of an Earthly Paradise* (Chicago, 1944)

Ælfric, *Lives of the Saints*, ed. W. W. Skeat. Early English Text Society, 2 vols. (London, 1881)

Anon., 'Popular Medicine in Germany', *Chamber's Journal* (1878), 783–4

Appelbaum, Stanley, *Medieval Tales and Stories* (Toronto, 2000)

Arnade, Peter J., *Realms of Ritual: Burgundian Ceremony and Civic Life in Late Medieval Ghent* (Ithaca, NY, 1996)

—— *Beggars, Iconoclasts, and Civic Patriots: The Political Culture of the Dutch Revolt* (Ithaca, NY, 2008)

Arnold, T. J. I., *Veelderhande geneuchlijcke dichten, tafelspelen ende refereynen* (Utrecht, 1977)

Astington, John, 'Malvolio and the Eunuchs', *Shakespeare Survey* 46 (1994), 23–35

Bakhtin, Mikhail M., *Problems of Dostoevsky's Poetics*, trans. Caryl Emerson (Minneapolis, 1984)

—— *Rabelais and his World*, trans. Helene Iswolsky (Bloomington, IN, 1984)

Baldwin, Elizabeth, 'Chaucer, Medieval Drama and a Newly Discovered Seventeenth-Century Play: The Survival of Medieval Stereotypes?', in *Farce and Farcical Elements*, ed. Wim N. M. Hüsken, Konrad Schoell and Leif Søndergaard (Amsterdam, 2002), 85–102

Barbazan, Etienne, and Dominique Martin Meon, *Fabliaux et contes des poètes françois des XI, XII, XIII, XIVe et XVe siècles* (Paris, 1808)

Barnes, Jonathan, *Early Greek Philosophy* (Harmondsworth, 2001)

Bax, Dirk, *Ontcijfering van Jeroen Bosch* (The Hague, 1949)

Bayless, Martha, *Parody in the Middle Ages: The Latin Tradition* (Anne Arbor, 1996)

Bense, Johan, *A Dictionary of Low Dutch Elements in the English Vocabulary* (The Hague, 1939)

Beyaert, Marc, *Opkomst en bloei van de Gentse rederijkerskamer Marien Theeren* (Ghent, 1978)

Biemans, Jos, Hans Kienhorst, Willem Kuiper and Rob Resoort, *Het Handschrift-Borgloon* (Hilversum, 2000)

Bisson, Lillian M., *Chaucer and the Late Medieval World* (New York, 1998)

Blamires, Alcuin, Karen Pratt and C. William Marx, *Woman Defamed and Woman Defended: An Anthology of Medieval Texts* (Oxford, 1992)

Bloch, R. Howard, *Medieval Misogyny and the Invention of Western Romantic Love* (Chicago, 1991)

Blommaert, P., 'Beknopte geschiedenis der Kamers van Rhetorica te Gent', *Belgisch museum voor de Nederduitsche tael- en letterkunde en de geschiedenis des vaderlands* (1837), 417–44

Blommaert, P., 'Van dat niemen en can ghedoen hi en es begrepen', *De Dietsche warande* I (1855), 134–6

Bloomfield, Morton, *Piers Plowman as Fourteenth-Century Apocalypse* (New Brunswick, NJ, 1961)

Blouw, Paul Valkema, 'The Van Oldenborch and Vanden Merberghe Pseudonyms, or, Why Frans Fraet had to die', *Quaerendo* 22 (1992), 165–96, 245–72

Boccaccio, Giovanni, *The Decameron*, trans. G. H. McWilliam (Harmondsworth, 1972)

Boekenooghen, G. J., *Die evangelien vanden spinrocke* (The Hague, 1910)

Boerma, Nicolaas, 'Mit dem Schiff nach Schlaraffenland', *Arbeitskreis Bild Druck Papier* 8 (2003), 37–49

Bohn, Henry, *A Polyglot of Foreign Proverbs* (London, 1867)

Boitani, Piero, *English Medieval Narrative in the Thirteenth and Fourteenth Century* (Cambridge, 1982)

Bolte, Johannes, 'Georg Schans Gedichte vom Niemand', *Zeitschrift für vergleichende Litteraturgeschichte* 9 (1896), 73–88

Bote, Hermann, *Till Eulenspiegel: His Adventures*, trans. and ed. Paul Oppenheimer (London, 2001)

Bourqui, Claude, *Polémique et stratégies dans le Dom Juan de Molière* (Paris, 1992)

Boutkan, Dirk, 'Pregermanic Fish in Old Saxon Glosses: On Alleged Ablaut Patterns and Other Formal Deviations', in *Speculum Saxonum: Studien zu den kleineren altsächsischen Sprachdenkmälern*, ed. Arend Quak (Amsterdam, 1999), 11–26

Bowring, John, *Brieven* (Leeuwarden, 1830)

Braekman, Willy L., *Medische en technische Middelnederlandse recepten. Een tweede bijdrage tot de geschiedenis van de vakliteratuur in de Nederlanden* (Ghent, 1975)

—— *Hier heb ik weer wat nieuws in d'hand: marktliederen, rolzangers en volkse poëzie van weleer* (Brussels, 1990)

—— *Middeleeuwse witte en zwarte magie in het Nederlands taalgebied* (Ghent, 1997)

—— 'Een "Konstboecxken" met een spotrecept door een "ongeleerden sottoer" (ca. 1595)', *Volkskunde: tijdschrift voor de studie van de volkscultuur* 105 (2004), 327–45

Brandeis, Arthur, *Jacob's Well, an Englisht Treatise on the Cleansing of Man's Conscience*. London, 1900)

Brandt Corstius, J. C., *Geschiedenis van de Nederlandse literatuur* (Utrecht, 1959)

Braudel, Fernand, *Civilization and Capitalism, 15th–18th Century: The Perspective of the World* (Berkeley, 1992)

Brecht, Martin, *Martin Luther: Shaping and Defining the Reformation, 1521–1532* (Minneapolis, 1990)

Bredero, Gerbrand Adriaensz, *Spaanschen Brabander*, ed. C. F. P. Stutterheim (Culemborg, 1974)

Brewer, Derek, ed., *Medieval Comic Tales* (Cambridge, 2008)

Brinkman, Herman, *Dichten uit liefde: literatuur in Leiden aan het einde van de middeleeuwen* (Hilversum, 1997)

Brom, Gerard, *Schilderkunst en litteratuur in de 16e en 17e eeuw* (Utrecht, 1957)

Brown, Andrew and Graeme Small, *Court and Civic Society in the Burgundian Low Countries c.1420–1530* (Manchester, 2007)

Brugman, Johannes, *Verspreide sermoenen*, ed. A. van Dijk (Antwerp, 1948)

Buitendijk, W. J. C., *Het calvinisme in de spiegel van de Zuidnederlandse literatuur der Contra-Reformatie* (Groningen, 1942)

Bunte, Wolfgang, *Juden und Judentum in der mittelniederländischen Literatur (1100–1600)* (Bern, 1989)

Burckhardt, Jacob, *The Civilization of the Renaissance in Italy*, trans. S. G. C. Middlemore, ed. Peter Burke and Peter Murray (Harmondsworth, 1990)

Burgon, John William, *The Life and Times of Sir Thomas Gresham*, 2 vols. (London, 1839)

Burns, J. H., *The Cambridge History of Medieval Political Thought c.350–c.1450* (Cambridge, 1988)

Burrows, Daron Lee, *Two Old French Satires on the Power of the Keys: L'Escommeniement au lecheor and Le Pardon de foutre* (London, 2005)

Busken Huet, Conrad, *Het land van Rembrand* (Haarlem, 1946)

Calmann, Gerta, 'The Picture of Nobody: An Iconographical Study', *Journal of the Warburg and Courtauld Institutes* 23 (1960), 60–94

Campbell, Eva M., *Satire in the Early English Drama* (Columbus, OH, 1914)

Carroll, William C., *Fat King, Lean Beggar: Representations of Poverty in the Age of Shakespeare* (Ithaca, NY, 1996)

Chambers, E. K., *The Medieval Stage* (Oxford, 1903)

Chaucer, Geoffrey, *The Riverside Chaucer*, gen. ed. Larry D. Benson (Oxford, 1990)

Chomel, Noel, *Algemeen huishoudelijk-, natuur-, zedekundig-, en konst- woordenboek*, 7 vols. (Leiden, 1778)

Cobby, Anne Elizabeth, *Ambivalent Conventions: Formula and Parody in Old French* (Amsterdam, 1995)

Coigneau, Dirk, *Refreinen in het zotte bij de rederijkers*, 3 vols. (Ghent, 1980–3)

—— *Mariken van Nieumeghen* (Hilversum, 1996)

—— '"Den Boeck" van Brussel: een geval apart?', *Jaarboek de Fonteine* 49–50 (1999–2000), 31–44

Cooke, Thomas D., Peter Whiteford and Nancy Mohr McKinley. 'XXIV: Tales', in *Manual of the Writings in Middle English, 1050–1500*, ed. Albert Hartung, 11 vols. (New Haven, 1967–2005), IX (1993), 2957–3592

Coppens, Christian, *Reading in Exile: The Libraries of John Ramridge, Thomas Harding, Henry Joliffe, Recusants in Louvain* (Cambridge, 1993)

Cowell, Andrew, *At Play in the Tavern: Signs, Coins, and Bodies in the Middle Ages* (Ann Arbor, MI, 1999)

Craig, Hardin, *English Religious Drama of the Middle Ages* (Oxford, 1960)

Cross, T. P., and W. A. Nitze, *Lancelot and Guenevere: A Study of the Origins of Courtly Love* (New York, 1970)

Curtius, Petrus, *Pappa Rerum Maxime Vulgarium Congesta per Locos in Puerorum Gratiam* (Antwerp, 1570)

Daan, Jo, *Wieringer land en leven in de taal* (Wieringen, 1981)

Dammer, Raphael, and Benedikt Jessing, *Der Jedermann im 16. Jahrhundert: die Hecastus-Dramen von Georgius Macropedius und Hans Sachs* (Berlin, 2007)

David, E. Randolph, 'Abbot Joachim of Fiore: A Reformist Apocalyptic', *Fearful Hope: Approaching the New Millennium*, ed. Christopher Kleinhenz and Fannie LeMoine (Madison, WI, 1999)

Davidson, Clifford, *Fools and Folly* (Kalamazoo, 1996)

Davidson, Clifford, Martin W. Walsh and Ton J. Broos, eds., *Everyman and its Dutch Original, Elckerlijc* (Kalamazoo, 2007)

Davies, J. C., 'The History of Utopia: A Chronology of Nowhere', in *Utopias*, ed. Peter Alexander and Roger Gill (London, 1984), 1–17

Davis, Natalie Zemon, *Society and Culture in Early Modern France* (Stanford, 1987)

D'Avity, Pierre, *The Estates, Empires, and Principallities of the World*, trans. Edward Grimeston (London, 1615)

De Bruyn, Eric, *Symboliek van de Hooiwagen-triptiek en de Rotterdamse Marskramer-tondo verklaard vanuit Middelnederlandse teksten* ('s-Hertogenbosch, 2004)

De Bruyn, Lucy, *Woman and the Devil in Sixteenth-Century Literature* (Tisbury, 1979)

De Castelein, Matthijs, *De const van rhetoriken* (Oudenaarde, 1986)

De Cervantes Saavedra, Miguel, *El ingenioso hidalgo Don Quijote de la Mancha*, ed. Francisco Rodríguez Marín (Santiago, 2005)

De Coster, Charles, *La Légende et les aventures héroiques, joyeuses et glorieuses d'Ulenspiegel et de Lamme Goedzak au pays de Flandres et ailleurs* (Paris, 1869)

De Jager, J. L., *Volksgebruiken in Nederland: een nieuwe kijk op tradities* (Utrecht, 1981)

De Jongh, E., *Tot lering en vermaak. Betekenissen van Hollandse genrevoorstellingen uit de zeventiende eeuw* (Amsterdam, 1976)

De Keyser, P., 'Het kluchtig sermoen van Bacchus', *Nederlandsch tijdschrift voor volkskunde* 30 (1925), 109–19

—— *Hein van Aken, Van den coninc Saladijn ende van Hughen van Tabaryen* (Leiden, 1950)

De Potter, F., and J. Broeckaert, *Geschiedenis der stad Aalst*, 2 vols. (Ghent, 1875)

De Roovere, Anthonis, *De gedichten van Anthonis de Roovere*, ed. J. J. Mak (Zwolle, 1955)

De Troyes, Nicolas, *Grand parangon des nouvelles nouvelles*, ed. Krystyna Kasprzyk (Paris, 1970)

De Vooys, C. G. N., 'Een ongedrukte bundel refereinen van 1524', *Tijdschrift voor Nederlandse taal- en letterkunde* 21 (1902), 66–117

—— *Verzamelde letterkundige opstellen* (Antwerp, 1947)

De Vreese, Willem, 'De legende van Sint-Haringus', *Het boek* 11 (1922), 299–304

Decker, Therese, and Martin Walsh, 'Three Sotternien: Farcical Afterpieces from the Hulthem Manuscript', *Dutch Crossing* 48 (1992), 73–91

—— *Mariken van Nieumeghen: A Bilingual Edition* (Columbia, 1994)

Delmelle, J., 'Géographie littéraire du Brabant. La Hesbaye thioise', *Le Folklore Brabançon* 145–8 (1960), 569–70

Delsaerdt, Pierre, *Suam quisque Bibliothecam* (Leuven, 2001)

Denifle, H., 'Ursprung der Hisoria des Nemo', *Archiv für Literatur- und Kirchen-Geschichte des Mittelalters* 4 (1988), 345–6

Dewolfs, J., 'Historiek van processies en ommegancken van Onze-Lieve-Vrouw ten Poel-. Tienen', *De Brabantse folklore* 26 (1975), 145–55

Dronke, Peter, 'Profane Elements in Literature', in *Renaissance and Renewal in the Twelfth Century*, ed. Robert L. Benson, Giles Constable and Carol D. Lanham (Cambridge, MA, 1982), 569–92

Droz, Eugénie, and H. Lewicka, *Le Recueil Trepperel*, 2 vols. (Geneva, 1961)

Dugaw, Diane, *Deep Play: John Gay and the Invention of Modernity* (Cranbury, NJ, 1991)

Duke, Alistair, *Reformation and Revolt in the Low Countries* (New York, 2003)

Duveger, J., 'Lutherse predicatie te Brussel en het process tegen een aantal kunstenaars (april–juni 1527)', *Weltenschappelijke tijdingen* 36 (1971), 221–8

Dyer, Christopher, *Making a Living in the Middle Ages: The People of Britain 850–1520* (London, 2003)

Eco, Umberto, 'Frames of Comic "Freedom"', in *Carnival!*, ed. Thomas A. Sebeok and Marcia E. Erikson (Berlin, 1984), 1–9

Erasmus, Desiderius, *Collected Works of Erasmus*, gen. ed. Ron Schoeffel, 89 vols. (Toronto, 1974–)

—— *Stultitiae Laus*, ed. John F. Collins (Bryn Mawr, PA, 1991)

Erenstein, R. L., 'De invloed van de commedia dell'arte in Nederland tot 1800', *Scenarium* 5 (1981), 91–106

Erné, B. H., and L. M. van Dis, *De Gentse spelen van 1539*, 2 vols. (The Hague, 1982)

Exquemelin, Alexandre, *The Buccaneers of America*, trans. Alexis Brown (Harmondsworth, 1969)

Forster, Leonard, 'Literary Relations between the Low Countries, England and Germany', *Dutch Crossing* 24 (1984), 16–31

Foucault, Michel, *Madness and Civilization: A History of Insanity in the Age of Reason*, trans. Richard Howard (London, 1989)

Frank, Grace, *The Medieval French Drama* (Oxford, 1954)

Freud, Sigmund, *Jokes and their Relation to the Unconscious*, trans. James Strachey (Harmondsworth, 1991)

Frey, Albert R., *A Dictionary of Numismatic Names* (New York, 1917)

Frijhoff, Willem, and Marijke Spies, *Dutch Culture in a European Perspective*, 2 vols. (Assen, 2004)

Furrow, Melissa, *Ten Fifteenth-Century Comic Poems* (New York, 1985)

Geeraedts, Loek, *Het volksboek van Ulenspieghel* (Antwerp, 1948)

Geirnaert, N., 'De miniatuur met de Drie Santinnen. Een nieuwe datering van het cartularium van de Brugse rederijkerskamer van de Drie Santinnen', *Brugs ommeland* 23 (1983), 243–8

Gibson, Walter S., *Bruegel* (Oxford, 1977)

—— 'Some Flemish Popular Prints from Hieronymus Cock and his Contemporaries', *The Art Bulletin* 60 (1978), 673–81

—— 'Artists and Rederijkers in the Age of Bruegel', *The Art Bulletin* 63 (1981), 426–46

—— *Pieter Brueghel and the Art of Laughter* (Berkeley, CA, 2006)

Gilman, Sander, *Parodic Sermon in European Perspective: Aspects of Liturgical Parody from the Middle Ages to the Twentieth Century* (Philadelphia, 1974)

—— *Seeing the Insane* (Lincoln, NA, 1996)

Ginzburg, Carlo, *The Cheese and the Worms: The Cosmos of a Sixteenth-Century Miller*, trans. John Tedeschi and Anne Tedeschi (Baltimore, 1980)

Glourieux, G., and A. Rouzet, 'Les Velpuis á Louvain. Formation d'un atelier', in *Ornamentation typograpique et bibliographie historique*, ed. Marie-Thérèse Isaac (Brussels, 1988), 67–85

Goethe, Johann Wolfgang, *Maxims and Reflections*, trans. Elisabeth Stopp, ed. Peter Hutchinson (Harmondsworth, 1991)

Goudriaan, Koen, Jaap van Moolenbroek and Ad Tervoort, eds., *Education and Learning in the Netherlands, 1400–1600: Essays in Honour of Hilde de Ridder-Symoens* (Leiden, 2004)

Grauls, Jan, *Volkstaal en volksleven in het werk van Pieter Bruegel* (Brussels, 1957)

Green, Jonathon, *Slang down the Ages: The Historical Development of Slang*, rev. edn (London, 2003), 282–3

Green, Otis Howard, *Spain and the Western Tradition: The Castilian Mind in Literature from El Cid to Calderón* (Madison, WI, 1968)

Grimm, Jacob and Wilhelm, *Deutsches Wörterbuch*, 2 vols. (Leipzig, 1860)

Guiette, Robert, *Forme et senefiance: études médiévales* (Geneva, 1978)

Gunn, Steven, David Grummitt and Hans Cools, *War, State, and Society in England and the Netherlands 1477–1559* (Oxford, 2007)

Hanawalt, Barbara A., *'Of Good and Ill Repute': Gender and Social Control in Medieval England* (Oxford, 1998)

Harrebomée, P. J., *Spreekwoordenboek der Nederlandsche taal*, 3 vols. (Hoevelaken, 1990)

Hayden-Roy, Priscilla, *'Till Eulenspiegel* – Transgressions against Convention: Interpreting the Parasite', *Daphnis* 20 (1991), 7–31

Heeroma, K., *Liederen en gedichten uit het Gruuthuse-handschrift* (Leiden, 1966)

Heinsius, Daniël, *Nederduytsche poemata*: facsimile-uitgave van eerste druk 1616 (Bern, 1983)

Helbig, Jean, *De glasschilderkunst in België, repertorium en documenten*, 2 vols. (Antwerp, 1951)

Hellinga, Lotte, and Clemens de Wolf, *Laurens Janszoon Coster was zijn naam* (Haarlem, 1988)

Heppner, Albert, 'The Popular Theatre of the Rederijkers in the Work of Jan Steen and his Contemporaries', *Journal of the Warburg and Courtauld Institutes* 3 (1939–40), 22–48

Hermans, Jos and Marc Nelissen, *Charters of Foundation and Early Documents* (Leuven, 2005)

Hermans, Theo, *A Literary History of the Low Countries* (Rochester, NY, 2009)

Hodges, Laura F., *Chaucer and Clothing: Clerical and Academic Clothing in the General Prologue* (Cambridge, 2005)

Hofman, E., 'Liederen en refreinen van Frans Fraet?', *Spiegel der letteren* 42 (2000), 227–58

Hollaar, Henk J., *Spelen van sinne vol schoone allegatien, drijderley referyenen – De Rotterdamse spelen van 1561* (Delft, 2006)

Hooper, James, 'Stickpenny', *Notes and Queries* 10 (1905), 70

Hornback, Robert, *The English Clown Tradition from the Middle Ages to Shakespeare* (Cambridge, 2009)

Huisman, Anneke, and Johan Koppenol, *Daer compt de Lotery met trommels en trompetten! Loterijen in de Nederlanden tot 1726* (Hilversum, 1991)

Hummelen, W. M. H., *Repertorium van het rederijkersdrama 1500–ca. 1620* (Assen, 1968)

—— 'Types and Methods of the Dutch Rhetoricians' Theatre', in *The Third Globe. Symposium for the Reconstruction of the Globe Playhouse*, ed. C. Walter Hodges, S. Schoenbaum and Leonard Leone (Detroit, 1979), 164–89

Hüsken, Wim N. M., *Noyt meerder vreucht – compositie en structuur van het komisch toneel in de Nederlanden voor de Renaissance* (Deventer, 1987)

—— '"Van incommen en begheert men scat noch goet": Cornelis Everaert and the Rosary', *European Theatre 1470–1600. Traditions and Transformations*, ed. Martin Gosman and Rina Walthaus (Groningen, 1996), 119–29

—— '1 augustus 1541: de klucht *Tielebuys* van Willem Vrancx wordt als welkomstspel gespeeld op het landjuweel van Diest. De kluchtentraditie in de Nederlanden', in *Een theatergeschiedenis der Nederlanden. Tien eeuwen drama en theater in Nederland en Vlaanderen*, ed. R. L. Erenstein (Amsterdam, 1996), 106–11

—— 'Civic Patronage in Early Fifteenth-Century Religious Drama in the Low Countries', in *Civic Ritual and Drama*, ed. Alexandra F. Johnston and Wim N. M. Hüsken (Amsterdam, 1997), 107–23

Hüsken, Wim N. M., 'Cornelis Everaert and the Community of Late Medieval Bruges', in *Drama and Community. People and Plays in Medieval Europe*, ed. Alan Hindley (Turnhout, 1999), 110–25

—— *De spelen van Cornelis Everaert*, 2 vols. (Hilversum, 2005)

—— 'Wie wás Cornelis Everaert nu eigenlijk?', *Jaarboek van de maatschappij der Nederlandse letterkunde* (2006), 138–41

——, B. A. M. Ramakers and F. A. M. Schaars, *Trou moet blijcken. Bronnenuitgave van de boeken der Haarlemse rederijkerskamer 'de Pellicanisten'*, 8 vols. (Assen, 1992–8), VII: *Boek G* (1997), 389–22

Hyams, Henri, *Antonio Moro, son oeuvre et son temps* (Brussels, 1910)

Infantes, Víctor, *Las danzas de la muerte: génesis y desarrollo de un género medieval* (Salamanca, 1997)

Isidorus Hispalensis, *Etymologiarum sive Originum*, ed. W. M Lindsay (Oxford, 1911)

Jacquot, J., 'Panorama des fetes et ceremonies du regne', in *Les Fêtes de la Renaissance*, ed. J. Jacquot, 2 vols. (Paris, 1958–60), II: *Fêtes et ceremonies au temps de Charles quint* (1960), 413–91

Janik, Vicki K., *Fools and Jesters in Literature, Art, and History: A Bio-bibliographical Sourcebook* (Westport, CT, 1998)

Janssens, Frederik, *Straatnaamgeving* (Leuven, 1983)

Jeanneret, Michel, *A Feast of Words: Banquets and Table Talk in the Renaissance*, trans. Jeremy Whiteley and Emma Hughes (Chicago, 1991)

Jeay, Madeleine, and Kathleen Garay, *The Distaff Gospels* (Peterborough, Ontario, 2006)

Jerome, *The Principal Works of St. Jerome*, trans. W. H. Fremantle, ed. Philip Schaff, Select Library of Nicene and Post-Nicene Fathers Second Series VI (New York, 1893)

Johnston, Alexandra F., 'Traders and Playmakers: English Guildsmen and the Low Countries', in *England and the Low Countries in the Late Middle Ages*, ed. Caroline M. Barron and Nigel Saul (New York, 1995), 99–114

—— 'The Continental Connection: A Reconsideration', in *The Stage as Mirror: Civic Theatre in Late Medieval Europe*, ed. A. E. Knight (Cambridge, 1997), 7–24

Jonckbloet, W. J. A., *Geschiedenis der Nederlandsche letterkunde*, 2 vols. (Groningen, 1889)

Jones, Malcolm, 'The Parodic Sermon in Medieval and Early Modern England', *Medium Ævum* 66 (1997), 95–114

—— *The Secret Middle Ages* (Stroud, 2002)

Juvenal, *Persi et Juvenalis Saturae*, ed. W. V. Clausen, 3rd edn (London, 1992)

Kaijser, Dick, 'Het laatmiddeleeuwse spotsermoen', *Spektator* 13 (1983), 105–27

Kalff, G., *Trou moet blycken: tooneelstukken der zestiende eeuw, voor het eerst naar de handschriften uitgegeven* (Groningen, 1889)

—— *Geschiedenis der Nederlandsche letterkunde*, 7 vols. Section 3 (Groningen, 1906–12)

—— 'Bijlage I. Speech by the moderator. Toespraak van den voorzitter', *Handelingen en mededeelingen van de maatschappij der Nederlandsche letterkunde* (1921), 7–18

—— *Middelnederlandsche epische fragmenten* (Arnhem, 1968)

—— *Het lied in de middeleeuwen* (Arnhem, 1972)

Kantorowicz, Ernst H., *The King's Two Bodies: A Study in Mediaeval Political Theology* (Princeton, NJ, 1957)

Kat, J. F. M., *De verloren zoon als letterkundig motief* (Amsterdam, 1952)

Katritzky, M. A., *The Art of Commedia: A Study in the Commedia dell'Arte 1560–1620* (Amsterdam and New York, 2006)

Keersmaekers, A., 'Geschiedenis van de Antwerpsche rederijkerskamers in de jaren 1585–1635', *Bijdragen tot de geschiedenis* 4 (1952), 123–56, 187–227

Keller, Rudi, *A Theory of Linguistic Signs* (Oxford, 1998)

Kendrick, Laura, 'Medieval Satire', in *A Companion to Satire*, ed. Ruben Quintero (Oxford, 2007), 52–69

Kerby-Fulton, Kathryn, *Reformist Apocalypticism and Piers Plowman*, Cambridge Studies in Medieval Literature 7 (Cambridge, 1990)

Kienhorst, H., 'Middelnederlandse Verzamelhandschriften als codicologisch object', in *Middeleeuwse verzamelhandschriften uit de Nederlanden*, ed. Gerard Sonnemans (Hilversum, 1996), 39–60

Klein, Jan Willem, '"Het getal zijner jaren is onnaspeurlijk". Een herijking van de dateringen van de handschriften en fragmenten met Middelnederlandse ridderepiek', *Tijdschrift voor Nederlandse taal- en letterkunde* 111 (1995), 1–23

Knuvelder, G. P. M., *Handboek tot de geschiedenis der Nederlandse letterkunde*, 4 vols. (Malmberg, 1948–53)

Koch, Mark, 'The Desanctification of the Beggar in Rogue Pamphlets of the English Renaissance', in *The Work of Disimilitude*, ed. David G. Allen and Robert A. White (Newark, DE, 1992), 91–104

Koopmans, Jelle, *Quatre sermons joyeux* (Geneva, 1984)

—— *Recueil de sermons joyeux: édition critique avec introduction, notes et glossaire* (Geneva, 1988)

Koopmans, Jelle, and Paul Verhuyck, *Sermon joyeux et Truanderie* (Amsterdam, 1987)

Kramer, Femke, 'Rigid Readings of Flexible Texts: The Case of Sixteenth Century Comic Drama', in *Aspects of Genre and Type in Pre-modern Literary Cultures*, ed. Bert Roest and Herman L. J. Vanstiphout (Leiden, 1999), 33–46

—— *Mooi vies, knap lelijk: grotesk realisme in rederijkerskluchten* (Hilversum, 2009)

Kruyskamp, C., *Dichten en spelen van Jan van den Berghe*

Kruyskamp, C. (ed.), *Martinus Nijhoff* (The Hague, 1950)

—— *De Middelnederlandse boerden voor het eerst verzameld* (The Hague, 1957)

Kurath, Hans, and Sherman M. Kuhn, *Middle English Dictionary* (Ann Arbor, MI, 2001)

Lambert, Malcolm D., *Medieval Heresy: Popular Movements from the Gregorian Reform to the Reformation* (Oxford, 2002)

Lambrecht, Joos, *Het naembouck van 1562. Tweede druk van het Nederlands-Frans woordenboek*, ed. René Verdeyen (Droz and Paris, 1945)

Lawrence, C. H., *The Friars: The Impact of the Early Mendicant Movement on Western Society* (London, 1994)

Leendertz, P., 'Eenige geneuchlijcke dichten', *Tijdschrift voor Nederlandse taal- en letterkunde* 20 (1901), 59–80

Leff, Gordon, *Heresy in the Later Middle Ages: The Relation of Heterodoxy to Dissent, c.1250–c.1450* (Manchester, 1999)

Lehmann, Paul, *Die Parodie im Mittelalter* (Munich, 1922)

Lerer, Seth, 'British Library MS Harley 78 and the Manuscripts of John Shirley', *Notes and Queries* 235 (1990), 400–3

Lerner, Robert, *The Heresy of the Free Spirit in the Later Middle Ages* (Berkeley, 1972)

Limberger, Michael, 'No Town in the World Provides More Advantages: Economies of Agglomeration and the Golden Age of Antwerp', in *Urban Achievement in Early Modern Europe: Golden Ages in Antwerp, Amsterdam and London*, ed. Patrick

O'Brien, Derek Keene, Marjolein 't Hart and Herman van der Wee (Cambridge, 2001), 39–62

Lindow, Wolfgang, *Bin kurtzweilig Lesen von Dil Ulenspiegel* (Stuttgart, 1978)

Lindsay, David, *Ane Satyre of the Thrie Estaitis*, ed. Roderick Lyall (Edinburgh, 1989)

Livingston, Charles Harold, *Le Jongleur Gautier le Leu: étude sur les fabliaux* (London, 1951)

Lodder, F. J., *Lachen om list en lust. Studies on the Middle Dutch Comic Verse Narratives. Studies over de Middelnederlandse komische versvertellingen* (Ridderkerk, 1997)

Luijten, Hans, and Marijke Blankman, *Minne- en zinnebeelden: een bloemlezing uit de Nederlandse emblematiek* (Amsterdam, 1996)

Lumiansky, R. M., and David Mills, *The Chester Mystery Cycle*, Early English Text Society, ss 3, 2 vols. (London, 1974)

Lunsford, Virginia W., *Piracy and Privateering in the Golden Age Netherlands* (Aldershot, 2005)

Luther, Martin, *Selections*, ed. John Dillenberger (New York, 1961)

MacCracken, Henry Noble, and Merriam Sherwood, *Lydgate's Minor Poems*, Early English Text Society, os 192, 2 vols. (London, 1911–34)

Maher, W. B., and B. Maher, 'The Ship of Fools: *Stultifera navis* or *Ignis fatuus*', *American Psychologist* 37 (1982), 756–61

Maistner, M. L. W., *Thought and Letters in Western Europe, AD 500–900*, rev. edn (London, 1957)

Mak, J. J., *Vier excellente cluchten,* Klassieke Galerij 46 (Antwerp, 1950)

—— *Rhetoricaal Glossarium* (Assen, 1959)

—— 'Everaert', in G. J. van Bork and P. J. Verkruijsse, *De Nederlandse en Vlaamse auteurs van middeleeuwen tot heden met inbegrip van de Friese auteurs* (Weesp, 1985), 197

—— and Dirk Coigneau, 'Jan van den Berghe', in G. J. van Bork and P. J. Verkruijsse, *De Nederlandse en Vlaamse auteurs van middeleeuwen tot heden met inbegrip van de Friese auteurs* (Weesp, 1985), 70

Man, M. G. A. de, 'De voormalige Middelburgsche rederijkerskamer het Bloemken Jesse onder de kenspreuk in minnen groeyende, en hare gildepenningen', *Jaarboek van het Kon. Ned. genootschap voor munt- en penningkunde* (1917), 1–40

Mann, Jill, *Chaucer and Medieval Estates Satire: The Literature of Social Classes and the General Prologue to the Canterbury Tales* (Cambridge, 1973)

Mareel, Samuel, 'Entre ciel et terre: le théâtre sociopolitique de Cornelis Eveaert', *European Medieval Drama* 12 (2008), 93–108

Marijnissen, R., 'De Eed van Meester Oom. Een voorbeeld van Brabantse jokkernij uit Bruegels tijd', in *Pieter Bruegel und seine Welt*, ed. O. von Simson and M. Winner (Berlin, 1979), 51–61

Marnef, Guido, *Het Calvinistisch bewind te Mechelen 1580–1585*, Standen en landen 87 (Kortrijk, 1987)

Marnix van Sint Aldegonde, Philips, *De werken van Ph. van Marnix van Sint Aldegonde*, 2 vols. (Brussels, 1858)

Marx, Karl, *Early Writings*, trans. and ed. T. B. Bottomore (New York, 1964)

Matarasso, Pauline, *The Cistercian World: Monastic Writings of the Twelfth Century* (Harmondsworth, 1993)

McDonnell, Ernest W., *The Beguines and Beghards in Medieval Culture* (New York, 1969)

Meadow, Mark, 'Volkscultuur of humanistencultuur? Spreekwoordenverzamelingen in de zestiende-eeuwse Nederlanden', *Volkskundig bulletin* 19 (1993), 208–40

Meertens, P. J., *Letterkundig leven in Zeeland in de zestiende en de eerste helft der zeventiende eeuw* (Amsterdam 1943)

Meeus, Marius, *Wat betekent arbeid? Over het ontstaan van de westerse arbeidsmoraal* (Assen, 1989)

Meijer, Reinder P., *Literature of the Low Countries: A Short History of Dutch Literature in the Netherlands and Belgium* (The Hague, 1978)

Melters, Johannes, *Ein frölich gemüt zu machen in schweren Zeiten: der Schwankroman in Mittelalter und Früher Neuzeit* (Berlin, 2004)

Merceron, Jacques E., 'Obscenity and Hagiography in Three Anonymous *Sermons Joyeux* and in Jean Molinet's *Saint Billouart*', in *Obscenity: Social Control and Artistic Creation in the European Middle Ages*, ed. Jan M. Ziolkowski (Leiden, 1998), 332–44

—— *Dictionnaire thématique et géographique des saints imaginaires, facetieux et substitutes en France et en Belgique francophone* (Paris, 2002)

Meyer, Paul, 'Melanges de poesie française, iv: Plaidoyer en faveur des femmes', *Romania* 6 (1877), 499–503

Midelfort, H. C. Erik, 'Reading and Believing: On the Reappraisal of Michel Foucault', in *Rewriting the History of Madness: Studies in Foucault's Histoire de la folie*, ed. Arthur Still and Irving Velody (London, 1992), 105–10

—— 'Madness and Civilisation in Early Modern Europe: A Reappraisal of Michel Foucault', in *Michel Foucault: Critical Assessments*, ed. Barry Smart (London, 1998), 117–33

Mohl, Ruth, *The Three Estates in Medieval and Renaissance Literature* (New York, 1933)

More, Thomas, *Complete Works*, 14 vols. (New Haven, 1963–97)

Moser, Dietz-Rüdiger, *Fastnacht-Fasching-Karneval: das Fest der 'Verkehrten Welt'* (Cologne, 1986)

Moser, Nelleke, *De strijd voor rhetorica: poëtica en positie van rederijkers in Vlaanderen, Brabant, Zeeland en Holland tussen 1450 en 1620* (Amsterdam, 2001)

Moxey, Keith P. F., 'Pieter Bruegel and the Feast of Fools', *The Art Bulletin* 64 (1982), 640–6

Muir, Lynette R., *Love and Conflict in Medieval Drama: The Plays and their Legacy* (Cambridge, 2007)

Muller, J. W., 'Ze(e)rden, scheren, sarren', *Tijdschrift voor Nederlandse taal- en letterkunde* 45 (1926), 15–22

—— 'Reinaert-studiën. III. Aernout en Willem. B. Het dubbel auteurschap van Reinaert I A en B', *Tijdschrift voor Nederlandsche taal- en letterkunde* 53 (1934), 127–67

Muller, J. W., and L. Scharpé, *Spelen van Cornelise Everaert*, 3 vols. (Leiden, 1898–1920)

Murray, Alexander, *Reason and Society in the Middle Ages* (Oxford, 1978)

Muscatine, Charles, *Medieval Literature, Style and Culture* (Columbia, 1999)

Nagel, Norman, 'Luther and the Priesthood of All Believers', *Concordia Theological Quarterly* 61 (1997), 283–4

Nolan, Barbara, 'Promiscuous Fictions: Medieval Bawdy Tales and their Textual Liaisons', in *The Body and the Soul in Medieval Literature,* ed. Piero Boitani and Anna Torti (Cambridge, 1998), 79–106

Noomen, Willem, and Nico van den Boogaard, *Nouveau recueil complet des fabliaux*, 10 vols. (Assen, 1983–98)

Notermans, J., 'Ambachtslieden en Rederijkers spelen in Tricht toneel', *Handelingen van de Kon zuidned maatschappij voor taal- en letterkunde en geschiedenis* 12 (1958), 211–22

O'Conor, Norreys Jephson, *Godes Peace and the Queenes: Vicissitudes of a House, 1539–1615* (London, 1934)

Oliphant Old, Hugh, *The Reading and the Preaching of the Scriptures in the Worship of the Christian Church* (Grand Rapids, MI, 1998–2004)

Otto, Beatrice K., *Fools are Everywhere* (Chicago, 2001)

Ouvry, B., 'Officieel ceremonieel te Oudenaarde, 1450–1600', *Handelingen van de Geschied- en oudheidkundige kring van Oudenaarde* 22 (1985), 25–64

Paris, Gaston, *Mediaeval French Literature*, trans. Hannah Lynch (London, 1903)

Parsons, Ben, 'Dutch Influences on English Literary Culture in the Early Renaissance, 1470–1650', *Literature Compass* 4 (2007), 1577–96

Parsons, Ben, and Bas Jongelen, '*A Play of Three Suitors*: A Neglected Version of the "Entrapped Suitors" Story (ATU 1730)', *Folklore* 119 (2008), 62–74

—— 'The Refrein and the Chambers of Rhetoric in the Early Modern Low Countries', *European Medieval Drama* 12 (2008), 185–210

—— 'Better than a Sack Full of Latin: Anticlericalism in the Middle Dutch *Dit es de Frenesie*', *Church History and Religious Culture* 89 (2009), 431–53

Partridge, Eric, *Dictionary of Catch-Phrases from the Sixteenth Century to the Present Day* (London, 1986)

Patterson, Lee, *Chaucer and the Subject of History* (Madison, WI, 1991)

—— 'Feminine Rhetoric and the Politics of Subjectivity: La Vielle and the Wife of Bath', in *Rethinking the Romance of the Rose: Text, Image, Reception*, ed. Sylvia Huot and Kevin Brownlee (University Park, PA 1992), 367–421

Pauli, Johannes, *Schimpf und Ernst*, ed. Johannes Bolte (Berlin, 1924)

Pepys, Samuel, *The Shorter Pepys*, ed. Robert Latham (London, 1993)

Perry, Jenkins, *Dialogus inter Militem et Clericum* (London, 1925)

Pettegree, Andrew, *Reformation and the Culture of Persuasion* (Cambridge, 2005)

Pikhaus, P., *Het tafelspel bij de rederijkers*, 2 vols. (Ghent, 1988–9)

Pleij, Herman, 'De sociale funktie van humor en trivialiteit op het rederijkerstoneel', *Spektator* 5 (1975–6), 108–27

—— *Het gilde van de Blauwe Schuit: literatuur, volksfeest en burgermoraal in de late middeleeuwen* (Amsterdam, 1979)

—— *Een nyeuwe clucht boeck: een zestiende-eeuwse anekdotenverzameling* (Muiderburg, 1983)

—— 'Literatuur als medicijn in de late middeleeuwen', *Literatuur* 2 (1985), 25–32

—— *De sneeuwpoppen van 1511. Literatuur en stadscultuur tussen middeleeuwen en moderne tijd* (Amsterdam, 1988)

—— 'De zot als maatschappelijk houvast in de overgang van middeleeuwen naar moderne tijd', *Groniek* 23 (1990), 19–39

—— *Nederlandse literatuur in de late middeleeuwen* (Utrecht, 1990)

—— *Sprekend over de middeleeuwen* (Utrecht, 1991)

—— 'Eind juli 1551 – Op het zottenfeest van Brussel wordt Meester Oom als vorst in een massaspel beëdigd – De stedelijke feestviering van bevrijdend ritueel naar gecontroleerd schouwtoneel', in *Een theatergeschiedenis der Nederlanden. Tien eeuwen drama en theater in Nederland en Vlaanderen*, ed. R. L. Erenstein (Amsterdam, 1996), 112–19

—— 'Anna Bijns als pamflettiste? Het refrein van beide Maartens', *Spiegel der letteren* 42 (2000), 187–225

—— *Dreaming of Cockaigne*, trans. Diane Webb (New York, 2001)

Pleij, Herman, 'Novel Knowledge: Innovation in Dutch Literature in the Fifteenth and Sixteenth Century', in *Making Knowledge in Early Modern Europe: Practices, Objects, and Texts, 1400–1800*, ed. Pamela H. Smith and Benjamin Schmidt (Chicago, 2007), 109–26

—— *De eeuw van de zotheid: over de nar als maatshcappelijk houvast in de vroegmoderne tijd* (Amsterdam, 2007)

—— *Het gevleugelde woord: geschiedenis van de Nederlandse literatuur, 1400–1560* (Amsterdam, 2007)

Pohl Perry, Sigrid, 'The Secret Voice: Clandestine Fine Printing in the Netherlands, 1940–1945', in *The Holocaust and the Book: Destruction and Preservation*, ed. Jonathan Rose (Boston, MA, 2001)

Proctor, Robert Collier, *Jan van Doesborgh: Printer at Antwerp* (London, 1894)

Prins, Johanna C., *Medieval Dutch Drama: Four Secular Plays and Four Farces from the Van Hulthem Manuscript*. Early European Drama in Translation 4 (Asheville, NC, 2000)

Pugliatti, Paola, *Beggary and the theatre in early modern England* (Aldershot, 2003)

Purvis, Alston W., *H. N. Werkman* (London, 2004)

Rabelais, François, *Gargantua*, ed. R. Calder (Geneva, 1970)

Ramakers, Bart, 'Voor stad en stadgenoten: Rederijkers, kamers en toneel in Haarlem in de tweede helft van de zestiende eeuw', in Ramakers, *Conformisten en rebellen: Rederijkerscultuur in de Nederlanden (1400–1650)* (Amsterdam, 2003), 109–24

—— 'Between Aea and Golgotha: The Education and Scholarship of Matthijs de Castelein', in Koen Goudriaan, Jaap van Moolenbroek and Ad Tervoort, eds., *Education and Learning in the Netherlands, 1400–1600: Essays in Honour of Hilde de Ridder-Symoens* (Leiden, 2004), 179–200

——, ed., *Conformisten en rebellen: Rederijkerscultuur in de Nederlanden (1400–1650)* (Amsterdam, 2003)

Revah, I. S., *Les Sermons de Gil Vicente. En marge d'un opuscule du professeur Joaquim de Carvalho* (Lisbon, 1949)

Rey-Flaud, Bernadette, *La Farce ou la machine a rire: theorie d'un genre dramatique 1450–1550*, Publications romanes et françaises, 167 (Geneva, 1984)

Robbins, Rossell Hope, ed., *Historical Poems of the XIVth and XVth Centuries* (London, 1959)

Rombauts, Philippe-Felix, and Theodoor van Lerius, *De Liggeren en andere historische archieven der Antwerpsche Sint Lucasgilde, onder zinspreuk: wt ionsten versaemt*, 2 vols. (Antwerp, 1961)

Roobaert, E., 'Jan Welravens, alias Oomken, schilder en rederijker to Brussel', *Bulletin, Musées royaux des beaux-arts* 3–4 (1961), 83–100

Root, Jerry, 'The Old French Fabliau and the Poetics of Disfiguration', *Medievalia et Humanistica* 24 (1997), 17–32

Rosenwald, Lessing J., and Frederick Richmond Goff, *Early Printed Books of the Low Countries: The Lessing J. Rosenwald Collection* (Washington, DC, 1958)

Rotgans, Lukas, *Boerekermis*, ed. L. Strengholt (Gorinchem, 1968)

Round, Nicholas G., 'Juan Ruiz and Some Versions of *Nummus*', in *The Medieval Mind: Hispanic Studies in Honour of Alan Deyermond*, ed. Ian Macpherson and Ralph Penny (London, 1999), 381–400

Rozik, Eli, *The Roots of Theatre: Rethinking Ritual and Other Theories of Origin* (Iowa City, 2002)

Ryckaert, R., 'Een Antwerpse brief aan Symmachus. Analyse van het "Totten goetwillighen leser" in de Antwerpse Spelen van sinne (1562)', *Spiegel der letteren* 46 (2004), 1–32

Sachs, Hans, *Schwanken*, ed. Adelbert von Keller, 20 vols. (Stuttgart, 1860–90)

Sacré, M., 'Het voormalig Dorpstooneel in Brabant volgens onuitgegeven bewijsstukken', *De Brabander* 1 (1919), 3–8

Salman, J., *Een handdruk van de tijd: de almanak en het dagelijks leven in de Nederlanden 1500–1700* (Zwolle, 1997)

Scheurleer, D. F., *Een devoot ende profitelyck boecxken* (The Hague, 1889)

Schmidt, Ariadne, 'Van de lusten geproefd. Wellust in het weduwebeeld in de vroegmoderne periode. Twee eeuwenoude weduwebeelden', *Jaarboek voor vrouwengeschiedenis* 20 (2000), 65–83

Schöll, Konrad, *Das komische Theater des französischen Mittelalters*: *Wirklichkeit und Spiel* (Munich, 1975)

Schotel, G. D. J., *Geschiedenis der rederijkers in Nederland*, 2 vols. (Amsterdam, 1862–71)

Schouteet, A., 'Inventaris van het archief van de Brugse rederijkersgilden van de H. Geest, van de Drie Santinnen en van het H. Kruis op het Stadsarchief van Brugge', *Handelingen van het Genootschap voor geschiedenis Société d'émulation te Brugge* 114 (1977), 380–2

Scribner, Robert W., *Popular Culture and Popular Movements in Reformation Germany* (London, 1987)

Serrure, C. P., *Vaderlandsch museum voor Nederduitsche letterkunde, oudheid en geschiedenis*, 5 vols. (Ghent, 1855–63)

Sicking, Louis, *Neptune and the Netherlands: State, Economy, and War at Sea in the Renaissance* (Leiden, 2004)

Simons, Walter, *Cities of Ladies: Beguine Communities in the Medieval Low Countries 1200–1565* (Philadelphia, 2003)

Simpson, James, *Reform and Cultural Revolution, 1350–1547*, Oxford English Literary History 2 (Oxford, 2004)

Sonnemans, Gerard, 'What's in a name? Het belang van opschriften in verzamelhandschriften', in *Middeleeuwse verzamelhandschriften uit de Nederlanden*, ed. G. Sonnemans (Hilversum, 1996), 61–78

Southworth, John, *Fools and Jesters* (Stroud, 2000)

Spaans, Joke, 'Public Opinion or Ritual Celebration of Concord? Politics, Religion and Society in Competition between the Chambers of Rhetoric at Vlaardingen in 1616', in *Public Opinion and Changing Identities in the Early Modern Netherlands: Essays in Honour of Alastair Duke*, ed. Judith Pollmann and Andrew Spicer (Leiden, 2007), 189–210

Speakman Sutch, Susie, 'Dichters van de stad – de Brusselse rederijkers en hun verhouding tot de Franstalige hofliteratuur en het geleerde humanisme (1475–1522)', in *De macht van het schone woord: literatuur in Brussel van de 14de tot de 18de eeuw*, ed. Jozef Janssens and Remco Sleiderink (Leuven, 2003), 141–59

Spies, Marijke, 'Developments in Sixteenth-Century Dutch Poetics. From "Rhetoric" to "Renaissance"', *Renaissance-Rhetorik*, ed. Heinrich F. Plett (Berlin, 1993), 72–91

—— 'Rhetoric and Civic Harmony in the Dutch Republic of the Late Sixteenth and Early Seventeenth Century', *Rhetorica Movet: Studies in Historical and Modern Rhetoric in Honor of Heinrich F. Plett*, ed. Peter Lothar Oesterreich and Thomas O. Sloane (Leiden, 1999), 57–72

Sprunger, Keith L., *Dutch Puritanism: A History of English and Scottish Churches of the Netherlands* (Leiden, 1982)

Spufford, Peter, *Money and its Use in Medieval Europe* (Cambridge, 1989)

Steenbergen, G. J., *Het landjuweel van de rederijkers* (Leuven, 1951)

Sterck, J. F. M., 'Onder Amsterdamsche humanisten', *Het boek* 9 (1920), 161–74

Stock, Ursula, *Die Bedeutung der Sakramente in Luthers Sermonen von 1519* (Leiden, 1982)

Stoett, F. A., *Nederlandsche spreekwoorden, spreekwijzen, uitdrukkingen en gezegden*, 2 vols. (Zutphen, 1923–25)

—— *Drie kluchten uit de zestiende eeuw* (Zutphen, 1932)

Strietman, Elsa, and Robert Potter, *Een esbattement van smenschen sin en verganckelijcke schoonheit / Man's Desire and Fleeting Beauty*, Leeds Medieval Studies, Middle Dutch Texts and Translations Series 1 (Leeds, 1994)

Stroman, Ben, *De Nederlandse toneelschrijfkunst: poging tot verklaring van een gemis* (Amsterdam, 1973)

Szittya, Penn R., 'The Antifraternal Tradition in Middle English', *Speculum* 52 (1977), 287–313

—— *The Antifraternal Tradition in Medieval Literature* (Princeton, 1986)

Tawney, R. H., *Religion and the Rise of Capitalism* (New York, 1926)

Te Winkel, Jan, *De ontwikkelingsgang der Nederlandsche letterkunde*, 2 vols. (Haarlem, 1922)

Ten Brink, Jan, *Geschiedenis der Nederlandsche letterkunde* (Amsterdam, 1897)

Ter Braak, Menno, *Verzameld werk.*, ed. M. van Crevel, H. A. Gomperts and G. H. 's-Gravesande, 5 vols. (Amsterdam, 1950–80)

Ter Laan, K., *Letterkundig woordenboek voor noord en zuid* (The Hague, 1952)

Test, George, *Satire: Spirit and Art* (Gainesville, 1991)

Thorne, Tony, *Dictionary of Contemporary Slang* (New York, 1990)

Thorpe, Benjamin, *Northern Mythology: North German and Netherlandish Popular Traditions and Superstitions* (London, 1852)

Tigges, Wim, '*The Land of Cokaygne*: Sophisticated Mirth', in *A Companion to Early English Literature*, ed. N. H. G. E. Veldhoen and Henk Aertsen (Amsterdam, 1988), 97–104

Treharne, Elaine, ed., *Old and Middle English, c.890–c.1400: An Anthology*, 2nd edn (Oxford, 2004)

Twycross, Meg, and Sarah Carpenter, *Masks and Masking in Medieval and Early Tudor England* (Aldershot, 2002)

Tydeman, William, *The Medieval European Stage, 500–1550* (Cambridge, 2001)

Unger, Richard W., *The Art of Medieval Technology: Images of Noah the Shipbuilder* (New Brunswick, NJ, 1991)

Uther, Hans-Jorg, *The Types of International Folktales*, Parts I–III, 3 vols. (Helsinki, 2004)

Vaananen, Veikko, 'Le "Fabliau" de Cocagne', *Neuphilologische Mitteilungen* 48 (1947), 3–36

Van Aken, Hein, *Die rose*, ed. Eelco Verwijs (Utrecht, 1976)

Van Autenboer, E., *Volksfeesten en rederijkers te Mechelen 1400–1600* (Ghent, 1962)

—— 'Een landjuweel te Antwerpen in 1496?', *Jaarboek de Fonteine* 29 (1978–9), 125–50

—— 'De Lelikens wten Dale. Rederijkerskamer van Zoutleeuw', *Eigen Schoon en de Brabander* 68 (1985), 249–70

Van Boekel, L., 'Een zestiende-eeuwsche Liersche rederijker, Ambrosius van Molle', *Tijdschrift voor geschiedenis en folklore* 4 (1941), 83–136

—— 'Jeronimus van der Voort. Een zestiende-eeuwsche Liersche rederijker', *Tijdschrift voor geschiedenis en folklore* 6 (1943), 5–80

Van Boheemen, F. C., and T. C. J. van der Heijden, *Retoricaal memoriaal: bronnen voor de geschiedenis van de Hollandse rederijkerskamers van de middeleeuwen tot het begin van de achttiende eeuw* (Delft, 1999)

Van Bork, G. J., and P. J. Verkruijsse, *De Nederlandse en Vlaamse auteurs van middeleeuwen tot heden met inbegrip van de Friese auteurs* (Weesp, 1985)

Van Bruane, Anne-Laure, 'Printing Plays: the Publication of the Ghent Plays of 1539 and the Reaction of the Authorities', *Dutch Crossing* 24 (2000), 265–84

—— 'Sociabiliteit en competitie. De sociaal-institutionele ontwikkeling van de rederijkerskamers in de Zuidelijke Nederlanden (1400–1650)', in Bart Ramakers, ed., *Conformisten en rebellen: Rederijkerscultuur in de Nederlanden (1400–1650)* (Amsterdam, 2003), 45–64

—— 'Repertorium van rederijkerskamers in de Zuidelijke Nederlanden en Luik 1400–1650', in *Digitale bibliotheek voor de Nederlandse letteren* (2005), online at www.dbnl. org/tekst/brua002repe01_01/

—— '"In principio erat verbum": Drama, Devotion, Reformation and Urban Association in the Low Countries', in *Early Modern Confraternities in Europe and the Americas*, ed. Christopher F. Black and Pamela Gravestock (Aldershot, 2006), 64–80

—— '"Of the King's Edict I do You no Command": Vernacular Literary Networks and the Reformation in the Low Countries', *Archive for Reformation History* 99 (2008), 229–55

—— *Om beters wille: rederijkerskamers en de stedelijke cultuur in de Zuidelijke Nederlanden (1400–1650)* (Amsterdam, 2008)

Van Bueren, Truus, and Jeanne Verbij-Schillings, 'Een rijkgeschakeerde cultuur: de Hollandse kunstproductie in opdracht van hof, kloosters en steden', in *Geschiedenis van Holland*, ed. Thimo de Nijs and Eelco Beukers, 3 vols. (Hilversum, 2002–3), I: *Tot 1572* (2002), 197–258

Van de Graft, C. C., *Middelnederlandsche historieliederen* (Ypres, 1904)

Van Delft, Dirk, *Heike Kamerlingh Onnes. Een biografie. De man van het absolute nulpunt* (Amsterdam, 2005)

Van den Berghe, Jan, 'The Voluptuous Man', trans. Peter King, *Dutch Crossing* 28 (1986), 53–107

Van der Heijden, M. C. A, *Hoort wat men u spelen zal: toneelstukken uit de middeleeuwen* (Utrecht, 1968)

Van der Kooi, Jurjen, 'De vrijers in de kast', in *Van Aladdin tot Zwaan Kleefaan: lexicon van sprookjes:ontstaan, ontwikkeling, variaties,* ed. A. J. Dekker, Theo Meder and Jurjen van der Kooi (Leuven, 1997), 387–90

Van der Meersch, D. J., *Kronyk der rederykkamers van Andenaerde, van de vroegste tyder af tot omtrerit den Jare 1830* (Ghent, 1844)

Van der Noot, Jan, *Het bosken en het theatre*, ed. W. A. P. Smit (Utrecht, 1979)

Van der Poel, Dieuwke, 'The *Romance of the Rose* and I: Narrative Perspective in the *Roman de la Rose* and its Two Middle Dutch Adaptations', in *Courtly Literature: Culture and Context*, ed. Keith Busby and Erik Kooper (Amsterdam, 1990), 573–85

Van der Sluijs, P., 'Enkele kanttekeningen met betrekking tot de Bossche rederijkerskamers', *Varia Historica Brabantica* 6–7 (1978), 187–205

Van der Stock, Jan, and Hans Nieuwdorp, 'Het Christusbeeld van de Meir te Antwerpen. Een meesterwerk van de gebroeders De Nole uit de vergeetboek', *Revue belge d'archéologie et d'histoire de l'art* 55 (1986), 69–96

Van der Wurf-Bodt, Coby, *Van lichte wiven tot gevallen vrouwen: Prostitutie in Utrecht vanaf de late middeleeuwen tot het eind van de negentiende eeuw* (Utrecht, 1988)

Van Dijk, Hans, 'The Drama Texts in the Van Hulthem Manuscript', in *Medieval Dutch Literature in its European Context*, ed. E. Kooper, Cambridge Studies in Medieval Literature 21 (Cambridge, 1994), 283–96

Van Dixhoorn, Arjan, 'Burgers, branies en bollebozen. De sociaal-institutionele ontwikkeling van de rederijkerskamers in de Noordelijke Nederlanden (1400–1650)', in Bart Ramakers, ed., *Conformisten en rebellen: Rederijkerscultuur in de Nederlanden (1400–1650)* (Amsterdam, 2003), 65–85

—— 'Writing Poetry as Intellectual Training. Chambers of Rhetoric and the Development of Vernacular Intellectual Life in the Low Countries', in Koen Goudriaan, Jaap van Moolenbroek and Ad Tervoort, eds., *Education and Learning in the Netherlands, 1400–1600: Essays in Honour of Hilde de Ridder-Symoens* (Leiden, 2004), 201–22

—— 'Repertorium van rederijkerskamers in de Noordelijke Nederlanden 1400–1650', in *Digitale bibliotheek voor de Nederlandse letteren* (2005), online at www.dbnl.org/tekst/dixh002repe01_01/

—— 'Epilogue', in *The Reach of the Republic of Letters: Literary and Learned Societies in Late Medieval and Early Modern Europe*, ed. Arjan van Dixhoorn and Susie Speakman Sutch, 2 vols. (Leiden, 2008), 2: 423–62

—— *Lustige geesten: rederijkers in de noordelijke nederlanden (1480–1650)* (Amsterdam, 2009)

Van Duyse, Prudens, *De rederijkkamers in Nederland, hun invloed op letterkundig, politiek en zedelijk gebied*, 2 vols. (Ghent, 1900–2)

Van Eeghem, Willem, 'Rhetores Bruxellenses', *Revue belge de philologie et d'histoire* 15 (1936), 47–78

—— *Drie schandaleuse spelen (Brussel 1559)* (Antwerp, 1937)

—— 'Cornelis Everaert op het Landjuweel te Gent (1539)', *Toneelgids* 25 (1938), 1–7

Van Elslander, A., *Het refrein in de Nederlanden tot 1600* (Ghent, 1953)

—— 'Lijst van Nederlandse rederijkerskamers uit de XVe en XVIe eeuw', *Jaarboek de Fonteine* 18 (1968), 29–60

Van Elslander, A., V. Speeckaert and J. Vuyst, 'Lijst van Zuid-Nederlandsche rederijkerskamers uit de XVe en XVIe eeuw', *Jaarboek de Fonteine* 2 (1944), 9–31

Van Es, G. A., *Piramus en Thisbe. Twee rederijkersspelen uit de zestiende eeuw* (Zwolle, 1965)

Van Even, Edward, *Het landjuweel van Antwerpen in 1561: eene verhandeling over dezen beroemden wedstrijd tusschen de rederijkkamers van Braband* (Ghent, 1861)

Van Hemelryck, Tania, 'Classé X en moyen français . . . Des saints facétieux', *Le Moyen français* 50 (2003), 93–114

Van Hout, Cornelis Meesz., *sMenschen sin en verganckelijcke schoonheit*, ed. Cornelis Schmidt (Zwolle, 1967)

Van Kampen, Hinke, Herman Pleij, Bob Stumpel, Annebel Venmans and Paul Vriesema, *Het zal koud zijn in 't water als 't vriest: Zestiende-eeuwse parodieen op gedrukte jaarvoorspellingen tekstuitg. met inleiding en commentaar* (The Hague, 1980)

Van Kol, Nellie, *Kinderversjes* (Alkmaar, 1923)

Van Leeuwen, Jacoba, 'Praise the Lord for this Peace! The Contribution of Religious Institutions to the Ceremonial Peace-Proclamations in Late Medieval Flanders', in *The Use and Abuse of Sacred Places in Late Medieval Towns*, ed. Paul Trio and Marjan de Smet (Leuven, 2006), 47–70

Van Leuvensteijn, Arjan, and Jeanine Stuart, *WD Hooft Door-trapte Meelis en J. Light Noozeman Klaartje. Edited by Arjan van Leuven Steyn and Jeanine Stuart. Noozeman Lichte Klaartje*, Stichting Neerlandistiek VU Amsterdam (Münster, 1999)

Van Maerlant, Jacob, *Van den lande van ouer zee*, ed. Garmt Stuiveling (Amsterdam, 1967)

Van Mander, Karel, *Het schilder-boeck: facsimile van de eerste uitgave* (Utrecht, 1969)

Van Mierlo, S. J., '"Den boem der Schriftueren" en het geval Jacob van Middeldonck', in *Verslagen en mededelingen van de Koninklijke Vlaamse academie voor taal- en letterkunde* (1939), 889–905

Van Mierlo, Jozef, *Geschiedenis van de letterkunde der Nederlanden*, 2 vols. (Brussels, 1939–40)

Van Moerkerken, P. H., *De satire in de Nederlandsche kunst der middeleeuwen* (Amsterdam, 1904)

Van Rensch, J., 'Broederschappen in Maastricht 1400–1850', *Hemelse trektochten. Broederschappen in Maastricht 1400–1850*, ed. T. J. van Rensch, A. M. Koldeweij, R. M. de la Haye and M. L. de Kreek (Maastricht, 1990), 7–88

Van Stipriaan, René, *Leugens en vermaak: Boccaccio's Novellen in de kluchtcultuur van de Nederlandse Renaissance* (Amsterdam, 1996)

Van Thijn, F., 'Eedt van Meester Oom', in G. J. van Bork and P. J. Verkruijsse, *De Nederlandse en Vlaamse auteurs van middeleeuwen tot heden met inbegrip van de Friese auteurs* (Weesp, 1985), 188

Van Veerdeghem, François, *Leven van Sinte Lutgart (tweede en derde boek)* (Leiden, 1899)

Van Vloten, J., 'Jacob van Oostvoorne (Contribution to Clarification of Several Questions Maerlant) (Bijdrage tot toelichting van verschillende Maerlants-vragen)', *De taal- en letterbode* 1 (1870), 83–93

Van Zuylen, Rogier Adriaan, *Inventaris der archieven van de stad 's Hertogenbosch* ('s-Hertogenbosch, 1863–76)

Vandecasteele, M., 'Letterkundig leven te Gent van 1500 tot 1539', *Jaarboek de Fonteyne* 16 (1966), 3–57

Vander Straelen, J. B., 'Geschiedenis der Rederykkamer de Violieren of Violettebloem, onder zinspreuk: wt jonsten versaemt, te Antwerpen', *Het taelverbond* 9 (1853), 240

Vander Straeten, E., *Le Théâtre villageois et Flandre*, 2 vols. (Brussels, 1874–80)

Veldhorst, Natascha, *De perfecte verleiding: muzikale scènes op het Amsterdams toneel* (Amsterdam, 2004)

Verdam, J., 'Het haar van den hond', *Tijdschrift voor Nederlandse taal- en letterkunde* 12 (1893), 141–9

Verduin, Leonard, 'The Chambers of Rhetoric and Anabaptist Origins in the Low Countries', *Mennonite Quarterly Review* 34 (1960), 192–6

Vergara, Alejandro, *Patinir: Essays and Critical Catalogue* (Madrid, 2007)

Verwijs, Eelco, *Van vrouwen ende van minne, Middelnederlandsche gedichten uit de 14de en 15de eeuw* (Groningen, 1871)

Visser, Pieter, *Broeders in de geest: de doopsgezinde bijdragen van Dierick en Jan* (Deventer, 1988)

Vooys, C. G. N., 'Rederijkersspelen in het archief van "Trou moet blijcken"', *Tijdschrift voor Nederlandse taal- en letterkunde* 45 (1926), 265–86

—— 'Rederijkersspelen uit het archief van "Trou moet Blijcken"', *Tijdschrift voor Nederlandse taal- en letterkunde* 47 (1928), 161–205

—— 'Rederijkersspelen uit het archief van "Trou moet blijcken" (Slot)', *Tijdschrift voor Nederlandse taal- en letterkunde* 49 (1930), 1–25

Vorselman, Gheeraert, *Eenen nyeuwen coock boeck: kookboek samengesteld door Gheeraert Vorselman en gedrukt te Antwerpen in 1560*, ed. Elly Cockx-Indestege (Wiesbaden, 1971)

Wack, Mary, *Lovesickness in the Middle Ages: The Viaticum and its Commentaries* (Philadelphia, 1990)

Waite, Gary K., *David Joris and Dutch Anabaptism, 1524–1543* (Waterloo, Ontario, 1990)

—— 'Reformers on Stage: Rhetorician Drama and Reformation Propaganda in the Netherlands of Charles V, 1519–1556', *Archiv für Reformationsgeschichte* 83 (1992), 209–39

—— *Reformers on Stage: Popular Drama and Religious Propaganda in the Low Countries* (Toronto, 2000)

—— 'On the Stage and in the Streets: Rhetorician Drama, Social Conflict and Religious Upheaval in Amsterdam, 1520–1550', in Bart Ramakers, ed., *Conformisten en rebellen: Rederijkerscultuur in de Nederlanden (1400–1650)* (Amsterdam, 2003), 162–73

Wakefield, Walter, and Austin Evans, *Heresies of the High Middle Ages* (New York, 1991)

Walsh, Martin W., '"Martín y muchos pobres": Grotesque Versions of the Charity of St Martin in the Bosch and Bruegel Schools', *Essays in Medieval Studies* 14 (1997), 107–20

Wardropper, Bruce, 'Belgium', in *The Reader's Encyclopedia of World Drama*, ed. John Gassner and Edward Quinn (New York, 1970), 59–65

Waterschoot, W., *Jan van der Noot: de poeticsche werken* (Ghent, 1975)

Weller, Dennis P., Cynthia von Bogendorf Rupprath and Mariët Westermann, *Jan Miense Molenaer: Painter of the Dutch Golden Age* (Raleigh, 2002)

Welsford, Enid, *The Fool: His Social and Literary History* (London, 1968)

Wesseling, Ari, 'Dutch Proverbs and Ancient Sources in Erasmus's *Praise of Folly*', *Renaissance Quarterly* 47 (1994), 351–78

Westermann, Mariët, *The Amusements of Jan Steen: Comic Painting in the Seventeenth Century* (Zwolle, 1997)

Westers, Oscar, *Welsprekende burgers* (Nijmegen, 2003)

Whiting, Barlett J., and Helen W. Whiting, *Proverbs, Sentences and Proverbial Phrases from English Writings Mainly before 1500* (Cambridge, MA, 1968)

Willebrands, Marleen, *De verstandige kok. De rijke keuken van de Gouden Eeuw* (Bussum, 2006)

Willems, J. F., 'Cornelis Everaert, tooneeldichter of Bruges', *Belgisch museum voor de Nederduitsche tael- en letterkunde en de geschiedenis des vaderlands* 6 (1842), 41–51

William of Saint-Amour, *De Periculis Novissimorum Temporum*, ed. G. Geltner, Dallas Medieval Texts and Translations 8 (Leuven and Paris, 2007)

Williams, Alison, *Tricksters and Pranksters: Roguery in French and German Literature of the Middle Ages and the Renaissance* (Amsterdam, 2000)

Williams, Arnold, 'Chaucer and the Friars', *Speculum* 28 (1953), 499–513

Witsen Geysbeek, P. G., *Biographisch anthologisch en critisch woordenboek der Neder-duitsche dichters*, 6 vols. (Amsterdam, 1821–7)

Wolf, Johann Wilhelm, *Wodana* (Ghent, 1851)

Wolfensburger, Wolf, 'Eulogy for a Mentally Retarded Jester', *Mental Retardation* 20 (1982), 269–70

Woodbridge, Linda, *Vagrancy, Homelessness, and English Renaissance Literature* (Urbana and Chicago, 2001)

Worp, J. A., *Geschiedenis van het drama en van het tooneel in Nederlan*, 2 vols. (Groningen, 1903–7)

—— *Geschiedenis van den Amsterdamschen schouwburg 1496–1772* (Amsterdam, 1920)

Wright, Thomas, *The Political Songs of England: From the Reign of John to that of Edward II* (London, 1839)

—— *Latin Poems Commonly Attributed to Walter Mapes*, ed. Thomas Wright (London, 1841)

—— *Political Poems and Songs Relating to English History: From the Accession of Edw. III to that of Ric. III*, Rolls Series, 2 vols. (London, 1859–61)

Wright, Thomas, and James Halliwell, *Reliquae Antiquae* (London, 1841–3)

Young, Douglas C., *Rogues and Genres: Generic Transformation in the Spanish Picaresque and Arabic Maqāma* (Newark, 2004)

Ypes, Catharina, *Petrarca in de Nederlandse letterkunde* (Amsterdam, 1934)

Yunck, John, *The Lineage of Lady Meed: The Development of Mediaeval Venality Satire* (Notre Dame, IA, 1963)

Zeydel, Edwin Hermann, *Vagabond Verse: Secular Latin Poems of the Middle Ages* (Detroit, 1966)